MOON

T0031788

RHODE
ISLAND

LIZ LEE

Contents

© MOON.COM

To New York City

To Stonington and Mystic

Watch Hill

Avondale

Misquamicut

WESTERLY

Westerly

78

3

95

Ashaway

Hopkinton

Yawgoog Pond

165

138

Rockville

HOPKINTON

Hope Valley

Wyoming

Millville

216

CHARLESTOWN

SOUTH COUNTY

91

Carolina

Carolina Management Area

Shannock

RICHMOND

Block Island Sound

Watchaug Pond

1

Ninigret Pond

Charlestown

Kenyon

138

EXETER

NEW SHOREHAM

Block Island

SOUTH KINGSTOWN

Burlingame State Park

Worden Pond

West Kingston

Wakefield

Peace Dale

2

Exeter

Galilee

Point Judith

108

NARRAGANSETT

Narragansett

1A

Saunderstown

Wickford

138

ATLANTIC OCEAN

Beavertail State Park

Fort Adams State Park

NEWPORT

Jamestown

JAMESTOWN

Newport

MIDDLETOWN

Middletown

114

PORTSMOUTH

138

East Bay

Sakonet

LITTLE COMPTON

Little Compton

Adamsville

N

0   5 km
0   5 mi

RHODE ISLAND

CONNECTICUT

MASSACHUSETTS

To Hartford

To I-395

DAVIS LODGE TURNPIKE

6

14

44

To Worcester

Slatersville

Woonsocket

To Boston

George
Washington
Management
Area

Pascoag Reservoir

BURRILLVILLE

100

Pascoag

Harrisville

Oakland

Mapleville

102

5

146

7

WEST GREENWICH

Rice City

Hopkins
Hollow

Summit

102

Coventry
Center

COVENTRY

Anthony

Foster Center

FOSTER

North
Foster

GLOCESTER

Cherry Valley

Clayville

SCITUATE

101

Chepachet

44

Harmony

Scituate
Reservoir

North
Scituate

6

Greenville

SMITHFIELD

NORTH
SMITHFIELD

Georgiaville

99

LINCOLN

146

Lonsdale

Valley
Falls

122

Berkeley

114

CUMBERLAND

Blackstone River

WOONSOCKET

North
Attleboro

295

11

Arcadia
Management
Area

3

Big River
Management
Area

95

EAST
GREENWICH

WEST
WARWICK

2

CRANSTON

JOHNSTON

295

NORTH
PROVIDENCE

PROVIDENCE

EAST
PROVIDENCE

Pawtucket

Rumford

Attleboro

95

To Boston

4

NORTH
KINGSTOWN

East Greenwich

Goddard Memorial
State Park

1

Apponaug

WARWICK

TF GREEN
AIRPORT

Warwick

Cranston

Narragansett
Bay

Riverside

114

6

BARRINGTON

Warren

136

BRISTOL

Bristol

Prudence
Island

South Prudence
State Park

Passage

East

195

44

Portsmouth

Tiverton

24

TIVERTON

To Cape
Cod

To Boston

195

Fall
River

79

DISCOVER

Rhode Island

Contrary to what Rhode Island locals might tell you, nothing within the state's boundaries is actually "far away" from anything else. Rhode Island comprises only about 1,500 square miles (over 500 of which are in territorial waters), and one can easily drive from one end of the state to the other in about an hour. But despite the relative ease with which one might cross a state line, there is something about Rhode Island that makes it difficult to leave. In fact, this tendency of Rhode Islanders to stay put has become something of a joke over the years; local gift shops have taken to selling bumper stickers and T-shirts depicting an anchor chained to the phrase "I never leave Rhode Island."

The anchor, of course, is part of the state's official insignia, a symbol representing steadfastness and hope. And like so much of Rhode Island's history, culture, people, and landscape, it also represents an inextricable link to the sea.

The ocean permeates everything in Rhode Island, from the sandy beaches and inland farms to city streets where seagulls can still be heard crying overhead and salty breezes blow in from the bay. In Rhode Island, the ocean creates jobs, supplies, food, and provides recreation and respite from the daily grind. It's

Clockwise from top left: sailboat in South County at sunset; sunflower near the Providence River; a monarch butterfly at Sachuest Point National Wildlife Refuge; Sakonnet Light at sunset; RISD Museum of Art; a seaside sculpture made from washed up logs and fishing rope.

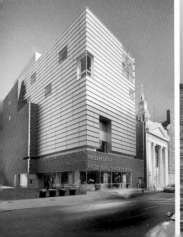

where the state gets its official name (after all, an island can't exist without the sea), and it's where it gets its nickname as well—the Ocean State.

Perhaps this is why Rhode Islanders live for summer, when rising temperatures and sunny skies make the coast that much more appealing. But as with all New England states, Rhode Island has appeal in every season. Autumn means brilliant bright-orange and red foliage, and apple picking and hayrides at family-run orchards. Spring is an excuse to seek out the diaphanous pink blooms of the cherry blossom trees at one of more than over two-dozen state parks. Even in the coldest winter months, visitors can enjoy the ineffable beauty of the Atlantic from behind the windowpanes of cozy seaside B&Bs or simply find warmth in the diversity and vibrancy of Providence or Newport—two of the nation's most historic cities.

And the best thing about Rhode Island? Everything is a day trip—which sort of makes it difficult to leave.

Clockwise from top left: Waterplace Park and Riverwalk at dusk; thousands of daffodils along the Clay Head Trail in spring; grapevines at Sakonnet Vineyards; a colorful doorway in Warren.

6 TOP
EXPERIENCES

1 **Wander the Cliff Walk in Newport:** Nature lovers and history buffs alike will enjoy this 3.5-mile coastline trail (page 103).

2 **Visit the Newport Mansions:** Newport's wealthy elite was so overcome with their own opulence that they gave their sprawling estates names like "Rosecliff," "The Breakers," and "Chateau sur Mer." Once you see them, you'll understand why (page 98).

>>>

3 **Enjoy Beaches across the State:** Rhode Islanders take their beaching very seriously, and it shows: It's a salty, sundrenched satisfaction that is not easy to replicate (page 21).

>>>

4 **Get Artistic:** Providence is called the Creative Capital because of art experiences like the impressive pyrotechnic installation *WaterFire*, but there are fantastic galleries and museums throughout the state (page 34).

5 **Cycle the State:** Admire the scenic and popular East Bay Trail or the isolated and beautiful Block Island on two wheels (page 147 and page 174).

6 **Drink and Dine:** Mouthwatering Italian dishes in Providence, seafood fresh from sandy shores, and thirst-quenching craft brews are just some of the tasty delights to enjoy (page 23 and page 60).

Planning Your Trip

Where to Go

In terms of tourism, little Rhode Island is a land of separate communities. You don't so much vacation in Rhode Island as you do in Providence, Newport, South County, or Block Island. That being said, if you spend time in any one part of Rhode Island, you'll find it quite simple to venture over to any other town in the state, which are all just a short drive away.

Providence and Vicinity

Providence somehow manages to feel like the cool college town it is while maintaining a very genuine blue-collar vibe at the same time. It also offers a culinary experience you may expect of a city several times its size, some beautifully preserved colonial and 19th-century architecture,

and a youthful, unconventional, and thriving music, art, and club scene, largely due to the presence of **Brown University, the Rhode Island School of Design (RISD),** and **Johnson & Wales.**

Greater Providence encapsulates a diversity of environments that reward day trips, drive-throughs, and even longer stays. The **Blackstone River Valley** features recreational opportunities, thanks to the historically notable Blackstone River.

Newport

Newport, known for its posh luxury hotels and elite seaside estates, offers the lodging and dining variety you might expect of much larger East

the Block Island Ferry

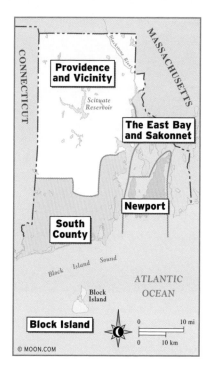

© MOON.COM

Block Island

Block Island is both beautiful and accessible, thanks to a conservancy that preserves more than a quarter of the island's open spaces. You'll find **historic bed-and-breakfasts and inns** here, including several mammoth **Victorian hotels,** as well as some of the most breathtaking stretches of coastline in the state.

The East Bay and Sakonnet

East Bay is a great weekend destination: **Warren** is an antiques hub with a few excellent restaurants, while **Bristol** offers charming inns and museums. Sakonnet makes a great day trip as it's laced with country roads and contains a handful of fun shops, cafés, roadside farm stands, and a bit of beach access. Alas, there are hardly any accommodations in Sakonnet's two towns, **Little Compton** and **Tiverton,** but it's a short drive from either Aquidneck Island or Bristol.

South County

This part of Rhode Island offers a mix of **colorful beach towns** studded with condos, motels, and guesthouses along with quieter interior communities known for **lush forests,** rippling ponds and rivers, and great hiking. The coastal area tends to be seasonal and is best visited from spring through summer. This is a very family-friendly part of Rhode Island, owing to its busy beaches with kid-oriented diversions, from water sports and whale watches to carousels and miniature golf.

Coast cities, and yet it's a fairly small place that's easy to navigate. It's a well-preserved colonial seaport community and a living-history museum of the Gilded Age, with **stunning mansions** situated on rocky cliffs. But you needn't be rich to enjoy the natural beauty of Newport's scenic coastline and sandy beaches.

She Never Came mural by BEZT in Providence

When to Go

Rhode Island is a **year-round** destination, but if you're planning to take advantage of the Ocean State's vast access to the water, focus your visit around the warmest months, generally from mid-May through mid-October and especially from **mid-June through Labor Day.** Keep in mind, however, that in Newport, Block Island, and South County, you'll be competing with throngs of other sea lovers for space and parking at the beach, in restaurants, and at hotels.

Newport and parts of South County have made an effort to attract **off-season** visitors; museums have begun keeping longer winter hours, and many hotels offer special rates in the off-season. Block Island, however, has few hotel options and even fewer dining options in winter.

The best compromise could be to visit in the shoulder season—in **May, before Memorial Day,** when the days are often warm and sunny, or in **September, after Labor Day,** when the ocean is at its warmest.

Because the **colleges** in **Providence** infuse downtown and College Hill with energy when the schools are in session, some visitors prefer fall, spring, and even winter in the state capital, which can seem empty in summer when there aren't as many students. While Providence can sometimes be uncomfortably hot and muggy in July and August, it's only a 45-minute drive to most of the state's beaches, making it a completely reasonable place to make your home base for a summer visit. Winters are not brutal, but the state does get socked by the occasional snow or ice storms, and the wind and frigidity can be uncomfortable from December through March.

The most bewitching and **scenic seasons** in Rhode Island are **spring,** when the entire state is abloom with greenery and flowers, and **fall,** when the foliage changes color, and the woods light up with brilliant swamp maples.

The Best of Rhode Island

With a week to explore Rhode Island, you can easily see the state's key towns and cities and enjoy a sampling of its major attractions. This approach begins in Providence and then steers you down through the state's coastal hubs, ending in Bristol, just an hour's drive from Providence. It's not difficult to manage this tour in just five to six days by using Providence and Newport as your bases and spending one night instead of two on Block Island, but to fully soak up the region's appeal, plan to take seven full days to get around.

Providence

DAY 1

Providence's renaissance has occurred largely around its downtown riverfront, so spend your first day getting acquainted with the area. Spend some time checking out the shops and cafés in **Downcity**, then walk over to **Waterplace Park**, where you can take a gondola ride during the warmer months. On many Saturday evenings from March through November you can also watch the dazzling *WaterFire*, a dramatic display of bonfires set in cauldrons along the river.

In the same day, you can cross the river to **College Hill**, home to Brown University and the Rhode Island School of Design as well as several other attractions, some of them related to the neighborhood's academic institutions. Must-sees include the **RISD Museum of Art** and the **Providence Athenaeum.** Be sure to stroll along Benefit Street, which is lined with gorgeous colonial and Victorian homes, and check out the excellent shopping, gallery-hopping, and inexpensive dining along both Thayer and Wickenden Streets.

DAY 2

On your second day, venture out to **Roger Williams Park**, which is an easy 4 -mi (6.4-km) drive or bus ride south from downtown. This sprawling green park contains **Roger Williams**

Federal Hill in Providence

historic houses on Thomas Street in Providence

Castle Hill Lighthouse in Newport

Park Zoo and the excellent **Museum of Natural History,** which includes a planetarium, making it an especially nice option if you have kids in tow. Alternatively, make a day trip north of the city to **Slater Mill Historic Site,** a linchpin of the American Industrial Revolution, located in downtown Pawtucket, a 15-minute drive north of Providence. Finish off the day with dinner and a stroll through **Federal Hill,** Providence's Little Italy, or check out one of the many other eclectic and highly acclaimed restaurants in the **West Side** neighborhood.

Newport
DAY 3
You should not visit Newport without taking a road trip along winding **Ocean Drive,** which meanders along the waterfront and affords close-up views of some of this small city's prettiest homes. Spend the rest of your first day becoming acquainted with the compact and highly walkable downtown, checking out the shops and the well-preserved colonial and Victorian architecture of **Historic District,** or

enjoying the exhibits at the excellent **Newport Art Museum.**

DAY 4
Save your second day in Newport for touring the massive summer homes of the Gilded Age along Bellevue Avenue, the most famous of which is **The Breakers.** After the imposing Breakers, if you have time to see only one other mansion, your best bet is **The Elms.** If you're a tennis fan, you might consider a visit to the **International Tennis Hall of Fame** and its museum.

If mansions aren't your thing, head north to visit the towns of **Portsmouth** and **Middletown,** where sightseeing highlights include the **Norman Bird Sanctuary, Sachuest Point National Wildlife Refuge,** and **Green Animals Topiary Garden,** as well as some of the best sandy beaches in the state.

South County
DAY 5
Laid-back South County contains some of Rhode Island's best beaches as well as copious

Rhode Island may be tiny, but it contains over 400 miles (645 km) of coastline, along which you'll find more than 100 public and private beaches. If sunbathing and swimming are on your agenda but you're not sure where to begin, here are some suggestions to get you started.

Best for Recreation: In Westerly, **Misquamicut State Beach** is one of the largest in the state. It's got a playground and a large concession stand with a shaded pavilion, and is situated amidst the motels, gifts shops, candy stores, water slides, mini-golf courses, arcades, and other amusements along Atlantic Avenue.

Best for Surfing: An easily accessible beach break makes **Narragansett Town Beach** in South County a popular spot with both seasoned and beginner surfers. The swell here ranges from between 2-8 feet, and a sunken barge just offshore along the northern stretch of the beach creates some nice right-breaking waves. Ample parking is available, but will cost between $10-$15 between Memorial Day and Labor Day (parking is free in the off-season).

Best for Families: If you're traveling with kids, try **Easton's Beach** (often called **First Beach** by locals), a 0.75-mi (1.2-km) stretch of sandy shoreline located right at the beginning of the Cliff Walk in Newport. The beach is also home to a carousel, a playground, an aquarium, a skateboard park, and a snack bar to keep children amused. Just a few minutes farther east is **Third Beach,** which is set back in a cove, meaning there aren't many waves so it's an ideal spot for taking a dip with small children.

Best for Avoiding Crowds: South Shore Beach in Little Compton has fun waves to splash around in or surf, and relatively sparse

crowds even in the high season—it's also one of the only beaches that permit bonfires in the evenings. Farther south, **Charlestown and Blue Shutters Town Beaches** are both smaller with less commotion.

Best for Joining the Crowds: Scarborough Beach in Narragansett is often the most crowded in the state and is popular with just about everyone. Also in Narragansett, **Roger Wheeler State Beach** is a local favorite, with nice facilities, a concession stand, a picnic area, and a bathhouse. This is a relatively small stretch of golden sand, and doesn't take long to fill up with beach-goers on sunny summer days.

opportunities for hiking, boating, swimming, and sunbathing. It's also where you catch the ferry to the next place on this tour, Block Island.

A great way to make the most of a day in South County is to drive along the shore, beginning in the quaint Victorian seaside town

of **Watch Hill** and continuing along Route 1A and U.S. 1 (and some side roads) through such charming seaside communities as **Weekapaug, Misquamicut, Charlestown, Galilee,** and **Point Judith.** A bit north, Narragansett is home to the **South County Museum,** which preserves the legacy of a gentleman's farm, and the **Gilbert Stuart Museum,** the home of George Washington's foremost portraitist. Don't feel like you have to spend the day sightseeing, however—when you find the beach that matches your personality, whether that's kid-friendly Watch Hill, pristine Charlestown, or raucous Misquamicut, feel free to pull out that towel and sunbathe.

Block Island
DAY 6
Beautiful and isolated Block Island, just 10 mi (16 km) or so south of the mainland, feels a world away from the rest of the state. Far less developed than other New England island retreats, such as Martha's Vineyard and Nantucket, Block Island is home to numerous nature preserves as well as some of the grandest Victorian seaside resorts in the country. While it's possible to visit for an afternoon, you'll want to spend a night and really get the feel of the island. Go for a bike ride, hike along the grounds of **Southeast Light** or through **Rodman's Hollow** preserve, grab an ice-cream cone at **Aldo's,** or simply laze away your time reading in a lounge chair at **Crescent Beach.**

The East Bay and Sakonnet
DAY 7
End your tour of Rhode Island with a visit to the quiet East Bay area, which you can reach from Newport more scenically by making a short detour through Sakonnet, a small patch of villages bordering Massachusetts and the ocean and home to the state's best winery, **Sakonnet Vineyards.** If the vineyard doesn't appeal to you, consider a trip to **Goosewing Beach and Nature Preserve,** a great place to watch the sunset or observe the enormous flocks of piping plover and other birds that congregate here.

Head north to reach the East Bay, where the main towns are Bristol and Warren. Bristol may be relatively small, but it's home to some historic attractions, including **Blithewold Mansion and Arboretum,** as well as a charming downtown neighborhood. Head to **Warren** for dinner at one of the several hip and eclectic restaurants that have cropped up here in recent years.

windblown sand on Block Island

Food in the Ocean State

Rhode Island has a few quirky food items that locals find completely ordinary but which might cause confusion for the uninformed tourist. Here are some of the most commonly encountered—and uniquely delicious—items for which the Ocean State is known.

- **Quahogs** are hard-shell clams found in abundance on Rhode Island's sandy shores, inlets, and salt ponds. These tasty bivalves can be found on restaurant menus all over the state, but they taste even better if you dig them yourself. Popular "quahogging" spots include the **Point Judith Salt Pond** in Galilee, and **Ninigret Pond** in Charlestown. Note: shellfishing licenses are required for out-of-state residents and can be obtained through the RI DEM: www.dem.ri.gov.

- **Stuffies,** a common menu item at many restaurants, are quahog shells stuffed with a mixture of minced clams and breadcrumb stuffing usually containing onions, celery, garlic, spices, and herbs. They are especially delicious with a bit of fresh-squeezed lemon juice and hot sauce. Exceptionally good stuffies can be found at the **Matunuck Oyster Bar** in East Matunuck (a gorgeous view of the salt pond makes them taste that much better) (629 Succotash Rd., 401/783-4202, www.rhodyoysters.com, 11:30am-10pm daily).

- **Coffee Milk** is the official state drink; it's a rather self-explanatory mixture of milk and coffee syrup, which is a rarity in other states but can be found on grocery shelves throughout Rhode Island. Any Rhode Island diner worth its salt will have coffee milk on the menu—try the **Modern Diner** in Pawtucket (364 East Ave., 401/726-8390, www.moderndinerri.com, 6am-2pm Mon.-Sat., 7am-2pm Sun.), just over the Providence line.

- **A Cabinet** is Rhode Island-ese for what is basically a milkshake: blended ice cream and milk. Coffee cabinets with Autocrat coffee syrup are a local favorite, but you can get them in a variety of flavors, locally made, at **Gray's Ice Cream** in Tiverton (16 East Rd., Tiverton, 401/624-4500,

stuffies

www.graysicecream.com, 6:30am-9pm daily summer, call for off-season hours).

- **Hot wieners** or New York System wieners are famous staples of Rhode Island food culture and can be found at several New York System diners throughout the state. This strange, tiny hot dog is served on a steamed bun and tastes best when ordered "all the way," which means loaded with chopped onions, celery salt, yellow mustard, and seasoned meat sauce. The legendary **Olneyville New York System** in Providence (18 Plainfield St., 401/621-9500, www.olneyvillenewyorksystem.com) is the best spot to enjoy them.

- **Del's** is the locally favored brand of frozen lemonade slush sold from trucks and lemonade stands all over the state. Look for the yellow and green striped Del's umbrella stands or trucks that park at beaches during the summer, or head to **1260 Oaklawn Avenue** in Cranston, where the first Del's Lemonade stand opened in 1948.

Weekend Getaway

Newport ranks among the most appealing long-weekend destinations in New England, but lesser-known coastal towns to the south—like Narragansett, Charlestown, and Wickford—offer a down-to-earth charm that appeals to broader sensibilities. Spend a day soaking up the gorgeous views and rich history of posh Newport, then head to South County for a truly relaxing day in one of Rhode Island's smaller, more laid-back beach communities.

Saturday
NEWPORT

Begin on **Ocean Drive,** the famously scenic route that loops around for about 10 mi (16 km), edging the sea and passing dramatic summer homes. Then continue onto tree-shaded **Bellevue Avenue,** the main thoroughfare of Newport's Gilded Age, studded with palatial mansions that have been converted into house-museums. Both **The Breakers** and **The Elms** are among the best mansions to tour.

Several lanes headed east from Bellevue provide access to the **Cliff Walk,** a rocky path that runs along a bluff and affords exceptional views of Rhode Island Sound as well as the backyards of several waterfront estates; definitely plan to hike along at least a section of this path if the weather permits. After that, you might just want to spend the rest of the afternoon swimming and lounging in the sand at **Easton's Beach,** but if there's rain in the forecast, consider checking out the exhibits at the **Newport Art Museum.** Plan on an early-ish dinner at the cozy **Perro Salado** in Washington Square. Then give yourself enough time to end the day by heading over the bridge to Jamestown, where you can watch the sunset from the rocky cliffs at **Beavertail State Park.**

The Breakers

Kid Stuff

Traveling with kids isn't always as easy as the guidebooks make it sound, but Rhode Island is, in fact, as ideal a place to do it as any, thanks to its balance of education and fun. A plethora of aquariums, zoos, carousels, arcades, beaches, and baseball games guarantee that any time of year is a good time to pack up the minivan: Spring is wonderful for outside strolls in the parks; summer begs for cooling dips at the beach; fall is foliage and festival time; and winter is when you can head for the indoor museums. These are the top sights and activities for kids:

- **Roger Williams Park Zoo** is world class, housing more than 957 species, a children's farmyard exhibit, a carousel, a natural history museum and planetarium, and a playground right in Providence.

- **Green Animals Topiary Garden** in Portsmouth is a seven-acre estate overlooking Narragansett Bay, where 21 of the 80 trees have been sculpted into giant animals.

- **The Providence Children's Museum** offers first-rate opportunities for education through play, with interactive exhibits focusing on science, nature, technology, and art.

- **Gray's Ice Cream** in Tiverton is a famed fixture of Rhode Island as much for its history (it has been around for 80-plus years) as for its rum-raisin flavor.

topiaries created from Yew bushes at Green Animals Topiary Garden

- **Save the Bay Exploration Center and Aquarium** in Newport is where wee ones can check out rare calico lobsters, among other sea creatures.

- **Atlantic Beach Park** in Misquamicut brings smiles to thousands of just-from-the-beach kids every summer with its 1915 carousel, amusement rides, and video arcade by the sea.

Sunday
SOUTH COUNTY

Head over to the mainland this morning for a surf or paddleboard lesson at **Narragansett Town Beach,** where board and wetsuit rentals are available right in the parking lot on summer days. Satisfy the hunger you've worked up out on the waves with brunch at **Crazy Burger Juice Bar & Café,** also located in Narragansett Pier.

After brunch, head south on Route 1 into Charlestown and spend the afternoon browsing at **The Fantastic Umbrella Factory,** a compound of curiosity shops surrounded by an exotic-animal petting zoo, greenhouses, and an enchanting bamboo forest. From here you're within minutes of several gorgeous beaches—**Matunuck, Moonstone, and Charlestown,** to name a few. Pack a picnic and take a stroll during sunset, then head to Matunuck for an 8pm show at **Theatre-by-the-Sea** or live music at the **Ocean Mist Beach Bar.**

Watersports

Newport is the undisputed center for sailing on the Eastern Seaboard, and one of the best places in the world to harness the wind and the waves with a charter or a personal lesson. A combination of stunning natural beauty and experienced yachters means you won't have a hard time putting together the perfect sailing experience. Browse the list of charter companies on **DiscoverNewport.org** to find a captain or **Sail Newport** to book a lesson.

sailing along Newport Harbor

DEEP-SEA FISHING

The waters of Block Island Sound run with the bluefish and striped bass, making it a perfect place to experience a deep-sea fishing expedition. Despite the decline of the New England fishing industry, little Galilee is still one of the top 20 fishing ports in the country, and it teems with experienced anglers who can take you out to enact your own personal Hemingway novel. Try **Frances Fleet,** which charters bluefish, striped bass, and tuna trips.

SURFING AND STANDUP PADDLEBOARDING

There's no better way to enjoy the water in Rhode Island than with a tranquil (or exhilarating) surfing or paddleboarding session. For surfboard rentals and lessons, stop by **Narragansett Surf and Skate in Narragansett.** If you're more of a SUP person, check out **Paddle Surf RI** in Westerly and leave the stress behind as you paddle out onto some calm, glassy water.

CANOEING AND KAYAKING

Not all of the water-sports action in the state occurs offshore. Rhode Island's network of pristine rivers, especially in the western and southern sections of the state, makes for some great kayaking and canoeing. One of the best spots is the crystalline **Wood River** in the state's southwest corner. Traveling its full length is an all-day affair through 14 mi (22.5 km) of pristine woodland, with some good rapids along the way. Several good put-ins, however, offer shorter trips, including the relatively smooth 6 mi (9.7 km) run from Hope Valley Road Landing to Alton Dam. To plan the best trip, contact the **Kayak Centre of Rhode Island.**

Stay in South County in one of the modest seaside hotels or take the 35-minute drive back to Newport.

Monday

If you're headed west toward Connecticut, consider spending your last morning hiking the trail at **Long Pond-Ell Pond Nature Preserve** in Hopkinton on your way out of town. The trail here includes excellent views from a rocky cliff overlooking the water, and some eye-popping color when the rhododendrons are in season. If you're headed back north to T. F. Green Airport, follow Route 1 and stop off in Wickford to spend the morning kayaking through **Wickford Harbor,** where rentals and guided tours are available at the Kayak Centre of Wickford.

Providence and Vicinity

As the third-largest metropolitan area in New

England, Providence offers an exciting contrast to the quiet beauty of Rhode Island's more rural areas.

Once famed for its jewelry, silverware, and textile manufacturing, the city, like so many others, was hit hard by the industrial decline of mid-20th century America, as manufacturing fled to cheaper labor markets overseas. But in recent decades, local government has spent millions in an effort to revitalize the city's image, reinventing downtown and transforming a muddled city center into a picturesque walking district that invites exploration.

Highlights

Look for ★ to find recommended sights, activities, dining, and lodging.

★ **Waterplace Park and Riverwalk:** This park and four-acre walk along the Providence River is the centerpiece of Providence's dramatic downtown renaissance (page 32).

★ **Downcity:** With its high concentration of small businesses, great restaurants, and beautiful buildings, Downcity is the historic center of Providence (page 34).

★ **Federal Hill:** Famous for its abundant restaurants and storied Mafia history, Providence's Little Italy is filled with cobblestone walkways, boutique shops, and cocktail lounges (page 36).

★ **The Providence Athenaeum:** Housed in a beautiful Greek Revival building on Benefit Street, this historic library dates back to 1831 and was a favorite hangout of writers H. P. Lovecraft and Edgar Allan Poe (page 41).

★ **Prospect Terrace Park:** Roger Williams's tomb lies just beneath a 15-foot-tall statue of the founding father at the edge of this urban park (page 41).

★ **RISD Museum of Art:** More than a college art gallery, this world-class museum offers an overview of art history dating back thousands of years, with works by artists ranging from Claude Monet to Winslow Homer (page 42).

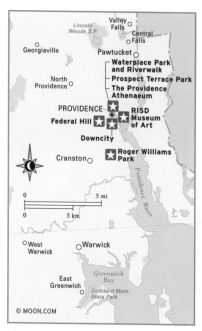

★ **Roger Williams Park:** This 430-acre urban green space includes a botanical center, a Victorian-style rose garden, a carousel, a first-rate zoo, a museum of natural history, and a planetarium (page 46).

Providence and Vicinity

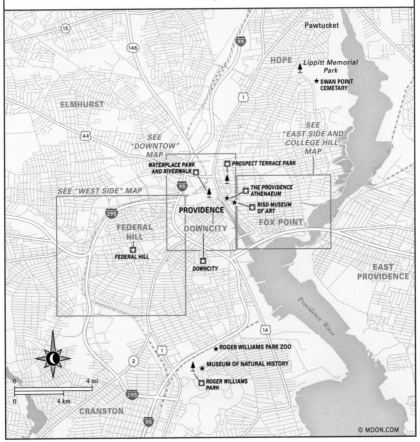

Pawtucket · HOPE · Lippitt Memorial Park · SWAN POINT CEMETERY · ELMHURST · SEE "DOWNTOW" MAP · SEE "EAST SIDE AND COLLEGE HILL" MAP · WATERPLACE PARK AND RIVERWALK · PROSPECT TERRACE PARK · SEE "WEST SIDE" MAP · THE PROVIDENCE ATHENAEUM · RISD MUSEUM OF ART · PROVIDENCE · DOWNCITY · FOX POINT · FEDERAL HILL · FEDERAL HILL · DOWNCITY · EAST PROVIDENCE · Providence River · ROGER WILLIAMS PARK ZOO · MUSEUM OF NATURAL HISTORY · ROGER WILLIAMS PARK · CRANSTON · 0 4 mi · 0 4 km · © MOON.COM

Building on the innovative prowess of institutions like Brown University and the Rhode Island School of Design (RISD), Providence now enjoys a reputation as an up-and-coming hub for young professionals and artists, defined by its diversity and distinct New England charm, as well as a budding economy that fuses technology, art, education, and commerce.

Evidence of revitalization efforts can be found all over the city, from the museums, galleries, and carefully restored architecture of downtown to the trendy neighborhoods of the West Side, where artisanal coffee shops, cocktail lounges, and colorful community gardens have been steadily taking the place of once-abandoned storefronts and lots.

Culinarily speaking, Providence is brimming with talent and energy, spurred on by a healthy competition between restaurants with adventurous menus, inspired atmospheres, and critically acclaimed chefs. This

Previous: the statue of Roger Williams at Prospect Terrace Park; the Providence Athenaeum; a gallery at RISD Museum of Art.

exceptional culinary scene, along with endless arts and culture venues and thoughtfully planned urban spaces, make Providence a perfect weekend getaway destination.

ORIENTATION

Providence is separated into East Side and West Side by the Providence River, which flows through the middle of town. On the **East Side,** College Hill rises sharply, with Brown University and the Rhode Island School of Design anchoring its slopes. The south boundary of the East Side is Fox Point, once known for its thriving Portuguese community and now increasingly home to the many students that attend Brown, RISD, and Johnson & Wales.

West of the river, a relatively flat network of curving streets forms **downtown,** home to many of the city's major hotels, restaurants, and cultural attractions. Just south of downtown lies the Jewelry District, which was separated from downtown by I-195 until 2013, when the highway was relocated. This relocation project freed up about 40 acres of land, some of which is now home to new office buildings and residential units, while some is still under development. As a result, the character of the Jewelry District, a former manufacturing hub known for its mishmash of bars, restaurants, and industrial space, is currently in flux.

West of downtown, just across I-95, are the many residential neighborhoods that form the city's **West Side,** including Broadway and the Armory District, Federal Hill, and Olneyville.

Just south lay the Elmwood and Washington Park neighborhoods, collectively known as the **South Side,** characterized by their many stately (and sometimes timeworn) Victorian homes as well as a vibrant Latino community.

The mostly residential neighborhoods of Smith Hill, Mount Pleasant, and Wanskuck, sometimes referred to as the North End, are just north of the State House, and are home to both Providence College and Rhode Island College.

PLANNING YOUR TIME

While it's true that many of Providence's main attractions can be seen in a day, the city is best experienced over the course of a few days, especially for travelers looking to take full advantage of the city's exceptional arts and culture scene and superlative restaurants. If you're a shopper, a foodie, an aficionado of historic preservation, a theatergoer, a gallery hopper, or a live-music fan, you'll easily find plenty here to keep you busy for several days.

The area just outside Providence is better suited to day trips than overnight stays. After your second or third day in Providence, it's worth the short drive north to see the state's Blackstone Valley region, especially if outdoor adventure is more your thing. Here you'll find plenty of opportunities for hiking, kayaking, and bicycling along the river.

HISTORY

The history of Providence is closely linked to the history of Rhode Island. The city's founder, Roger Williams, an early proponent of the separation of church and state, was found guilty of heresy and banished from the colony of Massachusetts in 1636. He sought refuge among the southern Native American tribes, acquiring a written deed in 1638 from the chiefs of the Narragansett people, Canonicus and Miantonomoh.

The residents of Providence took particularly strong exception to financial demands leveled by the English crown on Rhode Island. In 1772, they burned the British tax ship the *Gaspée,* and three years later held their own tea party, modeled after Boston's, on March 2, 1775.

By 1820, Providence's population stood at about 12,000, having doubled since the Revolution—it was the seventh-largest city in the young republic, and remained a commercial powerhouse for quite some time, in part because of the early industrial successes of the textile mills in Pawtucket. One rather unusual industry, jewelry manufacturing, remains a staple of the city's economy to this day. To support the factories, the city opened its doors

Downtown

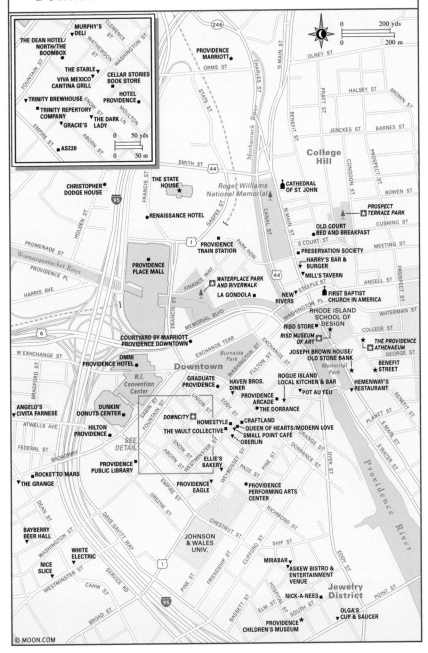

THE DEAN HOTEL/NORTH/THE BOOMBOX
MURPHY'S DELI
CLEMENCE ST
MATHEWSON ST
WASHINGTON ST
THE STABLE
VIVA MEXICO CANTINA GRILL
CELLAR STORIES BOOK STORE
FOUNTAIN ST
TRINITY BREWHOUSE
HOTEL PROVIDENCE
SNOW ST
MOULTON
TRINITY REPERTORY COMPANY
THE DARK LADY
GRACIE'S
EMPIRE ST
ABORN ST
AS220

0   50 yds
0   50 m

246
PROVIDENCE MARRIOTT
ORMS ST
CHARLES ST
N MAIN ST
OLNEY ST

0   200 yds
0   200 m

PRATT ST
HALSEY ST
BROWN ST
BENEFIT ST
JENCKES ST
BARNES ST

College Hill

STATE ST

Mohassuck River

SMITH ST
44
Roger Williams National Memorial
CATHEDRAL OF ST. JOHN

CONGDON ST
BOWEN ST
PROSPECT ST

CUSHING ST

CHRISTOPHER DODGE HOUSE
THE STATE HOUSE
95
HOLDEN ST
FRANCIS ST
GASPEE ST
CANAL ST
N MAIN ST
PROSPECT TERRACE PARK

RENAISSANCE HOTEL
OLD COURT BED AND BREAKFAST
S COURT ST
MEETING ST

PROMENADE ST
Woonasquatucket River
PROVIDENCE PL
1
PARK ROW
PROVIDENCE TRAIN STATION
PRESERVATION SOCIETY
HARRY'S BAR & BURGER
MILL'S TAVERN
ANGELL ST

HARRIS AVE
PROVIDENCE PLACE MALL
FINANCE WAY
WATERPLACE PARK AND RIVERWALK
LA GONDOLA
44
STEEPLE ST
NEW RIVERS
FIRST BAPTIST CHURCH IN AMERICA
WASHINGTON PL

6
FRANCIS ST
MEMORIAL BLVD
WATERMAN ST
RHODE ISLAND SCHOOL OF DESIGN
COLLEGE ST
PROSPECT ST

W EXCHANGE ST
COURTYARD BY MARRIOTT PROVIDENCE DOWNTOWN
EXCHANGE TERR
Burnside Park
WASHINGTON ST
EXCHANGE ST
FULTON ST
RISD STORE
RISD MUSEUM OF ART
JOSEPH BROWN HOUSE/OLD STONE BANK
THE PROVIDENCE ATHENAEUM
GEORGE ST

OMNI PROVIDENCE HOTEL
BRADFORD ST
Downtown
Memorial Park
BENEFIT STREET

R.I. Convention Center
GRADUATE PROVIDENCE
HAVEN BROS. DINER
ROGUE ISLAND LOCAL KITCHEN & BAR
HEMENWAY'S RESTAURANT

ANGELO'S CIVITA FARNESE
ATWELLS AVE
DUNKIN' DONUTS CENTER
SABIN ST
UNION ST
EDDY ST
PROVIDENCE ARCADE
POT AU FEU
THE DORRANCE
PLANET ST
S MAIN ST

HILTON PROVIDENCE
FOUNTAIN ST
DOWNCITY
HOMESTYLE
CRAFTLAND
QUEEN OF HEARTS/MODERN LOVE
SMALL POINT CAFÉ
OBERLIN
ORANGE ST
S WATER ST

FEDERAL ST
SEE DETAIL
SNOW ST
ABORN ST
WESTMINSTER ST
THE VAULT COLLECTIVE
WEYBOSSET ST
PAGE ST
PINE ST
DORRANCE ST
DYER ST
Providence River

BROADWAY
DEAN ST
PROVIDENCE PUBLIC LIBRARY
ELLIE'S BAKERY

ROCKET TO MARS
THE GRANGE
EMPIRE ST
PROVIDENCE EAGLE
PROVIDENCE PERFORMING ARTS CENTER
RICHMOND ST

GREENE ST
CHESTNUT ST
SHIP ST
EDDY ST
POINT ST

BAYBERRY BEER HALL
WASHINGTON ST
DAVE GAVITT WAY
JOHNSON & WALES UNIV.
CLIFFORD ST

WHITE ELECTRIC
NICE SLICE
WESTMINSTER ST
CAHIR ST
SERVICE RD
1
PINE ST
FRIENDSHIP ST
MIRABAR
ASKEW BISTRO & ENTERTAINMENT VENUE
HOSPITAL ST
Jewelry District

BROAD ST
95
BASSETT ST
ELM ST
SOUTH ST
NICK-A-NEES
OLGA'S CUP & SAUCER
PROVIDENCE CHILDREN'S MUSEUM

© MOON.COM

to immigrants, mostly of Italian, Portuguese, French-Canadian, and Swedish descent, who formed ethnic enclaves throughout the city.

Providence endured a steady economic decline beginning with the Depression and lasting through World War II and well into the 1970s. The city had nowhere to go but up by the time a plucky and ambitious new mayor named Vincent "Buddy" Cianci Jr. took office, spurring a dramatic renaissance that has resulted in the dynamic city we see today. The city reclaimed its waterways by uncovering two rivers that had been paved over a century ago, crowning them with Venetian-inspired foot and auto bridges. More recently, the city has lured artists and restaurateurs to revitalize its downtown, a transformation that is still under way.

Sights

DOWNTOWN
The State House
A good place to begin a walk around the city is the grounds of Providence's white-marble-domed **State House** (bounded by Francis, Gaspee, and Smith Sts., 401/222-3983, www.sos.ri.gov/publicinfo/tours, 8:30am-4:30pm Mon.-Fri., guided tours at 9am, 10am, 11am, 1pm, and 2pm, Mon.-Fri., free). Built in the late 1890s by McKim, Mead, and White, this striking work of white Georgia marble sits on several acres of sprawling green lawn. The enormous dome ranks among the largest freestanding domes in the world. Free tours of the interior last just under an hour. Highlights include a replica of the Liberty Bell and one of the most famous portraits of George Washington by Rhode Island artist Gilbert Stuart.

★ Waterplace Park and Riverwalk
South of the State House, the imposing facade of Providence Place Mall and the four-acre **Waterplace Park and Riverwalk** anchor the city's much-touted renaissance. Once a large tidal basin, the area was filled in 1892 by the Providence and Worcester Railroad and laid over with rail lines and yards. In 1994, the Moshassuck and Woonasquatucket Rivers were uncovered and lined with 1 mi (1.6 km) of cobblestone walkways connected by Venetian-style pedestrian bridges.

One of the more unusual ways to take in the revitalized riverfront is by gondola. Contact **La Gondola** (One Citizens Plaza, 401/421-8877, www.gondolari.com, 10am-10pm Sun.-Thurs., 10am-11pm Fri.-Sat., $89-179/2 people) for a ride aboard one of its Venetian-style boats. The 45-minute ride runs the length of the landscaped Riverwalk. You supply the beverages, alcoholic or not, and up to six people, and the gondolier will serenade you with love songs. It's smart to make reservations, especially on weekend evenings, but it's still possible to ride without reservations. Just show up at the landing by Citizens Plaza, and if the gondola is available, you're free to book a 15-20-minute excursion; the price for this shorter trip is $40 per person. It's customary to tip your gondolier 15-20 percent.

About 10 evenings per year, generally Saturdays May through October, **Waterfire Providence** (401/273-1155, www.waterfire.org) dazzles spectators with more than 100 bonfires set in cauldrons on pylons along the rivers. The project of artist and creator Barnaby Evans, the fires burn from sunset to midnight to the sounds of classical and New Age music, while the aroma of burning cedar, oak, and pine lends a distinct ambience to the ritual.

---

1. the State House 2: Westminster Street shopping district 3: the Providence Children's Museum 4: Waterplace Park and Riverwalk

The Creative Capital and Beyond

The continuum of creative juice that flows through Rhode Island's various communities is due largely in part to the wellspring of talent attracted by institutions like the Rhode Island School of Design and Brown University. For generations, the city has attracted artists and creative types of every ilk, many of whom stayed on after graduation to found small businesses, participate in public art projects, or simply live and work in a state that prides itself on supporting the arts. This is particularly evident in Providence, where there seem to be artist studios on every block, but it also extends further out to nearly every community in the state. If you're looking to take in some of the best visual and performing art Rhode Island has to offer, start in the capital and make your way south.

COLLEGE HILL

- No trip to Providence is complete without stopping in to see what's on display at the RISD Museum (224 Benefit St., 401/454-6500, www.risdmuseum.org), which houses more than 86,000 works of art, with galleries devoted to ancient Greek, Roman, and Egyptian artifacts, costumes and textiles, and Asian, decorative, and contemporary art. Don't leave without seeing the nine-foot tall statue of Buddha, a 12th-century wooden sculpture that is the largest of its kind in the United States, or the many breathtaking woodblock prints by Hokusai and his contemporaries.

- While you're on this side of town, consider also checking out the David Winton Bell Gallery (64 College St., 401/863-2932, www.brown.edu) at Brown University, whose collection includes works by artists from Rembrandt and Matisse to Robert Motherwell and Aaron Siskind.

DOWNTOWN

Things get especially interesting once you step outside the boundaries of Providence's formal institutions of higher learning and head downtown, where a closely related yet slightly more unhinged art scene thrives.

- Pay a visit to AS220 (115 Empire St., 401/831-9327, www.as220.org) and check out the "unjuried, uncensored" art on exhibit at one of four galleries operated by this nonprofit arts organization and cornerstone of the local art scene.

- If you're looking for a more participatory experience, check their website for weekly drop-in classes like figure drawing and printmaking. If you're looking for art to take home, pop in to

★ Downcity

Downcity (sometimes also called the Downcity Arts District) is bordered roughly by Sabin Street to the west, Pine Street to the east, and Empire Street to the south. After decades of economic decline, this downtown neighborhood underwent a makeover beginning in the early 2000s, when the city began an intensive—and quite successful—revitalization effort.

The neighborhood is home to many of the city's most vibrant small businesses, shops, restaurants, and hotels, most of which are concentrated on the main drags of Weybosset, Westminster, and Washington Streets. Here you can take in a touring Broadway show, catch productions at one of the smaller regional theater companies, shop for locally made gifts at one of the boutiques on Westminster Street, stay up late and catch some live music at one of the best venues in the city, or simply stroll and enjoy the wealth of beautiful 19th-century and early-20th-century commercial architecture.

Craftland (212 Westminster St., 401/272-4285, www.craftlandshop.com), where an array of locally made crafts, gifts, prints, and jewelry can be found.

- WaterFire (401/273-1155, www.waterfire.org, Saturdays May-Oct.): This ecological art installation created by a scientist-turned-artist is the Creative Capital's pièce de résistance. On select nights throughout the year, eighty fragrant bonfires are lit on Providence's rivers; creating a complete sensory experience that is not to be missed.

WICKFORD

One could easily spend days checking out the galleries in Providence alone, but the coastal art communities in Rhode Island tend to appeal to different sensibilities, with windswept watercolors, plein-air paintings, and whimsical sketchbook exhibits full of lighthouses and coastlines pervading the artistic landscape.

- The Wickford Art Association (36 Beach St., 401/294-6840, www.wickfordart.org) is a prime example of this, and also a great resource for those looking to drop in on classes like figure drawing, portraiture, and watercolor. The galleries here feature rotating exhibits by talented local artists, many of whom have been making art in the community since the association was established in 1962.

NEWPORT

- From Wickford, head over the bridge to Newport and stop in at the Newport Art Museum (76 Bellevue Ave., 401/848-8200, www.newportartmuseum.org), which has a permanent collection that focuses specifically on the role played by New England artists in the development of American art. Highlights here include works by Newport artist Howard Gardiner Cushing, whose sublime early-20th-century portraits of his wife Ethel hang alongside oils by 19th-century landscape artist William Trost Richards, George Bellows, and others. The museum also graciously hosts community events throughout the year, such as film screenings, murder mystery parties, live music, artist talks, and classes.

- Newport is also home to the National Museum of American Illustration (492 Bellevue Ave., 401/851-8949, www.americanillustration.org), where you can view an impressive collection of art created for books, periodicals, advertisements, and new media. Works by artists like Norman Rockwell, Andrew Wyeth, and Winslow Homer are on display in the galleries, housed in Vernon Court, a Gilded Age French château that is a work of art in and of itself.

Downcity is also home to the Providence Arcade (65 Weybosset St., 401/454-4568, www.arcadeprovidence.com), the nation's oldest indoor shopping mall, which was built in 1828 and reopened in 2013. With its Greek Revival columns, skylighted roof, and cast-iron railings, the Arcade is worth a walk through just for the architecture alone, but it's also home to a number of locally owned shops and restaurants, as well as 48 "microlofts" on the second and third floors.

The Providence Public Library (150 Empire St., 401/455-8000, www.provlib.org, 12:30pm-8:30pm Mon. and Thurs., 9:30am-5:30pm Tues., 12:30pm-5:30pm Fri., 9:30am-2:30pm Sat., 1pm-5pm Sun.) hosts art exhibits, film screenings, classes, and events but is also worth checking out just for its gorgeous interior. In 2013, after years of renovations, the library reopened the doors of its adjacent Washington Street wing, an impressive Venetian Renaissance-inspired building built circa 1900. The building's grand marble staircases and floors, cast-iron moldings, chandeliers, and murals make it well worth a walk-through.

Just around the corner from the library you'll find **AS220** art space (115 Empire St., 401/831-9327, www.as220.org, noon-1am Tues.-Sat.) a nonprofit complex of gallery spaces, artist studios, performance venues, and learning labs, which has also had a considerable hand in the revitalization of the Downcity neighborhood.

Providence Children's Museum

The **Providence Children's Museum** (100 South St., 401/273-5437, www.childrenmuseum.org, 9am-5pm daily, $12), located in the Jewelry District, offers a cool range of hands-on exhibits, including a children's garden that takes visitors through a touch-friendly tour of trees, shrubs, and plants native to Rhode Island; a puppetry workshop, a water-play environment where kids can learn about ice, mist, and the scientific ways of water, and a toddler-oriented area called Littlewoods, in which participants can scamper through simulated caves and climb trees.

WEST SIDE

West of downtown is the collection of residential neighborhoods and small business districts that make up Providence's West Side. The last few decades have brought significant changes to these neighborhoods, many of which were less than desirable places to live as recently as the 1990s, but are now burgeoning hipster enclaves replete with record stores, bicycle-repair shops, community gardens, and excellent coffee shops. Rents have increased, but the neighborhood shows relatively little sign of the cultural homogenization that so often comes with urban gentrification.

★ Federal Hill

Federal Hill, Providence's Little Italy, begins just west of where Atwells Avenue crosses I-95. You'll know you've found it when you pass under the lighted **Federal Hill Arch,** from which an Italian pinecone hangs as a symbol

of welcome. For about 15 blocks you'll find the shops and Italian restaurants for which the neighborhood is known, not to mention dry-goods stores and a few random tattoo parlors and hookah bars as well.

It's not hard to imagine crime bosses and characters from *The Sopranos* sauntering along Atwells Avenue, Federal Hill's main drag, probably because for years the neighborhood was a well-known hub for organized crime. Maybe there's a Mafia presence here these days, maybe there isn't; unquestionably there have been mob-related busts here in the past. What you will find along **Atwells Avenue,** and the cobblestone paved hub **De Pasquale Square,** are terrific restaurants and deli counters that seem right out of a Roman streetscape. Years ago, local filmmaker Michael Corrente brought a bit of fame to the neighborhood by using it as the location for the movie *Federal Hill.*

Atwells Avenue is best explored on foot, not just because of its enticing shops and cobblestone walkways but because traffic and parking here can be a nightmare, especially on weekend evenings. If walking isn't an option, most restaurants offer valet parking—just be prepared to sit in traffic.

Broadway and the Armory District

Just south of Federal Hill are Broadway and Westminster Streets, which both run parallel to Atwells Avenue. The sections of Broadway and Westminster between I-95 and Route 6 are home to some of the city's best restaurants, coffee shops, and a smattering of great vintage stores and excellent record shops. Because of its proximity to the very stately Cranston Street Armory Building, the neighborhood is sometimes referred to as the "Armory District."

Just west of the Federal Hill and Broadway neighborhoods is Olneyville, a historic and culturally diverse community, known for its crumbling mill buildings and the many artists who've taken up residence in them over the years. While the low rents and spaciousness

West Side

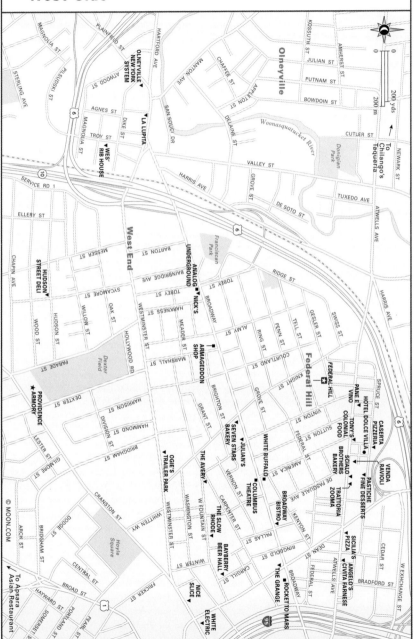

Olneyville

West End

Federal Hill

Woonasquatucket River

To Chilango's Taqueria

To Apsara Asian Restaurant

© MOON.COM

Streets and points of interest:

OLNEYVILLE NEW YORK SYSTEM
LA LUPITA
WES' RIB HOUSE
HUDSON STREET DELI
ANALOG UNDERGROUND
NICK'S
ARMAGEDDON SHOP
PROVIDENCE ARMORY
OGIE'S TRAILER PARK
SEVEN STARS BAKERY
JULIAN'S
THE AVERY
WHITE BUFFALO
COLUMBUS THEATRE
THE SLOW RHODE
BAYBERRY BEER HALL
NICE SLICE
WHITE ELECTRIC
PANE E' VINO
HOTEL DOLCE VILLA
TONY'S COLONIAL FOOD
CASERTA PIZZERIA
PASTICHE FINE DESSERTS
SCIALO BROTHERS BAKERY
VENDA RAVIOLI
TRATTORIA ZOOMA
BROADWAY BISTRO
SICILIA'S PIZZA
ANGELO'S CIVITA FARNESE
THE GRANGE
ROCKETTO MARS

that once made the mills so attractive to artists are becoming scarce (several of the mills were converted into luxury condos, or razed to make way for parking lots and shopping malls in the early 2000s), the arts community here is still highly visible. (See the shopping and food sections of this chapter for more about these neighborhoods.)

EAST SIDE AND COLLEGE HILL

The city's East Side is divided from downtown by the Moshassuck River north of about Thomas Street, and then the Providence River south of that. Rising steeply to the east just past the river is College Hill, home to Brown University and the Rhode Island School of Design, as well as the heart of Providence's dynamic profusion of colonial and 19th-century architecture.

North and South Main Streets

Several attractions line the waterfront just across the river at the base of College Hill.

ROGER WILLIAMS NATIONAL MEMORIAL

You can get a real sense of modern Providence's humble origins by visiting the site of the original natural springs where Roger Williams established a settlement, now the **Roger Williams National Memorial** (282 N. Main St., 401/521-7266, www.nps.gov/rowi, dawn-dusk daily). This 4.5-acre plot and the visitors center (9am-5pm daily, free) dates from 1730, making it one of the oldest structures in the city; it's easily accessible from downtown hotels and lies just a few blocks east of the State House via Smith Street. With its shaded pine groves and manicured lawn, the park today serves as a peaceful urban green space for downtown's white-collar workforce, college students, and anyone else looking for a respite from the noise and chaos of the city.

CATHEDRAL OF ST. JOHN

Just across from the Roger Williams National Memorial stands an elegant example of

Georgian ecclesiastical architecture, the Episcopal **Cathedral of St. John** (271 N. Main St., 410/331-4662, www.episcopalri.org), which also contains a number of Gothic elements, from tall lancet windows to a Gothic belfry. John Holden Greene designed the church in 1810, but the congregation dates back much earlier, when Gabriel Bernon established King's Chapel here with Nathaniel Brown. The adjoining cemetery contains graves of many of the city's early luminaries.

FIRST BAPTIST CHURCH IN AMERICA

Although it lacks the height of the downtown skyscrapers, the **First Baptist Church in America** (75 N. Main St., 401/274-4500, www.fbcia.org) nevertheless affects a dramatic influence on the city's skyline. Roger Williams established this parish in 1638, making it the nation's first such congregation. Interestingly, within just a few years, Williams parted ways with the Baptist Church, unable to reconcile his membership of any "earthly church" with his own devout beliefs in the New Testament. In 1700, member Pardon Tillinghast, who built the city's first wharf, constructed a meetinghouse for the congregation—at his own expense—along North Main Street. This structure was succeeded by a larger church in 1726 and, in 1775, by the present Baptist church, whose triple-tiered spire rises to 185 feet.

SOUTH MAIN STREET

College Street marks the transition from North to South Main Streets. South Main contains a mix of historic residences, restaurants and a few shops, vintage redbrick commercial structures, and new offices. Structures worth noting as you stroll along include the 1774 **Joseph Brown House** (50 S. Main St.), the home of one of the four famous Brown siblings. Joseph Brown took to architecture and designed this staunch redbrick city home with a widow's walk on the roof; he also designed the First Baptist Church and the Old Market House. Note the **Old Stone Bank**

East Side and College Hill

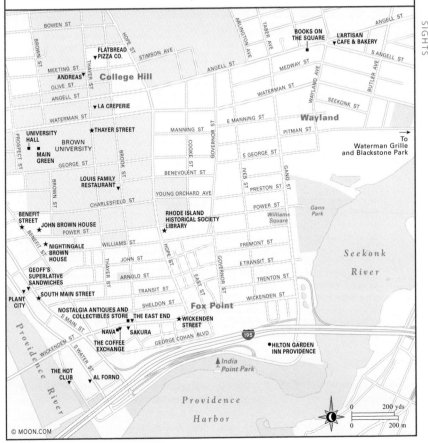

BOWEN ST
BROWN ST
HOPE ST
FLATBREAD PIZZA CO.
STIMSON AVE
MEETING ST
THAYER ST
ANDREAS
College Hill
OLIVE ST
ANGELL ST
LA CREPERIE
WATERMAN ST
UNIVERSITY HALL
THAYER STREET
BROWN UNIVERSITY
MAIN GREEN
PROSPECT ST
GEORGE ST
BROOK ST
LOUIS FAMILY RESTAURANT
BROWN ST
CHARLESFIELD ST
BENEFIT STREET
JOHN BROWN HOUSE
BENEFIT ST
POWER ST
NIGHTINGALE BROWN HOUSE
WILLIAMS ST
THAYER ST
JOHN ST
HOPE ST
GEOFF'S SUPERLATIVE SANDWICHES
ARNOLD ST
SOUTH MAIN STREET
TRANSIT ST
PLANT CITY
S MAIN ST
NOSTALGIA ANTIQUES AND COLLECTIBLES STORE
SHELDON ST
Fox Point
THE EAST END
WICKENDEN STREET
NAVA
SAKURA
GEORGE COHAN BLVD
THE COFFEE EXCHANGE
WICKENDEN ST
S WATER ST
THE HOT CLUB
AL FORNO
Providence River

ARLINGTON AVE
TABER AVE
ANGELL ST
BOOKS ON THE SQUARE
L'ARTISAN CAFE & BAKERY
S ANGELL ST
MEDWAY ST
WAYLAND AVE
BUTLER AVE
WATERMAN ST
SEEKONK ST
E MANNING ST
Wayland
MANNING ST
GOVERNOR ST
PITMAN ST
COOKE ST
E GEORGE ST
BENEVOLENT ST
IVES ST
YOUNG ORCHARD AVE
PRESTON ST
GANO ST
POWER ST
Gano Park
RHODE ISLAND HISTORICAL SOCIETY LIBRARY
Williams Square
FREMONT ST
GOVERNOR ST
EAST ST
E TRANSIT ST
Seekonk River
TRENTON ST
WICKENDEN ST
195
HILTON GARDEN INN PROVIDENCE
India Point Park

To Waterman Grille and Blackstone Park

Providence Harbor

0   200 yds
0   200 m

© MOON.COM

(86 S. Main St.), former home of the Providence Institution for Savings, which was the city's first savings bank and one of the country's oldest. The imposing gilt-domed neoclassical building dates to 1898.

Benefit Street

Sometimes called the city's "Mile of History," **Benefit Street** runs parallel to North and South Main Streets, just a block east but in most places many feet higher in elevation. During Providence's heyday as a colonial shipping center, and then throughout the 19th century's industrial periods, wealthy city residents built their homes along or just off Benefit Street, which remained fashionable well into the early 20th century. After World War II, however, and coinciding with the migration of former urban dwellers into suburbs, which affected most large U.S. cities, many of the old homes along Benefit Street were boarded up, and others were subdivided into boarding houses and cheap apartments. During the city's renaissance, which began in earnest in the late 1970s, the Providence Preservation Society began to restore Benefit Street house by house. Walking through the neighborhood today, it's hard to believe that it

Buddy Cianci and the Providence Renaissance

Providence legend **Buddy Cianci** was one of the longest-serving mayors of a major U.S. city and the first Italian American mayor of Providence. He was also one the country's most controversial political figures, inspiring everything from outrage to fascination—and even a high-profile documentary film about his life, released in 2006.

There's no question that a good deal of the credit for the city's so-called renaissance goes to Cianci, who was convicted in 1984, while in office, of kidnapping and then beating up his estranged wife's boyfriend with a fire log and burning him with a lit cigarette. He spent the term of his five-year suspended sentence as the host of a radio talk show, which drew fantastically high ratings. In 1991, Cianci ran for mayor again and won, this time capturing 97 percent of the vote—astounding when you consider he was a convicted felon and a Republican in a mostly Democratic and liberal state (although on most social issues, Cianci has a thoroughly progressive record). But, true to form, Cianci apparently went right back to his shady ways.

In 2002, he was convicted again, this time of one "racketeering conspiracy charge accusing him of masterminding a criminal scheme that took bribes for favors, including tax breaks, jobs, and sweetheart deals on city-owned land," according to the *Providence Journal*. It was the culmination of an investigation into city officials that the FBI called Operation Plunder Dome, after which Cianci was sentenced to five years and four months in prison. He resigned as mayor a few days later and began serving his sentence at Elkton Federal Correctional Institution in Ohio. Released in 2007, Cianci promptly returned to the airwaves with a radio show, and as a local TV news commentator.

While Cianci is often given much of the credit for the Providence we know today, there is a troubling side to his character, to say the least. He ran for mayor again in 2014 and lost to Jorge Elorza, a young law professor and former housing court judge whose campaign platform appealed more to a younger generation of voters who were presumably less impressed with Cianci's track record. It was the first time he'd had ever been defeated in a mayoral race, and, for many, the election marked the end of an era. He passed away in 2016.

was ever blighted—all told, you'll find about 200 buildings that date to the 18th and 19th centuries along Benefit Street, which is strung with vintage gas lamps and lined by brick sidewalks between Olney Street to the north and Wickenden Street to the south.

Providence Preservation Society (21 Meeting St., 401/831-7440, www.ppsri.org), offers both guided and self-guided walking tours of the neighborhood. At certain times during the year, the general public gets a glimpse inside some of these exceptional examples of homes built in the colonial era through Victorian times, and sometimes into the elaborate gardens that surround them. In June, you can attend the **Festival of Historic Houses,** a two-day event of house and garden tours along Benefit Street.

One of the first you'll come to as you

walk north from Transit or James Streets is the immense **Nightingale-Brown House** (357 Benefit St., 401/863-1177, www.brown.edu, 9am-4pm Mon.-Fri. Memorial Day-Labor Day, free). Colonel Joseph Nightingale built the enormous square hip-roofed house in 1792, Brown University founder Nicholas Brown bought the house in 1814, and his son John Carter Brown amassed an unrivaled collection of artifacts and documents here that traced the New World's early history. (This collection is now housed at the library at Brown University that bears his name.) The house remained in the Brown family into the 1980s and is now, appropriately enough, part of Brown University. Much of the building today is home to offices for Brown's Center for Public Humanities, however, museum collections are still on view here, like the 18th century imported China that was used by the Brown family for everyday meals throughout the 1900s.

A distinct departure from the many fine residences along Benefit Street, the formidable concrete **Old Arsenal** (176 Benefit St.) was designed in 1840 by James Bucklin, the same architect who designed downtown's Arcade and the Providence Athenaeum. Behind the imposing Gothic Revival facade of white stucco with a giant green wooden door that looks like something out of "Jack and the Beanstalk," it housed troops during both the Dorr Rebellion and the Civil War.

Until the construction of the present-day State House near Providence Place Mall, Rhode Island's General Assembly met at the **Old State House** (150 Benefit St., 401/277-2678, www.preservation.ri.gov, 9am-4pm Mon.-Fri.), a brick-and-sandstone structure dating to 1762 (its wooden predecessor burned down in 1758). From its first days, it served not only as the political center but also the social and commercial heart of the colony. In a juxtaposition of politics and commerce, the first floor was an open goods market while politicians assembled upstairs to debate and pass laws. On May 4, 1776, the young assembly passed what is considered the first declaration of independence in the United States, the Rhode Island Independence Act. Surprisingly, the state used this humble building as its capitol until 1900, when the current grand building was constructed. Today the building serves as the headquarters for the Rhode Island Historical Preservation and Heritage Commission, and visitors are welcome to pop in during office hours, 9am-4pm Monday through Friday.

In the 1790 colonial house at **88 Benefit Street,** now a private home, lived the object of Edgar Allan Poe's affection. She was a young widow named Sarah Helen Whitman, and the poet dedicated the famous works "To Helen" and "Annabel Lee" to her. Poe had corresponded with Whitman, herself a poet, for a few years and finally met her when he came to lecture at the Franklin Lyceum. The two

became immediately and seriously smitten with one another, but Whitman objected to Poe's habitual carousing and boozing—ultimately, she broke off their engagement and left him because of his inability to distance himself from the bottle. Shortly thereafter, the penniless and drunken Poe died in Baltimore.

★ Providence Athenaeum

Among the oldest libraries in North America, the **Providence Athenaeum** (251 Benefit St., 401/421-6970, www.providenceathenaeum. org, 10am-6pm Mon.-Fri., 10am-2pm Sat., free), dates to 1753 and contains rare and fascinating works, like seven volumes of the original double elephant folio edition of John J. Audubon's *Birds of America.* Works by Robert Burns, an early-19th-century study of Egypt commissioned by Napoleon titled *Description de l'Égypte,* and several books from 14th-century Europe are additional highlights of the Rare Books Collection.

The Athenaeum was established in 1831 and moved into this beautiful Greek Revival structure in 1838. In the late 1840s, Edgar Allan Poe and Sarah Whitman spent many an hour discussing literature and admiring one another's works in the Athenaeum's corridors. In addition to priceless original literary volumes and a comprehensive modern collection that can be viewed by any visitor (and taken out on loan by members), the Athenaeum houses several rare artworks, including *The Hours,* a famous painting by Newport-born miniature painter Edward G. Malbone.

★ Prospect Terrace Park

Farther up College Hill at the intersection of Congdon and Bowen Streets is perhaps the most romantic outdoor space in the city, lofty **Prospect Terrace Park,** a grassy rectangle with a wrought-iron fence that's perched high above downtown, providing an exceptional view of the city. It's also the burial site of Roger Williams, whose large granite statue stands at the edge of the park, overlooking downtown. Surrounding the park are more of the neighborhood's gorgeous houses, and it's a relatively short walk southeast to Brown University's commercial strip along Thayer Street, meaning you could walk off your dinner and stroll to the park just in time for one of the best sunset views in Providence.

John Brown House

Perhaps the most imposing of the neighborhood's many impressive homes is the Rhode Island Historical Society's **John Brown House** (52 Power St., 401/273-7507, www.rihs.org, 1pm-4pm Tues.-Fri., 10am-4pm Sat. Apr.-Nov., 10am-4pm Sat. Jan.-Mar., $10 adults, $6 children). The sixth U.S. president, John Quincy Adams, described this as "the most magnificent and elegant private mansion I have seen on this continent." Exquisitely restored and furnished top to bottom, it still looks swanky today—few American housemuseums from this period rival it. Inside you'll find a first-rate assemblage of colonial furnishings and decorative arts.

John Brown, a wealthy merchant and slave trader, began construction on the three-story Georgian mansion in 1786. For many decades during the building's first century, attending a party at the Brown House was obligatory for society types and academics. In 1941, the house was bequeathed to the Rhode Island Historical Society, which set about reproducing the interior's original colors and French wallpaper. Furnishings include many created by local artisans William Clagget, a clockmaker, and Goddard-Townsend, a Newport firm that specialized in high-quality colonial wood furnishings.

Rhode Island School of Design (RISD)

The campus of the prestigious **Rhode Island School of Design**, or **RISD** (pronounced "RIZ-dee"), occupies many of the blocks along Benefit Street from College to Waterman Streets; there are also buildings down the hill along Main Street and up a block on Prospect Street. The school opened with a very practical vocational aim: to train students in the ways of textile arts and design as well as in

related fields represented in Providence, such as jewelry design and manufacture, and machine works and design. Through the years, the school has gained considerable prestige not only for its applied design courses but for training some of the nation's leaders in fine and graphic arts, interior design, costume-making, and the like. An arty buzz permeates the campus and nearby streets, and no doubt it has helped to influence the similarly subversive tone of neighboring Brown University, which is perhaps the most countercultural of the Ivy League schools.

Keep an eye out for signs marking RISD's Office of Admissions, which occupies a brilliant Italianate edifice called the **Woods-Gerry Mansion** (62 Prospect St., 401/454-6141, 10am-5pm Mon. and Fri.-Sat., 10am-4pm Tues., 2pm-5pm Sun., free). The building contains galleries with rotating art exhibits, and in back you can walk through a small sculpture garden.

★ RISD MUSEUM OF ART

The **RISD Museum of Art** (224 Benefit St., 401/454-6500, www.risd.edu/museum.cfm, 10am-5pm Tues.-Sun., $15 adults, free under 18) offers a true survey of works from around the world and spanning many centuries. The collection varies widely, with several works by Monet gracing the French impressionist area and an excellent collection of mostly 18th- and 19th-century American artists such as Frank Benson, Thomas Cole, Winslow Homer, and John Singer Sargent. Rotating exhibitions vary considerably but in recent years have included fresh themes like *What Nerve! Alternative Figures in American Art, 1960 to the Present,* and *Bona Drag: An Incomplete History of Drag and Cross-Gender Performance in Film and Video Art.*

Brown University

Few educational institutions can claim a greater degree of recognition, both nationally and internationally, than **Brown University**, which has a stately campus that dominates the upper slope of College Hill.

"I Am Providence":
The Legacy of H. P. Lovecraft

A bust of H.P. Lovecraft sits inside the Providence Athenaeum.

In keeping with the trope of the starving artist, legendary horror and science-fiction writer H. P. Lovecraft was penniless and largely unknown at the time of his death in 1937. Born and raised on the East Side of Providence by parents who both suffered from mental illnesses, Lovecraft was forever altered by the fear-riddled and anxiety-provoking experiences of his childhood, eventually growing into the famously reclusive and uneasy man who would write such classics of the horror/sci-fi genre as *The Call of Cthulhu*, and *Whisperer in the Darkness*. Today, appreciation and influence of Lovecraft's work can be found throughout pop culture, from Black Sabbath songs to episodes of *South Park*.

Lovecraft was influenced by his more famous predecessor (and Providence frequenter) Edgar Allan Poe, creating tales of weird fiction before the horror/sci-fi genre existed as such. Much of his work was informed by a lifelong fascination with the sciences—astronomy in particular—and major themes in his work include threats to civilization, dark and mythical beings, and occult-like underworlds. It's fitting then that Lovecraft has accumulated somewhat of an occult following himself, especially in Providence, where there's an **H. P. Lovecraft Memorial Square** (Angell St. at Prospect St.) on the East Side, and where there are annual celebrations of his birth at **The Ladd Observatory** (210 Doyle Ave., 401/863-2323), and of his death at the **Swan Point Cemetery** (585 Blackstone Blvd., 401/272-1314, www.swanpointcemetery.com). In 1977, fans placed a commemorative headstone at Lovecraft's gravesite bearing the phrase "I AM PROVIDENCE," a line from his extensive collection of personal letters.

In 2013, the first annual **NecronomiCon Providence** (www.necronomicon-providence. com) took place, billing itself as the "International Conference and Festival of Weird Fiction, Art, and Academia," dedicated to exploring the life and works of Lovecraft and his contemporaries. Highlights include a Lovecraft walking tour, live performances inspired by weird fiction and art, a book and comics sale, author readings, panel discussions, and a "Cthulu Prayer Breakfast." The festival takes place during the third week of August to commemorate the author's birthday, August 20, 1890.

The seventh college founded in what became the United States, Brown began in 1764 in the East Bay community of Warren with the name Rhode Island College, under the guidance of Reverend James Manning. Despite its Baptist leanings, an early edict related to the school's operations was that "into this Liberal and Catholic Institution shall never be admitted any Religious Tests but on the Contrary all the Members Hereof shall forever enjoy full free Absolute and uninterrupted Liberty of Conscience." In 1770, a permanent location for the college was established on the east side of Providence on eight acres of what is now College Hill.

Today, Brown enjoys a reputation for being a flashy jet-set school of hipsters and dilettantes—depending on your point of view, a welcome relief to the sometimes overly tweedy Ivy League rivals Harvard and Yale. Inarguably, Brown fosters a deeply liberal and somewhat countercultural collective philosophy, where avant-garde arts and studies of on-the-edge literary and social theories thrive. Brown was headed by Ruth Simmons between 2000-2012, making it the first Ivy League institution to appoint a black president.

CAMPUS BUILDINGS

On Brown's central hub, the **Main Green,** you can admire the elegant Georgian architecture of the original **University Hall.** But the university's picturesque hilltop campus incorporates nearly every popular civic architectural style of the past two centuries. Colonial and then Greek Revival architecture (note James C. Bucklin's 1835 **Manning Hall** and also the 1840 **Rhode Island Hall**) dominates the style of those buildings created until the late 1880s, when the aesthetic shifted to accommodate the Victorian movement. A new spate of building during the 1960s and 1970s produced more modern structures such as the **List Art Building,** where you'll find the **David Winton Bell Gallery** (List Art Center, 64 College St., 401/863-2932, www.brown.edu, 11am-4pm Mon.-Wed. and Fri., 1pm-9pm Thurs., 1pm-4pm Sat.-Sun., free),

showing both contemporary and historic exhibitions.

THAYER STREET

Brown's commercial college strip centers on **Thayer Street,** from about Bowen Street south to Waterman Street. Even in summer, when relatively few students are on campus, Thayer Street is lively and youthful, with coffeehouses, sandwich shops, ethnic restaurants, bookstores, a few school buildings, and a fun vibe that befits the entertainment district nearest Brown and RISD.

WICKENDEN STREET

You'll find another corridor of arty shops, antique stores, restaurants and cafés along the slightly less trafficked **Wickenden Street** between Benefit Street and Gano Street. Wickenden Street runs east-west across Fox Point, at the southern end of College Hill fronting Providence Harbor. India Point, at the southeastern tip of this neighborhood, has for many years been the center of the city's Portuguese community, and because of its cute restaurants and shops it draws folks from all over. The street is home to one of Providence's oldest and most beloved coffee shops and roasters, **The Coffee Exchange** (207 Wickenden St., 401/273-1198, www.thecoffeeexchange.com, 6am-9pm daily).

Eighteen-acre **India Point Park** (India St., www.providenceri.com), accessible either from exit 2 off I-195 or by heading south on Gano Street or South Main Street from Wickenden Street, provides the city's only frontage on Narragansett Bay, right at the bay's head, where it meets the Seekonk and Providence Rivers. Here you'll find the northern entrance point of the East Bay Bike Path, which extends about 14 mi (22.5 km) to the southeast into Bristol. The park has a small network of paved trails suitable for biking or

1: RISD Museum of Art 2: the statue of Roger Williams at Prospect Terrace Park 3: a quiet corner in the Providence Athenaeum 4: Urs Fischer's *Untitled (Lamp/Bear)* sculpture on the Brown University campus

strolling and a few grassy fields for tossing a ball or Frisbee.

NORTH AND EAST OF COLLEGE HILL

North of the intersection with Wickenden Street, Hope Street has several cool shops and restaurants, plus some fine old homes.

Rhode Island Historical Society Library

The **Rhode Island Historical Society Library** (121 Hope St., 401/273-8107, www.rihs.org, 10am-5pm Wed.-Fri., free) is worth a stop if you have even a casual interest in genealogy or early state history. Documents pertaining to Rhode Island, including all manner of birth, death, and marriage records, date as far back as the days of Roger Williams. There are also prints, paintings, photos, and other historical items. The society sponsors 90-minute city walking tours June through mid-October with a focus on history, the waterfront, architecture, art, and similar topics.

Blackstone Boulevard

BLACKSTONE PARK

Just north of Wayland Square is the hilly 40-acre **Blackstone Park,** a grassy, tree-shaded park ideal for a stroll. It has a couple of ponds and several walking paths, plus some nice spots for a picnic. The mostly upper-middle-class residential neighborhood surrounding the park contains some impressive stucco, wood-frame, and redbrick homes from the early part of the 20th century, all with neat gardens and perfectly manicured lawns.

SWAN POINT CEMETERY

From the northern end of Blackstone Park, west down Irving Avenue, is the southern end of Blackstone Boulevard, a broad tree-lined avenue with a wide grassy median that's usually abuzz with joggers, walkers, and cyclists. A little more than 1 mi (1.6 km) north on Blackstone Boulevard, on the right, is the entrance to the 210-acre **Swan Point Cemetery** (585 Blackstone Blvd., 401/272-1314, www.

swanpointcemetery.com, 8am-5pm Oct.-May, 8am-7pm Apr.-Sept.), laid out in 1875. This is one of the country's foremost garden cemeteries. Visitors are encouraged to bicycle (slowly), walk, or drive the grounds, which are laced with beautiful gardens. Among the famous Rhode Islanders buried here are horror writer H. P. Lovecraft and Civil War general Ambrose Burnside.

LIPPITT MEMORIAL PARK

A short distance north along Blackstone Boulevard is **Lippitt Memorial Park,** a pretty little slice of greenery with a grand old central fountain and ample seating. The jogging path up the median of Blackstone Boulevard terminates where Hope Street becomes East Avenue, right across the street from **Three Sisters Ice Cream** (1074 Hope St., 401/273-7230, www.threesistersri.com, Mon.-Thurs., 7am-9pm, Fri. 7am-10pm, Sat. 8am-10pm, Sun. 8am-9pm).

SOUTH SIDE

The **South Side** of Providence contains the mostly residential neighborhoods of Elmwood and Washington Park. The area is home to a number of enormous, and sometimes crumbling, Victorian homes as well as a large and vibrant Latino community. Much energy has been invested here over the last decade; many historic homes have been purchased and restored or razed to make way for community gardens, and colorful murals grace the sides of many community buildings.

★ Roger Williams Park

Roughly 4 mi (6.4 km) south of downtown is the city's largest urban oasis, the 430-acre **Roger Williams Park** (1000 Elmwood Ave., 401/785-3510, https://rwpconservancy.org grounds 7am-9pm daily), the home of Roger Williams Park Zoo. Visitors can bike, skate, or walk nearly 10 mi (16 km) of paved roads (open to auto traffic, but only at low speeds, and there's usually ample room for all people and vehicles to maneuver). Unpaved trails also meander into the greenery around the 10 lakes (many where you can rent small boats). Roger Williams's great-great-granddaughter, Betsey Williams, donated the land for this park in the 1870s, and it retains its splendid Victorian layout, created by designer Horace W. S. Cleveland in 1878. The look and ambience borrows heavily from the most famous of 19th-century park designers, Frederick Law Olmsted.

One of the most architecturally significant structures in the park, the redbrick colonial revival **Casino** dates to 1896. It has impressive views from its veranda over the restored music bandstand and Roosevelt Lake. With a ballroom crowned by 20-foot ceilings and ornate plaster friezes and trim, it is a fine example of the park's success in restoration and a favorite place for weddings and parties. Surrounding the casino and extending throughout several parts of the park are lovely rose and flower gardens as well as a Japanese garden. The park also includes its own **Botanical Center** (Tues.-Sun. 11am-4pm, $5 adults, $2 children 6-12), home to the largest public indoor display garden in New England, with two greenhouses and over 150 different species of plants.

In the summer, there is occasional live music at the **Benedict Temple to Music,** a beautiful stone column amphitheater overlooking one of the park's ponds. If you've got kids, visit the reproduction vintage carousel at **Carousel Village** (noon-6pm weekdays, 11am-6pm weekends), which also has a miniature-golf course, bumper boats, minitrain rides, and other amusements.

MUSEUM OF NATURAL HISTORY

Roger Williams Park is home to the **Museum of Natural History** (401/785-9457, http://www.providenceri.gov/museum, 10am-4pm daily, museum $2, museum and planetarium $3), which contains a planetarium and more than 250,000 objects and artifacts collected during the past two centuries—at any given time, just 2 percent of the museum's holdings are on display. These include preserved mollusk shells, birds, mammals, rocks, minerals, and—a particular strength—fossils from the region's coal age. The museum displays cultural artifacts, mostly from North America, including baskets, textiles, tools, and carvings—but with significant representation from Africa, Oceana, and other parts of the world. Perhaps more stimulating is the attached **Cormack Planetarium,** where a dazzling computerized star projector offers a memorable lesson in astronomy.

the gazebo at Roger Williams Park

The 35-minute shows are presented at 2pm Saturday and Sunday, and at 2pm daily July through August.

ROGER WILLIAMS PARK ZOO

The **Roger Williams Park Zoo** (1000 Elmwood Ave., 401/785-3510, www.rogerwilliamsparkzoo.org, 10am-5pm Apr.-Sept., 10am-4pm Oct.-Mar., $17.95 adults, $12.95 children) has more than 1,000 animals of more than 165 species. It's the third-oldest zoo in the nation, and has been ranked among the nation's 10 best. Major exhibits include Australasia, with its kangaroos, wallabies, and alligators; Fabric of Africa, featuring zebras, elephants, wildebeests, and giraffes; and Tropical America, home to monkeys, flamingos, snakes, and a giant anteater.

Other animals on display include the South American giant river otter and the Titi monkeys at the Faces of the Rainforest exhibit, and moon bears, snow leopards, and red pandas along the Marco Polo Adventure Trek. Other exhibits include the Natural Wetlands Trail, the Fabric of Africa, a children's petting zoo, and the educational zoo laboratory.

Entertainment and Events

NIGHTLIFE

A high concentration of college students and creative types makes for an interesting late-night scene in Providence, where there's something happening to suit everyone's tastes on almost any given night. Whether you're in the mood for a dark dive bar with a pool table and a jukebox, buffalo wings and *Monday Night Football,* or an avant-garde dance party with a drag queen DJ, you won't have much trouble finding somewhere you feel comfortable.

Downcity and the adjoining **Jewelry District** have the greatest concentration of the city's nightspots, including big dance clubs with tipsy college kids and revelers from the suburbs as well as excellent live-music venues drawing first-rate acts, both local and international. The city prides itself on its local music scene, which is ever-evolving thanks to a steady influx of new talent from the local colleges. Providence also has a thriving gay scene, with several popular clubs that draw in patrons from all over southern New England.

Bars

In the Jewelry District, young and old convene for the excellent jukebox at **Nick-a-Nee's** (75 South St., 401/861-7290, 3pm-1am Sun.-Thurs., 3pm-2am Fri.-Sat.), which hosts pool tournaments and occasional live music in a space that's laid back, unpretentious, and fun. A quick walk over the Point Street Bridge will get you to **The Hot Club** (575 South Water St., 401/861-9007, www.hotclubprov.com, noon-1am Mon.-Thurs. and Sun., noon-2am Fri.-Sat.), a staple Providence hangout spot situated on the mouth of the Providence River, directly across from the iconic smokestacks of the National Grid power building.

The West Side offers no shortage of bars either. Martini sippers will love the dark, art deco-inspired interior of **The Avery** (18 Luongo Sq., www.averyprovidence.com, 4pm-midnight Mon.-Fri., 5pm-midnight Sat.-Sun.), but craft beer lovers should head around the corner to **Bayberry Beer Hall** (381 W. Fountain St., 401/383-9487, www.bayberrybeerhall.com, 4pm-11pm Mon.-Thurs., 4pm-midnight Fri., 10am-midnight Sat., 10am-3pm Sun.) to check out their ever-rotating selection of New England-brewed draft beers and made-from-scratch food. A more wholesome option can be found at **The Grange** (166 Broadway, 401/831-0600, www.providencegrange.com, 9am-10pm Sun.-Mon. and Wed.-Thurs., 9am-11pm Fri.-Sat.), which has an impressive, locally sourced artisanal cocktail menu and a sweet lounge with wooden swings. A few blocks away, **Ogie's Trailer Park** (1155 Westminster St.,

401/383-8200, www.ogiestrailerpark.com, 4pm-1am Mon.-Thurs., 4pm-2am Fri.-Sat., noon-1am Sun.) offers cocktails and snacks (tater tots!) in a decidedly kitschy, trailer-park inspired atmosphere.

If karaoke is your thing, The Boombox (122 Fountain St., 401/861-0040, www. singboombox.com, 5pm-1am Wed.-Thurs., 5pm-2am Fri.-Sat., 7pm-1am Sun.) is not to be missed. Situated downstairs at the Dean Hotel, it's the city's first and only karaoke bar, with a small main lounge and five private rooms that can be rented out for parties. Even if you don't sing, it's fun to just sit and sip a drink while others take the mic and serenade you.

Live Music

The city's main venue for commercial touring music acts is the Dunkin' Donuts Center (1 LaSalle Sq., at Broadway and Atwells Ave., 401/331-6700, www.dunkindonutscenter. com)—sometimes referred to as "the Dunk"—in the western end of downtown. But seeing as Providence has its own celebrated music scene, visitors won't need to pay exorbitant ticket prices or sit in nosebleed seats to in order to see a great show.

A show at the West Side's Columbus Theatre (270 Broadway, 401/621-9660, www. columbustheatre.com) is always a treat. This 1926 venue has been lovingly restored and much lauded as an exceptional setting—both aesthetically and acoustically—in which to take in a show from the latest up-and-coming indie, folk, and occasional comedy acts.

Look to Dusk (301 Harris Ave., 401/714-0444, www.duskprovidence.com) for punk, metal, and indie bands, both local and touring. For mostly local acts in a variety of genres, check the calendars at AS220 (115 Empire St., 401/861-9190, www.as220.org) downtown, or Askew (150 Chestnut St., 401/272-5722, www.askewprov.com), in the Jewelry District.

Gay and Lesbian

The Providence Eagle (124 Snow St., 401/421-1447, www.providenceeagle.com,

3pm-2am Sun.-Wed., 3pm-2:30am Thurs.-Sat.) is a popular downtown gay bar with a rotating schedule of music, karaoke, and dance parties in a cozy setting. Recent events include live wrestling, a leather party, and a Pride kickoff celebration.

Just down the street, Mirabar (15 Elbow St., 401/331-6761, www.mirabar.com, 3pm-1am Mon.-Thurs., 3pm-2am Fri.-Sat., 1pm-1am Sun.) is the definitive men's club with a small dance floor and cocktail bar. It tends to draw a fairly young crowd and can get pretty wild on busier evenings.

The Dark Lady (19 Snow St., 401/274-6369, 9pm-1am Sun.-Thurs., 2pm-3am Fri.-Sat.) located on a quiet side street on the edge of downtown, is a cozy hangout with fun dance parties and occasional live music. Probably the most popular of the gay bars in town is The Stable (125 Washington St., 401/272-6950, 2pm-3am Mon.-Fri., noon-4am Sat.-Sun.) known for its friendly bartenders, amazing drag shows, and a relaxed but super fun atmosphere.

THE ARTS

Providence enjoys a rich performing arts scene, with a slew of theaters that range from big-time showcases of pre-Broadway shows and national touring acts to inexpensive avant-garde local workshops that will challenge your sensibilities. It's a good destination for people who like to take chances—there's no shortage of educated and progressive, even a bit jaded, audiences. Not an evening passes in Providence without the opportunity to watch some out-there abstract dance piece, catch an obscure foreign film at one of the art cinemas, or see a courageous new dramatic work by the next wunderkind in the city's theater scene.

If you plan on hanging out downtown, the beloved AS220 (115 Empire St., 401/831-9327, www.as220.org, noon-1am Tues.-Sat.) features an eclectic mix of entertainment, from poetry slams and punk rock to adult spelling bees and industrial noise acts. The crowd (and the cocktail menu) is just as diverse.

AS220: Building an Arts Empire

AS220 (115 Empire St., 401/831-9327, www.as220.org) was founded in 1985 with just $800 and idealist dreams of a creative community free from the trappings and limitations of high-art culture. Thirty years later, founder Bert Crenca's aspirations of creating an "unjuried, uncensored" art space have been realized tenfold; today AS220 is a multimillion-dollar nonprofit with a stellar reputation and a major hand in revitalizing the downtown arts and entertainment district in Providence.

Creating accessible space for artists to live and work is at the core of AS220's mission—it owns and operates nearly 60 live/work studios at three different properties in the Downcity neighborhood—but its various gallery spaces, performance venues, youth programs, and community workshops are what's really had a major hand in putting Providence on the map as an artist-friendly city. If you're not in town in August for AS220's annual **Foo Fest**, a day-long block party with live bands, workshops, a zine fair, and lots of artistic spectacle, you can check out the galleries any day of the week.

Visitors should start at **AS220's Main Gallery** (115 Empire St., 401/831-9327, www.as220. org, noon-1am Tues.-Sat.) which features monthly (unjuried and uncensored, of course) rotating art exhibits in a wide range of disciplines, from audio/visual installations and black-and-white photography to self-portraits made completely from hand-sewn beads and sequins. The gallery doubles as a performance space, where you can catch local and national touring bands, spoken-word poetry, and live theater on any given night. It's connected to an excellent bar and café, **AS220 Foo(d)**, and is right next door to two of its other performance venues, the **Black Box**, which hosts experimental theater, and **Psychic Readings**, where you can catch live music and performance art that might be a bit stranger than on the main stage. A dance studio on the second floor offers drop-in classes from ballet and salsa to tai chi and lunchtime yoga.

Just around the corner, pop in to the **Project Space** inside of the Dreyfus building (93 Mathewson St.), where rotating installations completely transform three small rooms into otherworldly works of art. Artist-run classes, workshops, and printmaking studios are also located in the Dreyfus, which was previously a hotel dating back to 1890. While classes and most live shows here require a cover charge, the galleries, artist talks, and various other events are generally free and open to the public.

You can also look to the city's colleges for a wide range of dance, theater, music, and other arts performances, with **Rhode Island College** (600 Mt. Pleasant Ave., www.ric.edu/pfa) offering some of the best works. It's always worth checking its website to see what's playing and where; visit the school's Bannister Gallery for rotating art exhibits. In the city's North End, this school doesn't always get the same attention as some of Providence's larger educational institutions, but its arts program is notable.

Also check to see what's happening at **Providence College** (401/865-2218, www.providence.edu), whose **Blackfriars Theatre** (11 Cunningham Sq., 401/865-1000, www.providence.edu/theatre) produces some first-rate plays. At **Brown University** (www.brown.edu), the acclaimed music department presents concerts in a wide range of disciplines, from chamber music to jazz. Plays and other performing arts are scheduled regularly at the school's **Dill Performing Arts Center** (77 Waterman St., 401/863-2838).

Theater

The **Providence Performing Arts Center** (220 Weybosset St., 401/421-2787, www.ppacri.org) ranks among New England's top venues for concerts, children's theater, and Broadway-style musical comedies—plus ballet, opera, and classical music. Throughout the year, top recording stars and performers like Diana Krall, David Sedaris, Josh Groban, and even astrophysicist Neil DeGrasse Tyson grace the stage here, and national touring musicals have included *Hamilton* and *Hello, Dolly!*, *Cinderella* and *Sesame Street Live*.

The Tony Award-winning **Trinity Repertory Company** (201 Washington St., 401/351-4242, www.trinityrep.com) presents seven classic and contemporary plays annually with a season running September through June. It also puts on an annual holiday production of *A Christmas Carol*.

The **Columbus Theatre** (270 Broadway, 401/621-9660, www.columbustheatre.com) is a gorgeously restored Italianate revival theater with a history dating back to 1926. Since then, it's been home to many forms of entertainment, from vaudeville and opera to art house and pornography. In 2009, the theater fell on hard times and was forced to close. It reopened in 2012 under new leadership and now hosts first-rate national indie acts as well as local performers in its ornately-muraled main theater and its more intimate upstairs venue.

Music and Dance

The **Rhode Island Philharmonic** (667 Waterman Ave., East Providence, 401/242-7070, www.ri-philharmonic.org) has been a cultural mainstay in Providence since 1945, featuring notable guest conductors from time to time, plus artists such as Debbie Reynolds and Marvin Hamlisch. The Philharmonic presents a classical series, three fully staged operas, a pop series, and several family-oriented pieces.

The Lincoln-based modern-dance rep company **Fusionworks** (401/334-3091, www.fusionworksdance.org) performs at venues throughout the state and elsewhere in the Northeast.

Festival Ballet Providence (825 Hope St., 401/353-1129, www.festivalballet.com) is the city's mainstay for classical, neoclassical, and contemporary dance.

Film

Try to catch a movie at the **Avon Cinema** (260 Thayer St., 401/421-0020, www.avoncinema.com), an art deco theater dating back to 1938, which shows indie, foreign,

and sometimes commercial movies, with occasional special midnight screenings. At Providence Place Mall you'll find the 16-screen **Providence Place Cinemas 16** (800/315-4000) and the **IMAX theater** (www.imax.com), which shows larger-than-life features on a six-story screen with a mind-blowing (perhaps ear-splitting) 12,000-watt surround-sound system.

FESTIVALS AND EVENTS
Summer

In June, Providence's dynamic gay and lesbian community celebrates **RI Pride Fest** (401/467-2130, www.prideri.com), which takes over many of the streets downtown each year with live music, outdoor stages, and a parade. Also in June, is the **Festival of Historic Houses** (www.providencehousetour.com), a two-day event of house and garden tours along Benefit Street. In early July, one of the city's most vibrant ethnic communities throws an **Annual Cape Verdean Independence Day Celebration** (India Point Park, 401/222-4133), which gives attendees a chance to sample authentic Cape Verdean foods, observe arts and crafts exhibits, and listen to music and storytelling. In August, local arts nonprofit AS220 hosts the annual **Foo Fest** (Empire St. between Washington and Westminster Sts., 401/831-9327), a daylong festival featuring bands, craft and activity booths for adults and children, a maker fair, and lots of delicious food and drink. Begun in 1997, the **Rhode Island International Film Festival** (various locations in Providence and neighboring towns, 401/861-4445, www.rifilmfest.org) has grown into a highly prestigious event showing more than 265 films; it's held every August.

In 2015, the first-ever **PVD FEST** (various locations downtown, www.pvdfest.com) took place in June, with the promise of being "a new signature event for the Creative Capital." Since then, the even has grown into an annual weeklong celebration known for its awe-inspiring mix of street theater, live music, installations and participatory art, and pure spectacle from around the world.

Fall

In the middle of September, about 30 of the city's ethnic communities gather for the **Annual Rhode Island Heritage Festival** (Roger Williams National Memorial, North Main St., 401/222-4133, www.preservation. ri.gov/heritage) to share traditional song and dance, arts and crafts demonstrations, and food. In early November, bring out your inner decorator at the **Annual Fine Furnishings—Providence** (Rhode Island Convention Center, 401/816-0963), which focuses mostly on the handcrafted furnishings

and decorative arts of New England artisans. You'll find a nice range of both traditional and contemporary wares in all price ranges.

Winter and Spring

Yachting and sailing enthusiasts gear up for the coming season in late January or early February at the **Rhode Island Boat Show** (Rhode Island Convention Center, 401/739-4040, www.riboatshow.com), where dealers show off the latest sailboats, powerboats, and equipment. In April, the convention center hosts the **RI Home Show** (401/272-0980, www.ribahomeshow.com), which features a flower and garden exhibit as well as an energy expo.

Shopping

Providence offers a great selection of unusual shops along with the chains you'd find anywhere. A nice thing about the city's Gap, Victoria's Secret, and other chains is that the vast majority are contained within a well-designed urban shopping mall, Providence Place. This mammoth structure anchors downtown and overlooks the well-landscaped riverfront, and it's close to several hotels and within walking distance of the universities.

Beyond the mall, Providence has a number of great design shops, galleries, art-supply stores, indie book and record shops, vintage clothiers, and home-furnishings and gift boutiques. These are geared as much toward visitors as they are to the city's artists, students, academics, and hipsters. Providence lures creative types, who often end up opening offbeat and innovative businesses in town. And while this isn't necessarily an ideal city for bargain hunters, you'll often find decent deals on antiques and art, and at the student-oriented spots you'll have no trouble homing in on discount threads, used books and records, and other low-priced odds and ends.

DOWNTOWN

Apart from the mall, downtown's most engaging retail spots are located mostly in the **Downcity Arts District** on Westminster Street and its offshoots. Parking here can be tricky but once you find it, the neighborhood is a great place to explore on foot.

Providence Place Mall

Opened in 1999, **Providence Place Mall** (1 Providence Pl., 401/270-1000, www. providenceplace.com, 10am-9pm Mon.-Sat., 11am-6pm Sun.) is an immense four-story atrium mall with a 16-screen Showcase Cinema multiplex and an IMAX theater along with a fairly standard upscale mix of apparel, home-furnishing, and other chain shops. The top-floor 700-seat food court has all the standards, with ice cream, burgers and fries, Mexican, sushi, Italian, and Chinese eateries. The ground level is lined with sit-down chain restaurants, most of them are jam-packed on weekend evenings. You can exit I-95 directly

1: the Avon Cinema 2: Cellar Stories Bookstore 3: the Providence Arcade, the nation's oldest indoor shopping mall 4: gifts and treasures at NAVA on the East Side

into the mall parking garages, and the mall is within walking distance of the riverfront, State House, convention center, and even College Hill—especially on warm days, plenty of shoppers wander out and explore the city. Stores include the usual chains—Macy's, Gap, Sephora, Loft, Bed Bath & Beyond, Brooks Brothers, J. Crew—equaling about 150 stores.

Books

Cellar Stories Bookstore (111 Mathewson St., 401/521-2665, www.cellarstories.com, 10am-6pm Mon.-Sat.) is the largest used and antiquarian bookstore in the state, specializing not only in hard-to-find and out-of-print books but also magazines and periodicals. It's often dusty and disorganized in a charming sort of way—a very easy place to lose track of time.

Clothing and Accessories

For the ladies, a stop at the adorable and expertly curated Queen of Hearts (220 Westminster St., 401/421-1471, www.queenofheartsprovidence.com, 11am-6pm Mon.-Wed., 11am-8pm Thurs.-Sat., 11am-5pm Sun.) is a must, especially if you're in the market for locally designed and made clothing and accessories. Its sister store, Modern Love (222 Westminster St., 401/421-1471, www.queenofheartsprovidence.com, 11am-6pm Mon.-Wed., 11am-8pm Thurs.-Sat., 11am-5pm Sun.), is right next door and carries a great selection of eclectic and very hip shoes. Both stores cater to a younger crowd, or at least those with youthful sensibilities.

The Providence Arcade (65 Weybosset St., 401/454-4568, www.arcadeprovidence.com), the nation's oldest indoor shopping mall, is home to a number of great little shops, including Carmen & Ginger (401/274-1700, www.carmenandginger.com, 11am-5:30pm Tues.-Wed., 11am-7pm Thurs.-Sat., 11am-3pm Sun.), an upscale vintage shop selling everything from clothes and jewelry to lighting, home decor, and antique cameras, and Lovecraft Arts and Sciences Council (401/264-0838, 11am-6:30pm Mon.-Sat., 11am-4pm Sun.), a storefront gallery and

weird emporium selling new and used fiction, sci-fi, fantasy, horror, and topical nonfiction books.

Antique and Vintage

It's easy to lose track of time at The Vault Collective (235 Westminster St., 401/250-2587, 11am-7pm daily Apr.-Dec., 11am-6pm daily Jan.-Mar.) where various vendors have set up shop to create a one-stop vintage emporium. Expect a high-quality selection of one-of-a-kind vintage items including graphic tees from the 1970s, 1980s, and 1990s, boho leather boots, belts, and bags, and all manner of denim and flannel from decades past.

Gifts

If you're looking for one-of-a-kind gifts, or just something special for yourself, Craftland (212 Westminster St., 401/272-4285, 11am-5pm Mon.-Sat., noon-5pm Sun.) is the place. Locally made prints, cards, jewelry, and other ephemera give it a brick-and-mortar Etsy store sort of feel, and the salespeople are always friendly and eager to help.

Home Decor

For home furnishing and decor, check out Homestyle (229 Westminster St., 401/277-1159, 10am-6pm Mon.-Sat., noon-5pm Sun.), which carries cool, albeit pricey, housewares, gifts, home accessories, and furnishings.

THE EAST SIDE

Several commercial strips are on the East Side, beginning at the base of College Hill along South Main Street, and also in the Brown University retail corridor along Thayer Street. Wickenden Street, at the southern tip of the East Side, also has some cute stores, and you'll find a small shopping district around Wayland Square, just east of Brown University and Hope Street.

It's no surprise that Providence has some excellent sources for art supplies, including, most prominently, the RISD Store (30 N. Main St., 401/454-6464, www.risdstore.com, 8:30am-7pm Mon.-Fri., 10am-5pm Sat.-Sun.), which also has one of the best selections of art books and periodicals in the city.

Antique and Vintage

Wickenden Street has a few good antique stores, the most prominent being **Nostalgia** (236 Wickenden St., 401/400-5810, www. nostalgiaprovidence.com, 11am-7pm daily), a multiple-dealer establishment with three floors and about 50 co-op vendors selling vintage furniture, art, clothing, and home decor. It's a fun place to get lost in, and the selection ranges from high-end turn-of-the-century antiques to fun and inexpensive vintage pieces from the 1970s.

Books

In Wayland Square, check out **Books on the Square** (471 Angell St., 401/331-9097, www. booksq.com, 9am-9pm Mon.-Sat., 10am-6pm Sun.), which has a broad selection of fiction and nonfiction and is particularly strong on feminist, gay and lesbian, political, and children's books. You can sit in a comfy armchair and flip through books before buying them, or seek advice from one of the always-helpful staff members.

Gifts

Up Hope Street, you'll find one of the city's most beloved gift shops, **Frog and Toad** (795 Hope St., 401/831-3434, 11am-6pm Mon.-Sat., 11am-6pm Sun.), which stocks locally made jewelry, pottery, specialty soaps, funky imported furniture and crafts, and even its very own line of hilariously tongue-in-cheek hand-made letterpress gift cards. Also check out **NAVA** (197 Wickenden St., 401/453-6282, www.shopnava. com, 11am-6pm Mon.-Wed., 11am-7pm Thurs.-Sat., 11am-5pm Sun.), a cute little shop specializing in unique and often handmade jewelry, clothing, candles, cards, and more.

THE WEST SIDE

Most of what the West Side has to offer in terms of shopping is located on or just off Broadway on a 1 mi (1.6 km) stretch in between the I-95 and Route 6 overpasses, where

you'll find a smattering of great restaurants to check out when you're done.

Antique and Vintage

Lovers of vintage Americana, mid-century modern furniture, and kitschy kitchenware from eras gone by will want to stop in at **Rocket to Mars** (144 Broadway, 401/274-0905, 11am-6pm Wed.-Sat., 11am-5pm Sun.) or at least walk by and check out its incredible window displays.

Books

Ada Books (717 Westminster St., 401/573-2980, www.ada-books.com, 12:30pm-5:30pm Wed.-Fri., noon-5pm Sat., noon-4pm Sun.), named for a character in a Vladimir Nabokov novel, is a cozy little shop specializing in zines and indie comics (many of which are by local authors and artists), art and literary magazines, poetry, and film. Check the website for periodic in-store readings from local and national writers.

Gifts

Just down the street from Rocket to Mars, you'll find **White Buffalo** (267 Broadway, 1pm-5pm Mon., noon-6pm Tues.-Fri., 11am-6pm Sat., 11am-5pm Sun.), a cleverly curated gift shop selling handmade jewelry and handbags, vintage clothing, antiques, art prints, and children's clothes and toys. The shop owner here has excellent taste—it'll be hard to leave empty-handed.

Music

If record collecting is your thing, there are two excellent shops on Broadway: **Armageddon Shop** (436 Broadway, 401/521-6667, www. armageddonshop.com, noon-8pm Mon.-Sat., noon-6pm Sun.) specializes in punk, hardcore, garage, metal, and noise rock; **Analog Underground** (504 Broadway, 401/274-4123, 11am-7pm, Wed.-Sat., 11am-5pm Sun.) leans more toward experimental, psychedelic, reggae, lo-fi dance, and jazz. Both stores do a nice job of avoiding the intimidating, snobby record store cliché, so don't be afraid to ask for help.

Sports and Recreation

Providence is relatively hilly, so merely maneuvering around the city on foot or by bike qualifies as a recreational pursuit. Beyond that, within the city limits you'll find a handful of venues for sports and enjoying the outdoors, but with so many large parks and recreation areas within a 15-mi (24-km) radius, many residents get their exercise elsewhere. In addition to the activities described below, keep in mind the city's many exceptional parks, including Roger Williams Park, India Point Park, and Blackstone Park.

BICYCLING AND JOGGING

There aren't any great spots for mountain biking within Providence city limits (although you'll find several good spots nearby), but the city does have some nice routes for conventional biking. Keep in mind that this is a busy city with narrow streets and a high volume of auto traffic, and you'll have some very steep hills to contend with.

Joggers face some of the same issues but can enjoy one span that bikers will find less useful. Beginning either by the Capitol grounds or at nearby Providence Place Mall, you can jog along the restored riverfront, a 2-mi (3.2-km) loop if you take it all the way down to Bridge Street.

Within Providence, few roads seem better suited to cyclists and joggers than wide, tree-lined **Blackstone Boulevard,** which has designated bike lanes and runs about 1.5 mi (2.4 km) from Hope Street south to Blackstone Park, past handsome old homes and the entrance to Swan Point Cemetery. You can make a nice triangular loop out of this area, using Blackstone Boulevard as one leg, Hope Street as the longest leg (it meets with Blackstone near the Pawtucket border), and any of the many cross streets closer to Brown University as the shortest leg. Broadway on the West Side

also has designated bike lanes, and the city has gotten progressively more bike-friendly over the last decade.

From Providence and just outside, you also have access to several off-road bike paths. The 14.5-mi (23.3-km) **East Bay Bike Path** (www.eastbaybikepath.com) is accessible from India Point Park and runs along the Narragansett Bay all the way into Bristol. The **Woonasquatucket River Greenway** (www.wrwc.org/greenway.php) extends 5.4 mi (8.7 km) of off-road track into Johnston and can be accessed from Riverside Park (Allepo St. at Bosworth St.). The **Washington Secondary Bikepath** (www.dot.ri.gov) offers 19 mi (31 km) of flat terrain along a former railway bed between Providence and Coventry. Parking is on the Cranston-Providence border just off Garfield Avenue.

You can rent bikes through the Uber-owned **Jump** bike-sharing service (www.jump.com/cities/providence). Just look for the bright orange, pedal-assisted electric bikes at various hubs throughout the city and pay through the Uber app. Rental costs $2 for the first half-hour, and $0.07 per minute after that. Bike rentals are also available at **Providence Bicycle** (725 Branch Ave., 401/331-6610, www.providencebicycle.com, 10am-6pm Mon.-Fri., 10am-5pm Sun., $30/day), which is in northern Providence but worth the trip if you're a devotee of cycling.

BOATING, CANOEING, AND KAYAKING

Although not the boating hub that Newport, the East Bay, or South County are, Providence does have some access points that lead directly into Narragansett Bay, including some excellent areas for kayaking. Unfortunately, there are no kayak or canoe rentals in town; you'll have to venture down to South County or East Bay for those. You can take sailing classes

($25-75) geared to all levels of ability and experience at the **Community Boating Center** (109 India St., India Point Park, 401/454-7245, www.communityboating.com, 9am-5pm Mon.-Fri.), which has a boathouse and a fleet of about 50 boats.

GOLF

Donald Ross, known for designing municipal courses in cities throughout New England, laid out **Triggs Golf Course** (1533 Chalkstone Ave., 401/521-8460, http://triggs. us, 6:30am-dusk daily, $29 for 9 holes, $49 for 18 holes) in the 1930s. It's a relatively affordable, reasonably well-maintained course with cart and club rentals.

Goddard Park Beach Golf Course (Ives Rd., Goddard State Park, 401/884-9834, 7:30am-dusk daily, $12-14) is a nine-hole public course that's open mid-April through late November.

ICE-SKATING

A favorite spot in the winter (Nov.-Mar.) is the **Providence Skating Rink** (2 Kennedy Plaza, 401/331-5544, www.theprovidencerink. com, 10am-10pm daily Nov.-Mar., $7 adults, $4 children and seniors), which has public skating several times daily. This outdoor rink, twice the size of the famous one in Rockefeller Center, anchors downtown Providence, right by the bus station and close to the Riverwalk—it's good fun as much for taking to the ice as it is for watching skaters on a brisk day. Late spring-early fall, the focus shifts to roller-skating. Year-round, lessons in both of these balancing arts are given; you can also rent equipment (skate rental is $4-7) at the large pavilion and admission booth at the end of the rink, which has lockers, a pro shop, a snack

bar, and some private party rooms that revelers sometimes rent for birthdays and special events.

SPECTATOR SPORTS
Basketball

With all the schools in Providence, you'd think there would be more opportunities to catch live college sporting events, but few of these institutions have notable athletic programs. A major exception is the **Providence College** Friars (401/865-1000, www.friars. com), a men's basketball team that frequently ranks near the top of the Big East Conference. Games are held at the **Dunkin' Donuts Center** (1 LaSalle Sq., box office 401/331-6700).

Hockey

Providence itself has but one pro sports team, the **Providence Bruins** (401/273-5000, www. providencebruins.com), an American Hockey League farm club that's a feeder for the NHL's Boston Bruins. The season runs October through early April, and tickets cost $20-30. Games are held at the **Dunkin' Donuts Center**.

Roller Derby

The **Providence Roller Derby** (www. providencerollerderby.com) is an all-female nonprofit league that puts on a great show. Team members have names like "Oxford Coma" and "Mini Meat" and usually perform with personalities to match. It's an entertaining alternative to the more traditional sporting events, and you can catch the home bouts a few times each summer right downtown at the **Providence Skating Rink** (2 Kennedy Plaza).

Food

Providence has long been home to many ethnic groups with rich culinary traditions, including Italians, Portuguese, Latin Americans, and Asians, making for an endless variety of food. Providence's own **Little Italy,** on Federal Hill, enjoys a reputation among the best in the world outside Italy, and Indian, Thai, and sushi restaurants flourished here long before they became commonplace elsewhere. **Seafood** plays a vital role in local cuisine, and as an international port, Providence has always had access to exotic ingredients.

In addition, the city's arty element and throngs of students have created a desire, if not a need, for cheap and innovative foods—it doesn't hurt that quite a few of those students and their professors are affiliated with the superb culinary arts program at Johnson & Wales University, home to the world's largest culinary archive. After decades in which Providence took a backseat to larger cities like Boston and New York, it seems the rest of the country is finally catching on: In 2015, Providence was named the number 2 food city in America by *Travel & Leisure* magazine.

Seafood

One of the most sought-after reservations for date-nighters, ★ **New Rivers** (7 Steeple St., 401/751-0350, www.newriversrestaurant.com, 5pm-11pm Mon.-Sat., $18-28) is an elegant, candlelit spot housed in a 1793 mill along the river on the edge of downtown. The menu is as exquisite as the atmosphere: think squid ink cavatelli with Rhode Island lobster, shrimp, and herbs, or grilled quail, truffle roasted sunchokes, foie gras, and Brussels leaves. The restaurant is equally serious about its bar menu, incorporating many lesser-known and small-production wines, craft brews, and distilleries that have been hand selected to complement the cuisine.

Hemenway's Seafood Grill and Oyster Bar (121 S. Main St., 401/351-8570, www.hemenwaysrestaurant.com, 11:30am-10pm Mon.-Thurs., 11:30am-11pm Fri.-Sat., noon-9pm Sun., $17-35) is the place to go for fresh seafood. There's little that's pretentious or contrived about the food here—just fresh and simply prepared, like the scampi over linguine, fried shrimp dinners, lobster mac 'n' cheese, baked scrod with seafood crumbs, and, of course, sublimely delicious fresh-shucked oysters—14 varieties are served here. The big, often noisy dining room has large plate-glass windows that overlook South Main Street, and because of its proximity to the downtown financial district, the crowd here tends to be of the suit-and-tie variety.

The atmosphere at ★ **Oberlin** (186 Union St., 401/588-8755, 5pm-11:30pm Thurs.-Mon., closed Tues.-Wed., $6-30) is airy and artsy, and the critically-acclaimed food is not to be missed. Named one of Bon Appétit's best new restaurants in 2016, Oberlin has made a name for itself by serving up wildly creative takes on fresh-caught local seafood. The menu features ever-changing dishes like mussels marinated with green garlic, chili, and sweet potato, and raw bluefish with garlic chive capers and dill. If you're not into seafood, don't worry—the house-made pasta dishes (and the wine list) are to die for as well.

French

A warm, romantic eatery in a quiet downtown alley, **Pot au Feu** (44 Custom House St., 401/273-8953, www.potaufeuri.com, 5pm-9pm Tues.-Sat., $16-23 in the bistro, $20-40 in the salon) is the city's seminal French restaurant. It opened in the early 1970s and seems to grow more popular each year. Depending on your mood or your budget, opt either for the classic bistro fare of the cozy basement space, where a classic bouillabaisse and the signature crème brûlée vie for your attention, or splurge on the suave, special-occasion-worthy upstairs salon. Here try roast duckling, foie gras, and similarly rich French standbys.

American

Housed in an historic building once home to a Federal Reserve Bank, The Dorrance (60 Dorrance St., 401/521-6000, www. thedorrance.com, 5pm-midnight Tues.-Thurs., 5pm-2am Fri.-Sat., $16-32) impresses with high ornate ceilings, opulent chandeliers, and a long luxurious bar (with an equally luxurious cocktail menu). Favorites include fresh Rhode Island scallops, roasted chicken, and fresh ricotta cavatelli. At the bar, fresh New England oysters on the half shell pair perfectly with the Up & Cumber cocktail—a fusion of organic vodka, elderberry liqueur, fresh lime juice, and ginger beer.

The fashionable Downcity option that caters to a see-and-be-seen crowd but is nevertheless unpretentious, ★ Gracie's (194 Washington St., 401/272-7811, www. graciesprov.com, 5pm-10pm Tues.-Sat., $31-50) is one of the city's favorite "special occasion" spots, known for its sterling service, inviting contemporary dining room, and exceptionally creative and well-crafted food that relies heavily on organic ingredients. You could kick things off with the Hudson Valley foie gras with spring dug parsnip, walnut, golden raisins, rhubarb, and maple before trying the entrée of dry aged creekstone ribeye with potato crusted yolk, asparagus, chanterelles, and Banyuls Bordelaise sauce.

Inside the historic Arcade building, you'll find Rogue Island (65 Webosset St., 401/831-3733, www.rogueislandgroup.com, 4pm-11pm Mon., noon-11pm Tues., noon-midnight Wed.-Fri., 9am-midnight Sat., 9am-4pm Sun., $8-25), offering up a self-described "approachable farm-to-table" food in an informal atmosphere. The menu changes daily depending on what's in season, but expect mouth-watering options like grilled pork chops with fried Brussels sprouts and roasted fingerling potatoes, and short rib grilled cheese with housemade fig jam.

Vegan

Occupying a 10,000 square foot building just across from the newly-opened Providence River pedestrian bridge, Plant City (334 South Water St., 401/429-2029, www. matthewkenneycuisine.com/plant-city-pvd, 7am-11pm Mon.-Wed., 7am-1pm Thurs.-Sat., 7pm-midnight Sun., $5-24) is a self-described "integrated, plant-based food and lifestyle brand." In more practical terms, it's a vegan food hall, featuring a bar, a Mexican restaurant, a pizza joint, and a café with delicious pastries, breakfast bowls, wraps, sandwiches, and coffee. Opened by celebrity chef Matthew Kenney in the spring of 2019, the food here is good enough that even the die-hard meat-eaters among us will find something to love. At the café, try the T-Blat, a BLT made with smoky tempeh bacon, avocado, and chipotle mayo.

Asian Fusion

The highly acclaimed ★ North (122 Fountain St., www.foodbynorth.com, 5:30pm-midnight daily, $6-25) lives up to all the hype, with its mishmash of regional and globally-inspired small plates, unusual cocktails, and relaxed, communal atmosphere. Housed in the same building as the uber-hip Dean Hotel, North's seasonally influenced menu changes nightly, but staple favorites include the tiny ham biscuits (so delicious), and raw oysters with horseradish vinegar. North does not take reservations, but dishes like Dan Dan noodles with mutton, squid, fermented chili and black pepper, or roasted scallops with snap peas, nasturtium, and sunflower *hozon* make it well worth the wait you might encounter on busy weekend evenings.

Japanese

There is nothing quite like a steaming-hot bowl of ramen to warm you up on a cold day, but you won't need to use the weather as an excuse to check out Ken's Ramen (69 Washington St., www.kens-ramen.com, lunch noon-3pm Tues.-Sat., dinner 6pm-10pm Tues.-Thurs. and 5:30pm-11pm Fri.-Sat., $2-13), a minimalist "artisan" noodle bar serving

Rhode Island's Craft Beer

In the 1990s, Providence underwent a cultural and socioeconomic makeover of sorts, a triumphant revival for which it was nicknamed the "Renaissance City." That renaissance had a profound effect on the city's burgeoning culinary scene, and more recently is spilling over into the world of microbreweries, several of which have cropped up over the years just outside Providence and beyond.

In Pawtucket, beer enthusiasts should check out **The Guild** (461 Main St., 401/724-1241, www.theguildri.com, tastings: 4pm-10pm Tues.-Thurs., noon-am Fri.-Sat., noon-6pm Sun.). Hidden away in part of a converted warehouse, this brewery turned beer hall offers a rotating draft selection of small batch craft beers from around New England. The atmosphere is airy and industrial, with lots of communal tables, oversized bar games (like giant Jenga!), and various food trucks parked outside in the courtyard. Just down the road, Foolproof Brewery (241 Grotto Ave., 401/721-5970, www.foolproofbrewing.com, tastings: 4pm-8pm Thurs.-Fri., 1pm-9pm Sat., 1pm-8pm Sun., tours: 1pm-4pm hourly, Sat., $10) creates delicious brews in cool cans—try the Raincloud Robust Porter or the Farmhouse Ale.

There are several other breweries located within a 45-minute drive of Providence. **Grey Sail Brewery** (63 Canal St., Westerly, 401/212-7592, www.greysailbrewing.com, 3pm-8pm Wed.-Fri., 3pm-8pm Fri., noon-8pm Sat.-Sun.) has a Flying Jenny pale ale that is a local favorite, and **Whaler's Brewing** (1070 Kingstown Rd., South Kingstown, 401/284-7785, www.whalersbrewing.com, 4pm-10pm Tues.-Sat., 11:30am-7pm Sun.), where you'll want to pick up a growler of one of their award-winning IPAs. Just over the bridge, head to **Newport Craft Brewing** (293 JT Connell Rd., Newport, 401/849-5232, www.newportcraft.com, private tours by appointment only) for its Rhode Trip IPA, or the stronger Rhode Rage double IPA.

In fact, Rhode Islanders have gotten so serious about their craft beers that you can now hop on the **Rhode Island Brew Bus** (401/232-4232, www.therhodeislandbrewbus.com) for a guided tour of the state's local breweries and beer-centric bars, with pickup locations in Providence. Tours generally cost $70 per person, and usually include 3-4 breweries, wineries, and/or distilleries as well as food, guided tours, and tastings. If the bus is too pricey for you, you can find a cold **Narragansett** (www.narragansettbeer.com) tall boy at just about any bar in the state for just $2-3. It's not fancy, but it still enjoys a reputation as New England's oldest beer, founded in Cranston, Rhode Island in 1890.

Japanese soups with a modern flare. Noodle bowls come with bean sprouts, kikurage mushrooms, scallions, and nori and your choice of either Char Siu pork belly or pulled chicken. The hip but often very noisy atmosphere pairs well with chilled sake or one of Ken's top-shelf whiskeys.

Mexican

Viva Mexico Cantina (129 Washington St., 401/369-7974, www.vivamexicocantinagrill.com, 10am-10pm Mon.-Wed. and Sun., 10am-midnight Thurs., 10am-1am Fri.-Sat., $5-15) serves breakfast, lunch, and dinner every day, with a menu offering all of the standard

Mexican fare plus some more adventurous dishes like *Lengua Guizada*—sautéed beef tongue with onions and tomato sauce—and *Barbacoa de Chivo*—seasoned shredded goat meat. Housed in the historic Mercantile Block building next to a gay bar and underneath a slew of artist studios, the atmosphere is aptly colorful and laid back—a perfect place to share a pitcher of margaritas.

Comfort Food

Trinity Brewhouse (186 Fountain St., 401/453-2337, www.trinitybrewhouse.com, 11:30am-1am Mon.-Thurs., 11:30am-2am Fri., noon-2am Sat., noon-1am Sun., $8-22)

brews several beers and serves a wide range of snack foods and light entrées, including pulled-pork barbecue sandwiches and shepherd's pie. You'll find decent burgers and also some veggie options like falafel salad and margherita pizza. The crowd upstairs tends to be an eclectic mix of working-class folks, families, and white-collar 9-to-5ers, while the noisier pub downstairs caters more to students and service industry folks.

If you should find yourself out late at night downtown, **Haven Bros. Diner** (Kennedy Plaza, 401/603-8124, 11pm-3am Mon.-Thurs., 11pm-4am Fri.-Sat., $2-5) is a somewhat legendary favorite for a post-bar-hopping snack. This lovably gruff hangout is actually a diner on wheels, which the owners park outside city hall into the wee hours. Founded in 1888 as a horse-drawn lunch wagon, it is one of the oldest diners in America. Swing by after the bars let out on a weekend night and you will surely be treated to some spectacle to complement that greasy burger and coffee milk.

Cafés and Sandwich Shops

Small Point Café (230 Westminster St., 401/228-6999, www.smallpointcafe.com, 7am-6pm Mon.-Fri., 7:30am-6pm Sat.-Sun., $4-10) in Downcity serves delicious organic, fair-trade coffee, tea, and espresso, plus soups and sandwiches, pastry, and bagels made with organic ingredients in a light, comfortable atmosphere. This is a popular study spot for students taking advantage of the comfy couches and free Wi-Fi, and also a great spot to people watch the passersby on Westminster Street.

In the Jewelry District, **Olga's Cup and Saucer** (103 Point St., 401/831-6666, www. olgascupandsaucer.blogspot.com, 7am-4pm Mon.-Fri., 9am-3pm Sat.-Sun., baked goods $2-6, lunch $7-10) produces delicious artisanal breads, apple-hazelnut pies, lemon-blueberry pudding, chocolate-almond marble cake, and coconut oat-crisp cookies. It's a nice spot to enjoy a pastry, bagels, and fresh coffee—especially during the warmer months when the garden patio is open.

As the sister store to the excellent Gracie's Restaurant, tiny ★ **Ellie's Bakery** (61 Washington St., 401/228-8118, www. elliesbakery.com, 7am-3pm Tues., 7am-3pm and 5pm-9pm Wed.-Sun., 7am-3pm; and 5pm-9pm, Fri.-Sat., $6-24) serves tea coffee, breakfast, lunch, and very fancy pastries—like lemon curd and ricotta brioche, orange blossom and rhubarb bread, and ginger sandwiches with lemon cream cheese frosting. Pastry chef Melissa Denmark is one of the many women who are rising stars in the Providence culinary scene.

Since 1929, downtown office workers have relied on **Murphy's Delicatessen** (100 Fountain St., 401/621-8467, www. murphysprovidence.com, 11am-1am Mon.-Thurs., 11am-2am Fri., 9am-2am Sat., 9am-1am Sun., $4-15) for filling sandwiches. Favorites include the lobster salad roll; the artery-clogging corned beef, pastrami, salami, and Swiss; and Murphy's Reuben with Irish corned beef. Several burgers are offered, as well as some veggie options.

WEST SIDE

Italian

Providence has one of the most prominent Little Italy neighborhoods in the country. You could easily spend a week or so sampling the specialties of every grocery, trattoria, pizza place, and food shop on Federal Hill, but here are a few places to start.

Not to be missed is ★ **Angelo's Civita Farnese** (141 Atwells Ave., 401/621-8171, www.angelosri.com, 11:30am-9pm Mon.-Sat., $4-16), which could survive on any street in Providence, but here on Federal Hill it's a star among the cheaper eateries. Expect heaping portions of traditional red-sauce fare in this boisterous place with communal seating. There's not much in the way of ambience, but it's fun and delicious!

Pane e Vino (365 Atwells Ave., 401/223-2230, www.panevino.net, 4:30pm-10pm Mon.-Fri., 4pm-10pm Sat., 3pm-9pm Sun., $10-38) is upscale in feel more than in price. The high caliber of cooking is impressive, from a starter of littleneck clams with a

garlic-tomato broth and cannellini beans to a main course of gnocchi with a rich port wine-wild boar sauce. Desserts here are excellent, and the wine list includes more than two-dozen varieties by the glass.

You can't miss the notably all-pink exterior of **Zooma Trattoria** (245 Atwells Ave., 401/383-2002, www.trattoriazoomari.com, 11:30am-10pm daily, $9-38), named for lyrics from the Louis Prima song "Angelina." The art-filled restaurant with high ceilings and elegant furnishings excels at creative regional Italian fare, from fresh pastas to authentic pizzas. There's also a first-rate wine list heavy on both Italian and North American vintages.

There are many options for pizza on Federal Hill. **Caserta's** (121 Spruce St., 401/621-3618, https://casertapizzeria.com, 9:30am-10pm Tues.-Sun., 9:30am-11pm Fri.-Sat., $4-20) serves amazingly delicious traditional Italian pizza in a relaxed, family-friendly atmosphere. Open since 1953, Caserta's is somewhat of a Providence institution. **Sicilia's** (181 Atwells Ave., 401/273-9222, www.siciliaspizzaprovidence.com, 10am-2am Mon.-Wed., 10am-3am Thurs.-Fri., 10am-midnight, Sat., 10am-2am, Sun., $7-19) is famous for its very indulgent stuffed-crust pizzas (the fried zucchini stuffed-crust is to die for). ★ **Nice Slice** (767 Westminster St., 401/453-6423, www.niceslice.com, 11am-11pm Sun.-Thurs., 11am-midnight Fri.-Sat., $3-23), located a few streets over from Federal Hill, serves pizza by the slice if you're just looking for a snack, plus whole pies with vegan-friendly options and a surprisingly delicious gluten-free crust available upon request.

For dessert, head to **Pastiche** (92 Spruce St. 401/861-5190, www.pastichefinedesserts.com, 8:30am-6pm Tues.-Thurs., 8:30am-11:30pm Fri.-Sat., 10am-10pm Sun., $2-7), a European-style café with amazing cakes, pastries, and espresso. A working fireplace makes this a cozy and very romantic spot on cold days. Favorites include the lemon mousse tart, carrot cake, and cannoli.

If you're looking for something to take home with you, you can buy fantastic handmade ravioli in about 75 varieties at ★ **Venda Ravioli** (275 Atwells Ave., 401/421-9105, www.vendaravioli.com, 8:30am-7pm Mon.-Sat., 8:30am-5pm Sun.), one of the most inspired delis in any Italian neighborhood in the country. **Tony's Colonial Food** (311 Atwells Ave., 401/621-8675, www.tonyscolonial.mybigcommerce.com 8:30am-6pm daily) is a tempting *salumeria* with just about every kind of gourmet grocery item imaginable. Family-owned since 1916, **Scialo Bros. Bakery** (257 Atwells Ave., 401/421-0986, www.scialobakery.com, 8am-7pm Mon.-Thurs., 8am-8pm Fri.-Sat., 8am-5pm Sun.) fires up its brick ovens daily to produce delicious Italian bread, biscotti, cakes, and pastries.

American

Check out ★ **The Slow Rhode** (425 West Fountain St., 401/351-0006, 5pm-1am daily, $6-15) if you're looking for simple, fresh small plates, excellent cocktails, and daily specials with a creative flair. The open garage door and small patio create a breezy, laidback atmosphere in the warmer months, while the dimly lit interior is cozy warm in winter. The menu might include anything from a fresh plate of local veggies, to a fried chicken sandwich on a buttermilk biscuit with herbed aioli and pickles, depending on the season.

A quirky bistro serving mod-Californian cuisine, **Julian's** (318 Broadway, 401/861-1770, www.juliansprovidence.com, 9am-11pm Mon.-Sat., 8am-9pm Sun., $11-22) serves brunch and dinner seven days a week. The dining rooms are filled with unusual art, and there's a glass-encased Pez dispenser collection to ponder in the restroom. The menu features everything from juicy steaks to vegan specialties, and the bar has an excellent (albeit pricey) selection of craft beers and cocktails. Be warned: wait times for weekend brunch sometimes exceed an hour.

1: the patio at The East End restaurant 2: a coffee house on the East Side 3: Trinity Brewhouse in downtown Providence 4: Plant City

For a memorable brunch or dinner, don't miss ★ **Nick's** (500 Broadway, 401/421-0286, www.nicksonbroadway.com, brunch 8am-3pm Wed.-Sun., dinner 5:30pm-10pm Wed.-Sat., brunch $6-12, dinner $15-27). This small, bright, and airy open-kitchen restaurant is helmed by one of the city's culinary stars, Derek Wagner. Its seasonal, locally sourced menu features dishes like lemon-herb roasted Point Judith fluke with risotto of asparagus, kale, herbs, and Parmesan, or herb roasted chicken with spring vegetables, green lentils, and thyme. Nick's brunch is exceptionally good; create your own omelet or dig into the brioche French toast with Vermont maple syrup.

For very high-end comfort food in a charming and comfortable setting, **Broadway Bistro** (205 Broadway, 401/331-2450, www.broadwaybistrori.com, 5pm-11pm daily, $7-23) is a local favorite. Its unpretentious menu features dishes like strip steak with roasted corn risotto, seared bluefish with fingerling potatoes, and braised greens, or "PBR" beer-braised mussels with house-made sausage and wilted kale. This is the place to go if you're in the mood for a perfectly cooked steak paired with a nice spicy red from its short but excellent wine list.

Thai

If you're craving authentic Cambodian or Thai food, head to **Apsara** (716 Public St., 401/785-1490, www.apsarari.com, 10:30am-9:30pm Sun.-Thurs., 10am-10pm, Fri.-Sat., $5-13), a humble and very popular (and busy) place tucked away in the Elmwood neighborhood (not to be confused with Apsara Palace on the East Side). The pad Thai, scallion pancakes, Shanghai noodles, and vegetable satay are spectacular. The bubble tea menu and the very courteous staff make the experience that much nicer.

Mexican

In a simple, nondescript house down the hill from Federal Hill, ★ **Chilango's Taqueria** (447 Manton Ave. at Atwells Ave., 401/383-4877, 5pm-10pm Mon.-Tues. and Thurs., 11am-10pm Fri.-Sat., 1pm-9pm Sun., $5-10) is worth the drive for perhaps the most authentic down-home Mexican food in the state, plus a nice range of Mexican beers and tequilas. It's not fancy, but the food is out of this world.

For quick, inexpensive, and delicious Mexican food, head to **La Lupita** (1950 Westminster St., 401/331-2444, www.lalupitamex.com, 10am-9pm Mon.-Thurs., 10am-10pm Fri.-Sat., 10am-8pm Sun., $2-10) in Olneyville Square. Consistently delicious burritos and tacos with fresh ingredients make this family-run restaurant a favorite spot among the many Latino and Spanish-speaking families in the neighborhood as well as the artists and other delightful weirdos who live and work in the surrounding mills.

Comfort Food

A much different experience can be found at **Wes' Rib House** (38 Dike St., 401/421-9090, www.wesribhouse.com, 11:30am-2am Sun.-Thurs., 11:30am-4am Fri.-Sat., $6-20), a Kansas City-style barbecue joint that's been open on the West Side since 1973. Tucked among some crumbling mill buildings in Olneyville, Wes' is naturally best known for its BBQ ribs, but pescatarians will find BBQ salmon or catfish goes just as well with the baked beans and buttery corn bread. TVs behind the bar are usually tuned to whichever game happens to be on, and the late-night crowds can get rowdy on the weekends.

You can't leave Providence without stopping at ★ **Olneyville New York System**, (18 Plainfield St., 401/621-9500, www.olneyvillenewyorksystem.com, 11am-2am Mon.-Thurs., 11am-3am Fri.-Sat., noon-2am Sun., $4-10), a celebrated wiener joint that's been open since 1946. These tiny hot dogs served on steamed buns are meant to be ordered "all the way," which means they come loaded with yellow mustard, celery salt, chopped onions, and a mysterious meat sauce. If this doesn't appeal to your tastes, order a grilled cheese with French fries, and wash it down with a coffee milk, Rhode Island's official state drink.

Cafés and Sandwich Shops

★ **White Electric** (711 Westminster St. 401/453-3007, www.whiteelectriccoffee.com, 7am-6:30pm Mon.-Fri., 8am-5:30pm Sat., 9am-4pm Sun., $2-8) ranks high on the city's coffee circuit, and its light, airy, arty atmosphere makes for an all-around excellent coffee shop experience. Aside from great coffee, espresso, and teas, it also offers fresh-made pastries, bagels, and healthy and delicious sandwiches and salads.

Decent coffee and exceptional breads, pastries, and snacks can be found at **Seven Stars Bakery** (342 Broadway, 401/521-2200, www.sevenstarsbakery.com, 6:30am-6pm Mon.-Fri., 7am-6pm Sat.-Sun., $2-6), along with plenty of nice airy spaces to sit and chat, including sidewalk seating in the warmer months. Try the currant scones, lemon cakes (mini pound cakes soaked in fresh lemon-juice syrup), or sticky buns with toasted pecans, or grab a sandwich to go on a fresh-made baguette.

★ **Hudson Street Deli** (68 Hudson St., 401/228-8555, www.hudsonstreetdeli.com, 6:30am-5pm Mon.-Sat., 9am-4:30pm Sun., $3-9) has long been famous for its giant sandwiches served on pillowy, fresh-baked bread, but since coming under new ownership in 2014, it now offers fresh-pressed juices, organic fair-trade coffee and teas, and vegetarian options like tempeh bacon and kale salad. This is a favorite neighborhood hangout and the lines can get pretty deep on weekend mornings, but the sandwiches are worth it—try the "RI's Best Reuben," a classic combo of corned beef, Swiss cheese, house-made purple sauerkraut, and Russian dressing on pressed marble rye.

EAST SIDE

American

★ **Al Forno** (577 S. Water St., 410/273-9760, www.alforno.com, 5pm-10pm Tues.-Fri., 4pm-11pm Sat., $20-45) occupies a warehouse near Fox Point with two-story-tall dining room windows that offer views of the iconic smokestacks across the Providence River. This restaurant put the neighborhood on the culinary map in 1980—the *International Herald Tribune* named it the world's best restaurant for casual dining. So what's all the fuss? Chef-owners (and married couple) Johanne Killeen and George Germon have made a study of northern Italian cuisine, which they prepare using—whenever appropriate—wood-burning ovens or open-flame grilling. Classic dishes include the wood-grilled heritage pork chop with mashed potatoes, broccoli rabe, wild fennel and roasted figs. The wood-grilled pizzas are quite popular and offered by the slice as appetizers. Reservations are competitive—book well ahead if you can.

Classic upscale faire in a gorgeous setting can be found at **Waterman Grille** (4 Richmond Sq., 401/521-9229, www.watermangrille.com, 4pm-9pm Mon.-Thurs., 4pm-10pm Fri., 3pm-10pm Sat.-Sun., $10-40), situated along the Seekonk River in a former bridge gatehouse that dates back to 1871. Start with the endive and arugula salad topped with pine nuts and blue cheese, then move on to the wood-grilled filet mignon with mashed potatoes, roasted asparagus, and red wine jus.

Serving creative and superb contemporary American fare in a riotously loud but inviting dining room, **Mill's Tavern** (101 N. Main St., 401/272-3331, www.millstavernrestaurant.com, 5pm-10pm Mon.-Thurs., 5pm-11pm Fri.-Sat., 4pm-9pm Sun., $11-48) earns tremendous acclaim. Dishes such as lobster and English pea risotto with vanilla mascarpone have helped this stately spot on increasingly trendy North Main Street develop into one of the city's top venues for celebrating a special occasion.

The East End (244 Wickenden St., 401/233-9770, www.theeastendpvd.com, 11am-1am daily, $10-28) is a cute little bistro offering diverse dishes and award-winning cocktails with a slightly southern bent. A raw bar is offered year round but the rest of the menu changes seasonally, with surprise dishes like grilled squid chowder, Thai-style fried chicken, and melt-in-your-mouth crab biscuits. Whiskey enthusiasts will adore the insanely extensive list of bourbons, scotches, and ryes from all over the globe. Outdoor seating is available in the warmer months on the cozy garden patio.

Greek

A Thayer Street mainstay since the 1960s, casual yet snazzy **Andreas Restaurant** (268 Thayer St., 401/331-7879, www.andreasri.com, 11am-11pm Mon.-Fri., 10:30am-11pm Sat.-Sun., $12-28) is a lively, sometimes crowded Greek restaurant with a smartly furnished dining room and big windows overlooking the street. You can grab a lamb burger or grilled calamari appetizer, or opt for something more substantial, like flame-broiled salmon with olive oil or pastitsio casserole topped with béchamel sauce. There's also a nice wine list and sidewalk seating.

Indian

India (1060 Hope St., 401/421-2600, www.indiarestaurant.com, 11am-10pm Sun.-Thurs., 11am-11pm Fri.-Sat., $9-25) brings excellent Indian fare to the northeast side of town. In addition to the standbys, India offers some unusual options, like *papri chat*, an Indian take on nachos with chickpeas, onions, cilantro, yogurt, and tamarind chutney. Locals love it for its imaginative decor, with bright paintings, hanging Oriental rugs, a back patio with swings for seating, and live entertainment—belly dancers and free henna tattoos are offered on Friday and Saturday evenings.

Sushi

If you're in the mood for sushi, ★ **Sakura** (231 Wickenden St., 401/331-6861, www.sakuraprovidence.com, noon-10pm Sun.-Thurs., noon-11pm Fri.-Sat., $10-23) is one of the best spots in town. This East Side staple is BYOB and offers a choice between sushi bar, western table, or traditional tatami seating, making for a fun, comfortable, and casual experience. A professional (but sometimes

humorously curt) staff, solid reputation, and proximity to college housing neighborhoods keep Sakura busy year-round, so be sure to make a reservation if you have a large party, especially on weekend nights. The menu boasts fresh and often locally caught fish, with creative dishes you won't find anywhere else. Try the Providence Roll or the Red Sox Maki paired with a can of locally brewed Whalers IPA, available just across the street at **Campus Fine Wines** (127 Brook St., 401/621-9650, 11am-10pm Mon.-Thurs., 10am-10pm Fri.-Sat., noon-6pm Sun.).

Comfort Food

A creative take on the American burger joint, **Harry's Bar and Burger** (121 N. Main St., 401/228-7437, www.harrysbarburger.com, 11:30am-1am Sun.-Thurs., 11:30am-2am Fri.-Sat., $4-10) is the go-to place for simple but high-quality burgers and craft beer on the East Side. Burgers here are made from certified Hereford beef, served on soft potato rolls, and go nicely with the hand-scooped shakes and salt-and-pepper fries. The atmosphere is fun and hip, with walls painted to look like cowhide.

Old photographs, magazine collages, and original artwork cover the walls at **Louie's** (286 Brook St., 401/861-5225, www.louisrestaurant.org, 5am-3pm daily, under $10), a favorite Brown and RISD breakfast joint that's been family owned and operated for more than 60 years. Order the butter pancakes or the "Drunk Johnny," an omelet with corned-beef hash, onions, and cheese.

The large, open-concept dining room at **Flatbread Pizza Company** (161 Cushing St., 401/273-2737, www.flatbreadcompany.com, 11:30am-10pm daily, $6-20) sort of makes you feel like you're walking into a ski lodge, with its exposed wooden beams, hardwood floors, and a crunchy, hippie vibe. At the center of the room are the giant pizza ovens firing up house specialties like Mopsy's Kalua Pork Pie—a pizza with smoked free-range pork, organic chipotle BBQ sauce, fresh pineapple, Vermont goat cheese, mozzarella, Parmesan, and herbs.

Families with kids will love the "living room" area at the back of the restaurant, with comfy couches, children's books, and even shelves of records that you can browse through and give to the bartender to play for you.

Cafés and Sandwich Shops

★ **The Coffee Exchange** (207 Wickenden St., 401/273-1198, www.thecoffeeexchange. com, 6am-9pm daily, under $4) occupies an attractive Victorian house on Wickenden Street filled with posters, flyers, and coffee-related goods. The excellent coffee is roasted in-house, and a percentage of sales is donated to workers, many of them children who struggle to make a living employed on coffee farms in developing countries. When school is in session, the cozy interior and covered-deck patio can get a bit crowded with studying students from nearby Brown and RISD, but it's usually not hard to grab a table.

An excellent café and bakery with floor-to-ceiling windows and a sunny patio out on the side, **Seven Stars** (820 Hope St., 401/521-2200, www.sevenstarsbakery.com, 6:30am-6pm Mon.-Fri., 7am-6pm Sat.-Sun., $2-7) serves delicious ginger biscuits, individual-size lemon cakes, olive bread, gooey chocolate brownies, and ham-and-cheese calzones. It has a delightful garden patio open in the warmer months.

If you overlook its pretentious name,

★ **L'Artisan Café & Bakery** (9 Wayland Sq., 401/331-4444, www.lartisan-cafe.com, 6am-10pm daily, $2-9) is a near-perfect little coffeehouse—big windows, comfortable couches and chairs, and an outdoor patio in a charming neighborhood. Aside from expertly made coffee and espresso, the café offers house-made paninis (like mozzarella and pesto), wraps, soups, salads, and all kinds of baked goods, including scones, Danishes, and breakfast sandwiches. This is also one of the only cafés in town that offers beer and wine as well—it's a nice spot when you want to enjoy a glass of wine but want to avoid the bar scene.

The surly counter staff at **Geoff's** (401 South Main St., 401/751-2248, www.geoffsri. com, 10am-10pm daily, $8-13) cannot seem to deter folks from coming back for more amazing sandwiches and fresh, spicy pickles: try the Geoff, with hot pastrami and melted Swiss, or the R. J. Heim (named after a local weatherman), with hot turkey, Canadian bacon, melted Swiss, cranberry sauce, and Dijon mustard.

La Creperie (82 Fones Alley, 401/751-5536, www.creperieprov.com, 10am-11pm Mon.-Thurs., 10am-midnight Fri., 9am-midnight Sat., 9am-11pm Sun., $4-7) is a tiny spot down an alley off Thayer Street, but this homey little place serves very good sweet and savory crepes, and it stays open very late. Fresh-fruit smoothies are another house specialty.

Accommodations

When it comes to hotels, Providence is a seller's market. There simply aren't many properties given the city's size and rapidly growing popularity. But things are improving, and the city's hotels are uniformly excellent, most within walking distance of great shopping, dining, and culture. You'll also find several historic inns, from high-end luxury spots to a few that serve travelers on a somewhat limited budget. For more affordable accommodations, however, you'll have to venture outside

of town to nearby Warwick or Pawtucket, or Seekonk, Massachusetts.

It's fairly easy to get in and out of Providence, so consider a hotel in the outlying regions—even communities in the Blackstone River Valley or the East Bay are relatively convenient for exploring the capital. Staying in one of these nearby areas could save you $50-100 per night for a room that's comparable to what you'll find in the city, depending on the time of year.

Providence is a commercial, educational, and political hub—it hosts a fair number of conventions and can be especially busy on weekends during the school year and weekdays anytime. Book ahead for the best rates.

DOWNTOWN
$100-150

Situated in the center of downtown Providence, ★ **The Dean Hotel** (122 Fountain St., 401/455-3326, www.thedeanhotel.com, $110-250) has caused quite a stir since it opened in 2014. With its sleek design, custom-made furniture, and found-object decor, you'd never know this 52-room boutique hotel was once home to one of the city's seedier institutions—a strip club and brothel. The century-old building has maintained much of its historical charm while gaining considerable points on the hipness scale with the addition of four new hangout spots within: Faust, a traditional German-style beer hall; a swank cocktail lounge called The Magdalenae Room; artisanal java joint Bolt Coffee; and Providence's first and only karaoke lounge, The Boombox. *Condé Naste Traveler* named it one of the best new hotels of 2014, a considerable accolade for a lodging so cheap and convenient. College Hill, Downcity, and the Providence Place Mall are all just a short walk away.

Historic **Christopher Dodge House B&B** (11 W. Park St., 401/351-6111, www.providence-hotel.com, $129-179) occupies a gorgeously restored 1850s Italianate Victorian with a redbrick facade, pressed-tin ceilings, and beautifully crafted original woodwork, tall windows, and polished wide-plank floors. The eight-room property offers a nice range of rooms, the higher-end units with kitchenettes and some with gas fireplaces. Full breakfast and off-street parking are included. All rooms have cable TV and in-room phones. This is an upscale but relaxed property where you'll receive personal but unobtrusive service.

$150-250

The **Courtyard by Marriott Providence Downtown** (32 Exchange Terr., 401/272-1191 or 888/887-7955, www.courtyard.com, $139-199) closely resembles the historic tan-brick structures on Exchange Street beside it—aesthetically it's a nice property, and it's conveniently situated. The hotel has been phenomenally popular since it opened, with relatively reasonable rates for downtown. The 216 guest rooms are large and airy, and many have unobstructed views of the State House, Providence Place Mall, and Waterplace Park. Amenities include a business center and library, an indoor pool with a hot tub, a fitness center, and a small café.

The 274-room **Providence Hilton** (21 Atwells Ave., 401/831-3900, $175-225) offers a full fitness center, an indoor pool, and whirlpool tubs. The property is located at a busy intersection west of the convention center, so it's a close walk to downtown attractions, Johnson & Wales, Federal Hill, and all of the excellent downtown restaurants. Rates are lowest on weekends; at busy times they rise significantly.

That towering neoclassical skyscraper with peaked gables and a redbrick facade next to the mall in downtown Providence is the 564-room **Omni Providence Hotel** (1 W. Exchange St., 401/598-8000 or 800/937-8461, www.omnihotels.com/hotels/providence, $150-300). Interior elements include a massive glass-domed rotunda, marble, polished dark woods, and recessed lighting. Guest rooms mix reproduction French and British antiques with rich fabrics and wallpapers, and the oversized bathrooms boast plush fixtures and fancy soaps and shampoos. The hotel also has two restaurants, Fleming's and Centro, plus enclosed elevated walkways that connect to both the Providence Convention Center and Providence Place Mall.

The **Graduate Hotel** (11 Dorrance St., 401/421-0700, www.graduatehotels.com/providence, $135-275), formerly known as the Providence Biltmore, dates to 1922 and is an iconic fixture in the Providence skyline. The swank rooms got a makeover in 2019 when the hotel changed ownership, but the elaborate lobby still includes a soaring three-tiered atrium, vaulted gilt ceiling, and gurgling fountains. The hotel offers a gym, complimentary bike rentals, and a cozy ground-level coffee shop as well.

The **Providence Marriott** (1 Orms St., 401/272-2400 or 886/807-2171, www.marriott.com, $150-250) has plush rooms with desks and armchairs with ottomans, upscale bath amenities, a nice health club and indoor-outdoor pool, and a good restaurant with a summer outdoor pool deck and grill, the Bluefin Grille (401/553-0424). Parking is included. The only drawback of this property is that it's slightly north of downtown's attractions and restaurants—a 10-minute walk, which is unpleasant only if it's cold or wet outside. This 351-room hotel is just a short walk north of the State House, however, and it's right off I-95.

Over $250

One of the ritziest spots on the city's lodging scene, the boutiquey ★ **Hotel Providence** (311 Westminster St., 401/861-8000 or 800/861-8990, www.hotelprovidence.com, $250-350) occupies a late-19th-century building on formerly forlorn Westminster Street, now at the center of this downtown neighborhood's comeback. The 64 rooms and 16 suites are outfitted with tiger-maple furnishings, plush upholstered chairs and bedding, and original art. This is a hip, upscale, design-themed hotel that has become a fashionable fixture of downtown Providence. It's very close to the Johnson & Wales campus and the bars and dining of both Downcity and the Jewelry District. The ground floor hosts Backstage Kitchen + Bar, which offers al fresco dining in a festively lit courtyard.

In a restored 1920s building adjacent to the Rhode Island State House and the Providence Place Mall, the **Renaissance Providence Hotel** (5 Avenue of the Arts, 401/919-5000, www.renaissance-hotels.marriott.com, $200-400) is another swanky and massive lodging option, with 272 rooms, plush bedding, and a fancy bar located inside of what was originally intended to be a Masonic temple. This is a Marriot hotel with all of the usual amenities. It made headlines in 2011 when a video of a hotel employee quitting his job with the help of a marching band went viral.

WEST SIDE
$100-150

The only accommodation in the city's bustling Federal Hill neighborhood is the ★ **Hotel Dolce Villa** (63 De Pasquale Ave., 401/383-7031, www.dolcevillari.com, $100-200) on De Pasquale Square. A departure from the usual dark and heavy New England look, the decor feels distinctly contemporary, with stainless-steel appliances and white tile walls, white marble floors, linens, and modern furniture. A few of the rooms have balconies that overlook the lively café culture in the square below. Every suite comes with a fully equipped kitchen, flat-screen TVs, and, in the two-room suites, remote-control gas-burning fireplaces. This small operation with just 14 one- and two-bedroom suites is run like a full-service hotel, with a well-trained 24-hour staff and experienced management.

COLLEGE HILL AND THE WATERFRONT
$150-250

Hilton Garden Providence (220 India St., 401/272-5577, www.wyndham.com, $150-250) has an enviable location overlooking Providence Harbor. This mid-priced chain property is wedged between I-195 and an on-ramp, but you can't beat the convenience to India Point Park, the restaurants and coffee shops on Wickenden Street, and the campuses of Brown and RISD. The 136 rooms are fairly traditional and cookie-cutter, but they are clean and bright. Half have water views, and for an extra $10-20 you can get one with a whirlpool bath. The hotel has a restaurant, a small gym with whirlpool, and an outdoor pool with a terrace that has water views.

The **Old Court B&B** (144 Benefit St., 401/751-2002, www.oldcourt.com, $155-225) may have the most wonderful setting in Providence, in the heart of the historic Benefit Street neighborhood. Built as a rectory in 1863, it's a short walk to both downtown and the Brown and RISD campuses.

Rooms have museum-quality antiques and chandeliers, mostly from the Victorian era and early 20th century, and are refreshingly clutter-free, allowing the inn to strike a pleasing balance between a traditional B&B and a small luxury hotel. Considering the lavish furnishings, scenic and convenient location, and modern amenities, the Old Court represents a very smart value.

Transportation and Services

GETTING THERE AND AROUND

Getting There

AIR

Providence's international airport **T. F. Green Airport** (2000 Post Rd., Warwick, 888/268-7222 or 401/691-2471, www.pvdairport.com) is located south of the city and has regular flights from many U.S. and Canadian cities by United, Southwest, JetBlue, American, and other carriers.

BUS

The **Rhode Island Public Transit Authority (RIPTA)** (401/781-9400 or 800/244-0444, www.ripta.com) runs frequent buses from T. F. Green to downtown. In addition, **Peter Pan Bus Lines** (800/343-9999, www.peterpanbus.com) runs buses to Providence from throughout New England, stopping at 1 Peter Pan Way (north of town, off exit 25 from I-95) and downtown (1 Kennedy Plaza). **Greyhound** (800/231-2222, www.greyhound.com) also connects to Providence from many U.S. cities, also stopping at 1 Kennedy Plaza.

TRAIN

It's fairly easy to get to Providence by train aboard **Amtrak** (800/872-7245, www.amtrak.com). Trains stop in Providence on their way from Washington DC (6 hours), New York (3.5 hours), and Boston (40 minutes).

Getting Around

BUS

Bus travel is inexpensive and relatively convenient throughout the state on the **Rhode Island Transportation Authority (RIPTA)** buses (401/781-9400, www.ripta.com). Kennedy Plaza, in the heart of downtown, is the nexus for bus routes all over Rhode Island. Fares start at just $2 for any ride within 1 mi (1.6 km) of downtown (transfers are an additional $1.00), and $6 for a 1-day pass. Have some singles with you, as exact change is required. There are student discounts as well as monthly passes. Buses generally run 5:30am-midnight, and the Providence Visitors Center and the Convention and Visitors Bureau distribute free maps that detail popular routes.

The city's pleasant and inexpensive **LINK trolley** runs from Fox Point up through College Hill, past Thayer Street, and then west across downtown and over to Federal Hill, and also from the State House south through downtown and the Jewelry District, with a stop at the Providence ferry landing, terminating in the Southside at Blackstone. The fare is $2 for any ride on the system, and monthly and discount passes are offered. LINK trolleys make their appointed stops every 20 minutes.

CAR

The pace of driving in Providence is less chaotic than in Boston, but this is still a type A kind of place: People drive fast and use their horns. One-way, narrow, and crooked streets proliferate and can be confusing and frustrating (although they are charming to walk). Overall, if you're fairly used to driving and parking in urban environments, Providence is reasonably navigable.

Parking garages abound downtown but can be rather expensive (up to $10/hour). One strategy is to park at the 5,000-space, nine-level Providence Place Mall, which is within easy walking distance of most downtown attractions and is economical, but only if you get your parking ticket validated inside the mall. Parking costs just $2 for up to 5 hours; it's $10 for 5-8 hours, and $25 for 24 hours.

Providence is a relatively safe city, and you don't often hear of car thefts or break-ins, but they certainly can and do happen. You'll save a lot of money opting for street parking over garage or supervised-lot parking, but lock your doors, and don't leave anything valuable in plain view.

TAXI

People don't generally hail cabs on the street in Providence, but you can find them at major hotels and occasionally outside clubs at night. For trips to the airport or coming home late from a bar or restaurant, your best bet is Lyft (www.lyft.com/cities/providence) or Uber (www.uber.com/cities/providence) services, which are usually inexpensive dependable. If you'd rather take a traditional cab, try Providence Taxi at 401/255-2050.

SERVICES
Visitor Information

For maps, updates on the city's events, and all other visitor information, call or stop by the Providence Warwick Convention and Visitors Bureau (10 Memorial Blvd., 401/456-0200, www.goprovidence.com, 8:30am-5pm Mon.-Fri.). You can also drop in at the Providence Visitors Center (1 Sabin St., 401/751-1177, 8:30am-5pm Mon.-Sat.), another vast repository of brochures and information, located inside the Rhode Island Convention Center.

Medical Services

Some major hospitals include: Kent Hospital (455 Toll Gate Rd., Warwick, 401/737-7000 or 888/455-5368, www.kentri.org), Miriam Hospital (164 Summit Ave., Providence, 401/793-2500, www.miriamhospital. org), Rhode Island Hospital (593 Eddy St., Providence, 401/444-4000, www. rhodeislandhospital.org), and Our Lady of Fatima Hospital (200 High Service Ave., North Providence, 401/456-3000, www. fatimahospital.com).

You'll find pharmacies, many of them open until 9pm or 10pm, throughout the city; the leading chain is CVS (www. cvs.com). Pharmacies open 24 hours include East Providence CVS (640 Warren Ave., East Providence, 401/438-2272) and Walgreens (533 Elmwood Ave., Providence, 401/781-7930).

Banks

Banks are found all over the downtown area, in the college neighborhoods, and in areas frequented by tourists, and ATMs are scattered throughout the city.

Media

The city's (and the region's) daily newspaper is the Providence Journal (401/277-7700, www.projo.com). The paper has a decent website with information on local dining, arts, music, travel, and kids-oriented activities. A resource for metro Providence arts, dining, shopping, clubbing, and such similar diversions is Motif, which is often poorly written, but one of the only alt-weeklies left in the city. Also look to flashy and free Providence Monthly (www. providenceonline.com, 401/521-0023), a glossy magazine, for great features on the city along with first-rate dining, shopping, and nightlife coverage.

Other area papers include the twice-weekly Warwick Beacon (401/732-3100, www. warwickonline.com) and the Kent County Daily Times (401/821-7400, www.ricentral. com).

Internet is available for free in libraries, in most cafés, and at the FedEx Office (100 Westminster St., 401/331-1990), which also provides faxing and shipping services.

Tours

Providence River Boat Co. (575 S. Water St., 401/580-2628, www.providenceriverboat. com) offers water-taxi service, sightseeing cruises, and charter tours of the Providence waterfront and out into Narragansett Bay.

Outside Providence

It's an old joke in Rhode Island, since the state is so small, that everyone except those who live in the capital can simply describe their residence as "outside Providence." There is, however, a distinct part of the state that is more aptly called Greater Providence as opposed to, say, the East Bay or South County. While it may not have a cohesive identity as such, this section encompasses some dozen towns and cities and accounts for nearly half the area of the state. And while there may not be as many formal attractions as in other parts of the state, there are still several museums and a bevy of recreational opportunities in wild landscapes of forest, river, and wetlands.

The most appealing part of this region for visitors is the area directly north of Providence known as the Blackstone River Valley. This small corner of the smallest state has had an outsized influence on the history of the nation as a whole. It was here in the early 1800s in cities like Pawtucket and Woonsocket that industrious entrepreneurs began harnessing the power of the Blackstone River to create the nation's first textile mills.

To the west, the river valley merges with Rhode Island's "quiet corner," a half-dozen towns that have resisted development of any kind to remain a bucolic vision of what New England looked like 100 years ago. Here you'll find miles of backcountry roads lined with stone walls, orchards, farm stands, and historic homes. This area comes alive especially

historic Old Slater Mill on the Blackstone River in Pawtucket

Outside Providence

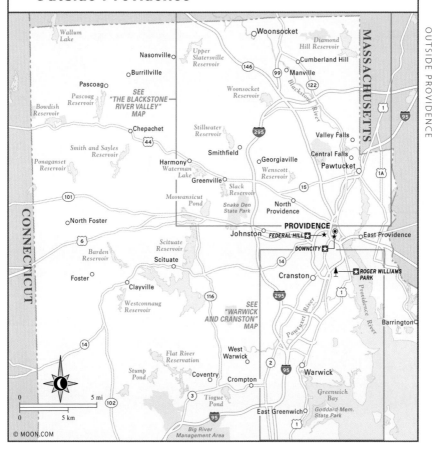

© MOON.COM

during foliage season, when colorful red maples and yellow beeches frame postcard-ready small-town tableaux.

By contrast, the coastal area south of Providence along Narragansett Bay is home to the urbanization of Rhode Island's two largest cities after Providence—Cranston and Warwick. While there are no formal attractions for visitors in either city, Warwick has some pretty neighborhoods on the bay worth driving through, as well as some pretty beaches that are the closest places to Providence to sunbathe or take a dip.

THE BLACKSTONE RIVER VALLEY

The part of Greater Providence with the most distinct cultural and historic identity is the **Blackstone River Valley**, which begins just north of Providence in Pawtucket and extends north to Woonsocket, encompassing a swath of nearby communities. In this area you can get a sense of how the nation shifted from an agrarian land of farmers, independent artisans, and skilled craftspeople to a full-fledged industrial powerhouse. Shortly after the War of Independence, complete mill

The Blackstone River Valley

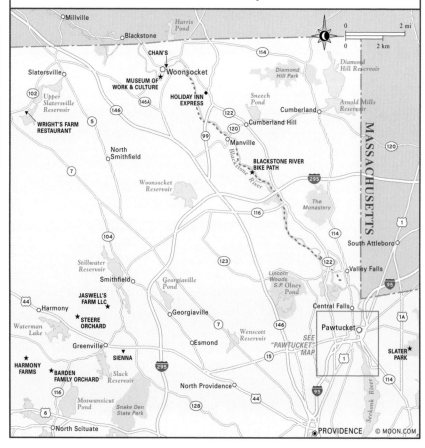

communities—with worker housing, community halls and churches, and massive mill buildings—sprang up all along the Blackstone River and its tributaries, from Pawtucket north through Woonsocket and across the Massachusetts border to Worcester, nearly 50 mi (81 km) away.

Sights

SLATER MILL HISTORIC SITE

For all intents and purposes, the American Industrial Revolution started at **Slater Mill** (Main St. and Roosevelt Ave., Pawtucket, 401/725-8638, www.slatermill.org, 10am-4pm Tues.-Sun., $12 adults, $8.50 children), a collection of mill buildings now preserved as a historic site along the Blackstone River. Young English immigrant Samuel Slater took a job in Ezekiel Carpenter's clothing shop, and by recalling the exact blueprints for water-powered textile machinery in his native country, developed the nation's first such textile factory. A 10,000-square-foot visitors center across from the mill provides orientation with a short video offering a stark view of mill life in Rhode Island.

The 5.5-acre site has several buildings, including the three-story **Wilkenson House,** built in 1810 on the site of an old metalworks, which contains a full machine shop on the ground floor and a re-creation of the mill's massive waterwheel in the basement. During the tour, you watch a nine-ton wooden waterwheel turn and spread the power through the building, the gears turning a series of pulleys that in turn power individual tools and machines.

Perhaps the most striking of the site's structures, the Old Slater Mill is a sturdy 1793 wooden structure, which looks especially striking when sunlight streams through its many soaring windows. Within just a few months of its construction, the factory had turned out the first cotton yarn produced in the New World. Inside, you'll find a few original machines from the period and many more authentic replicas that provide a clear sense of how these factories operated in the early days. Many of the machines were either designed or modified by Samuel Slater himself. At one end of the building, a small museum store sells penny candy and small gifts, including work by local artisans and fiber artists, as well as a selection of books on industrial history and textile crafts.

Moved here in 1962, having been spared destruction when I-95 was built through Pawtucket, the 1758 Sylvanus Brown house, a nicely restored gambrel-roof colonial, is also part of the tour. Demonstrations of flax-weaving are often given inside—a garden of flax was planted behind the house in 2000. (The golden-colored debris left after flax has been combed through a large metal hackle is called tow, hence the term *towheaded* to describe a blond-haired child.) Millwright Sylvanus Brown ran the house as a carpenter's shop during the late 1700s. It has been fully restored to its original appearance.

SLATER PARK

In the northeastern section of Pawtucket, near the Massachusetts border, lies Slater Park (401/728-0500, ext. 252, www.experiencepawtucket.org), which has entrances on both Newport Avenue and Armistice Boulevard. There are 18 picnic sites plus tennis courts, ball fields, gardens, and other diversions to while away an afternoon. Chief among them is a Looff Carousel (401/639-4237, 11am-5pm Sat.-Sun. June-Oct., $0.50 per ride), which dates to 1895. Charles I. D. Looff ranks among the earliest and most distinguished designers of carousels, and Slater Park's ride contains 50 whimsical characters.

HOPE ARTISTE VILLAGE

One of the most successful mill restorations in the area is in Pawtucket at the Hope Artiste Village (1005 Main St., 401/312-3850, www.hopeartistevillage.com), home to an eclectic mix of small businesses, artist studios, and hangout spots. The ground floor is anchored by a popular live music venue, The Met (401/729-1005, www.themetri.com), and also includes the Rhode Island Music Hall of Fame (401/225-8860, www.rhodeislandmusichalloffame.com, 8am-10pm daily, free), an archival project documenting the contributions of local musicians. Upstairs you'll find Breaktime Bowl and Bar (401/427-7006, www.breaktimebowlandbar.com, 4-10pm Tues.-Thurs., 4pm-1am Fri., noon-1am Sat., noon-8pm Sun.), a beautiful rustic style bowling alley (it's someone's job to manually reset the pins) with a pub food menu and a full bar. The mill is also home to a popular wintertime farmers market (www.farmfresh.org, 9am-1pm Sun., Nov.-May), and occasional open studio events throughout the year.

MUSEUM OF WORK AND CULTURE

Located in Woonsocket, the Rhode Island Historical Society's Museum of Work and Culture (42 S. Main St., 401/769-9675, www.rihs.org, 9:30am-4pm Tues.-Fri., 10am-4pm Sat., 1pm-4pm Sun., $8, free for children under 10) anchors Market Square and provides a vivid glimpse into the industrial history of Woonsocket and southern New England. The curators have designed imaginative interactive exhibits that capture the spirit and reveal the hardships of the city's history.

Pawtucket

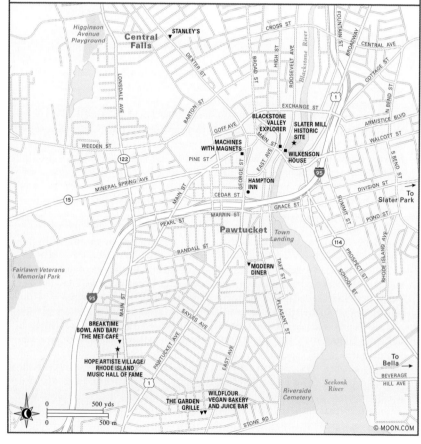

© MOON.COM

The museum traces the history of Woonsocket's French-Canadian immigration, providing a good sense of this insular community, its proud labor history, and its ardent preservation of customs and language. Exhibits recreate a 1920s textile mill shop, a farmhouse in rural Quebec, and a circa-1900 Catholic Church. One of the better exhibits takes you into a triple-decker. These three-story tenements were mostly built from the 1890s to about 1930 and are notable for their stacked three-story exterior porches; they're a common sight throughout urban Rhode Island and in many other parts of New England.

The museum tour ends with a presentation inside a re-created 1930s Independent Textile Union Hall. Many of the tapes and interactive exhibits are narrated by older town residents who lived through the city's labor strife of the early 20th century. You can read some of the touching letters immigrants sent back to their families in rural Quebec.

FARMS AND APPLE PICKING

It's always sad to see the summer end, but Rhode Islanders like to make the best of it by easing into autumn with sunny Sunday drives to the northwest corner of the state, where apple orchards and pick-your-own farms abound. A favorite is **Barden Family Orchard** (56 Elmdale Rd., North Scituate, 401/934-1413, www.bardenfamilyorchard.com), located about 25 minutes west of Providence via Route 6, where you can stroll through the gorgeous orchard, pick your own sweet varieties like honey crisps and Rome Beauties, or take the kids through the pumpkin patch to pick out their jack-o'-lantern to be. Similarly wholesome experiences can be had at **Jaswell's Farm** (50 Swan Rd., Smithfield, 401/231-9043, www.jaswellsfarm.com) and **Steere Orchard** (150 Austin Ave., Greenville, 401/949-1456, www.steereorchard.com), both about 25 minutes northwest of Providence via Route 6 and I-295, and **Harmony Farms** (359 Saw Mill Rd., North Scituate, 401/934-0741, www.harmonyfarmsri.com), a 20-minute drive on Route 6 headed west from Providence. All of these orchards offer hayrides during harvest season.

Entertainment and Events

There are two excellent music venues in Pawtucket, just a few miles north of downtown Providence. **The Met Café** (1005 Main St., 401/729-1005, www.themetri.com), which has been open in some form or another since 1975, books touring indie, folk, hip-hop, and blues acts of consistent quality. Just down the road at **Machines With Magnets** (400 Main St., 401/475-2655, www.machineswithmagnets.com), a recording studio that also houses an art gallery and performance venue, you can see some of the area's best local performers as well as occasional touring acts in an unconventional, thought-provoking setting.

Recreation

KAYAKING THE BLACKSTONE

The same powerful current that ran the mills also makes the Blackstone River a great spot for kayaking and, especially in spring when the river rises, white-water rafting. The Blackstone is a complex waterway for paddlers; you'll encounter dams, which require portaging, and unmarked spillways that can greatly alter the river's water level. Rangers at the **Blackstone River Valley National Heritage Corridor** (1 Depot Sq., 401/762-0250, www.nps.gov/blac, 8am-4:30pm Mon.-Fri.) offer a great deal of information on how to make the most of canoeing and kayaking as well as how to do so safely. You can also learn a great deal about the river's history, and the flora and fauna encountered along it.

BLACKSTONE RIVER BIKEWAY

The **Blackstone River Bikeway** (www.blackstoneheritagecorridor.org) follows parts of the Blackstone River and the old Blackstone Canal—it runs from Pawtucket 11 mi (17.7 km) north to Woonsocket but will someday connect all the way to Worcester. It's notable for its peaceful wooded scenery dotted with historic mill buildings. Another connection is currently in the works to hook up with the East Bay path in order to create a continuous route of more than 30 mi (48 km) of biking within the state. You can access it at several points, and you can park your car at lots in Lincoln (at both ends of Front Street, along the river) and at Blackstone State Park at the end of Lower River Road. You'll pass by some of the great old mills of the region, as well as vast meadows and some fairly mundane suburban stretches.

Food

This area is not known for its food, but you can find fairly simple and affordable restaurants that emphasize steak, pastas, and the region's famous "family chicken dinners." With such a diversity of ethnicities in the region, you'll also find several purveyors of authentic Portuguese, Italian, and French-Canadian food.

ITALIAN

It's one of the few restaurants in northern Rhode Island that could be called dressy, but even at **Bella** (1992 Victory Sq., Burrillville, 401/568-6996, www. bellarestaurantandbanquet.com, 4pm-9pm Wed.-Thurs., 11:30am-10pm Fri., 4pm-10pm Sat., noon-8pm Sun., $9-29) you can get by with casual attire. The spacious dining room of this Italian restaurant looks and feels like a banquet hall—the ambience is not especially distinctive, but it's pleasant. Specialties include grilled sirloin steak brushed with rosemary-infused oil and wild haddock with dried tomato and spiced olive oil. Pastas like homemade lasagna and gnocchi are a great option. You can mix and match several types of pasta with about 15 kinds of sauce (red or white clam, vodka, primavera, and so on).

In Smithfield, **Siena** (400 Putnam Pike, 401/349-4111, www.sienari.com, 4:30pm-9:30pm Tues.-Thurs., 4:30pm-10:30pm Fri.-Sat., 3pm-9pm Sun., $10-29) is a great bet for upscale, Italian cuisine. Try the saltimbocca—veal scaloppine sautéed with prosciutto, sage, garlic, and marsala wine, or the Branzino—a pan-seared Chilean sea bass fillet with ocean scallops and a creamy scallion sauce. The dining room is somewhat gaudy, with busy carpets and some unusual racehorse-themed art and sculpture, but the food is consistent.

VEGETARIAN

Open since 1996, ★ **The Garden Grille** (727 East Ave., Pawtucket, 401/726-2826, www.gardengrilleri.com, 11am-10pm Mon.-Sat., 11am-9pm Sun., $8-16) was the area's first (and for many years only) all-vegetarian restaurant, serving fresh fruit and vegetable juices, and sourcing organic ingredients from local farms long before the rest of the culinary world began to follow suit. Favorite menu items are the roasted butternut squash quesadilla, Korean tacos made with sweet chili glazed tempeh and vegan chipotle aioli, and the "Reggie's Raw Heaven" salad, a colorful blend of sliced mango, grapefruit, avocado, beet-infused jicama, cashew crumbles, and pomegranate vinaigrette over a bed of arugula.

CHINESE

Somewhat Americanized but plenty of fun is ★ **Chan's** (267 Main St., Woonsocket, 401/765-1900, www.chanseggrollsandjazz. com, 11:30am-10pm Mon.-Wed., 11:30am-10:30pm Thurs. and Sat., 11:30am-12:30am Fri. and Sun., $5-14), an elaborate, almost campy Chinese restaurant that's been around since 1905. People drive 30 minutes or more to check out the scene here, sample the tasty Szechuan fare, and listen to the lineup of live jazz and blues musicians who play here regularly. The menu is encyclopedic, with nods to just about every Chinese culinary tradition you can think of. Specialties include roast pork egg foo yong, beef sautéed with pickled ginger, egg drop soup, lobster with fried rice, and the Tahitian Delight (fresh sea scallops and tender chicken stir-fried in a light sauce with straw mushrooms, broccoli, carrot slices, and water chestnuts on a bed of pan-fried noodles).

COMFORT FOOD

Justly famous for introducing northern Rhode Islanders to the concept of "family chicken dinners," **Wright's Farm Restaurant** (84 Inman Rd., Nasonville, 401/769-2856, www. wrightsfarm.com, 4pm-9pm Thurs.-Fri., noon-9pm Sat., noon-8pm Sun., $8-14) presents family-style meals: heaping platters of chicken, green salad, fries, rolls, and pasta sides. The concept is so simple, so all-American: all-you-can-possibly-stuff-down-your-throat dinners that bring family members and friends together in a homey ambience. It's a huge place, with banquet seating for 1,600 patrons, plus a gift and toy shop that sells house-made specialties like Italian dressing, barbecue sauce, and fudge. It's a pretty amazing operation, with 75 ovens working away.

Modern Diner (364 East Ave., Pawtucket, 401/726-8390, www.moderndinerri.com, 6am-2pm Mon.-Sat., 7am-2pm Sun., $4-11), a crimson-and-cream Sterling Streamliner steel railroad-car diner attached to a Victorian house, serves excellent home-style food. It's a short drive from Slater Mill, and breakfast is served all day. Plenty of the state's diner aficionados rank this place among the best around. Cranberry-almond pancakes are a highlight, but you'll find a full slate of typical diner favorites. It's not open for dinner and accepts cash only.

For several decades, devotees of burgers and fries have been cramming into **Stanley's** (535 Dexter Ave., Central Falls, 401/726-9689, www.stanleyshamburgers.com, 11am-8pm Mon.-Thurs., 11am-9pm Fri.-Sat., $3-7); the patties here are freshly made and wonderful, grilled with several toppings (cheddar, mushrooms, onions); the French fries are prepared with just the right crispness.

CAFÉS AND SANDWICH SHOPS

The sister store to the Garden Grille just a couple of doors down, ★ **Wildflour Vegan Bakery and Juice Bar** (727 East Ave., 401/475-4718, www.wildflourbakerycafe.com, 7am-9pm Mon.-Thurs., 7am-10pm Fri., 8am-10pm Sat., 8am-9pm Sun., under $7) in Pawtucket is an oasis in a city otherwise devoid of independent coffee shops. You don't need to be vegan to enjoy the delicious pastries here, like the gluten-free chocolate peanut butter whoopie pie, the raw raspberry coconut "cheesecake," and the lemon lavender cupcakes. The fresh-pressed fruit and vegetable juices, herbal infusion teas, and organic fair-trade coffee are equally delicious. Big sunny windows, local art, and a handful of eccentric customers complete the experience.

Accommodations

Pawtucket may not be the most glamorous town, but its lodging choices are definitely an affordable alternative to some of Providence's pricier hotels.

$100-150

In addition to having comfortable rooms with all of the standard amenities, **Hampton Inn** (2 George St., Pawtucket, 401/723-6700, www.hamptoninn3.hilton.com, $100-200) is located less than 10 minutes away from downtown Providence, and is just a quick walk from downtown Pawtucket and Slater Mill. The setting leaves something to be desired (it's located just across from a highway on-ramp), but it's definitely convenient. The hotel also has a fitness center, a heated pool, and is pet friendly.

For those planning on spending time in the Woonsocket area, the **Holiday Inn Express** (194 Fortin Drive, 401/769-5000, www.ihg.com, $110-175) is a safe bet, with bland but comfortable rooms, a small gym, and an indoor heated pool. It's located about a 20-minute drive from downtown Providence, accessible via Route 146, and about 5 minutes to the Museum of Work and Culture and the Stadium Theatre, both in downtown Woonsocket.

Information and Services

VISITOR INFORMATION

Pamphlets, brochures, and visitor information are available on the towns north and northwest of Providence from the **Blackstone Valley Tourism Council** (175 Main St., Pawtucket, 401/724-2200 or 800/454-2882, www.tourblackstone.com).

TOURS

One interesting way to explore the region is on one of the cruises offered on the **Blackstone Valley Explorer** (175 Main St., Pawtucket, 401/724-2200, www.rivertourblackstone.com, $12 adults, $10 children), a 49-passenger riverboat with a canopy roof that runs up and down the Blackstone River June through mid-October. Several kinds of excursions are offered, departing from Central Falls and Woonsocket. Some of these are available only to groups and students, so it's best to call ahead for details. These tours give a particularly strong sense of the mix of rural and wildlife-inhabited lands that exist side-by-side with the great old mill villages of the past two centuries.

Getting There and Around

The Blackstone River Valley is easy to get around by car, although you can take the bus to several places, among them Pawtucket and Woonsocket. It's fairly easy to get to Slater Mill from Providence using public transportation—Bus 99 is your best bet; it runs regularly between Kennedy Plaza in Providence and downtown Pawtucket ($2 fare, about 15 minutes). If you're driving, note that I-295 cuts across the southeastern half of the Blackstone River Valley as it loops from I-95 south of Providence back up to I-95 north of it in Attleboro, Massachusetts. From Providence, Route 146 is a quick limited-access highway northwest to Woonsocket (about a 20-minute drive), and Pawtucket is an easy, 10-minute drive from downtown Providence via I-95.

WARWICK AND CRANSTON

On the opposite side of Providence from the Blackstone River Valley, Rhode Island's most densely populated suburbs, Warwick and Cranston, lie immediately south of the capital and contain high concentrations of indoor and strip malls, chain restaurants and motels, and busy roads lined with traffic lights. Warwick is also home to T. F. Green Airport, New England's third-busiest. Cranston has fewer strip malls, and lies immediately southwest of Providence and is easily reached via I-95 or Route 10.

Although it's crowded and somewhat dull, this patch of middle-class bedroom communities is not without charm. Both towns lie along Narragansett Bay and have several interesting and historic residential neighborhoods near the water. The towns also contain the nearest public beaches to Providence, and just south of Warwick, the all-American community of East Greenwich has a cute downtown with hip eateries and a smattering of cool boutiques.

Sights

It's almost incorrect to call Warwick a suburb—this full-fledged city is one of the state's most prominent communities, as it's home to Rhode Island's main airport and has a population of about 85,000 (second only to

Providence). Like many of the state's communities, Warwick actually comprises a slew of small village centers rather than one coherent core. Through the early 20th century, textile mills engaged in dyeing, bleaching, and finishing employed many of Warwick's workers, but even a century ago many residents commuted to Providence and other nearby towns, and it has remained a bedroom community ever since.

PAWTUXET VILLAGE

Pawtuxet Village, which lies on the Warwick Cranston border, contains a number of beautiful colonial homes, plus a cute smattering of shops and restaurants clustered around where Broad Street meets the Pawtuxet River. From Pawtuxet (not to be confused with Pawtucket, another city north of Providence), a party of local patriots attacked the grounded British revenue schooner *Gaspée,* one of several early acts of defiance against the crown in New England that ultimately led to the American Revolution. Since 1966, Pawtuxet has hosted the annual *Gaspée* Days celebration (401/781-1772, www.gaspee. org), held in late June, which features, among other events, a parade, a road race, fireworks, and a symbolic burning of the *Gaspée* in effigy.

GODDARD MEMORIAL STATE PARK

Goddard Memorial State Park (Ives Rd., 401/884-2010, free), the site of an ambitious tree-growing project undertaken by the late-19th-century owner of this land, Henry Russell, and continued by the subsequent owner, Colonel William Goddard. Today you can stroll or ride horseback through the park on more than 18 mi (29 km) of trails. C & L Stables (1095 Ives Rd., 401/886-5246, www. candlstables.info, 10am-6pm Tues.-Sun. in summer, by reservation only in winter) offers guided trail and beach horseback rides here daily for $30 an hour. There's also a fine beach along Greenwich Bay, numerous playing fields, bridle trails, picnic areas, changing facilities, and a nine-hole golf course.

Warwick and Cranston

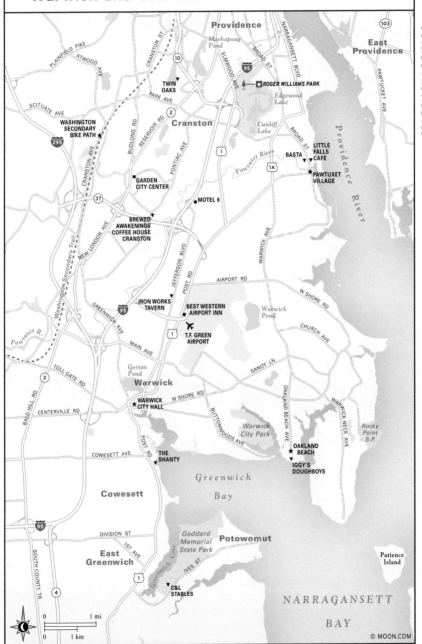

Concerts are given during the warmer months in the park's restored carousel pavilion, next to the beach.

Shopping

In Cranston, **Garden City Center** (Rte. 2, Cranston, 401/942-2800, www.gardencitycenter.com, 10am-9pm Mon.-Sat., noon-6pm Sun.) is an open-air shopping center with more than 70 upscale shops, including both local and chain operations. Good picks here include Anthropologie, J. Crew, Pottery Barn, Sephora, and more.

Sports and Recreation

BEACHES

Warwick has the best beaches in Greater Providence, including **Goddard Memorial State Park** (1095 Ives Rd., 401/884-2010 or 401/884-9620 in season, www.riparks.org) and 126-acre **Warwick City Park** (401/738-2000), which has a saltwater beach, changing facilities, bike paths, hiking, and ball fields. It's said, although not verified, that the very first clambake was held here in the late 1800s. Sheltered **Oakland Beach** (401/738-2000) at the southern tip of Oakland Avenue off Route 117 is a smaller swath of sand that's near several restaurants and bars; there's also a restored carousel, a big hit with kids. Technically it's okay to swim at these beaches, but on many days you'll find these beaches are closed for swimming due to high bacteria counts in the water. Check in with www.health.ri.gov/beaches for the latest closure before going in the water, and also consider the close proximity of the much more luxurious, open water South County beaches.

BOATING

Warwick is interior Rhode Island's boating capital, with more marinas, moorings, and slips than any other city in the state. Some of the larger marinas include **Apponaug Harbor Marina** (17 Arnold's Neck Dr., www.apponaugharbormarina.com 401/739-5005), **Brewer Yacht Club** (100 Folly Landing, 401/884-0544), **Greenwich Bay Marina** (1 Masthead Dr., 401/884-1810), and **Norton's Shipyard** (foot of Division St., 401/884-8828).

BIKING

The **Washington Secondary Bikepath** is the state's longest off-road bike path, with 19 mi (31 km) of flat terrain along a former railway bed, stretching from Cranston to Coventry. Parking is on the Cranston-Warwick border just off Pontiac Avenue (below I-295). The path is nicely shaded in many stretches, with some interesting scenery; you'll cross over streams and ponds, dilapidated factories, and old mill buildings along the way.

Food

Warwick has dozens of restaurants, many of them chains, and many of these lie along the busy Route 2 retail strip. Warwick, Cranston, and East Greenwich are somewhat upscale suburbs, so quite a few notable chefs have opened restaurants in this area in recent years, especially in East Greenwich's quaint downtown.

ITALIAN

The semi-upscale but family-friendly **Twin Oaks** (100 Sabra St., Cranston, 401/781-9693, www.twinoaksrest.com, 11:30am-11pm Sun. and Tues.-Thurs., 11:30am-midnight Fri.-Sat., $10-36) is a Rhode Island institution, founded in 1933 by an Italian American moonshiner whose speakeasy got busted during Prohibition. Today the restaurant's six dining rooms and three separate bars can accommodate 650 people. Despite its vastness, the place retains its homey, if rather antiquated feel—the main dining room overlooks a scenic lake, which makes up for the drab brown carpets and wood paneling. The menu is also vast, with seafood, steaks, and dozens of classic Italian pasta dishes. This is not the place to find an exotic culinary adventure, but it will definitely give you a taste of old-school Rhode Island culture.

For excellent Italian food, try ★ **Basta** (2195 Broad St. Cranston, 401/461-2300, www.bastaonbroad.com, 5pm-9pm Sun.-Thurs., 5pm-10pm Fri.-Sat., $12-30) in Pawtuxet Village. The white-tablecloth dining room is elegant but not stuffy, the martinis are ice cold, and the chicken Parmesan is to die for.

AMERICAN

The **Iron Works Tavern** (697 Jefferson Blvd., Warwick, 401/739-5111, www.theironworkstavern.com, 11:30am-10pm Mon.-Thurs., 11:30am-11pm Fri.-Sat., 3pm-10pm Sun., $7-13) is located at the former site of an ironworks factory, and the atmosphere here reflects this, with 14-foot ceilings, salvaged brick, and preserved wood beams creating an industrial but sophisticated feel in the bar as well as dining room. The unpretentious menu offers delicious (and very reasonably priced) entrées such as roasted Atlantic salmon with baby potatoes, broccolini, and lemon herb aioli, or bacon-infused meatloaf with garlic mashed potatoes and crimini mushrooms.

The **Shanty** (3854 Post Rd., Warwick, 401/884-7008, www.theshantyri.com, 4pm-10pm Sun.-Thurs., 4pm-11pm Fri.-Sat., 10am-3pm Sat.-Sun., $8-28) is an adorable little place in an otherwise bland section of Warwick. Exposed beam ceilings, industrial light fixtures, and antique hardwood booths create a cozy but modern vibe in the sunny dining room. Try the T.V. Dinner—a comfort food sampler that includes buttermilk fried cornish game hen, smoked cheddar mac 'n' cheese, tomato and cucumber salad, and a strawberry streusel cookie.

COMFORT FOOD

★ **Iggy's Doughboys** (889 Oakland Beach Ave., Warwick, 401/737-9459, www.iggysdoughboys.com, 11am-10pm Sun.-Thurs., 11am-11pm Fri.-Sun. summer, 11am-7pm Sun.-Thurs., 11am-8pm Fri.-Sat. winter, $3-9) might just serve the best clam cakes in the state—it's certainly fun to test them out against the many reputable competitors around Rhode Island. The original Iggy's opened in 1924 and has withstood hurricanes and recessions; the view out toward Newport Bridge, Jamestown, and across to the East Bay is outstanding—you'll actually feel as though you're down by the ocean. Standard fare includes chowder, stuffies, fried scallops, the famous Iggy Burger with sautéed peppers and onions, tuna grinders, meatball subs, and chicken wings. Iggy's also specializes in greasy little fried doughboys, which are dusted liberally with powdered sugar; a half-dozen costs just $2.95. The website has coupons discounting several items on the menu.

CAFÉS AND SANDWICH SHOPS

Grab a light lunch, pastries and baked goods, or excellent hot coffee at **Little Falls Café** (2166 Broad St., Cranston, 401/781-8010, 6am-3pm daily, under $8), a fun little coffeehouse in Pawtuxet Village, with small crowded tables, a wall for posters and flyers, and a close-knit, arty, community atmosphere.

Accommodations

Like Pawtucket, Warwick and Cranston may lack the charm and excitement of Providence, but they've got the upper hand when it comes to cheap places to stay.

$50-100

Just 3 mi (4.8 km) north of the airport are the region's least-expensive chain properties, the cheapest of which is the **Motel 6** (20 Jefferson Blvd., Warwick, 401/467-9800 or 800/466-8356, www.motel6.com, $60-100). It's perfectly fine if you just need a cheap, clean bed for the night.

$100-150

In Cranston, the 18-room **Edgewood Manor** (232 Norwood Ave., 401/781-0099, www.providence-lodging.com, $109-229) is a grand, early-1900s Greek Revival mansion with five beautifully crafted fireplaces and ornate architectural detailing. Guest rooms and suites carry out the building's lavish theme, with plush linens, Oriental rugs, four-poster beds, neatly framed paintings and prints, paneled walls, and high-style Victorian antiques.

Located next to the airport, the **Best Western** (2138 Post Rd., Warwick, 401/737-7400 or 800/251-1962, www.bwprovidence.com, $120-150) in Warwick has 103 units, including a few suites with wet bars and refrigerators. The property's slogan, "luxury for less," is a bit optimistic, but the rooms are pleasantly decorated as far as economy chains go, and the staff is helpful and friendly.

Getting There and Around

Warwick and Cranston are quick 15-20 minute drives from downtown Providence, easily accessible via I-95 South or heading south from the West Side via Elmwood Ave., Broad, or Cranston Streets. Many locations can be accessed by bus via **Rhode Island Public Transit Authority** (www.ripta.com); the 21 bus travels from downtown Providence to Garden City and the Warwick Mall, and the 14 West Bay route travels through the downtown section of East Greenwich via Main St.

Visitor Information

Pamphlets, brochures, and visitor information are available from the **Providence Warwick Convention and Visitors Bureau** (144 Westminster St., 401/456-0200, www.goprovidence.com). You can also get information on the Warwick and Cranston area from the **Warwick Tourism Office** (Warwick City Hall, 3275 Post Rd., 401/738-2000, ext. 6402, www.visitwarwickri.com).

Newport

With its tightly packed rows of immaculately restored colonial homes and impossibly narrow streets, Newport looks and feels every bit the quintessential New England maritime town.

The city's fascinating history, excellent beaches, upscale shopping district, and some of the most creative food in the state are what really put Newport on the map. For those interested in sailing, this is the place; whether you're interested in lessons, boat rentals, or charter services. Excellent surf breaks, prime saltwater fishing, and picturesque cliff walks also draw visitors from near and far. For those less nautically inclined, the museums, mansions, and restaurants can keep you occupied for days. Culturally speaking, Newport is predictably preppy

Highlights

Look for ★ to find recommended sights, activities, dining, and lodging.

★ **The Historic District:** Newport's most notable colonial neighborhood has enjoyed an astounding renaissance in recent years. It has the finest concentration of colonial architecture in New England (page 89).

★ **Newport Art Museum:** With a focus on Rhode Island art and artists, this museum makes its home in the Griswold House, an 1864 Modern Gothic mansion (page 94).

★ **Ocean Drive:** Arguably the most stunning shore drive on the East Coast, Ocean Drive reveals one gorgeous photo op after another (page 96).

★ **The Breakers:** Cornelius Vanderbilt's little summer cottage is the most stunning of all Newport's mansions—and that's saying a lot (page 101).

★ **Cliff Walk:** Stroll along this fabled oceanfront path, which fringes some of Newport's most expensive and famous mansions, including The Breakers and Rough Point (page 103).

★ **First and Second Beaches:** The soft white sand, crashing waves, and superb people-watching at two of Rhode Island's best beaches should not be missed (page 109).

and highbrow—which is what you might expect from a city where the Vanderbilts and Kennedys once spent their summer vacations.

Most visitors traveling from Providence will reach the island via Route 138, a road that bends around an off-ramp and somewhat dramatically reveals two stunning bridges spanning the sparkly waters of the Narragansett Bay. The Jamestown Verrazzano Bridge (circa 1922) connects motorists to the Island of Jamestown, where the road eventually continues to the Claiborne Pell Newport Bridge, which offers a dazzling view of blue ocean dotted by sailboats, seagulls, and small surrounding islands. Downtown Newport welcomes visitors with cute cobblestone walkways, the sparkling waters (and impressive yachts) of its adjacent harbor, and a lively shopping and dining district along historic Thames Street.

PLANNING YOUR TIME

Newport is one of the most popular destinations in the state, and you'll want to spend at least a weekend here to touch on the major sights and activities. It is possible to see Newport in one day by touring Ocean Drive, walking the waterfront, and taking in at least one mansion tour. But of all the waterfront communities in Rhode Island, this is one where you'll want to try to dedicate at least two full days, especially in the summer when you could easily spend an entire day just lounging on the beach.

Newport is really two cities in one—there's the tightly laid out downtown with its narrow one-way streets and rows of buildings dating from colonial through Victorian times, and then there's the sweeping, wealthy peninsula that juts south and east of all this, where expensive homes on large plots of land dominate the landscape. The downtown area is best explored on foot (especially in the summer when traffic is at its peak), but it's nice to have a car or at least a bicycle to explore the rest. One full

day to tour each of these areas, along with a little time set aside for the beach or a sail, is an ideal way to spend a weekend.

The catch is that Newport can be crowded in summer and on weekends just about any time of year, and hotel rates are among the highest in New England, so consider staying nearby and making several daytrips into town. Moderately priced motels and hotels are in nearby Middletown, and as the popularity of sites like Airbnb continue to rise, so too do the possibilities for less expensive lodging. Still, there's no way of getting around the fact that summer is a favorite time to visit but an awful time for traffic, getting a table at restaurants, and enjoying the city's attractions without enduring long lines or crowds. Consider visiting during shoulder seasons of May or September, or on a weekday, when you'll have much more room for exploring.

HISTORY

Settled in 1639, Newport began as one of early Rhode Island's typically tolerant colonies, a haven for those disenchanted with the religious and political conformity and ultimately oppressive Massachusetts colonies. With a strategic, sheltered harbor, however, it wasn't long before enterprising locals turned the young city into a corner of the infamous Triangle Trade with the West Indies and Africa. Much of Newport's early trading was slave oriented—in fact, Newport surpassed even Charleston, South Carolina, during the early years in the number of slaves that passed through its port.

Rhode Island's ban on slavery in 1774 did little to slow Newport's merchants, who continued to trade in rum, molasses, indigo, and other wares. The blow to the city's economic clout, and also its colonist pride, came at the beginning of the Revolutionary War, when British forces decided to occupy Newport. From 1776 to 1779 the city remained firmly under British control. Most of the population,

NEWPORT

Previous: a view of the Newport Bridge from Jamestown; The Breakers; Castle Hill Lighthouse along Ocean Drive.

Newport

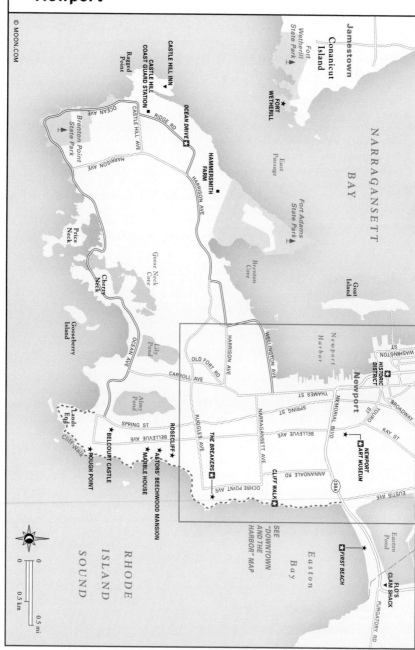

© MOON.COM

Jamestown
Conanicut
Island

Fort
Wetherill
State Park

FORT
WETHERILL ★

CASTLE HILL INN ▼

Ragged
Point

CASTLE HILL
COAST GUARD STATION ★

OCEAN AVE

CASTLE HILL AVE

RIDGE RD

OCEAN DRIVE ★

HAMMERSMITH
FARM ★

HARRISON AVE

HARRISON AVE

Brenton Point
State Park ▲

East
Passage

Fort Adams
State Park ▲

NARRAGANSETT
BAY

Price
Neck

Goose Neck Cove

Brenton
Cove

Goat
Island

Cherry
Neck

Gooseberry
Island

OCEAN AVE

Lily
Pond

HARRISON AVE

WELLINGTON AVE

Newport
Harbor

WASHINGTON ST

HISTORIC
DISTRICT ★

Newport

THAMES ST

TOURO

BROADWAY

OLD FORT RD

CARROLL AVE

Almy
Pond

SPRING ST

RUGGLES AVE

NARRAGANSETT AVE

SPRING ST

MEMORIAL BLVD

BELLEVUE AVE

KAY ST

Lands
End

Cliff Walk

BELCOURT CASTLE ★

ROSECLIFF ★

BELLEVUE AVE

ASTORS' BEECHWOOD MANSION ★

MARBLE HOUSE ★

ROUGH POINT ★

THE BREAKERS ★

OCHRE POINT AVE

ANNANDALE RD

NEWPORT
ART MUSEUM ★

CLIFF WALK ★

(138A)

EUSTIS AVE

RHODE
ISLAND
SOUND

Easton
Bay

SEE
"DOWNTOWN
AND THE
HARBOR" MAP

FIRST BEACH ★

Easton
Pond

FLO'S
CLAM SHACK ★

PURGATORY RD

0   0.5 km
0   0.5 mi

which was sympathetic to the war for independence, fled Newport, decimating trade. Even as it started to recover after the war, the shipping embargo imposed on New England during the War of 1812 effectively sealed Newport's fate as nothing more than a small-time port city.

For much of the 19th century, shipbuilding, naval exploits, and trade continued to play some role in Newport's fortunes, but Newport's greatest commodity continued to be its marvelous location at the tip of Aquidneck Island. Wealthy factory owners, rail and shipping tycoons, and other captains of industry began summering in this town that rarely became as hot in the summer as other parts of the Northeast. By the middle of the 19th century, almost any family with a big name, from Edith Wharton to the Vanderbilts, had a summer "cottage" (read: mansion) in the area south and east of downtown on Ocean Drive or Bellevue Avenue. And those who didn't had friends to visit here and were thus still a part of the town's culture. Since then, everyone from President Kennedy to Billy Joel has had homes here.

The city's brief stint as a pleasure village took a hit during the Depression. As fortunes fell and a spirit of fiscal conservatism took hold through World War II, many of Newport's mansions fell empty and were sold and subdivided into apartments, while others were shuttered completely. As weeklong summer vacations became increasingly popular with middle-class families after World War II, however, an increasing number of visitors began spending summers in Newport, and even more did so in the several motels just outside the city in Middletown.

Newport enjoyed a slow but steady resurgence from this point forward. Locals began to look around more and notice the city's incredible bounty of notable architecture, first by working toward the preservation of the city's grand "summer cottages." In 1967, tobacco heiress Doris Duke and others formed the Newport Restoration Foundation, which helped to preserve hundreds of important colonial houses. For at least the past 30 years, Newport has enjoyed a reputation as a yachting hub, an increasingly upscale vacation destination, and a favorite place for touring magnificent homes.

Sights

DOWNTOWN AND THE HARBOR

While the beaches and mansions are Newport's biggest attractions, the downtown waterfront has a substantial appeal as well, with its chorus line of blinding-white yachts moored in the harbor and flood of tourists on the cobblestone wharfs on summer afternoons. A good place to start is the **Newport Visitors Information Center** (23 America's Cup Ave., 800/326-6030, www.discovernewport.org), which is unusually comprehensive and useful. It is right at the northern entrance to downtown, adjacent to the city's bus terminal and the centrally located Newport Marriott. It's an excellent place

to begin your explorations of the city, and it has a large pay-parking lot and garage, making it a good spot to ditch your wheels (although on-street parking can be found in the adjacent neighborhoods for those who don't mind an extra walk). Newport's downtown and harbor area can be managed easily on foot, and you can take public transportation from the visitors center to other parts of the city, including Ocean Drive and the mansions on Bellevue Avenue.

★ Historic District

While Newport is best known for the mansions constructed in the late 19th century, the town has historically significant buildings stretching back more than 200 years, many of which are clustered around the area east of the waterfront. The neighborhood is flanked on this side by bustling **Thames Street**, the commercial hub of Newport's thriving downtown district, and the first place many tourists land upon arrival. The Upper Thames Street shopping district is the more boisterous section, with noisy bars and tourist stores, while Lower Thames tends more toward the small upscale boutiques and eateries. Both sections run parallel to the waterfront, anchoring the narrow cobblestone streets of the Historic District. West of Thames Street, wharves jut into Newport Harbor, interspersed with a mix of businesses, restaurants, and hotels.

MUSEUM OF NEWPORT

Before setting foot in any of the mansions, culture and history buffs should take a detour to the **Museum of Newport History** (Thames St., at the bottom of Washington Sq., 401/846-0813, www.newporthistory. org, 10am-5pm daily, $5 suggested donation), where the exhibits give a nice overview of the history of the city and southern Rhode Island. Housed in the historic Brick Market Place, the space is crammed with artifacts that trace the city's history, including decorative

pieces and artwork, vintage photos, and ship models. Other exhibits touch on the city's founding fathers, John Clarke and William Coddington, as well as on the indigenous Native Americans who lived here for many centuries and the diverse ethnic and religious makeup of Newport's earliest citizens, including Quakers, Jews, Portuguese, and African Americans.

April through September, a variety of guided walking tours (401/841-8770, www. newporthistorytours.org, $15 adults, $5 children under 12) that focus on the city's history leave from the museum. Themes include Jewish Newport, Colonial Newport, Rogues and Scoundrels, and Gold to Gilded.

TOURO SYNAGOGUE

Rhode Island's famous religious tolerance is symbolically—and beautifully—enshrined in **Touro Synagogue** (60 Touro St., 401/847-4794, www.tourosynagogue.org, check website for hours, $12 adults, free for children under 13). Not only is it the oldest Jewish house of worship in the United States, it's also one of the most impressive 18th-century buildings in New England. Like so many historic buildings on the Eastern Seaboard, the synagogue's brochure brags that George

Thames Street

Washington spent time here—in fact, it was here that he declared the new nation's position on religious freedom, pledging he would "give to bigotry no sanction, to persecution no assistance." If that connection helps draw visitors who may not otherwise venture into a synagogue, OK then, but Touro Synagogue should be on every visitor's short list of Newport attractions for its own historical, religious, and architectural significance.

UNITED BAPTIST CHURCH, JOHN CLARKE MEMORIAL

Also in the vicinity of Washington Square is the 1846 **United Baptist Church, John Clarke Memorial** (30 Spring St., 401/847-3210, 8:30am-noon Mon.-Fri.), located to the north and east of Colony House. The congregation was established in Portsmouth in 1638 by Dr. John Clarke, the very gentleman who obtained Rhode Island's Royal Charter in 1663 from King Charles II. Free guided tours of this rather austere but beautiful church are offered every Monday through Thursday between 8am and noon.

NEWPORT ARTILLERY CO. MUSEUM

For background on the Revolutionary War's Battle of Newport as well as other conflicts, visit the **Newport Artillery Co. Museum** (23 Clarke St., 401/846-8488, www.newportartillery.org, 10am-2pm Sat.-Sun., 5-7pm Wed.), which is housed in a cut-granite Greek revival building just south of Washington Square on Clarke Street. Military objects and artifacts from more than 100 nations fill these rooms, including 15 cannons spanning 150 years, one of them struck by Paul Revere in 1798. Other unique military artifacts include uniforms worn by former general and Secretary of State Colin Powell, the Vietnam War's General Westmoreland, and Egyptian president Anwar Sadat.

GREAT FRIENDS MEETING HOUSE

Near the corner of Farewell and Marlborough Streets, the **Great Friends Meeting House**

(401/846-0813, www.newporthistorical.org, open by appointment, $4) was once the largest and most prominent building in Newport, visible to ships arriving in Newport Harbor from some way out. With parts dating back to 1699, it is the oldest surviving house of worship in town and was expanded continuously over the subsequent two centuries. Quakers used it as the setting for the New England Yearly Meetings. The Society of Friends was an important influence on Newport society during the 17th and 18th centuries, a time when the then-radical religion was harshly persecuted in other parts of the New World. The central interior block of the building features massive, exposed framing timbers as well as the tiered bench seating and diamond pane windows typical of the period.

SEAMEN'S CHURCH INSTITUTE

Stop at the **Seamen's Church Institute** (18 Market Sq., just off Thames St., www.seamensnewport.org, 401/847-4260, 9am-4pm daily) to catch your breath and to admire this handsome building that has served the needs of seafarers for nearly a century. The building contains a small nondenominational chapel, a café, public restrooms with a coin laundry and showers, a library, and a small museum (with limited hours; call ahead).

SAMUEL WHITEHORNE HOUSE

While Newport has many homes and museums from the colonial and Victorian periods, the only house-museum from the Federal period is the **Samuel Whitehorne House** (416 Thames St., 401/847-2448, 10am-4pm Wed.-Sun., $8 adults, free for children under 12), a few blocks down Thames Street. The property is overseen by the **Newport Restoration Foundation** (51 Touro St., 401/849-7300, www.newportrestoration.org), an organization founded by the late heiress Doris Duke, who assembled an incomparable collection of Federal and colonial pieces from Newport's top cabinetmakers. She placed much of the collection in this house, which dates to 1811 and originally belonged to one of Newport's

Downtown and the Harbor

© MOON.COM

WICKHAM RD

CHASTELLUX AVE

COLUMBUS AVE

ROSENEATH AVE

HOUSTON AVE

CLINTON ST

MARCHANT ST

SIMMONS ST

King Park

WELLINGTON AVE

Spencer Park

BINNEY ST

Murphy Field

PALMER ST

HARRISON AVE

EASTNOR RD

ATLANTIC ST

CONNECTION ST

POTTER ST

OLD FORT RD

HAROLD ST

CARROLL AVE

CARROLL AVE

VAUGHAN ST

EARL AVE

THAMES ST

CAREY ST

HAMMOND ST

MCALLISTER ST

LEE AVE

DEAN AVE

HOLLAND ST

DEARBORN ST

S BAPTIST ST

POPE ST

INTERNATIONAL YACHT RESTORATION SCHOOL AND MUSEUM OF YACHTING ★

OCEAN DRIVE ✪

SPRING ST

RUGGLES AVE

Almy Pond Conservation Area

SPRING ST

BATEMAN AVE

Morton Park

MORTON ST

WEBSTER ST

HAZARD AVE

NARRAGANSETT AVE

DIXON ST

THE ELMS ★

PERRY ST

ISAAC BELL HOUSE ★

BELLEVUE AVE

CLAY ST

WARD AVE

SYLVAN ST

BERKELEY AVE

BOWERY ST

MIDDLETON AVE

CHEPSTOW ★

BELLEVUE AVE

VICTORIA AVE

NATIONAL MUSEUM OF AMERICAN ILLUSTRATION ★

SHEPARD AVE

CHATEAU-SUR-MER ★

LEROY AVE

MARINE AVE

RUGGLES AVE

LAWRENCE AVE

SALVE REGINA UNIVERSITY

ANNANDALE RD

GAMMELL RD

OCHRE POINT AVE

THE BREAKERS ★✪

CLIFF WALK ✪

Easton Bay

0   200 yds
0   200 m

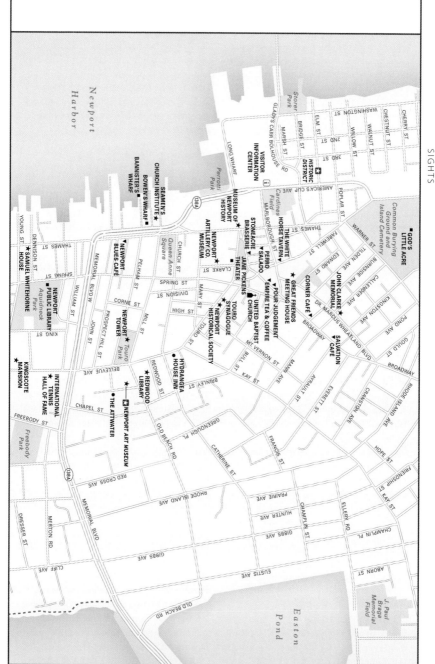

most successful shipping merchants, Samuel Whitehorne, who earned his fortune in rum distilling, shipping, and the slave trade. The house has all the classic elements of Federal architecture: a symmetrical hipped roof, a lavish formal garden, and a circular entryway.

INTERNATIONAL YACHT RESTORATION SCHOOL AND MUSEUM OF YACHTING

The **International Yacht Restoration School (IYRS)** (449 Thames St., 401/848-5777, ext. 227, www.iyrs.edu, 10am-5pm Mon.-Fri. by appointment, free) is a nonprofit with a mission to teach the "skills, history, and science needed to construct, restore, and maintain classic watercraft." The school has an impressive collection of fine old boats, including the IYRS flagship, the *Coronet*, which has sailed around the world and hosted such luminaries as Alexander Graham Bell and the king of Hawaii. The school is also home to the **Museum of Yachting** (noon-5pm Tues.-Fri., free), which exhibits art, historical artifacts, and excellent views of the harbor on the top floor of the Aquidneck Mill Building.

BELLEVUE AVENUE

Running parallel to Thames Street a few blocks east and up the hill from Newport Harbor, Bellevue Avenue had become a wealthy, exclusive retreat by the time of the Civil War. Each season, new arrivals built ever-larger summer cottages until development peaked around 1890-1914, generally referred to as Newport's Gilded Age. During these 25 years, unbelievably wealthy industrialists and high-society types built massive, fortress-like homes and threw parties that sometimes cost more than $250,000 a pop. Today, many of the grandest of these houses still stand, operated as house-museums and are open to the public.

Redwood Library

North of the intersection with Memorial Boulevard is the **Redwood Library** (50 Bellevue Ave., 401/847-0292, www. redwoodlibrary.org, 9:30am-5:30pm Mon.-Sat., 1pm-5pm Sun.), a neoclassical structure built in 1750 by one of the nation's first architects, Peter Harrison, and once frequented by Gilbert Stuart, William and Henry James, and Edith Wharton. It is the oldest lending library in the country and contains special collections focusing on 18th- and 19th-century fine and decorative arts, and architecture and historic preservation in New England.

Newport Tower

Across Bellevue Avenue and down Mill Street is the **Newport Tower** (also know as the Old Stone Mill), which anchors Touro Park. Much controversy surrounds this structure, which many locals had believed was built by Vikings 1,000 years ago, until improved forensic research cast doubt on this explanation. Another story is that one of the city's earliest residents and Rhode Island's first governor, Benedict Arnold, built the structure sometime in the 18th century. The structure is enclosed by a fence inside of Touro Park, and is more interesting for its controversial history than it is for being visually impressive.

★ Newport Art Museum

The **Newport Art Museum** (76 Bellevue Ave., 401/848-8200, www.newportart museum.org, 10am-5pm Tues.-Sat., noon-5pm Sun., $15 adults, $10 seniors, $6 students, free for youth under 18) displays the works of mostly regional artists, running the gamut from American impressionism to modern sculpture. Evocative seascapes by members of the Provincetown or Gloucester schools of artists grace the walls in the downstairs sitting rooms, and colonial-era portraits line the stairway of the museum, which is located inside the Griswold House, a gorgeously restored 1864 home with amazingly ornate woodwork. Across a sculpture-studded field, the Cushing House stages changing exhibits, some of them quite clever. One exhibition, for example, focused on Newport's connection to Japan, which was opened to U.S. trade in the 19th century by the city's own Commodore

A Brief History of Tennis

Tennis is an extremely old game, with roots in 11th-century France. But its present form dates to around the 1870s, when many wealthy Brits installed courts at their country manors. Similarly, as a wealthy leisure class was emerging in the United States, especially in New England, interest in tennis increased there.

In 1874, **British Major Walter Clopton Wingfield** devised **a new form of tennis** that combined the centuries-old game, which is now generally referred to as "court tennis" or "real tennis," with some characteristics of badminton, which has Native American origins. This variation, called lawn tennis, is the true ancestor of the game we play today, while real tennis is a comparatively obscure game played in few places.

Just a few years after its introduction into high society in New York, the **first men's tennis championship** in the United States was held at the **Newport Casino;** a women's championship was added in 1887. International competitions began in 1900 with the **Davis Cup,** which started as a men's tourney between the United States and England, although tennis had already developed a strong following in Australia, France, Holland, and many other nations.

Although tennis was something of a blue-blooded country-club activity during its first half-century, its popularity spread to the general public during, ironically, the Depression, when a number of federally funded New Deal programs led to the construction of tennis courts at public parks and schools.

Professional tennis, of course, has enjoyed an almost meteoric rise in popularity through the past three decades. One of the four major tournaments, the U.S. Open is the modern-day descendant of that first championship held in Newport in 1881. For about 35 years, the Newport Casino and its illustrious tournament served as the U.S. equivalent of Wimbledon, and it might still today if not for Newport's relative isolation from the Northeast's major population centers. In 1915, the U.S. Open was shifted from Newport to Long Island, New York.

Nevertheless, from 1915 onward an invitational tournament continued to be staged on **Newport's grass court,** and in 1954 the Newport Casino was converted into the home of the **National Tennis Hall of Fame.** Starting in 1976, the Newport Casino has hosted the Hall of Fame Tennis Championship (now sponsored by Campbell Soup), the only pro tournament in the nation still played solely on grass courts.

Matthew Perry; items on display included a full suit of samurai armor. A more recent exhibition focused on "the eternal feminine," featuring a private collection of art using the female as muse and icon—highlights included original and rare black and white photographs of art rock heroines Patti Smith and Yoko Ono.

International Tennis Hall of Fame

Tennis may have originated in England, but in the United States its history passes through Newport. The first U.S. National Lawn Tennis Championship, later known as the U.S. Open, was played on the grass-lawn tennis courts of the Newport Casino in 1881. Now that hallowed ground has become the **International Tennis Hall of Fame** (194 Bellevue Ave., 401/849-3990, www.tennisfame.com, 10am-6pm daily, $15, free for ages 16 and under, admission includes court access). Just south of Memorial Boulevard, the museum contains about a dozen exhibit rooms displaying memorabilia of the game, including an Andy Warhol portrait of Chris Evert, the original 1874 tennis patent granted by the queen of England to Major Walter Clopton Wingfield, and a gallery celebrating tennis champions of the early 20th century. The museum is unusual in that it remains a working tennis facility that's open to the public for play; this is the only lawn tennis facility in the country that's not a private club. There's also quite an extensive gift shop as well as a restaurant overlooking the courts.

National Museum of American Illustration

The **National Museum of American Illustration** (NMAI, 492 Bellevue Ave., 401/851-8949, www.americanillustration. org, 11am-5pm Thurs.-Sun. Memorial Day-Labor Day or by appointment year-round, $20 adults, $18 seniors, $10 children 5-12, children under 5 not admitted) is worth admiring from the outside and also interesting to tour, keeping in mind the limited hours of admission. This museum is housed in one of the grand mansions along Bellevue Avenue, the 1898 Vernon Court, which is modeled after a 17th-century château. John Merven Carrère and Thomas Hastings, also responsible for the New York Public Library and the Frick Collection, designed the mansion, noted for its marble Great Hall and its steep roof punctuated by nine tall chimneys. The museum was formed with a mission to preserve and present the nation's finest illustrated art—works commissioned to appear in magazines, books, advertisements, and other print products. The collection displays work by dozens of famous illustrators, among them Maxfield Parrish, Norman Rockwell, N. C. Wyeth, Charles Dana Gibson, Howard Chandler Christy, and many others. As you tour the mansion, you'll also see a vast array of decorative arts and period furnishings.

Salve Regina University

Just off the east side of Bellevue Avenue is the attractive campus of **Salve Regina University** (Ochre Point Ave., 401/847-6650, www.salve.edu). There are 18 historically significant buildings on the property, which is a few blocks east of Bellevue Cliff Walk. The school is heavily involved in preservation programs, sponsoring lectures and events to preserve its many prominent structures. The most famous building on campus is perhaps **Ochre Court,** one of the city's earliest grand summer cottages, completed in 1892 with a design by Richard Morris Hunt. Ochre Court was donated in 1947 to serve as the foundation of Salve Regina, and through the past few decades, several other summer cottages in the adjoining neighborhood have been donated to the school. Noted architects whose works are now part of the campus include H. H. Richardson, the father of Richardsonian Romanesque; Charles Eamer Kempe; and the firm of McKim, Mead, and White.

SOUTH NEWPORT

The southern portion of Newport is less densely populated; its high points are its verdant open spaces, beaches, and many sweeping views of the Atlantic Ocean.

★ Ocean Drive

One of the most famous scenic drives on the East Coast, 9.5-mi (15.3-km) Ocean Drive is a roughly C-shaped route that begins at the lower end of downtown, on Wellington Avenue at the intersection of Thames Street. Ocean Drive isn't one road but rather the name of a well-marked route that connects several roads. At least half the fun of this journey, which can take from an hour to half a day, depending on how often you stop, is simply peering out the window at the stunning homes, sandy beaches, and ocean views.

Still right in town on Newport Harbor, you'll pass little **King Park** on your right as you drive west along Wellington Avenue; this is the city's small but pleasant in-town beach. About 1 mi (1.6 km) farther along, you'll come to a National Historic Landmark and one of the most formidable coastal forts ever built in the United States, **Fort Adams** (Eisenhower House, Fort Adams State Park, 401/841-0707, www.fortadams.org, 10am-4pm daily late May-mid-Oct., grounds admission free, fort tours $15 adults, $8 for children, $40 families). The fort served the region from the 1820s through World War II, occupying a grassy point opposite downtown Newport, about 1 mi (1.6 km) across Newport Harbor. Today you can tour the bastions, officers' quarters, the enclosed 6.25-acre parade, and the exterior dry moat that helped prevent the fort from ever being compromised by an enemy. Entrance to the main fortification is by guided tour only, but admission to the grounds is free.

On leaving the park, continue back onto Harrison Avenue. Although it's no longer open to the public, **Hammersmith Farm** (off Harrison Ave., next to Fort Adams State Park) is home to an 1887 mansion that is one of Newport's most fabled properties. The site of Jacqueline Bouvier and John F. Kennedy's wedding reception in 1953, it became the "summer White House" for the first family after Kennedy became president. Once open for tours, the house was sold for $8 million to a private owner in 1999.

A short distance farther along Harrison Avenue, make a right onto Ridge Road and follow it around, passing the elegant Ocean Cliff Hotel. This road meets with Castle Hill Avenue, from which a small lane leads to the **Castle Hill Coast Guard Station** (75 Ridge Rd., 401/846-3676, tours by appointment during daylight hours). Back on the main route, you'll finally reach Ocean Avenue, which runs right along the water with mostly contemporary and colonial-style beach homes on the inland side of the street.

Where Ocean Drive turns nearly 90 degrees around Brenton Point, you'll find a parking area for **Brenton Point State Park**

(401/849-4562 May-Oct., 401/847-2400 year-round, www.riparks.com), a rugged, rocky promontory overlooking the ocean. You can picnic here or stroll along the beach, and it's also quite popular for kite-flying.

Continue on Ocean Drive along the waterfront back toward Newport, passing the Newport Country Club, some private beaches, and several gorgeous homes that range from century-old Victorian castles to rather recently built compounds with lavish decking and many-gabled roofs. Officially, Ocean Drive ends at Coggeshall Avenue, where a left turn will bring you back into lower downtown, about 2 mi (3.2 km) away. Make a right turn, however, and after following the road a short way, make a left onto Bellevue Avenue to begin a tour of the Newport mansions of the Gilded Age—in the reverse direction from most visitors, who approach the mansions from town.

Newport's Mansions

Much has been written about Newport's vast marble halls, and not all of it positive. As the railroad and steel tycoons began constructing their ostentatious summer homes at the end of the 19th century, they symbolized a new Renaissance in American architecture.

beautiful homes on Ocean Drive

Tour Newport's Mansions

With over 15 historic properties and 80 acres of gardens and parks, Newport's collection of sprawling mansions can seem an overwhelming tour indeed. If you're intent on seeing as many of them as possible, consider the following tips:

Buy tickets ahead of time. The crowds in high season can be crushing, so take advantage of some of the online packages available through the **Preservation Society of Newport County** (424 Bellevue Ave., 401/847-1000, www.newportmansions.org), which manages most of the major mansions (one exception is Belcourt Castle). While individual mansions can be pricey, the fees for combination tickets can be quite economical. For example, a ticket to The Breakers is $19 for adults ($5 children 6-17); however, combined The Breakers and one other mansion is $24 ($5 children). If you are a mansion freak, a ticket to see any five mansions is only $31 ($10 children). So try to gauge your interest in the mansions realistically beforehand to benefit from these savings.

Plan on touring three mansions per day. Tours are offered quite regularly at the largest mansions (approximately every 15 minutes during high season and every 30 minutes in spring). Times vary at many of the smaller mansions, but generally the wait time is no longer than 30 minutes. And because most tours are finished in under an hour and the mansions are within easy walking distance of one another (and transportation is provided in the form of natural-gas trolleys between the houses), it is quite reasonable to plan three mansion tours in one day. Some ambitious visitors opt to do four or five, but there are only so many gilded ceilings and marble hallways the human eye can gaze upon before they all start to blend together. To fully appreciate the level of grandeur and detail, it may be wisest to take in three tours per day, leaving time for a change of scenery—Newport's beaches, downtown, or parks. If you've got children, of course, you'll need to reduce that further to one or two mansions at most. (A good alternative, included in the combination ticket, is a tour of the Green Animals Topiary Garden in Portsmouth.)

Invest in a good map or guide. The society produces probably the best map to the Cliff Walk and Bellevue Avenue, which includes a level of detail down to each individual building in the area, color-coded by type (private home, house museum, university building), along with step-by-step information about the Cliff Walk and the locations of bus and trolley stops. Many other publishers and organizations produce their own maps and guides to the area; they are readily available at local bookshops and convenience stores.

The mansions are **wheelchair** accessible; **baby strollers,** however, are not allowed.

Finally, the New World would have palaces to rival those of the Old World—built not by kings but by captains of industry. And while they might give a nod to the classical forms of Europe in style, they implemented the most advanced technology—electric lighting, hot and cold running water—that American ingenuity could conjure. Within a few short years, however, as the excesses of the Gilded Age spawned a Progressive backlash, no less an authority than novelist Henry James derided the Newport cottages as "white elephants"—beautiful but useless symbols of excess. Some modern architects continue to turn up their noses at the extravagant tastes of the robber barons

of the day, who seemed to choose the most garish forms of decoration in their homes that they could find.

Still, there's nothing like the impact of walking into some of these homes, in which every element seems calculated to impress. The Astors, Vanderbilts, and other millionaires of the time literally spared no expense in constructing their masterpieces, lavishing the same care and attention on these architectural endeavors as they did in constructing their multimillion-dollar businesses. While the initial reaction of most visitors is one of sheer, overwhelming amazement, closer inspection reveals countless pleasures in the details. There's not a single sconce or column that's free of adornment—each wall panel, and in some cases each ceiling tile, is decorated with some family crest or symbol designed to bless the fortunes of its creator. Even the most cynical viewer of the selfishness of wealth has to feel some awe in the beauty of so many well-thought-out design elements coming together in a harmonious whole. Lovers of antiques and historic homes may feel they've died and gone to architectural heaven. The **Preservation Society of Newport County** (401/847-1000, www.newportmansions.org) operates tours of most of the houses. Several different tour possibilities are available, including combination tickets that provide a discount.

ROUGH POINT

Some people get rich for being famous; others are famous for being rich. Heiress Doris Duke—the title is practically part of her name—belongs to the latter category. In 1925, when she was just 12 years old, she inherited $100 million on the death of her father, a tobacco and electricity magnate. She led a colorful life, to say the least, traveling around the world, working as a foreign correspondent during World War II, and famously romancing a number of men, marrying and divorcing three of them. Today, her legacy is best seen in the field of historic preservation through her establishment of the Newport Restoration Foundation, which started the city's preservation boom in the 1960s. Since then, it has helped fully restore more than 80 threatened structures in Newport, including the mansion where Duke herself spent the summers, **Rough Point** (680 Bellevue Ave., 401/847-8344, www.newportrestoration.com, 10am-5pm Tues.-Sun., $20 adults, free for children under 13).

A grand mansion built in 1889 for Frederick W. Vanderbilt, the home occupies a rocky point overlooking the ocean. James B. Duke, Doris's father, bought the estate in 1922 but lived in it for just three years before his death. Inside, you'll find a collection of

rare Ming vases and ceramics, plus original paintings by Renoir, Van Dyck, and portraitist Joshua Reynolds. There is also a phenomenal collection of furniture and antiquities, rare among Newport mansions.

Guided tours are included with admission and offered daily at 10:30am and 11:30am, and 1:30pm and 3:30pm.

KINGSCOTE MANSION AND THE ISAAC BELL HOUSE

The first mansion you find as you travel south down Bellevue Avenue is also historically one of the first to establish the trend of Newport as a summer vacation spot for the rich and powerful. **Kingscote Mansion** (Bowery Ave. at Bellevue Ave., 401/847-1000, www.newportmansions.org, 10am-4:30pm daily late June-early Sept., $18 adults, $8 children) was the brainchild of George Noble Jones, a wealthy Georgia plantation owner who wanted a grand seaside residence to escape the Southern heat during summer. He commissioned architect Richard Upjohn to build him a truly unique and modern residence—Upjohn's Gothic Revival cottage, all asymmetrical gables, dormers, and drip moldings, represented the cutting edge of English architecture at the time—a reaction against the staid classical forms of Greek Revival that were otherwise in vogue. Today the home stands as one of the only examples of its style and size. Completed in 1841, Kingscote set the tone that other mansions were to follow over the next 75 years. One of its most impressive features, however, was added in 1881: the dining room by the architectural firm Mead, White, and McKim, a breathtaking hall with a cork ceiling and what is believed to be the earliest-ever installation of Tiffany stained glass windows, that manages to be grand and intimate at the same time.

Next door, Mead, White, and McKim went on to build the **Isaac Bell House** (Bellevue Ave., 401/847-1000, www.newportmansions.org, 10am-4:30pm daily late June-early Sept., $18 adults, $8 children), a less imposing residence that nevertheless ranks among the

The Gilded Age

Around 1850, real estate speculators began buying up the land south and east of downtown, and Bellevue Avenue was extended south toward the water. This development triggered the period of wealth in Newport that would come to be known as "The Gilded Age." Wealthy New Yorkers and Bostonians began building summer cottages in this new section of Newport, and each summer the newest structures dwarfed the previous ones both in size and opulence. Many Southerners also built homes in this increasingly exclusive summer colony. The value of land skyrocketed, and the boom continued through the late 1850s.

LET THE PARTY BEGIN

After a short-lived recession, civic leaders decided to throw a sumptuous party for summering bigwigs as well as the many past Newport residents who had not been back for some time. The ball was a huge success, and the tradition of summer entertaining continued to grow each subsequent year. Predictably, the **Civil War** interrupted Newport's growth as a resort, but as soon as it ended, grand summer life in Newport returned stronger than ever.

Into the 1880s, the presence of Newport's **superrich part-time residents** began to pay off in the form of significant investments in infrastructure improvements. A city water system was inaugurated in 1881, and private telephone service came the following year. Electric trolley service, which ran from Commercial Wharf up over Bath Street (now Memorial Boulevard) to Easton's Beach, became a reality in 1889. Upper-class leisure activities also made inroads during these years, with the earliest national tennis matches commencing in 1881, followed by polo and then golf tournaments. The little city by the sea, virtually bereft of industry or commercial clout, became a powerhouse owing to its sterling reputation as a playground for the rich and famous.

THE IN CROWD

In the Gilded Age, **Harry Lehr** and **Mrs. William Astor** became the leading society players in Newport, more or less controlling every aspect of the social season, determining who could move in the city's most desirable circles and who should be kept down. The so-called **"400,"** a social **precursor** of sorts **to today's Forbes 500,** were those individuals fortunate enough to attend the ball held each summer in the ballroom of the Astor home. To be on this list could easily legitimize a person's social standing; to be excluded from it could scar one's reputation irreparably.

The outrageous antics of Newport's society mavens gradually began to wear on those outside looking in, most significantly the press. The gossip writers of the time took great glee in reporting each and every excess, from the time that Harry Lehr and Mrs. Stuyvesant Fish held a party at which a diminutive trained monkey was booked as the guest of honor, to the **infamous dog gala,** when Lehr invited about **100 canines** and their owners to a lavish sit-down meal where thousands of dollars were spent on food. The public reaction to these displays was finally such that the summer party-throwers began to exercise more restraint, but the over-the-top parties still continued for many years to come.

nation's most impressive examples of shingle-style architecture. Completed in 1883, it is a quirky house even by Newport standards, with bamboo-style porch columns and an open floor plan inspired by the grand houses of Japan. Three narrow brick chimneys rise from the many-gabled roofline. A single ticket is good for both Kingscote and the Isaac Bell House.

THE ELMS

The first real eruption of grandeur on Bellevue Avenue is also one of the most appealing of Newport's mansions. **The Elms** (424 Bellevue Ave., 401/847-1000, www.newportmansions. org, 10am-5pm daily early Apr.-mid-June, 10am-6pm daily mid-June-early Sept., 10am-5pm daily early Sept.-late Nov., 10am-4pm daily late Nov.-Dec., $18 adults, $8 children) is a near-perfect copy of an 18th-century French château, built for coal tycoon Edward J. Berwind in 1901. The grounds comprise 10 acres of landscaped parkland containing about 40 species of trees, plus dignified marble statuary and perfectly groomed shrubs. The interior, almost cozy compared to some mansions, abounds with gadgets as The Elms was among the earliest Newport homes to be lighted and run by electricity. Tours are self-guided with digital audio players, a format that allows you to walk through the house in 30-90 minutes, depending on how many specific topics you choose to hear about.

CHEPSTOW

Just north of the Salve Regina campus on Narragansett Avenue, **Chepstow** (401/847-1000, www.newportmansions.org, 10am-4:30pm daily late June-early Sept., $16 adults, $7 children 6-17, free for children under 6) is another early Newport mansion. An Italianate villa designed by George Champlin Mason and completed in 1860, its exterior is harmonious if less grand than some of its cousins. The esteemed collection of Hudson River School paintings, however, is worth the price of admission. A descendant of Lewis Morris, a signatory of the Declaration of Independence, owned this cottage.

CHÂTEAU-SUR-MER

Continuing the taste for all things French following the Civil War, **Château-sur-Mer** (424 Bellevue Ave., 401/847-1000, www.newportmansions.org, 10am-5pm daily early Apr.-mid-June, 10am-6pm daily mid-June-early Sept., 10am-5pm daily early Sept.-late Nov., 10am-4pm daily late Nov.-Dec., $18 adults, $8 children) might be considered the missing link between the large homes such as Kingscote and Chepstow and the true mansions like The Breakers and Rosecliff. It was first built in a blocky château style in 1852 for merchant and Far East importer William S. Wetmore. After he died, however, his children decided the home needed a makeover, commissioning architect Richard Morris Hunt to update it to a more modern style. Hunt transformed both interior and exterior into a grand ensemble of the most fashionable European designs. Before those pesky Vanderbilts moved to Newport in the 1890s, this massive home was the largest residence in Newport. The interior impresses immediately with a stairway out of *Gone with the Wind* and a morning room demonstrating intricate woodwork. Behind the house you can stroll through a colonial revival garden pavilion and a Victorian-inspired park with century-old copper beech trees and weeping willows.

★ THE BREAKERS

Each of Newport's mansions is an undeniably overwhelming display of wealth, beauty, and design, but even among such over-the-top grandeur, the most lavish of them all is **The Breakers** (44 Ochre Point Ave., 401/847-1000, www.newportmansions.org, 9am-5pm daily Apr.-late June, 9am-6pm daily late June-early Sept., 9am-5pm daily early Sept.-Nov., 9am-4pm daily late Nov.-Dec., $26 adults, $8 children), completed in 1895 as the summer home of steamship and railroad giant Commodore Cornelius Vanderbilt II, the first among equals of "the 400," the nickname for the elite New York social circle that ran the country back in the day. Designed by an international dream team of architects, the house has no less than 70 rooms and is a dead ringer for Italy's most opulent 16th-century palazzos. Alas, Vanderbilt only enjoyed one summer of good health here—after a stroke in 1896, he died a few years later in 1899.

His children, however, more than enjoyed the estate, including the impressive 13-acre grounds, which overlook Cliff Walk and the Atlantic Ocean—it was the sound of the waves smashing against the rocks below that gave The Breakers its name. Inside, rooms are constructed with ample amounts of semiprecious stones, rare marble, baccarat crystal chandeliers, and even platinum leaf on the walls (platinum is the rarest and most expensive metal in the world for its ability to not tarnish). In the bathrooms, four faucets provide

both hot and cold freshwater and saltwater, and the marble baths were so thick that servants had to fill and drain them several times with hot water before they'd hold enough heat. Then there is the 45-foot-high Great Hall, as grandiose a room as there ever was and the site of countless soirees during The Breakers's heyday. At some of them, it's said, guests slid down the polished banister on dining trays.

ROSECLIFF

More French influence is evident down the street at **Rosecliff** (548 Bellevue Ave., 401/847-1000, www.newportmansions.org, 10am-5pm daily early Apr.-mid-June, 10am-6pm daily mid-June-early Sept., 10am-5pm daily early Sept.-late Nov., 10am-4pm daily late Nov.-Dec., $18 adults, $8 children), built by Stanford White in 1902 and inspired by the Grand Trianon section of the palace at Versailles, France. Originally commissioned by Theresa and Hermann Oelrichs, it has been featured in a handful of movies, including the 1974 version *The Great Gatsby* and *Amistad*.

As her husband increasingly preferred the more laid-back social life out West, the home became more and more the domain of "Tessie" Fair Oelrichs, a colorful silver heiress from Nevada who became the center of Newport society for many years. Luckily, Oelrichs knew how to throw a party, and the house is remembered for having hosted a magic-themed party at which Harry Houdini entertained the guests, as well as many other outlandish events. A tour highlight is walking through the largest ballroom in Newport (and that's saying a lot in this city).

MARBLE HOUSE

Another modest little Vanderbilt home is **Marble House** (596 Bellevue Ave., 401/847-1000, www.newportmansions.org, 10am-5pm daily early Apr.-mid-June, 10am-6pm daily mid-June-early Sept., 10am-5pm daily early Sept.-late Nov., 10am-4pm daily late

Nov.-Dec., $8 adults, $8 children), built in 1892 by Richard Morris Hunt for Cornelius Vanderbilt's grandson once removed, William K. Vanderbilt, who commissioned the home as a present for his wife, Alva, for her 39th birthday (which makes you wonder what he gave her for her 40th). True to its name, it's now filled with nearly half a million cubic feet of marble and includes on its grounds a Chinese teahouse built by Alva that overlooks the crashing waves of the Atlantic below. After The Breakers, this is one of Newport's most-visited house-museums—visitors can't seem to get enough of the stairwells, columns, and floors of Italian, American, and African marble.

TOP EXPERIENCE

★ CLIFF WALK

The two finest things Newport has to offer—its natural seaside beauty and the architectural relics of the Gilded Age—collide along the seaside **Cliff Walk** (www.cliffwalk.com), arguably one of the country's grandest strolls. Beginning at the western end of Easton's Beach (also known as First Beach), the 3.5-mi (5.6-km) path runs between the rocky beach and many of the town's most impressive mansions. The area is a designated National Historic District and was deemed a National Recreational Trail in 1975, making it a double-whammy of natural and artificial glory. For many who walk it, the Cliff Walk is an opportunity to gaze at fancy estates and experience the same ocean views that mesmerized Newport's wealthy summer visitors at the turn of the 20th century. It is also a wonderful nature trail, abundant with opportunities for bird-watching and admiring fields of wildflowers.

There are a number of access points along Cliff Walk, but none are near ample public parking except the beginning of the trail at Easton's Beach, so the other points are limited to pedestrians and cyclists. Sheppard Avenue, Webster Street, and Wetmore Avenue intersect the walk about midway and have some

1: The Elms 2: The Breakers, as seen on the Cliff Walk 3: Rosecliff 4: a view from the Cliff Walk

NEWPORT
ENTERTAINMENT AND EVENTS

limited street parking, and Narragansett Avenue, about 0.5 mi (0.8 km) into the walk, has the most parking of any intersecting streets. During the summer, a bus runs up and down Bellevue Avenue—the main paved road that parallels the walk—and you can take the bus to any of the cross streets that lead to the walk.

Less than 1 mi (1.6 km) into the walk, at the end of Narragansett Avenue, you'll come to the **40 Steps,** a sharply descending stone stairway that goes nearly to the sea below; from a small promontory at the base of the steps you can watch the waves smashing against the rocks. Soon after 40 Steps, the path meanders by some of Newport's most famous mansions, including The Breakers, Rosecliff, Astor's Beechwood, and Marble House. Soon after, on the right and just above the path, you'll see the ornate red Chinese teahouse commissioned by Marble House's owner, Alva Vanderbilt. At this point the Cliff Walk cuts through a short tunnel before emerging again for another fairly well-maintained stretch and then a second tunnel.

Once you emerge from this final tunnel, Cliff Walk becomes a scramble on the wild side, as it hugs the rocky shoreline by a series of large private homes. This span is aptly nicknamed **Rough Point,** and rather crude and ugly chain-link fences separate the path from the private properties. Northeasters

and hurricanes have taken their toll on Cliff Walk's southern reaches, and in some places the seawall has been ripped out. It's all entirely passable, and it's generally not too steep or high, but you do want to wear sturdy shoes. As you cut around the southeastern tip of the peninsula, you'll be able to see the Doris Duke estate, Rough Point, just off Bellevue where it bends from south to west.

As the Cliff Walk turns west around the southeastern tip of Newport, you'll come to Ledge Road, a short dead-end that shoots south off Bellevue Avenue. At this point you might think the path has come to an end—indeed, a short walk up Ledge Road does lead you back to where buses pass along Bellevue Avenue. However, it's also entirely possible to climb along the jagged rocks, treading carefully, for a short distance around the southwestern tip of this small peninsula. After a little more than 0.25 mi (0.4 km) of cutting your own trail, the official Cliff Walk resumes, now in a northerly direction along the western end of the peninsula. To your left, looking northwest, you'll see the exclusive **Bailey's Beach,** and before long you'll reach the eastern edge of this fabled stretch of sand.

For a detailed sense of the entire walk's history and highlights, the official website (www.cliffwalk.com) has detailed maps and 360-degree panoramas of some of the most beautiful spots along the trail.

Entertainment and Events

NIGHTLIFE

For a relatively small city, there's much to do in Newport at night, especially during the summer months.

Bars and Pubs

Bar hoppers and beer connoisseurs should start out at **Pour Judgement** (32 Broadway, 401/619-2115, www.pourjudgementnewport. com, 11am-1am Mon.-Fri., 11:30am-1am Sat., 10am-1am Sun.), a popular hangout with an

excellent selection of craft beer and an unpretentious, friendly vibe. Just a few blocks north you'll find **Salvation Café** (140 Broadway, 401/847-2620, www.salvationcafe.com, 4:30pm-midnight daily), a bar and restaurant with fun, colorful decor, and a mostly young, hip crowd. In the summertime, the outdoor patio and tiki bar is a bonus. Both locations are favorites with locals and a great alternative to the downtown and harbor hangouts, which can get crowded with tourists.

If crowded with tourists is more your scene, check out the **Boom Boom Room** (1 Bannister's Wharf, 401/849-2900, 11:30am-1am daily), located below the Candy Store at Bannister's Wharf, which draws a fairly mainstream crowd for dancing to DJ-spun Top 40 hits and disco. Upstairs in the bar at **Candy Store** (401/849-2900, 11:30am-midnight, daily) yachting enthusiasts and Newport socialites trade gossip and cruise over wines by the glass and fancy cocktails.

Live Music

At the **Newport Blues Cafe** (286 Thames St., 401/841-5510, www.newportblues.com, 7pm-1am Tues.-Sun., shows usually start at 10pm), a restaurant-lounge housed in the former Newport National Bank building dating back to 1892, you can catch live music from acclaimed artists most nights of the week, from jazz and blues to standup comedy and indie rock. Indie acts—some big names, but mostly local—also play regularly at **One Pelham East** (270 Thames St., 401/847-9460, www.thepelham.com, 3:30pm-1am Mon.-Fri., 1:30pm-1am Sat.-Sun.) which caters to a younger crowd. Usually packed on summer nights, it can be a comfortable spot to catch fall and winter acts, too.

Parlor Bar & Kitchen (200 Broadway, 401/848-9081, www.parlornewport.com, 5pm-1am Mon.-Thurs., 10am-1am Sat.-Sun.) is also a good bet for live rock, folk, jazz, and reggae bands, most of which are local. Decent food and a pool table make this a good bet even on nights when no live music is booked.

THE ARTS

Considering Newport's glittering legacy of sophisticated and wealthy summer visitors along with its well-endowed visual arts scene, the city is relatively lacking when it comes to the performing arts.

One of the most popular entertainment venues is the **Newport Playhouse and Cabaret Restaurant** (102 Connell Hwy., near the foot of Newport Bridge, 401/848-7529, www.newportplayhouse.com), which presents several generally light theatrical performances each year April through December. The show comes with a substantial buffet dinner, and the theater has a full liquor license. Although it's mostly used as an art-house cinema, the **Jane Pickens Theater** (49 Touro St., 401/846-5252, www.janepickens.com) also hosts occasional live performances and local musicians.

Different kinds of concerts are sometimes held at the city's house-museums, churches, and at Salve Regina University. It's best to check with the **Newport County Convention and Visitors Bureau** (23 America's Cup Ave., next to the bus terminal, Newport, 401/849-8098 or 800/326-6030, www.discovernewport.org) for details on what's happening where.

FESTIVALS AND EVENTS
Summer

Kicking off the season in June, a behind-the-fence look at many Newport properties is offered on the **Secret Garden Tour** (www.secretgardentour.com), which is also held again in September.

A variety of venues host the **Newport Music Festival** (www.newportmusic.org), which has been going strong since the late 1960s. The event runs for roughly two weeks each July and presents about 60 chamber-music and other classical concerts at some of the city's most famous mansions, including The Elms, The Breakers, Marble House, Salve Regina's Ochre Court, and Rosecliff. Some of the concerts are held in ballrooms and indoor spaces, while others are presented under tent cover on the lush grounds.

Also in July, the International Tennis Hall of Fame hosts the **Tennis Hall of Fame Open** (www.tennisfame.com), a major draw on the Association of Tennis Professionals tour and the only grass-court professional tennis tourney in the country.

One of the crowning events of the summer in Newport is the **Newport Folk Festival** (www.newportfolk.org), a three-day event held at the sprawling, seaside Fort Adams

Newport Folk Festival

Every August, Newport's already impressive number of summer visitors swells by leaps and bounds thanks to the global draw of the renowned Newport Folk and Jazz Festivals.

Since its inception nearly six decades ago, the Newport Folk Festival has made a name for itself by hosting legendary artists and legendary performances; from the famous "Dylan goes electric" show of 1965, and the songwriting workshop hosted by Joni Mitchell and James Taylor in 1969 to the 2005 "Pixies go acoustic" performance and the duet between Beck and Ramblin' Jack Elliot in 2013.

Cofounded in 1959 by jazz producer George Wein and folk music heroes Pete Seeger, Theodore Bikel, Oscar Brand, and Albert Grossman, the festival went on to gain a reputation as a platform for introducing unknown talents to the world at large. Artists like Joan Baez, Bob Dylan, and Kris Kristofferson all got their starts at Newport Folk, and many others have gained critical acclaim since the festival roster began branching out to include acts from the alternative country, indie, folk-punk, world, and Americana genres. Today the festival is one of the most popular outdoor music festivals on the Eastern Seaboard, drawing music lovers from all over the world.

Before there was the Folk Fest, George Wein and several Newport socialites founded the Newport Jazz Festival in 1954, known for its mix of well-known performers and up-and-coming musicians. Over the decades, legends like Miles Davis, Duke Ellington, Billie Holiday, and Frank Sinatra have graced its stages, and today the three-day series of concerts and events packs in hundreds of performances, from organ trios and vocalists to Brazilian duos and big-band productions on multiple stages.

Both festivals take place on successive weekends at Fort Adams State Park, which is situated on a peninsula surrounded by sparkling ocean waters—a setting that truly adds to the magic of the performances. The park has strict rules about what attendees may bring in, so when packing, bear in mind that no glass containers, alcohol, pets, bikes, or beach umbrellas are permitted. Children are welcome, and there are plenty of inexpensive kids' meals at the concession stands. Tickets for the Folk Fest often sell out long before the lineup is even announced—check www.newportfolk.org for tickets and info. Tickets for Jazz Fest are usually easier to come by and can be purchased in advance at www.newportjazzfest.org.

State Park in late July. It's one of the nation's top folk festivals and has drawn dozens of major artists through the years; recent performers include Bob Dylan, Gillian Welch, Jeff Tweedy, Joan Baez, Neko Case, and Roger Waters. The following weekend in August, the hugely popular Newport Jazz Festival (401/848-5055, www.newportjazzfest.org) is also held at Fort Adams. Big international acts congregate here alongside promising up-and-comers to entertain jazz enthusiasts. Recent performers include Bobby McFerrin, Dr. John, and Arturo Sandoval; past performers included Duke Ellington and Miles Davis.

Fall

In early October, check out the Norman Bird Sanctuary Harvest Fair (www.normanbirdsanctuary.org), a 2-day celebration of fall, with children's games, hayrides, and craft vendors.

Winter and Spring

All through mid-November until Christmas, the holiday season sees the town's mansions decked out even more elaborately than usual; heavyweights such as Marble House and The Breakers are festively dressed in white lights and Christmas decorations for Christmas at the Newport Mansions (401/847-1000, www.newportmansions.org, late Nov.-early Jan., admission cost varies for different mansions). All through December is the annual Christmas in Newport Celebration (www.christmasinnewport.org), which fills the waterfront and historic districts with thousands of white lights and Christmas music from live bands and choruses.

Shopping

There is no shortage of shopping in Newport, especially downtown along Thames Street and the lanes and wharves just off of it. Two of the wharves in Newport function today as mini malls that jut into the harbor. Dozens of mostly independent art galleries and clothing, jewelry, and gifts shops can be found here, and some of the usual high-end chain businesses as well.

Most of the house-museums along Bellevue Avenue have gift shops, and the proceeds help to keep these mansions running. Books on local and regional architecture and decorative arts, prints, and housewares are among the most common items you'll find in these shops.

Another Newport retail specialty is decorative and practical wares with a nautical bent, from the requisite ship's wheel and scrimshaw kitsch to high-quality maritime paintings and prints, sailing clothing and gear, and antique barometers, ships' clocks, and similar items. Quite a few artists live in or near Newport and have their creations represented at galleries around town.

SHOPPING DISTRICTS
Downtown
BANNISTER'S WHARF

Bannister's Wharf (off Thames St., www.bannistersnewport.com) has several high-end shops, like **Royale Male** (22 Bannister's Wharf, 401/849-5990, 11:30am-5pm Mon.-Sat., noon-5pm Sun.), which specializes in British and European clothing and accessories for "the discriminating customer." If you're looking for something to wear out to dinner, turn to **Mandarine** (16 Bannister's Wharf, 401/848-9360, 10am-8pm Mon.-Sat., 10am-5pm Sun.), which carries silk dresses, jewelry, suits, and accessories by designers from all over the world.

BOWEN'S WHARF

Bowen's Wharf (Thames St. at America's Cup Ave., 401/849-2243, www.bowenswharf.com, 10am-10pm Mon.-Sat., noon-7pm Sun.) is a bit smaller than Bannister's Wharf but has a mix of businesses, including **Alex and Ani** (1 Bowen's Wharf, 401/849-3002, www.alexandani.com, 10am-6pm Mon.-Thurs.,

NEWPORT
SHOPPING

Alex and Ani retail store

10am-7pm Fri.-Sat., 11am-5pm Sun.) and **Soap & Water** (16 Bowen's Wharf, 401/619-5514, www.soapandwaternewport.com, 10am-9pm Sun.-Thurs., 10am-11pm Fri.-Sat.), a high-end bath products boutique, and about 20 other shops, restaurants, harbor tour companies, and galleries.

THAMES STREET

Before hitting the surf, hit the shelves and racks of **Helly Hansen** (154 Thames St., 877/666-8742, www.hellyhansen.com, 9am-10pm daily). The boating gear selection ranges from base layers to keep you warm on windy sails to fully waterproof parkas and snuggly soft shell jackets. For designer digs without the high price tags, try **Wish** (435 Thames St., www.shopwishnewport.com, 401/848-0202, noon-4pm Sun.-Tues., 10am-5pm Wed.-Sat.), a designer consignment boutique that caters to a younger crowd and carries both casual and evening wear.

All manner of antiques and vintage goods can be found at the **Armory Antique Marketplace** (365 Thames St., 401/848-2398, www.armoryantiquesnewport.com, 10am-5pm daily). Here you can peruse the aisles for everything from vintage furniture and dinnerware to antique artwork and pottery in this massive 6,000-square-foot antique mall located in the very cool Newport Armory building. In the same building, you'll find **The Leeside Antiques** (401/662-2629, 10am-5pm Mon.-Thurs., 10am-6pm Fri. and Sun., 10am-7pm Sun.), a smaller vintage shop specializing in estate jewelry, silver, and crystal.

Thames Glass (688 Thames St., 401/846-0576, www.thamesglass.com, 10am-5pm Mon.-Sat., noon-5pm Sun.) carries the hand-blown glasswork of Newport artist Matthew Buechner; you can take glassblowing lessons here, too.

Bellevue

Bellevue Avenue has its own "luxury" shopping district (www.bellevueshopping district.com), and this one definitely caters to the Newport socialite crowd, so if you're not content with window shopping, be prepared to spend some money. If you're trying to capture that "Newport lady" look, try **CK Bradley** (182 Bellevue Ave., 401/619-3912, www.ckbradley.com, 10am-6pm daily) where you can find women's clothing, handbags, and jewelry with a nautical, East Coast flair. At **Bellevue Kids** (206 Bellevue Ave., 401/846-7700, 10am-5:30pm Mon.-Sat., 11am-4pm Sun.) specializes in unique and high-end duds and toys for children, from newborns through age 10. Bellevue is also home to several art galleries, jewelry stores, beauty salons, and women's clothing boutiques that specialize in resort wear.

Broadway

The Broadway neighborhood is a nice change of pace, especially if you're shopping on a limited budget. At **Closet Revival** (30 Broadway, 401/845-0592, www.closetrevivalnewportri.com, 11am-5pm daily) you can find funky vintage and one-of-a-kind clothing, hats, and other accessories from the 1950s and onward at very reasonable prices. A couple blocks away, new and vintage records and rock 'n' roll ephemera can be found at the very cool **Vinyl Guru** (152 Broadway, 401/374-0760, noon-6pm Wed.-Thurs., noon-7pm Fri.-Sat., noon-4pm Sun.), which carries everything from blues and punk, to indie, soul, and hardcore. Check out **Annex! Comics** (314 Broadway, 401/847-4607, 10am-6pm Mon.-Sat., noon-6pm Sun.) for new and old comics, pulp fiction and horror, action figures, and collectibles.

Sports and Recreation

BEACHES

Day-trippers from all over New England come to Newport for its gorgeous beaches. Newport and neighboring Middletown have been blessed with several largely undeveloped stretches of soft sand that are some of the most beautiful on the Atlantic Coast.

★ First Beach

The beach starts in Newport near the Middletown border with **Easton's Beach** (175 Memorial Blvd., 401/845-5810, www. cityofnewport.com)—otherwise known as **First Beach**, which curves between Easton's Pond and the Atlantic below the Cliff Walk. In addition to its picturesque setting, the beach is particularly good for families, with a bathhouse, a full restaurant, and lots of activities going on all the time.

Children's programs are held early on Thursday evenings, and other activities geared for kids take place daily at a miniature amusement park at the Easton's Beach Rotunda, which includes the popular **Easton's Beach Carousel** (10am-5pm daily mid-June-early Sept., $1 per ride or $5 for 10).

Rounding out the experience is the miniature aquatic petting zoo at the **Save the Bay Exploration Center** (175 Memorial Blvd., 401/324-6020, www.savebay.org, 10am-4pm daily Memorial Day-Sept., 10am-4pm Fri.-Sun. Oct.-Memorial Day, $8, free for children under 3). The educational facility is filled with tanks of local marine life, and while it's not big enough to offer an entire day's worth of activities, it makes for a fun stop on the way to or from the neighboring beach.

Daily parking for nonresidents costs $15 on weekday, $25 on holidays and weekends. The parking lot holds about 600 cars and fills up fast in summer. If you're staying for longer than a week, it's worth considering a nonresident parking sticker good for the entire season (Memorial Day-Labor Day) for $100.

Additional metered street parking is also available along the seawall, if you can find it.

★ Second Beach

While First Beach may be where all the action is, quite a few locals actually consider **Sachuest Beach**, also known as **Second Beach**, as the best beach in Newport (although it is technically in Middletown). A short distance east on Purgatory Road and Paradise Avenue, it's a 3-mi-long (4.8-km) crescent directly facing the Atlantic and sheltered by Eastern and Sachuest Points, making it ideal both for walkers and sunbathers. Daily parking, plenty of which is available in several lots, costs $20 on weekdays and $30 on weekends—prices that clearly reflect the beach's immense popularity; nonresidents can also buy a season parking pass for $140.

Third Beach

Finally, traveling down Sachuest Point Road and then bearing left will bring you to **Third Beach**, the least popular but no less beautiful stretch of sand that faces northeast toward the Sakonnet River, which opens to the Atlantic just south of here. The river keeps the water even warmer than most Rhode Island beaches, making this an excellent spot for a dip. The beach's location makes it a nice spot for families with young children, as there are fewer crowds and much safer surf. Parking rates are the same as Sachuest Beach, right down the road.

Other Beaches

Aquidneck Island has many other beaches, each with its own personality. The easiest to access from downtown Newport is **King Park** (Wellington Ave., 401/846-1398, free), right off Thames Street; it attracts swimmers, sunbathers, and picnickers, although it's small and its harbor-side setting is not the most relaxing of vistas. A better view can be had just

off of Ocean Drive on the edge of Newport Harbor at **Fort Adams State Park** (Harrison Ave., off Rte. 138, 401/847-2400, www.riparks.com/fortadams.htm, sunrise-sunset daily, free), which boasts 100-plus acres of manicured lawns, picnic spots, beaches, soccer fields, and boating and camping areas. Each year it's home to the area's folk and jazz festivals as well as a plenitude of private clambakes. Also on Ocean Drive, **Brenton Point State Park** has a medium-size parking area and a small pavilion with changing rooms. The beach is too rocky and rough for swimming, but it can be ideal for beachcombing and lying in the sun.

Perhaps the most intriguing beach in Newport is **Bailey's Beach,** which is really only accessible on foot, by bicycle, or by way of the Bellevue Avenue bus. In the late 19th century, Bailey's Beach became the ultra-exclusive playground for Newport's wealthiest summer residents—over the years, however, enough people protested about the restricted access that the city council intervened on their behalf. Much to the horror of local elitists, research into the original layout of Bellevue Avenue revealed that a good chunk of Bailey's Beach was in fact not legally private at all. A public easement was granted, finally giving the public access.

As you drive north along the eastern shore of Aquidneck Island, you'll come to a couple of other good beaches. **Sandy Point Beach** is a wide, peaceful expanse of sand along the Sakonnet River with picnic facilities, grills, and restrooms. Parking costs $10 on weekdays and $20 on weekends.

BICYCLING

Newport and the rest of Aquidneck Island are prime territory for bicycling. Any of the walking or driving routes described in this chapter are excellent for biking, as is all of Conanicut Island and Jamestown, especially

in and around Beavertail State Park. You can rent bicycles in Newport at **Newport Bicycle** (130 Broadway, 401/846-0773, www.newportbicycleri.com, 10am-6pm Mon.-Fri., 9am-6pm Sat., noon-5pm Sun., $35-50 per day). The staff here is extremely helpful and friendly, and they offer hybrids, road bikes, tandems, and even tot trailers for the kids.

BOATING

Newport is one of North America's great sailing and yachting hubs. There are several full-service marinas in town, including **Bannister's Wharf** (off Thames St. in Newport Harbor, 401/846-4500, www.bannistersnewport.com/marina.html), a relatively small facility in the heart of downtown, with gas, diesel, ice, electricity, showers, laundry, and a phone.

At Fort Adams State Park, **Sail Newport** (60 Fort Adams Dr., 401/846-1983 or 401/849-8385, www.sailnewport.org, office 9am-5pm daily year-round, dock office 8:30am-8:30pm daily late May-early Sept.) rents 19-22-foot sailboats ($120-150 for a three-hour rental) and provides professional instruction for all ages.

FISHING

From spring through fall, Newport is one of the Eastern Seaboard's best spots for saltwater fishing—you'll see surf casters up and down the beaches from Newport north along the Sakonnet River and all the way around Aquidneck Island, vying for Narragansett Bay's stripers and bluefish. Fishing from a boat in greater Newport's waters provides access to many more species, among them mahi-mahi, tarpon, trigger fish, Atlantic mackerel, flounder, and swordfish. There are about eight freshwater ponds on the island that are stocked with bass and trout, including Easton's Pond, which is just beyond Easton's Beach on the Newport-Middletown border.

You can rent equipment and buy bait at a number of locations. The **Saltwater Edge Fly-Fishing Company** (1037 Aquidneck

1: a view of Second Beach from Sachuest Point Road **2:** sailboats moored in a marina near Bannister's Wharf

Ave., 866/793-6733, www.saltwateredge. com, 9am-5pm Mon.-Fri., 9am-4pm Sat.-Sun.) is your one-stop shop for information and tackle for surf-casting or boat fishing in saltwater. If you're looking for a guide or would like to charter a boat, try the folks at **On the Rocks Charters** (401/359-3625, www.ontherockscharters.com), who operate a small but affordable light tackle fishing boat and have years of experience catching stripers, bluefish, bonito, and more in the Narragansett Bay waters off the coast of Newport.

SCUBA DIVING

For the very reason that the waters around Newport and Aquidneck Island have proven treacherous to ship captains for centuries, scuba divers love this part of Rhode Island. Lurking beneath the surface are countless coral reefs, ledges, and interesting—though potentially dangerous—formations, and there are plenty of sunken ships in these parts. For information on rentals, local laws and restrictions, and advice, contact **Bubbles Dive Center** (550 Thames St., 401/338-2250, www. bubblesdivecenter.net, 3pm-6pm Mon.-Fri., 9am-4pm Sat., 9am-2pm Sun.).

SURFING

There are a couple of decent surf breaks in Newport, the most accessible of which is right at **Second Beach** (or **Sachuest Beach**) on Sachuest Point Road. This is a nice, sandy beach break that's great for beginners and has plenty of parking, which, of course, means you'll have to share the waves with many other surfers, especially on crowded summer days. But it's also a great spot for off-season and evening surfing, when the parking lot is free and the crowds are significantly smaller.

Another popular break is **Ruggles**, named for its access point where Ruggles Avenue meets the Cliff Walk on the southeastern tip of the island. This is a cherished point break with locals, who tend to be a little territorial when it comes to their waves. It is not recommended for beginners.

Stop in to **Island Surf & Sport** (86 Aquidneck Ave., 401/846-4421, www. islandsports.com, 10am-6pm Mon.-Fri., 9am-6pm Sat., 10am-5pm Sun.) for information about board rentals ($20/hour, $80/day), surf lessons ($75/hour for private lessons, includes board and wetsuit rental), and breaks.

TENNIS

The **International Tennis Hall of Fame** (194 Bellevue Ave., 401/849-3990 or 800/457-1144, www.tennisfame.com) is the only place in the United States where any two travelers can drop in and play lawn tennis. Access to the "royal" court is included with admission to the museum ($15). There are 13 grass courts open May through October.

Food

Newport has plenty of fairly traditional seafood places, steak and chops houses, and even a few old dining rooms serving haute continental and French cuisine, but in more recent years, several establishments serving highly creative regional American and globally influenced cooking have opened. Many of these are located in the less touristy but increasingly hip Broadway neighborhood that begins on the eastern edge of downtown and extends northeast into Middletown.

Keep in mind that the vast majority of Newport's high-end formal restaurants have taverns or pubs attached that serve less-pricey food and demand much less fancy attire. Note that in the off-season, restaurants in Newport—and especially in the neighboring towns and on Block Island—greatly reduce their hours. Call ahead to check which meals are currently offered.

Seafood

Even hard-core vegetarians have a hard time leaving Newport without craving seafood, what with shellfish and lobster shacks at almost every turn. Those who heed the call will fare quite nicely at **The Mooring** (Sayer's Wharf, 401/846-2260, www. mooringrestaurant.com, 11:30am-10pm Sun.-Thurs., 11:30am-11pm Fri.-Sat., $14-65), particularly if they're able to nab a table with a view of the harbor and sunset. No one's breaking the culinary sound barrier in the kitchen, but it's a great place to eat oysters and watch the sun set—or sample the impressively lengthy wine list.

A favorite new spot for extremely fresh and creative seafood, **Midtown Oyster Bar** (345 Thames St., 401/619-4100, www. midtownoyster.com, 11am-9:30pm Sun.-Thurs., 11am-10:30pm Fri.-Sat., $8-28) is a massive three-floor restaurant with a modern-meets-colonial vibe. New England staples such as raw oysters, clam chowder, and stuffed quahogs are available, and more adventurous dishes like chargrilled octopus and shrimp tomatillo gazpacho are offered as well. Considerable culinary buzz and an enviable rooftop deck make this a popular destination, so expect crowds—especially in the high season.

American

For truly luxe dinner service, head to **Cara** (in The Chanler at Cliff Walk, 117 Memorial Blvd., 401/847-2244, www.thechanler.com/cara-restaurant, 5:30pm-9pm, daily, $95-135), which offers three-course prix fixe meals and six-course tastings that usually involve things like oysters, caviar, foie gras, and filet mignon.

Bar culture had to begin somewhere in this country, and **The White Horse Tavern** (26 Marlborough St., 401/849-3600, www.whitehorsenewport.com, 11am-9pm

Mon.-Thurs., 11am-10pm Fri.-Sat., 11am-9pm Sun., $29-48) may just be where it started. Opened in 1687 by the father of a pirate, the tavern features clapboard walls and huge ceiling beams typical of 17th-century architecture, but its menu, including grilled bruschetta and maple-glazed salmon, is surprisingly here-and-now. Take note, proper dress ("country club" or "business casual") is required.

The ★ **Castle Hill Inn** (590 Ocean Ave., 401/849-3800, www.castlehillinn. com, 11:30am-3pm and 5:45pm-9pm daily, $25-40), apart from having one of the most dramatic locations in the city, serves stellar regional American fare. Think cherry-glazed duck breast and fennel-pollen-scented Maine lobster risotto with a chocolate chip cookie dough soufflé for dessert. There are several dining rooms with views of Narragansett Bay, and cocktails and hors d'oeuvres can be ordered from the Adirondack chairs on the front lawn overlooking the water.

For an exciting dinner experience, try the **Newport & Narragansett Bay Railroad Dinner Train** (departs from 1 Alexander Rd., Portsmouth, 401/295-1203, www.trainsri. com, hours vary, $35-70). These rides are a throwback to the golden days of rail travel on the Newport & Narragansett Bay Railroad, each one lasting about 2.5 hours along 22 mi (35 km) of track looking out at Narragansett Bay. Both lunch and dinner rides are available, and the food is better than you might expect, given the logistics of preparing high-quality cuisine aboard a train. The menu varies based on the season, but diners can expect classic New England comfort food (think roasted turkey and baked butternut squash), and a winelist that pairs well with the beautiful scenery.

Craft beer enthusiasts will find what they're looking for at **Norey's** (156 Broadway, 401/847-4971, www.noreys.com, 4pm-1am Mon.-Sat., $8-23), a very cool bar and grill with a world-class rating by *Beer Advocate*.

The feeling here is warm and inviting, with wood paneling and arty light fixtures. The menu is simple and fresh, with a regional emphasis, like the local oysters steamed with Belgian beer and tomato sauce and juicy burgers made from free-range, local cattle. An extensive wine list and occasional live bands are additional reasons to put this on your list of places to check out.

A self-described "field-to-fork, chef-driven eatery," **Thames Street Kitchen** (509 Thames St., 401/846-8400, www.tsknpt.com, 5:30pm-10pm Wed.-Sun., $8-25) is a popular spot serving fresh, artisanal, and adventurous food in a hip, airy, and laid-back space on lower Thames. The menu changes often, but recent offerings include a halibut porterhouse with chermoula and grilled lemon. The wine list is small but interesting. Reservations are recommended.

Zelda's (528 Thames St., 401/849-4002, www.zeldasnewport.com, 3pm-1am Mon.-Fri., 1pm-1am Sat., 11am-9pm Sun. $15-30) has two identities—on one side it's an informal and always packed pub; on the other side you'll find a dark, romantic, and festive space that's more appropriate for a full meal. You can order from the same menu on either side. Specialties include seared rare ahi tuna with sesame seaweed salad, soba noodles, and wasabi ponzu, and chicken-fried lobster with garlic mashed potatoes and lobster gravy. Either space can get loud, which makes it a fun spot to hang out with friends; there's also a significant wine cellar.

French

Refined, traditional French food is served at the slightly formal and inviting **Restaurant Bouchard** (505 Thames St., 401/846-012, www.bouchardnewport.com, 5:30pm-9pm Wed.-Mon., $19-42), which occupies the ground floor of a small B&B. Fine china and crystal along with deft service set the tone for such rarefied French fare as sliced tender lamb with red wine and a hint of curry sauce, roasted duck with currants, sautéed chicken breast with a creamy morel mushroom sauce, and wild mushroom ravioli with a walnut oil-balsamic vinaigrette.

The interior of ★ **Stoneacre Brasserie** (28 Washington Sq., 401/619-7810, www.stoneacrebrasserie.com, 5:30pm-10pm Mon.-Thurs., 11:30am-3:30pm and 5:30pm-11pm Fri.-Sat., 10:30am-10pm Sun., $14-28) is similar to its menu: fresh, inviting, and inspired by a traditional French brasserie. The seasonal and locally sourced menu features dishes such as wild striped bass with corn succotash and blistered cherry tomatoes, and *moules et frite* with with white wine, garlic-herb butter, and aioli. The menus might be simple but they're expertly done and impossibly fresh. Amazing cocktails and a friendly, professional staff make this a sure bet.

Asian Fusion

The menu at ★ **Salvation Café** (140 Broadway, 401/847-2620, www.salvationcafe.com, 4:30pm-midnight daily, $12-25) verges on pan-Asian and sometimes dazzles, sometimes comforts, but always piques one's curiosity; the small plates are especially fun. Consider the crispy pork belly flatbread or the Mongolian BBQ baby back ribs with sesame napa slaw. This is one of Newport's oddest, hippest, and happiest little bistros, with a fun crowd and kitschy decor.

Brunch

One of the most popular brunch spots in town, the ★ **Corner Café** (110 Broadway, 401/846-0606, www.cornercafenewport.com, 7am-2:30am Mon.-Wed., 7am-9:30pm Thurs., 7am-10pm Fri.-Sat., 7am-4pm Sun., $5-15) is best known for its mouthwatering breakfast menu, which offers treats like Portuguese sweet bread French toast stuffed with fruit and sweet cream, and a "Parisienne" omelet with sliced turkey, blackberries, and crumbled blue cheese topped with powdered sugar. The BYOB lunch and dinner menu is likewise flavored by French, Irish, Portuguese, and west coast influences, and the dining room is cozy and inviting, with long banquettes on either wall and a wood stove that's fired up on cold days. Long waits are not unusual here, especially during brunch on the weekends.

Comfort Food

For amazing burgers and a fun, laid-back atmosphere, head to **Mission** (29 Marlborough St., 401/619-5560, www.missionnpt.com, 11am-10pm Mon., Wed.-Thurs., 11am-11pm Fri.-Sat., 11am-9pm Sun., $6-10), a cute little spot just off Broadway and a short walk from downtown. The menu is literally just burgers, dogs, and fries, with falafel thrown in the mix to keep the vegetarians happy, but what Mission does it does very, very well. All burgers come with special Mission sauce—an aioli with ketchup, cornichons, capers, fines-herbs, and brandy. The "mission" statement says it all: "Good grub. Good beer. Good vibes."

If you're craving barbecue, head to the **Smokehouse Cafe** (31 Scotts Wharf, 401/848-9800, www.smokehousenewport. com, 11:30am-midnight daily, $8-24), which serves a delicious smoked BBQ burgers, burritos, and sides like mac 'n' cheese or grilled corn on the cob. The dining rooms overlook the harbor, and there's an expansive waterfront patio, too.

Brick Alley Pub and Restaurant (140 Thames St., 401/849-6334, www.brickalley. com, 11:30am-9pm daily, $6-30) has long been a reliable, if usually quite crowded, standby for tasty comfort fare. The long menu includes lobster rolls, bacon burgers, fish tacos, and spinach fettuccine. The staff is friendly and fun, the crowd is lively and loud, and large windows and funky decor create a light, colorful atmosphere.

A true Rhode Island diner experience can be had at **Gary's Handy Lunch** (462 Thames St., 401/847-9480, 5am-3pm Mon.-Sat., 5am-1pm Sun., $4-10) a family-owned favorite in Newport for decades. The food is pretty straightforward greasy-spoon fare, but the service and atmosphere are the friendliest in town, as many locals will attest. This is a great spot to fill up on pancakes and bacon after a night on the town, and the food is inexpensive—just be aware that credit cards are not accepted, so hit the ATM before you dine.

Sushi

Sushi fanatics converge on **Sumo Sushi** (198 Thames St., 401/848-2307, 11:30am-10:30pm daily, $10-25) for exquisite Japanese food plus several Korean dishes and stews. Korean barbecue is one classic dish, as is spicy kimchi stew with beef, pork, vegetables, and tofu. Several Japanese teriyaki grills are also

Brick Alley Pub and Restaurant on Thames Street

offered. From the sushi side of the menu, maki rolls include spicy scallop, salmon skin and cucumber, pickled radish, and more than a dozen others. The sedate, warmly furnished dining room is a calm alternative to some of Thames Street's busier restaurants.

Japanese

The noodle bar fad has made its way to Newport at **Bóru Noodle Bar** (36 Broadway, 401/846-4200, www.borunoodlebar.com, 11:30am-10pm Tues.-Sun., $7-16), where traditional Japanese ramen bowls get dressed up in flavors like curry, sesame chicken, and even short ribs with cashews and basil. Try the seared tuna ramen with cold noodles and wasabi slaw, the Szechuan fried calamari with black bean chili sauce, or the delicious pork buns with hoisin, pickles, and radish. Bóru is fast and casual, with counter service and limited seating. It's a nice choice if you're craving hot, delicious food but are short on time (or cash).

Mexican

Headed by veteran chef Dan Hall, the inspired Mexican cuisine of ★ **Perro Salado** (19 Charles St., 401/619-4777, www.perrosalado. com, 5pm-10pm Mon.-Fri., 11:30am-10pm Sat., noon-10pm Sun., $10-26) is a true standout in Newport's talent-saturated restaurant scene. Housed in an 18th-century home, the dining room is casual, cozy, and colorful, and the menu is smart, creative, and fresh. Start with the po'boy tacos with the empanadas and jicama slaw, then try the lobster quesadilla with cotija cheese and arugula salad. Excellent margaritas, occasional live music, and a festively lit patio are additional reasons to stop here.

Cafés and Sandwich Shops

The best coffee in Newport can be found at ★ **Empire Tea & Coffee** (22 Broadway, 401/619-1388, ext. 1, www.empireteaand coffee.com, 6am-8pm daily, $2-8), a café and tearoom where you can also find bagels, pastry, and fresh pressed fruit and vegetable juices. Comfy couches and chairs, distressed hardwood floors, and a central location in the hip Broadway neighborhood make it a perfect rainy day hangout spot or a convenient stop for snacks and iced coffee on your way to the beach.

Megs' Aussie Milk Bar (111 Bellevue Ave., 401/619-4811, www.megsmilkbar.com, 8am-3pm Mon.-Sat., 8am-early afternoon, Sun., $3-11), named after the Australian counterpart to the bygone American soda fountain, is a cute and quirky café serving breakfast and lunch, plus tea, coffee, smoothies, and juices with an Australian flare. Treat yourself to an Aussie iced coffee (ice cream, double espresso, milk, and whipped cream), or a slow-roasted Aussie lamb sandwich with rosemary, balsamic, and feta cheese.

Accommodations

Newport's summer population booms, and it's always a good idea to plan as early as possible when you're thinking of visiting. Rooms sell out especially quickly for key summer events like the folk festival, the jazz festival, and the Newport Music Festival. At other times, you can almost always find a spot at one of the motels or hotels in neighboring Middletown, or you can base your operations in South County, a 20-30-minute drive from Newport over a pair of long bridges that span the Narragansett. Be warned that crossing the Newport Bridge will cost you $4 each way, but this is a small price to pay when you consider the sometimes offensively high cost of accommodations in Newport.

That being said, Newport has the greatest variety of hotel accommodations in the state, including dozens of inns and B&Bs. There are relatively few larger hotels in Newport,

Newport Time-Shares

Several area time-shares are available through Wyndham Resorts (855/421-4788, www. clubwyndham.com), which owns a number of resorts throughout the country, including four in Newport, and two more across the bay in Jamestown: the Bay Voyage Inn (150 Conanicus Ave., Jamestown, 401/423-2100) and Newport Overlook (150 Bayview Dr., Jamestown, 800/428-1932). If you're seeking seclusion and a stunning setting with great views back toward Newport, both are great picks. In Newport, the Wyndham Long Wharf (5 Washington St., Newport, 401/847-7800) is close to the waterfront and other attractions. Inn on the Harbor (359 Thames St., Newport, 855/421-6789) and Newport Onshore (405 Thames St., Newport, 855/421-4786) are additional options farther down Thames Street.

There are big advantages to choosing any of these five properties over a conventional hotel or inn, especially if you visit Newport often or are traveling with a family or group of friends. First, the locations and settings are top notch. The units themselves are in large, rambling shingle-clad buildings—in Newport they're mostly 4- to 5-story apartment buildings, while the Jamestown structures spread out more and feel house-like. There are studio, one-bedroom, two-bedroom, and three-bedroom properties available, and each property has a full slate of amenities, including pools, spas, exercise rooms, children's playgrounds, and the like. The units themselves are tastefully furnished and all have kitchens; the majority of them have water views, depending on the property, of course. These are not historic buildings, and some critics complain they lack character, but they do make a lot of sense for some travelers.

and those are very expensive, especially during the summer. If you're looking for mid- to low-end chain properties, try Middletown, a short drive away. Just over the Newport border along Route 138A in Middletown you'll also find a variety of oceanside inns, motels, and hotels offering a wide range of rates. Newport proper has relatively few oceanfront accommodations, although several properties downtown overlook the harbor. If you want to be within walking distance of hotels, shops, and nightlife, downtown Newport (see below) is your best option—but keep in mind that you'll pay for this privilege.

$150-250

The Inns on Bellevue (30 Bellevue Ave., 401/848-6242, www.innsonbellevue.com, $150-250) are some of the least expensive places in central Newport where it's possible to find an affordable room during the warmer months. All three of these late-19th-century converted homes are in a terrific location, with small but cute rooms decorated with a smattering of antiques. The main inn is located at the upper end of Bellevue Avenue near

where it meets Touro Street—you just can't find rooms this cheap in Newport in this location. The staff and the clientele tend to be young, outgoing, and very laid back.

Another first-rate pick is the handsome Serenity Inn (93 Pelham St., 401/845-9400, www.serenityinnnewport.com, $159-250). The 13 guest rooms in this stately 1855 sea captain's mansion are replete with chandeliers and working fireplaces, along with modern amenities like TVs and, in some rooms, two-person whirlpool tubs. There are fabulous views of the harbor, just two blocks away, from the rooftop sundeck. It's especially romantic to sit up here at night, looking down over quaint First Street, the nation's first gas-lighted street.

One of the most conveniently situated small downtown properties, the Black Duck Inn (29 Pelham St., 401/847-4400, www. blackduckinn.com, $159-359) looks across Thames Street toward myriad shops and restaurants of Bowen's Wharf. The inn takes its name from an infamous rum-running ship that smuggled bootleg liquor into Newport Harbor during the late 1920s. The interior contains a comfortable—if somewhat awkward—mash of chic modern decor with Victorian furniture. Most rooms have queen-size beds, and there's a two-bedroom suite that's nice for families or friends traveling together. Some units have hot tubs.

The enthusiastic innkeepers at La Farge Perry House (24 Kay St., 401/847-2223 or 877/736-1100, www.lafargeperry.com, $219-329) balance the inn's homey ambience with striking accents and decor. There are five suites, including the John La Farge, which contains convincing reproductions of paintings by the distinguished artist and former owner, for whom the inn is named. A mural of Newport from the turn of the 20th century decorates the dining-room walls, and deep, comfy armchairs fill the common areas. Depending on the season, iced tea or sherry is served during the afternoon in the formal parlor. The bright, sunny house is especially impressive when decked out with holiday decorations in December.

OVER $250

An elaborate, almost decadent Edwardian mansion oozing with character and run by friendly innkeepers Dennis Blair and Grant Edmondson, the ★ Hydrangea House Inn (16 Bellevue Ave., 800/945-4667, www.hydrangeahouse.com, $295-350) sits near the beginning of Bellevue Avenue, just up the hill from the harbor front. The house was built in 1876, and the lavish details of that period have been colorfully preserved. Among the more enticing units among the nine spacious guest rooms and suites, the Hydrangea Suite has a king-size canopy bed, a marble bath, a double whirlpool tub with its own fireplace, and Oriental rugs. Guests are treated to afternoon tea, chocolate-chip cookies before bed, and a full breakfast.

The Sarah Kendall House (47 Washington St., 800/758-9578, www.sarahkendallhouse.com, $250-350) is an 1871 Second Empire house with a high green turret and a porch full of comfy wicker seating overlooking the harbor and Newport Bridge. It's located just a few blocks north of the downtown harbor, so many shops and eateries are within an easy stroll. The guest rooms have hardwood floors and four-poster beds, and many units have working fireplaces. From the sitting room, lodged in the third-floor turret, terrific views are to be had of the water and Goat Island. Afternoon tea and full breakfast are provided.

A nice boutique property in the heart of downtown, the Mill Street Inn (75 Mill St., 800/392-1316, www.millstreetinn.com, $315-450) occupies a 19th-century mill which has high ceilings, exposed brick walls and wood beams, and a warm character that has been nicely preserved. There are 23 chic and modern suites, some with private decks that look out over downtown and the harbor; the upper-level townhouse suites have two floors. Continental breakfast, afternoon tea, and parking are included.

Just off of Bellevue Avenue, you'll find ★ The Attwater (22 Liberty St. 401/846-7444, www.theattwater.com, $300-450), a 12-room boutique B&B set on a quiet street in the middle of the historic district. This 1910 building was renovated in 2012, giving it a modern and colorful vibe while still paying homage to the city's rich history and culture. Thoughtful touches like arty jellyfish prints, bright turquoise accent furniture, and lamps made out of nautical rope combine for a "Newport unconventional" look. Hotel amenities include iPads and Apple TV, gas fireplaces in the king suites, a fitness room, spa services, super-plush kimono robes, and a café.

The Cliffside Inn (2 Seaview Ave., 401/847-1811 or 800/845-1811, www.cliffsideinn.com, $400-535) is one of Newport's most distinctive inns. The Second Empire mansion was built in 1880 and has 13 guest rooms as well as three rooms in a more contemporary cottage across from the inn's front lawn and gardens, all just steps away from the Cliff Walk. There are a total of 17 fireplaces in the main mansion. The Cliffside is noted for its valuable Victorian beds and other fine collectibles. Afternoon tea and a stunning formal breakfast complete the experience at this luxurious hotel.

The massive **Hotel Viking** (1 Bellevue Ave., 401/847-3300, www.hotelviking.com, $300-450) has a nice location equidistant from Broadway's hip restaurants, Bellevue's mansions, and Spring Street's antique shops. The 237 guest rooms are recently renovated and well-maintained. The hotel was built in 1926 and was one of New England's premier addresses for many years. Furnishings are reproduction Queen Anne and Chippendale, but the rooms have all the modern trappings you'd expect of a luxury full-service hotel. There's also a pool, a spa, and a rooftop bar with views of the harbor.

The extraordinarily sumptuous ★ **Castle Hill Inn** (590 Ocean Dr., 401/849-3800 or 888/466-1355, www.castlehillinn.com, $500-1,000) enjoys one of Newport's most enchanting settings, perched on a grassy promontory jutting into the ocean with outstanding views of Narragansett Bay. The small Castle Hill Lighthouse (circa 1890) warns ships from the rocks nearby. Accommodations are in the main Agassiz Mansion and three distinguished outbuildings. In the main building, the 1874 summer home of Harvard marine biologist Alexander Agassiz, there are 10 rooms, most of them quite large and all with well-chosen antiques—the sorts of pieces you might expect to find decorating one of the summer cottages along Bellevue Avenue. Typical features include bay views, marble whirlpool tubs, Oriental rugs, gas fireplaces, pitched ceilings, and stately beds with goose-down comforters and imported damask linens. It's easy to understand why these are some of the priciest rooms in Rhode Island.

Transportation and Services

GETTING THERE AND AROUND
Bus
Peter Pan Bus Lines (401/751-8800 or 888/751-8800, www.peterpanbus.com) offers service from Boston's Logan Airport via Boston several times daily; the cost is about $70 round-trip (about $50 round-trip if you're coming from Boston rather than from the airport). The ride takes about 90 minutes, not counting the short trip from Logan to Boston's South Station.

The **Rhode Island Transportation Authority (RIPTA)** (401/781-9400, www.ripta.com) has bus service from T. F. Green Airport to Newport, and also from Newport to Providence and to the University of Rhode Island in Kingston. Buses arrive in Newport at the station attached to the Newport Visitors Center on America's Cup Avenue, in the middle of downtown and within walking distance to many hotels and businesses.

Within Newport, RIPTA operates local bus and trolley services that run among downtown, the outlying shopping centers, the mansions on Bellevue Avenue, and Cliff Walk and Easton's Beach. The fare is $2 one way, $6 for an individual day pass, or $25 for a seven-day pass.

Car
Several car-rental companies maintain offices in the Newport area, including **Enterprise** (70 West Main Rd., Middletown, 401/849-3939 or 800/325-8007, www.enterprise.com) and **Budget** (707 W. Main Rd., Middletown, 401/847-0313, www.hertz.com).

Driving times to Newport from major cities are: from Providence, 45 minutes-1 hour; from Boston, 90 minutes-2 hours; from Cape Cod's Bourne Bridge, 1 hour-75 minutes; from Hartford, about two hours; from New York City, about three hours. Add at least 30 minutes to these times during busy periods, including most summer weekends. From Providence, Newport is accessible via I-95

South and 138 East. This route includes a $4 cash-only toll crossing the Newport Bridge. An alternative (toll-free) route is to take I-195 East into Massachusetts, then take exit 8A to Route 24 South, which hooks back into Rhode Island and eventually links up with Route 114 South into Newport.

Parking in Newport is not terribly difficult after Columbus Day through about Memorial Day, but the 3-4 months of summer can be a nightmare. Much of the angst, however, seems to come from locals and regulars who are so accustomed to finding ample parking in the off-season that they kick and scream when they can't find free or metered spots on the street during the warmer months. If you can stomach paying $15-20 for a parking space in summer, you won't have much trouble finding one. There are several large municipal and private garages around town, and you can park at the garage adjacent to the Gateway Information Center for the entire day if you're willing to shell out the cash.

Taxi

You can definitely get by in Newport without a car, using cabs, Lyft, or Uber for the few longer trips that might come up, and relying on sightseeing tour buses for trips out around Ocean Drive and to various outlying attractions. Local cab companies include **Orange Cab** (401/841-0030, www.newportcabs.com), and **Island Taxi** (401/846-2400, www.islandtaxinewport.com). Newport also has a pedi-cab service; **Newport Pedicab** (401/432-5498, www.newportpedicab.com) offers rides from May through September. It's a fun way to get around the downtown area, and the drivers are very friendly, knowledgeable sources of information about the city.

FERRY SERVICE
To Block Island

This service is provided late June through early September by **Interstate Navigation** (401/783-7996, www.blockislandferry.com). High-speed ferries leave Newport daily at 9:45am and 12:30pm; the sail time is about 1 hour. The one-way fare is $25.50 for adults ($50.50 round-trip), $13 for children, and $6 each way for bicycles. The terminal is at Perrotti Park (39 America's Cup Ave.) downtown.

To Jamestown

Even if you have a car, it's quite practical and pleasant to travel between Newport and Jamestown via the **Jamestown-Newport Ferry** (401/423-9900, www.conanicutmarina.com). From Jamestown, the boat leaves several times a day for Newport's Bowen's Wharf, right off Thames Street; it crosses to Goat Island, then back to Bowen's Wharf, and then returns to Jamestown, where it is based. The earliest boat leaves Jamestown at about 10am, and the last one returns at about 10pm. Fares are $26 round-trip for adults and $10 for children under 12.

During the morning and afternoon runs, the ferry from Jamestown makes an added stop at the 16-acre wildlife refuge of **Rose Island**, which also includes a lighthouse and an old military outpost named Fort Hamilton. The landing fee, if you'd like to explore it, is $13 per person. From Rose Island, the boat continues to Fort Adams, where you're also free to get out and wander around, and then continues to Bowen's Wharf and Goat Island.

VISITOR INFORMATION

Pamphlets, brochures, and visitor information are available from the **Newport County Convention and Visitors Bureau** (23 America's Cup Ave., next to the bus terminal, 800/326-6030, www.discovernewport.org), which also provides packages with discounted rates on lodging and restaurants and has a switchboard for last-minute hotel availability.

MEDICAL SERVICES

The area's major hospital is **Newport Hospital** (11 Friendship St., Newport, 401/846-6400, www.newporthospital.org). Local pharmacies include **CVS** (181 Bellevue Ave., and 289 Broadway, Newport, 401/846-7800, www.cvs.com).

BANKS

A handful of banks are found on Thames Street, and several ATMs are located on Thames Street and on Bellevue Avenue, as well as at the bus station and in convenience stores.

MEDIA

Most locals read the *Providence Journal* or the *Boston Globe* as their daily news source. Newport's local newspaper is the *Newport Daily News* (www.newportri.com).

Free **Internet access** is available in several local cafés, at the **Newport Public Library** (300 Spring St., 401/847-8720, www.newportlibraryri.org, noon-8:30pm Mon., 9am-8:30pm Tues.-Thurs., 9am-5:30pm Fri.-Sat.), and for guests only at the majority of hotels in town. Fax and shipping services are offered at **The UPS Store** (270 Bellevue Ave., Newport, 401/848-7600, www.theupsstore.com, 8am-6:30pm Mon.-Fri., 9am-5pm Sat.).

TOURS

Boat

Oldport Marine Services (Sayer's Wharf, 401/847-9109, www.oldportmarine.com) offers cruises along Narragansett Bay and through Newport Harbor on the MV *Amazing Grace*. These hour-long narrated tours ($22 adults, $18 seniors, $10 children) are offered daily mid-May through mid-October.

Sightsailing of Newport (32 Bowen's Wharf, 401/849-3333 or 800/709-7245, www.sightsailing.com) gives daily, narrated tours aboard sailboats of three different sizes that generally last 75-90 minutes.

Classic Cruises of Newport (Christie's Landing, 401/847-0298, www.cruisenewport.com, $30-35 pp) has daily cruises from Bannister's Wharf. These include the 72-foot schooner *Madeleine,* the high-speed Prohibition-era *Rumrunner II,* and the *Arabella,* a 155-foot sailing cruise yacht that makes three-night excursions out to Martha's Vineyard, Nantucket, and elsewhere in the Northeast.

Leaving from Bowen's Wharf, the schooner *Adirondack II* (401/847-0000, www.

sail-newport.com) also makes five 1.5-hour sightseeing trips around Newport Harbor, Fort Adams, and area lighthouses each day. Tickets are $35 per person.

There are several other sailing charters in town as well. **America's Cup Charters** (401/846-9886, www.americascupcharters.com) offers daily sunset cruises aboard actual America's Cup-winning yachts (adults, $88, children 10 years and under, $40). These tours sail around Narragansett Bay.

Walking Tours

Newport Historical Society Walking Tours (401/846-0813, www.newporthistorical.org) offers interesting walks through the city; these leave from the Museum of Newport History at Brick Market at various times throughout the week, May through October. The appeal of **Native Newporter** (401/662-1407, www.nativenewportertours.com) is right in the name—the owner-operated company comprises guides that reach back over three generations of Newport history. They present several forthright and factual Newport tours ($25-45) replete with an insider's knowledge of the city that can include one mansion tour. The best value is probably the group's special "Mansion Madness" tour ($95), which includes admission to *every* major mansion for one day of sightseeing. There's no set time limit, so the only limit to how many marble staircases and gilded chandeliers you can see is your own stamina and stomach for displays of conspicuous consumption.

Kids especially enjoy **Ghost Tours of Newport** (401/841-8600, www.ghostsofnewport.com, $17 adults, $10 children), which leave from the Newport Marriott. These lantern-led strolls show the dark and creepy side of the city.

Bus

Viking Tours of Newport (Gateway Visitors Center, 401/847-6921, www.vikingtoursnewport.com) provides narrated trolley tours of the city that include

Ocean Drive and the mansions along Bellevue Avenue. A standard tour is $25 per person; package deals that include tours of one or more of the mansions are also available.

Train

On the **Newport & Narragansett Bay Railroad Dinner Train** (departs from 1 Alexander Rd., Portsmouth, 401/295-1203, www.trainsri.com, hours vary, $35-70). you'll enjoy a breathtaking journey over tracks used for passenger service for roughly a century from the 1860s; they wend for 5 mi (8 km) along the shore of Narragansett Bay, well

beyond the Newport Naval Base, and then 5 mi (8 km) back. All fairs include dinner.

Air

The most thrilling way to see Newport is by jumping on a birdie with **Newport Helicopter Tours** (401/843-8687, www. newporthelicoptertours.com), which offers trips through the sky above Aquidneck. For a different perspective on Newport's mansions, a fly-by over The Elms, The Breakers, Rosecliff, and Marble House is available, and other tours include buzzing over a few lighthouses and scoping various islands at sunset. Tickets range $75-190 per person.

Greater Newport

Outside of Newport, the towns of Middletown and Portsmouth stretch north, characterized by green farms, orchards, and vineyards. West of Newport, just across the bridge, is Jamestown, an island community situated at the mouth of the Narragansett Bay. Each town has it's own charms and points worth visiting, and all three offer ocean views and very nice seaside New England vibes.

MIDDLETOWN

Part of Newport until 1743, Middletown is a pleasantly sleepy town offering not much to do except relax and admire the area's pristine beaches, historic homes, and natural scenery. Most visitors make their way here from Newport for the day for the beaches or birdwatching at the local bird sanctuary, or to take advantage of cheaper accommodations while touring Newport.

Sights

PURGATORY CHASM

The parking lot nearest Newport at Second Beach is a short walk from **Purgatory Chasm,** a 160-foot-deep fissure in the cliffs that ranges 8-15 feet in width at the top and 2-20 feet at the bottom. There's a small

parking area (maximum 30 minutes) at the short trail to the chasm itself. This narrow and perhaps overhyped geological feature, with a nice little wooden bridge over it, has been a curiosity for as long as anybody can remember. Still, it's fun to sit on the rocky promontory and admire the view down over Second Beach.

SACHUEST POINT NATIONAL WILDLIFE REFUGE

From Purgatory Chasm, continue east along Sachuest Road to reach **Sachuest Point National Wildlife Refuge** (Sachuest Point Rd.), which has a visitors center that's good for trail maps and local information. The center sits on a small bluff that affords nice views back toward Newport. Looking up the hill to the north of Newport, you'll also see the Gothic towers of St. George's prep school. Anglers appreciate the miles of rocky shoreline; the preserve also has some good hiking.

NORMAN BIRD SANCTUARY

A short distance up the hill along Third Beach Road is the entrance to the **Norman Bird Sanctuary** (583 Third Beach Rd., 401/846-2577, www.normanbirdsanctuary.

NEWPORT
GREATER NEWPORT

Greater Newport

0   1 mi
0   1 km

Bristol 136

BRISTOL

Bristol Harbor

Hog Island

114

MT. HOPE BRIDGE

MONTAUP COUNTRY CLUB ⛳

Tiverton

24

BRISTOL FERRY RD

E MAIN RD

Nannaquaket Pond

NARRAGANSETT BAY

PORTSMOUTH

Prudence Island

GREEN ANIMALS TOPIARY GARDEN ★

Portsmouth

114

West Passage

Conanicut Island

Aquidneck Island

BURMA RD

GREEN VALLEY COUNTRY CLUB ⛳

St. Mary's Pond

NEWPORT POLO CLUB ★

★ PRESCOTT FARM

138

W MAIN RD

WAPPING RD

Sakonnet River

NEWPORT STATE AIRPORT ✈

GREENVALE VINEYARDS ★

E MAIN RD

NEWPORT VINEYARDS ★

NEWPORT NATIONAL GOLF CLUB ⛳

N MAIN RD

EAST SHORE RD

Gould Island

NAVAL STATION NEWPORT

138

JAMESTOWN

Jamestown

East Passage

Middletown

MIDDLETOWN

214

SWEET BERRY FARM ★

GREEN END AVE

PALISADE AVE

JAMESTOWN COUNTRY CLUB ⛳

C. PELL NEWPORT BRIDGE

THE BAY VOYAGE INN ▼

Norman Bird Sanctuary ⛰

THE SHACK AT DUTCH HARBOR ▼

TRATTORIA SIMPATICO ▼

FLO'S CLAM SHACK ▼

Third Beach

HISTORIC DISTRICT 🏛

NEWPORT ART MUSEUM 🏛

138A

FIRST BEACH

PURGATORY CHASM

SECOND BEACH 🏛

Sachuest Point National Wildlife Refuge ⛰

Fort Wetherill State Park ⛰

Goat Island

Fort Adams State Park

Newport

OCEAN DRIVE

BELLEVUE AVE

Easton Bay

SEE "NEWPORT" MAP

RHODE ISLAND SOUND

FORT WETHERILL ★

HARRISON AVE

THE BREAKERS 🏛

NEWPORT

CLIFF WALK 🏛

Beavertail State Park ⛰

Brenton Point State Park

© MOON.COM

123

org, 9am-5pm daily, $7), which occupies a small hill overlooking Second and Third Beaches, Sachuest Point, and the ocean. The refuge encompasses more than 300 acres of farm fields, meadows, woodlands, and rocky ridges. In addition to hiking trails, the sanctuary boasts a small museum inside a historic barn, with exhibits about beach ecology and Native American history as well as live snakes, rodents, and raptors found in the sanctuary. Various educational walks and programs geared toward experts and novices, adults and families are offered throughout the year. During the spring and fall migrations, bird walks are held at 8am Sunday.

PRESCOTT FARM

On West Main Road, 1 mi (1.6 km) north from the intersection of Union Street, is the turn-off for Newport Restoration Society's third main property, **Prescott Farm** (2009 W. Main Rd., Middletown, 401/849-7300, www.newportrestoration.com, dawn-dusk daily year-round, free). This 40-acre farmstead, purchased by doyenne Doris Duke to preserve Aquidneck's farming history, makes an engaging alternative to the crowded mansions of Newport as well as an interesting look at agrarian culture during Newport's colonial times. Among the attractions here is a 1730s guardhouse that contains notable Early American furnishings from the 17th century and an original 1812 windmill, still used today to grind grain, that spent time on several farms in the area after it was first built and installed in Warren.

VINEYARDS

From where Old Mill Lane intersects with Wapping Road, it's roughly 1 mi (1.6 km) until you reach the right-hand turnoff for **Greenvale Vineyards** (582 Wapping Rd., 401/847-3777, www.greenvale.com, 10am-5pm Mon.-Sat., noon-5pm Sun.). Tastings at this attractive winery are held in a distinctive old gray building with a mansard roof. The breezes from the Sakonnet River keep things

pretty cool even on hot summer days, making it a nice excursion in July and August.

If you're still thirsty, the second of the area's wineries, **Newport Vineyards** (909 E. Main Rd., Rte. 138, Middletown, 401/848-5161, www.newportvineyards.com, 10am-8pm Tues.-Thurs., 10am-5pm Fri.-Sat., 11am-6pm Sun.-Mon.), is a short drive away on East Main Street, just across from the airport. On the property you'll also find a toy store, a garden center, an art gallery, and a small restaurant; a farmers market is held on the grounds Saturday morning June through October.

SWEET BERRY FARM

Pick-your-own farms are more popular in other parts of the state, but **Sweet Berry Farm** (19 Third Beach Rd., Middletown, 401/847-3912, www.sweetberryfarmri.com, 8am-7pm daily, Apr.-Dec.) is a great spot for this activity within a short drive of downtown Newport. In summer, go for strawberries and raspberries, then move on to cut flowers and vegetables as the months progress, and finally find pumpkins in the fall and Christmas trees in early winter.

Recreation
BEACHES

The Newport-Middletown border lies on the eastern end of **Easton's Beach**, otherwise known as **First Beach**. From there, Memorial Boulevard becomes Purgatory Road. You can reach **Second Beach**, a nice, sandy beach with fun waves for splashing around in, by bearing left onto Paradise Road and then quickly right onto Hanging Rocks Road—you'll see parking on the right.

Backtrack along Sachuest Road past Gardiners Pond, make a right onto Indian Avenue, and follow it to **Third Beach** Road, which leads to **Third Beach.**

Head north on Wapping Road until the road runs into Sandy Point Avenue; here a right turn leads down the hill to **Sandy Point Beach,** along the western shores of the Sakonnet River. This scenic beach is broad and flat and ideal for a picnic. In the other direction, Sandy Point Avenue runs west for about 0.5 mi (0.8 km) until hitting East Main Road (Route 138).

GOLF

The most popular and dramatic of the area's golf courses is the **Newport National Golf Club** (324 Mitchell's Lane, Middletown, 401/848-9690, www.newportnational.com, $65-150), which opened in 2003 and has quickly become one of the top destination golf courses in New England.

Food
SEAFOOD

Just near the Newport-Middletown border, **Johnny's Restaurant and Patio Bar** (240 Aquidneck Ave., Middletown, 401/847-2750, www.johnnysnewport.com, 6:30am-10pm daily, $14-22) is a spacious eatery with a water view—its greatest attribute—that can be enjoyed from an enormous patio. The menu presents a fairly standard variety of somewhat upscale seafood dishes, including grilled yellowfin tuna, baked scrod, and lobster salad; rack of lamb Grand Marnier is popular among the non-fish fare.

There is no shortage of fried seafood to be found in Newport and the surrounding towns, but the kitchen at ★ **Flo's Clam Shack** (4 Wave Ave., Middletown, 401/847-8141, www.flosclamshacks.com, 11am-9pm daily, $6-29) has been plating up clam cakes, stuffies, and fish-and-chips since the 1930s. Situated right on the Newport-Middletown border across from the beach, this crowded and rather ramshackle restaurant has a dining room decorated with nautical memorabilia, and an upstairs raw bar with a deck overlooking the Atlantic. It will be crowded in the summer, and it will be worth the wait.

SUSHI

There's above-average sushi to be found at **Sea Shai** (747 Aquidneck Ave., Middletown, 401/619-0968, www.seashai.com, 11:30am-10pm Tues.-Sun., $8-22), known for featherlight tempura, fresh sashimi, and decent

Korean dishes such as classic *bulgogi* (sliced barbecue beef).

CHINESE

Ching Tao (268 W. Main Rd., Rte. 114, Middletown, 401/849-2112, www.chingtaori.com, 11:30am-10pm Mon.-Thurs., 11am-10:30pm Fri.-Sat., noon-10pm Sun., $6-14) serves good if somewhat predictable Chinese food. Specialties include asparagus with pork ginger sauce, hot-and-spicy crispy tofu and seafood in a sizzling red-wine sauce, and mango chicken in a white-wine reduction.

Accommodations
$100-150

The **Sea Whale** (150 Aquidneck Ave., Middletown, 401/846-7071 or 888/257-4096, www.seawhale.com, $125-150) looks a bit dreary from the exterior, but this 16-unit motel faces directly onto Easton's Pond (white chaise lounges sit out back on the lawn overlooking the water). Rooms are basic but well kept, and those on the upper level have balconies; all of them face the pond and have cable TV, refrigerators, hair dryers, phones (with free local calls), and plenty of parking. It's a 10-minute walk to Easton's Beach, and you really can't beat the price for this location.

$150-250

The nicely maintained **Newport Courtyard Marriott** (9 Commerce Dr., Middletown, 401/849-8000, www.courtyard.com, $175-215) is a reliable chain property a few miles north of downtown Newport. There are 130 rooms and 10 suites, plus an indoor-outdoor pool, a hot tub, a small gym, and a laundry room; continental breakfast is included.

Rhea's Inn by the Sea (42 Aquidneck Ave., Middletown, 401/849-3548, www.rheasinn.com, $150-250) occupies a three-story cedar-shake building that's just a five-minute stroll from Easton's Beach. There are nine rooms with private baths, air-conditioning, cable TV, and phones—all the basics. Two of the rooms have separate living areas, and some have whirlpool tubs; there's a common area on each floor. This is a reliable, non-chain option.

Getting There

From downtown Newport, Middletown is just a quick, 10-minute drive headed east on Memorial Boulevard (138A). The RIPTA bus #60 runs from downtown Newport to Middletown for a $2 fare.

PORTSMOUTH

Rounding out the tip of Aquidneck Island, north of Middletown, the town of Portsmouth tends to get missed by many visitors to Newport, even though it claims to be nothing less than the "birthplace of American democracy." While that might seem like municipal hubris, it's actually not far off the mark: Founded in 1638 by religious heretics banished from Massachusetts Bay, including feminist preacher Anne Hutchinson, the town was the first to be ruled by its own members instead of the Crown of England. A bronze tablet erected on a rock at Founders Brook memorializes the so-called Portsmouth Compact that founded the independent community. Portsmouth today has its own rather modest summer colony, mostly along or just off Route 138, which runs down the eastern side of the town overlooking the Sakonnet River.

Sights

The **Green Animals Topiary Garden** (380 Cory's Lane, 401/847-1000, www.newportmansions.org, 10am-6pm daily Apr.-mid-Oct., $12 adults, $4.50 children 6-17), circa 1860, is one of the oldest topiary gardens in America, offering 80 shrubs and trees sculpted into whimsical shapes and animals, like teddy bears, a giraffe, a unicorn, and an elephant. Also on the grounds is a small museum of Victorian toys, and there's an extensive gift shop of toys, garden items, and the like. Green Animals admission is included with the combination ticket for Hunter House and several Bellevue Avenue mansions.

Recreation

GOLF

Montaup Country Club (500 Anthony Rd., Portsmouth, 401/683-0955, www.montaupcc.com, $37-47) is a good course. Another option is **Green Valley** (371 Union St., Portsmouth, 401/847-9543, www.greenvalleyccofri.com, $28-68); both have 18 holes, and Green Valley offers night golf.

POLO

Polo has been an important rite of Newport's summer social season since the 1880s. At the **Newport Polo Club** (250 Linden Lane, Portsmouth, 401/846-0200, www.nptpolo.com), visitors can watch matches on Saturdays June through September. These contests pit international teams from the United States and several other countries against one another. Matches start at 5pm June through August and 4pm in September; admission is $15. Part of the tradition is setting up "tailgate" picnics on the grounds—this is one of Newport's—and even New England's—most unusual weekly summer events.

Food

The **15 Point Road Restaurant** (15 Point Rd., Portsmouth, 401/683-3138, www.15pointroad.com, 5pm-9pm Tues.-Thurs., 5pm-9:30pm Fri.-Sat., 4pm-9pm Sun., $12-26) is a little cottage right by the beach at Stonebridge Marina in the Island Park section of Portsmouth. Popular with northern Aquidneck Island locals, this is also a great option for travelers seeking creative, deftly prepared cooking without the crowds and high prices of Thames Street. The staff at this handsome little neighborhood restaurant is friendly and easygoing. Seafood is a major player here, and the kitchen turns out a tender and delicious beef Wellington and a rich lobster casserole baked in sherry and cream and topped with puff pastry.

1: Portsmouth's Green Animals Topiary Garden
2: one of the hiking trails at Sachuest Point
3: the lighthouse at Beavertail State Park

Newport and the Slave Trade

By the end of the 17th century, Newport was one of the primary ports in North America, and a major hub for the trafficking of enslaved peoples from the western coasts of Africa. Although Rhode Island was the first of the 13 colonies to pass an abolition law banning African slavery in 1652, such laws would not be widely enforced until the end of the following century, and in the intervening years, merchants in Rhode Island controlled an estimated 60-90 percent of the slave trade in America.

Slavery in Rhode Island was spurred by the manufacturing of rum at one of over a dozen distilleries throughout the state, many of which were located in Newport and neighboring Jamestown. Rum was shipped to Africa and traded for enslaved African peoples, who were then brought to the Caribbean and traded for molasses, which was brought back to Rhode Island to produce more rum. This system, known as the Triangle Trade, also made it possible for enslaved peoples to be sold back into the colonies, thus a slave-based economy eventually took hold in Newport, where Africans and African Americans worked as servants in the mansions of wealthy aristocrats, and as laborers on the fields of neighboring South County farms.

Many of Rhode Island's early merchant families (Brown University is named for one such family) owe their financial prosperity to the trading of enslaved Africans, a phenomenon unprecedented in its brutality and lack of humanity. In recent years, historical preservationists have worked hard to research and document the traditions, history, and culture of African descendant families in Newport and greater Rhode Island, with a focus on celebrating the civic, political, business, and artistic contributions of African Americans in Rhode Island.

Several of the Newport area mansions regularly lead walking tours detailing the history of the Newport slave trade. Among them is **Linden Place** (500 Hope St., Bristol, 401/253-0390, www.lindenplace.org), 15 mi (24 km) north of Newport. Linden Place is the former home of the DeWolfs, one of the most prominent of Newport's slave-trading families. Newport's Common Burial Ground and Island Cemetery are also notable for containing **"God's Little Acre"** (Farewell St., 401/846-0432, www.colonialcemetery.com), home to one of the largest extant collections of grave markers of enslaved and free Africans and African Americans, dating back to the late 1600s.

A cute diner with a couple of U-shaped counters, red vinyl booths, and nautical photos on walls, **Reidy's** (3351 E. Main Rd., Portsmouth, 401/683-9802, 6am-8pm Mon.-Sat., 6am-6pm Sun., under $5-15) is a local gathering spot, especially for breakfast, served all day. The kitchen serves fairly typical diner fare plus some Greek and Portuguese specialties. Consider the excellent kale soup, veal parmigiana, tapioca pudding, clam cakes, stuffies, and homemade muffins.

Getting There

Portsmouth is about a 20-minute drive from Newport, via Route 114 North, or 138 East. The RIPTA #60 bus also runs from downtown Newport to central Portsmouth for a $2 fare.

JAMESTOWN

In the middle of Narragansett Bay between Newport and South County, the town of Jamestown occupies all of Conanicut Island, a cigar-shaped swath with a smaller island off its southwestern tip. With a full-time population of 6,000, the island is not at all densely populated, although improved bridges have been built in recent decades and southern Rhode Island has expanded in general, making Jamestown a full-time home for more people. Jamestown's small but thriving downtown area is situated adjacent to a small marina and offers some nice shops, art galleries, and restaurants, but the real draw here is the natural landscape.

Sights

At the southern tip of the island of Jamestown,

travelers will be rewarded with what is perhaps one of the most beautiful ocean views in the entire state at **Beavertail State Park** (Beavertail Road, 401/423-9941, www.riparks.com/Locations/LocationBeavertail.html, free). The park offers hiking trails and four designated lookout points from which to enjoy a dramatic, rocky coastline, shifting tidal pools, and panoramic views of the Atlantic. The Beavertail Lighthouse (circa 1856) sits at the far end of the park, marking the entrance to the Narragansett Bay. Those visiting between Memorial Day and Columbus Day can check out the **Beavertail Lighthouse Museum** (www.beavertaillight.org, 10:30am-4:30pm daily, early June-Labor Day, free), which features rotating exhibits about maritime science, technology, art, and culture, as well as information about the history of the lighthouse itself. The park is also a popular spot for saltwater fishing, and the more adventurous swimmer can usually find a spot to take a dip, so long as they're comfortable trekking down some fairly steep rocks.

At the southeastern tip of Jamestown, it's fun to explore **Fort Wetherill** (Fort Wetherill Rd., 401/423-1771, www.riparks.com, free), a former military training camp situated on 100-foot high granite cliffs overlooking the ocean. The park has picnic areas, boating, fishing, and hiking on over 60 acres—but the real fun is exploring the ruins of the training camp.

Recreation
WATER SPORTS
Sea kayaking is a very popular activity along Newport's winding shoreline and up and down the Sakonnet River—there are hundreds of inlets and quite a few islands to explore within reasonable paddling distance of Newport and the surrounding towns. The best source for rentals in the area is **Jamestown Outdoors** (35 Narragansett Ave., Jamestown, 401/924-2885, www.jamestownoutdoors.com, 11am-5pm Wed.-Sat., 11am-3pm Sun., $35/2 hours), which offers rentals of kayaks, and stand-up paddleboards.

FISHING
You can rent equipment and buy bait at a number of locations, including **Zeek's Bait and Tackle** (194 North Rd., Jamestown, 401/423-1170, 10am-7pm Mon.-Sat., 10am-6pm Sun.).

GOLF
Across Newport Bridge is **Jamestown Country Club** (245 Conanicus Ave., Jamestown, 401/423-9930, www.jamestown golf.com), a nine-holer that's an affordable option in a lovely setting.

Food
SEAFOOD
A casual longtime favorite in Jamestown, **Chopmist Charlie's** (40 Narragansett Ave., Jamestown, 401/423-1020, www.chopmistcharlie.com, 11:30am-9pm daily, $11-17) serves lunch and dinner, specializing in local seafood. Fairly straightforward and always fresh stuffies, calamari, shrimp steamed in beer, scampi, and seafood au gratin are doled out in generous portions.

ITALIAN
Little Jamestown has one of the best regional Italian restaurants around: ★ **Trattoria Simpatico** (13 Narragansett Ave., Jamestown, 401/423-3731, www.simpaticojamestown.com, 5pm-9pm Thurs.-Fri., 3:30pm-9:30pm Sat., 3:30pm-9pm Sun., $18-32). Typical entrees show the chef's skill with both healthful and globally inspired dishes. In fact, the Italian menu borrows heavily from the U.S. Southwest, Asia, and Latin America, from the spiced plum glazed pork ribs, to the Bolognese pie with local ricotta cheese, and smoked chicken spring rolls. The festively lit outdoor patio here is a favorite spot to see and be seen on summer nights, and a heated patio even stays open during the colder months.

MEXICAN
The Shack at Dutch Harbor (252 Narragansett Ave, Jamestown, 401/423-0630, www.dutchharborboatyard.com,

11am-5:45pm daily late June-early Sept., $4-12) is aptly named—it is literally the size of a tool shed, but the chefs in this tiny kitchen crank out some of the tastiest tacos in the state. The shack is a sister location of Tallulah's Tacos (it has locations in Providence and Newport as well) and is situated in a boat yard where you can enjoy locally caught fish, lobster, and shrimp tacos with spicy crema, fresh cilantro, and homemade guacamole at one of a few picnic tables overlooking the harbor.

CAFÉS AND SANDWICH SHOPS
In Jamestown, bright and sunny **Slice of Heaven** (32 Narragansett Ave., Jamestown, 401/423-9866, www.sliceofheavenri.com, 6am-3pm daily, $5-11), a friendly little bakery-café, packs them in for weekend brunch and breakfast served all day—try the panini sandwiches and wraps, lemon-ginger muffins, Grand Marnier French toast stuffed with berries and fresh whipped cream, and terrific ahi tuna salad. There's great people-watching from the deck out front.

Jamestown is also home to the **Village Hearth Bakery Café** (2 Watson Ave., Jamestown, 401/423-9282, www.villagehearthbakerycafe.com, 7am-2pm Fri., 8am-2pm Sat.-Sun. $3-10), a cute little café with a beautiful flower garden patio. The hours are limited but the coffee, and fresh-baked breads and pastries are some of the best on the island. Try the plum brandy muffins, veggie quiche, or the breakfast croissant filled with roasted spinach and asiago cheese.

Accommodations
$150-250
The **Lionel Champlin Guest House** (20 Lincoln St., Jamestown, 401/423-7469, www.

lcguesthouse.com, $125-160) is a 3-story Victorian guesthouse with bright and beautiful rooms, within a short walk from Jamestown's small but engaging downtown neighborhood. All rooms have private baths, Wi-Fi, and TVs, and rooms facing east offer nice views of the harbor. Rates are a small fraction of what you would pay for similar accommodations across the bridge in Newport, and the setting here is peaceful and serene.

Perched on Narragansett Bay, the **Bay Voyage Inn** (150 Conanicus Ave., Jamestown, 401/423-2100, www.wyndhambayvoyageinn.com, $159-250) is more resort than inn. With 32 suites (including kitchenettes and parlor areas), the Victorian-style building is also home to a pool, indoor whirlpools, a fitness center, and a recreation director to help arrange sailing, fishing, or biking excursions in the area.

Getting There
CAR
To get to Jamestown from Newport via car, simply head north and get on 138 West at the on-ramp at the north end of America's Cup Avenue and head over the Newport Bridge. The toll is $4 each way and the drive takes about 15 minutes.

FERRY
The **Jamestown-Newport Ferry** (401/423-9900, www.jamestownnewportferry.com) leaves several times a day from Newport's Bowen's Wharf, right off Thames Street; it crosses to Goat Island, then back to Bowen's Wharf, and then returns to Jamestown, where it is based. The earliest boat leaves Newport at about 11:30am, and the last one returns at about 9:30pm. Fares are $25 round-trip for adults and $10 for children under 12.

Block Island

Block Island's natural beauty and tranquility

foster relaxation and peace of mind, which is likely why the Nature Conservancy named it one of the 12 "Last Great Places" in the Western Hemisphere.

Stepping off the ferry onto Block Island's shore during the summer months can almost feel like being thrust into a party; not surprisingly, the roads that flank downtown's shoreline are lined with shops, restaurants, bars, and hotels. But not far outside of these commercial boundaries is an island experience defined instead by lush green space, pristine shoreline, and well-preserved historical landmarks.

Thanks in large part to the Block Island Conservancy, more than

Highlights

Look for ★ to find recommended sights, activities, dining, and lodging.

★ **Southeast Light:** Built in 1873, this Victorian-style lighthouse is one of the most photographed in New England. Any time of year, it's worth walking the grounds, and in summer you can actually climb the 50-foot staircase to the top for an amazing view (page 136).

★ **Mohegan Bluffs:** Towering nearly 200 feet above the Atlantic Ocean on the island's southeast shore, the Mohegan Bluffs are one of the most picturesque and storied sights on the island. Descend the steps to the secluded beach below, or stand atop for breathtaking views (page 137).

★ **Greenway Trails:** This 28-mi (45-km) network of trails is the best way to observe the island's fiercely guarded woodland and wildlife. (page 137).

★ **North Lighthouse:** Dating back to 1867, the secluded North Lighthouse is well worth the scenic walk required to reach it from the parking area. A small but interesting maritime museum is open to the public during the summer months (page 139).

★ **Crescent Beach:** No trip to Block Island is complete without a visit to one of its pristine white-sand beaches; this stretch just north of Old Harbor is the prettiest (page 144).

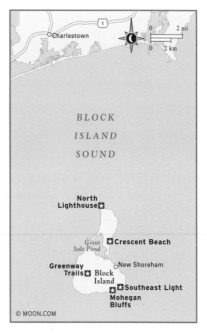

© MOON.COM

40 percent of the island is now protected from development. With a landmass of just under 10 square miles, and a year-round population of about 1,000 people, Block Island's charm lies not only in its natural beauty but also in its residents' resolute willingness to preserve that beauty by all means necessary. For this they are rewarded with unobstructed views of the Atlantic, miles of unspoiled hiking trails, and thriving wildlife populations.

Every summer, about 15,000 visitors descend on the town of New Shoreham, which encompasses the entire island. Block Island enjoys a reputation for being easygoing and accessible, free from the elitist vibe of its cousins to the east, posh Martha's Vineyard and Nantucket. Instead of being capped with the sprawling homes of wealthy summer residents, only the green fringe of conservation land tops the cliffs of Clay Head, the first glimpse of the island you'll likely see coming over on the ferry from Point Judith. Favorite pastimes here include leisurely bike rides, quiet hikes through conservation tracts populated with migratory songbirds, sunbathing along the miles of free public beaches, or kayaking the sparkling waters of Great Salt Pond.

HISTORY

Narragansett Indians were the only occupants of the island they called Manisses (MAN-iss-eez), a word meaning "little island of Manitou" or "little island of God," until the early 16th century, when explorer Giovanni da Verrazano first sighted it. Verrazano decided its character to be similar to the Greek island of Rhodes, inadvertently inspiring what would later become the name of the entire state. The current and rather inelegant moniker traces to Dutchman Adriaen Block, who visited in 1614. About 50 years later, a group of 16 British colonial families bought and settled what was then a territory within Massachusetts.

Block Island's history has been one of hardship and violence. During its first century,

pirates, privateers, and Frenchmen invaded the island regularly, robbing and terrorizing islanders at will. (It's still rumored that no less a seadog than Captain Kidd buried treasure on the north shore.) During the Revolutionary War, General George Washington had all of the islanders' livestock shipped to the mainland to keep it out of the hands of British ships. During the War of 1812, residents turned around and sold goods and produce to the enemy British.

Block Island's relative autonomy continued well into the 19th century, partly due to its lack of a suitable harbor, and the dangerous shoals and ledges of its surrounding waters. In fact, it's estimated that about half of all the shipwrecks in New England have occurred off Block Island—the total is roughly 500. A true anchorage wasn't created until 1878, when Old Harbor was born. That spurred a frenzied tourism boom, when its fame as "Bermuda of the North" spurred the construction of leviathan wood-frame hotels with sweeping mansard roofs, towering turrets, and long wraparound porches. In 1900, New Harbor was finally established at nearby Great Salt Pond when engineers dredged a permanent channel connecting it to the sea.

Almost as soon as it became popular, however, its brief fame as a tourist destination plummeted, with tough years following the Depression and World War II. It wasn't until the renewed popularity of New England's coastal islands and a nationwide embrace of historic preservation took hold, beginning in the 1970s, that Block Island began drawing major summer crowds again.

PLANNING YOUR TIME

While it's true that Block Island is accessible as a day trip from the mainland, those who have the means will want to spend at least one or two nights here, as it is best enjoyed at a slow pace. The local tourism board goes out of its way to promote the island as a year-round

BLOCK ISLAND

Block Island

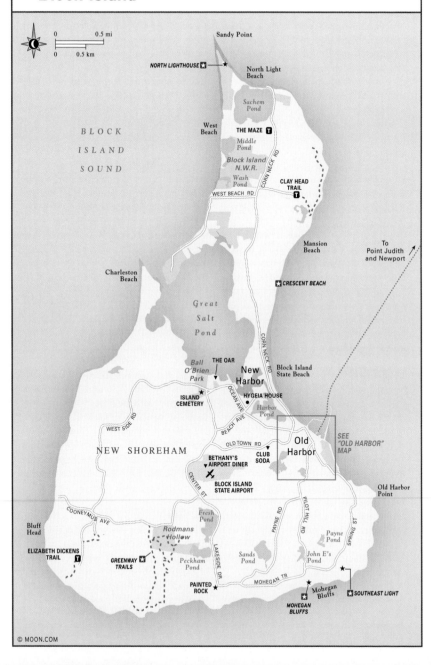

0   0.5 mi

0   0.5 km

Sandy Point

NORTH LIGHTHOUSE ★

North Light Beach

Sachem Pond

BLOCK ISLAND SOUND

West Beach

THE MAZE ▮

Middle Pond

Block Island N.W.R.

Wash Pond

CORN NECK RD

WEST BEACH RD

CLAY HEAD TRAIL ▮

Charleston Beach

Mansion Beach

CRESCENT BEACH ★

To Point Judith and Newport

Great Salt Pond

CORN NECK RD

Ball O'Brien Park

THE OAR

New Harbor

Block Island State Beach

ISLAND CEMETERY ★

OCEAN AVE

HYGEIA HOUSE ●

Harbor Pond

WEST SIDE RD

BEACH AVE

OLD TOWN RD

Old Harbor

SEE "OLD HARBOR" MAP

NEW SHOREHAM

BETHANY'S AIRPORT DINER ✕

CLUB SODA ▼

BLOCK ISLAND STATE AIRPORT

CENTER ST

Old Harbor Point

COONEYMUS AVE

Fresh Pond

Rodmans Hollow

PAYNE RD

PILOT HILL RD

Payne Pond

SPRING ST

Bluff Head

ELIZABETH DICKENS TRAIL ▮

GREENWAY TRAILS ★

Peckham Pond

LAKESIDE DR

Sands Pond

John E's Pond

PAINTED ROCK ★

MOHEGAN TR

Mohegan Bluffs ★

SOUTHEAST LIGHT ★

MOHEGAN BLUFFS ▣

© MOON.COM

destination, and the effort is more than just a marketing ploy. Granted, few hotels and even fewer restaurants remain open through the winter months, but the island still has much to offer for those who enjoy the quiet solitude and rugged beauty of the New England winterscape. Many local businesses "play it by ear" when it comes to their operating hours, meaning they open and close whenever they want, based on the time of year, etc. Call ahead to confirm hours, especially in the off-season.

Spring is breathtakingly scenic on Block Island, with bright yellow daffodils, red and purple tulips, and pearly white shadbush dotting the landscape. In part because of the absence of hardwood forests, there's less foliage drama in fall than in spring, when flowerbeds burst and beach shrubs and grasses turn emerald green. It is also prime season for bird-watching, when hundreds of species pass through on their way north to summer in Canada.

Last, and obviously not least, there's summer—*the* time to visit the island for the majority of visitors. Businesses are open, and activities like **fishing** and **sailing** are ideal. Of course, in summer you'll pay more for accommodations, especially on weekends, and you may endure long lines at the ferry, but there's no better time to enjoy the beaches, and no denying the infectious joy of summering on Block Island.

Sights

While there are a few formal sightseeing opportunities here, most of what Block Island has to offer comes in the form of natural beauty. It doesn't take long to make a quick drive of the island, which is only about 10 square miles. Even on a bike you can tour all of the major points of interest in one day, if you're feeling ambitious.

OLD HARBOR

Most visitors begin their explorations of Block Island in Old Harbor—allowing minimal time for browsing shops, you can easily tour this charming waterfront commercial district in an hour or two. Businesses are concentrated along **Water Street,** which sweeps alongside the harbor front; several lanes running perpendicular also contain a smattering of shops and restaurants.

For centuries, there was no harbor at all at Block Island. The U.S. government finally installed two breakwaters here in the 1870s, and Old Harbor was developed with lightning speed. Today Old Harbor is a National Historic District, one of the best preserves of Victorian seaside architecture in the country. There's little to do in Old Harbor outside of shopping, eating, and people watching, but check with the **Island Free Library** (9 Dodge St., 401/466-3233, www.islandfreelibrary.org) for events and activities. The library hosts a variety of programming for all ages year-round, including story hours, yoga, game nights, and craft classes—a great resource, especially for those visiting with children.

Walk south (left as you leave the ferry parking lot) and you'll come to just about the only major four-way intersection in Old Harbor, at Spring, Water, and High Streets. In the traffic island stands the *Statue of Rebecca,* a monumental fountain erected in 1896 by the Women's Christian Temperance Movement. Inspired by the biblical story of Rebecca at the well, the statue was intended to encourage islanders to stay away from alcohol, a lesson few heeded then or now.

At the very southern tip of Old Harbor stood the island's most famous and immense Victorian hotel, the Ocean View, which burned down in the 1960s. On the site now stands the **Ocean View Pavilion,** which looks out toward Crescent Beach and the ocean. It's a pretty spot for a stroll.

Old Harbor

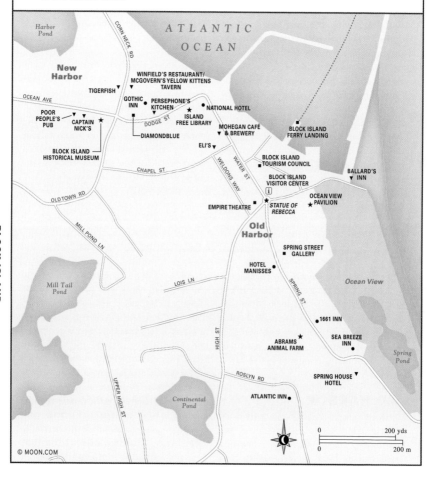

EXPLORING SOUTH FROM OLD HARBOR

Abrams Animal Farm

Particularly if you have kids along, be sure to visit the **Abrams Animal Farm** (Spring St. and High St., 401/466-2421, www.blockislandresorts.com, dawn-dusk daily, free), next door to Hotel Manisses. This exotic-animal farm and petting zoo is home to llamas, camels, Highland steers, and a zebu (a breed of cattle from India that is the oldest known), collected by the hotel's owner Justin

Abrams. Today the farm covers over six acres, and is also home to black swans, lemurs, and even a pair of kangaroos.

★ Southeast Light

Perched way up on the cliffs of Mohegan Bluffs on the south shore of the island is **Southeast Light**, the highest and most visible lighthouse on the New England coast, with a beam that can be seen 35 miles (56 km) out to sea. The lighthouse (122 Mohegan Trl., 401/466-5009, www.blockislandinfo.com/

island-events/southeast-light, 10am-4pm Sat.-Sun. late May-late June, 10am-4pm daily late June-early Sept., 10am-4pm Sat.-Sun. early Sept.-early Oct., free) looks more like a Gothic mansion than the traditional black-and-white tower. The brick keeper's house is attached to the structure, making the 52-foot structure look like a turret.

Part of the appeal for visitors is its history of migration. While the lighthouse was originally built 300 feet from the bluffs in 1878, erosion over time narrowed that gap to just 35 feet. In 1993, the Southeast Lighthouse Foundation spent more than $2 million to lift the entire structure on beams lubricated with Ivory soap in order to slide it back 300 feet from the edge. Inside, a small museum details the history of the structure and the move, supplemented by tours ($10 adults, $5 seniors and children 6-17, free for children under 6) every hour on the half-hour. At the rate the cliffs are receding, it seems likely the museum will one day include exhibits about a second heroic move back from the edge.

★ Mohegan Bluffs

Just beyond the lighthouse is a small parking lot that marks the entrance to the nearly 200-foot-high **Mohegan Bluffs**, the stretch of delicate outcropping that extends below nearby Southeast Light. This expanse of steep, crumbly cliffs derives its name from an infamous 16th-century battle in which 40 Mohegan Indians were purportedly driven off of the cliffs by the island's Manisses tribe. The view here is unlike any you'll find elsewhere in Rhode Island—it is startlingly gorgeous, and still unmarred by waterfront developments and commercial attractions. At **Payne Overlook,** just past the lighthouse, you can hike down wooden stairs to the beach where you'll encounter far fewer crowds than at Block Island's more central beaches.

You'll find an even more dramatic vista at **Second Overlook,** a few hundred yards past Payne Overlook. Few cyclists take the turnoff here, so you are likely to have the view all to yourself (although there is no beach access).

On clear days you can see all the way to the tip of Long Island's Montauk Point.

Rodman's Hollow

Continuing west along Mohegan Trail, which hugs the island's southern shore, you'll come to an intersection at Lakeside Drive. Here you'll find **Painted Rock,** one of the island's most colorful traditions. Legend has it that on Halloween night in 1962, the large rock, which sits on a small grassy island in the middle of the intersection, was painted as a prank. Since then, locals and visitors have painted it over so often that it now has nearly an inch and a half of paint covering it. At the rock, take the right onto Lakeside Drive, then a left onto Cooneymus Road, and you'll soon come to unpaved Black Rock Road, which leads to the island's most famous nature preserve, **Rodman's Hollow**. All told, it's about 3 mi (4.8 km) to get here from Southeast Light. The first property bought by Block Island Conservancy in the 1970s, this sunken glacial-outwash ravine has become an emblem of Block Island's crusade to preserve the island's natural spaces. A network of trails traverses the hollow and leads down the cliff to the sandy beach below. Among the trails there are some 40 different endangered species, most of the insect variety, as well as migratory birds looking for a rest on the Atlantic Flyway.

Island Cemetery

West of Rodman's Hollow on West Side Road is the ancient **Island Cemetery,** where headstones mark the passing of many of Block Island's earliest families. Names such as Ball, Rose, Dodge, and Champlin appear on dozens of these markers, several of which date to the 1600s. It's a stunning location, with nice views north out over New Harbor and Great Salt Pond.

★ Greenway Trails

Rodman's Hollow is just a piece of the vast network of hiking paths referred to as the **Greenway Trails**. Since the early 1970s,

groups like the Block Island Conservancy have been working hard to preserve the island's open spaces, and in the 1980s, they began building the trails as a means for the public to fully enjoy the bounty of the preserved rolling hills, grassy pastures, and unspoiled ocean views. Inspired by the walking trails of England, today the network comprises about 28 mi (45 km) and connects the various tracts of nature preserve that make up nearly 45 percent of the island.

Highlights include the towering ocean-view cliffs of **Clay Head Trail and the Maze**, a series of interconnected grassy pathways at the north end of the island where you'll find a lookout onto a secluded sandy beach, and, in the spring, an impressive show of thousands of daffodils if you wander long enough through the maze to find them. The Greenway is comprised of about 15 mi (24 km) and winds through the southern half of the island, with starting points on Lakeside Drive, and along Old Mill, Cooneymus, West Side, and Beacon Hill Roads. At the southwest corner of the island, you'll find the **Elizabeth Dickens Trail** (0.5 mi/0.8 km), named after an ornithologist known as "The Birdy Lady" of Block Island, who is often credited with being a forerunner of the island's conservation efforts. The trail crisscrosses the open fields that flank the edge of the bluffs.

The Greenway also includes beach hikes, less-challenging hikes for children, and trails surrounding swampy areas that are great for bird enthusiasts. Trailheads can be tricky to find, so you'll want to pick up a trail map, which can be found at the **Block Island Visitor Center** (1 Water St., 401/466-2982, www.blockislandchamber.com), located just steps away from the ferry landing. The Greenway is the best way to observe the island's fiercely guarded woodland and wildlife—just be sure to watch out for ticks, as deer

ticks (known to cause Lyme disease) are common on Block Island.

NEW HARBOR

The town's other concentration of civilization—or at least shops and restaurants—is the smaller New Harbor, which is "new" only in the relative sense (it was developed in the 1890s). Before this, Great Salt Pond had been a great freshwater pond, except when occasional storms breached the pond's land barrier and let in the ocean water. The breach was made permanent when a deep channel was dredged to open the new harbor. Today, especially in summer, you'll see upward of 1,500 boats moored on the one-square-mile pond.

Block Island Historical Museum

Just inland, at the corner of Old Town Road and Ocean Avenue, you can tour the **Block Island Historical Museum** (Old Town Rd., 401/466-2481, www.blockislandhistorical.org, 11am-4pm daily late June-early Sept., 11am-4pm on Sat.-Sun. in spring and fall, $10 adults, $8 seniors, free for children under 12), where exhibits—both permanent and temporary—illustrate the island's fanciful and fascinating history, with particular emphasis on the primary industries, fishing and farming. There are also several rooms set up in the style of the island's heyday of Victorian tourism. This 1850s Second Empire building also contains antiques donated by local families through the years. It's not a large museum, but it does well at explaining how Block Island developed into the community it is today.

NORTHERN BLOCK ISLAND

The town districts of Old and New Harbor are just under 1 mi (1.6 km) apart. Between them you can head north on Corn Neck Road to tour the narrow, northern tip of Block Island.

★ North Lighthouse

On the northern tip of the island you'll find **North Lighthouse** (Sandy Point, north end

---

1: shops and restaurants along the streets of Old Harbor **2:** friendly llamas at Abrams Animal Farm **3:** the view from the beach below Mohegan Bluffs **4:** Rodman's Hollow

of Corn Neck Rd., 401/466-3220, 10am-4pm daily, July 5-Labor Day, occasional weekends in Sept., $3), which is a 0.5 mi (0.8 km) walk up the beach from a small parking area. This granite beauty has stood guard above a boulder-strewn beach since 1867, and opened as a maritime museum in 1993 after many years of disuse and neglect. The exhibits inside detail the island's history of shipwrecks and dramatic rescues, and a small 9/11 memorial was installed on the grounds outside in 2002. A favorite time to walk along the pebbly beach to the lighthouse is at dusk, when the views of the sun setting over the horizon are magical.

In the parking area for the lighthouse, note **Settler's Rock monument,** which marks the spot where the island's first English settlers came ashore in 1661. Island residents placed it there in 1911 to mark the 250th anniversary of the colonization of the island. Across from this is **Sachem Pond**, a wildlife refuge replete with swans, red-winged blackbirds, and plenty of other migratory species, depending on the season.

Entertainment and Events

Relatively speaking, this is not a major party island, even in high season, but there are a number of favorite hangout spots frequented by seasonal hospitality industry employees and a fair share of islanders and visitors of all ages.

NIGHTLIFE

Probably the island's most popular club, **Captain Nick's Rock-N-Roll Bar** (34 Ocean Ave., 401/466-5670, www.captainnicksbi.com, 4pm-1am daily, late May-early Oct.), brings in live music on the weekends, and drums up pretty substantial crowds in the high season. Overflowing with lots of kitschy pirate decor, skeletons, tiki masks, nautical ephemera, and drink specials featuring Captain Morgan's rum, it tends to draw a boat-loving crowd of 30- and 40-somethings and up.

Up the hill a short walk from Captain Nick's, **Club Soda** (35 Connecticut Ave., 401/466-5397, 3pm-1am daily) is a local dive that draws a younger, more unconventional crowd to its subterranean bar for live bands, karaoke, arcade games, pool, and cheap drinks.

Another longtime favorite for live music is **McGovern's Yellow Kittens Tavern**

(214 Corn Neck Rd., 401/466-5855, www.yellowkittens.com, 11:30am-1am daily, late May-late Sept.), just around the corner, which brings in a mix of original and cover bands to perform for a somewhat younger crowd. It also has a pool table, darts, and video games.

Day or night, **Ballard's Restaurant** (42 Water St., 401/466-2231, www.ballardsinn.com, 10am-1am daily, late May-late Sept.) on Ballard's Beach showcases live bands and singers on its beachside stage, while tourists lounge and preen with cocktails and Coronas on the beach. This is definitely a see-and-be-seen crowd, drawing reinforcements yearly from the influx of young foreigners (many from Eastern Europe) who come to work in the restaurants and hotels.

Just a short walk from the ferry landing you'll find the **Poor People's Pub** (33 Ocean Ave., 401/466-8533, www.pppbi.com, 11:30am-1am daily), which hosts a live DJ dance party every Friday and Saturday night during the high season and a weekly Sunday "rehab" brunch with live music, in addition to assorted events throughout the year, like lip-sync battles and hotdog-eating contests.

In **Victoria's Parlor** (Spring St., 401/466-5844, www.springhousehotel.com, 6-10pm daily, early May-late Sept.), the decadent sitting room and lounge at the Spring House Hotel, you can order vintage port wines

1: part of Clay Head Trail 2: Southeast Lighthouse 3: daffodils on the Clay Head Trail 4: North Lighthouse

and cognacs among Oriental rugs and Victorian settees and armchairs. Similarly refined is the **Upstairs Parlor at the Hotel Manisses** (1 Spring St., 401/466-2421, www.blockislandresorts.com, 6-10pm daily, late May-late Sept.), a dark and clubby room decked in Victoriana and wicker where you can sip fine drinks and play chess.

CINEMA

The island also has a pair of movie theaters showing first-run films, the most interesting being the **Empire Theatre and Café** (17 Water St., 401/466-2555, www.empiretheaterblockisland.com, $12 adults, $10 children and seniors), a vintage roller rink turned movie venue that offers live music many evenings in addition to films. **Ocean West Theatre** (Champlin's Resort, 134 W. Side Rd., 401/466-2971, www.champlinsresort.com, $7) shows first-run movies at night plus matinees for kids on rainy days.

FESTIVALS AND EVENTS

June brings with it the **Block Island Music Festival** (www.blockislandmusic.com), a free event hosted by Captain Nick's, featuring bands from all over the northeast, and **Block Island Race Week** (www.blockislandraceweek.com), a long-running sailing regatta.

The island's largest event, **Experience Block Island** takes place during the last weekend in September. The event features lots of food, drink, and entertainment specials at venues around the island, but also includes special accommodation packages, outdoor adventure deals, and more.

Bird enthusiasts and naturalists flock to Block Island the first weekend in October for **Audubon Birding Weekend** (401/949-5454, www.asri.org). And just when you think the island has all but shut down for the year, the weekend after Thanksgiving kicks off the **Annual Christmas Shopping Stroll,** when local boutiques and shops display seasonal wares and gifts. That same weekend, there's a well-attended **Block Island Artist Guild Fair** held at Harbor Baptist Church.

You can usually get the latest on upcoming events in the pages of the *Block Island Times* or by checking with the chamber of commerce.

Shopping

ANTIQUE AND VINTAGE

Old Harbor abounds in gift stores and antiques. **Lazy Fish** (235 Dodge St., 401/497-3526, 10am-6pm daily June-Sept., call for off-season hours) sells affordable old furniture that has been attractively weathered by decades of salt and sun, as well as vintage children's toys, clothing, estate jewelry, and island artwork as well.

The owner of **Red Right Return** (Dodge St., 401/466-5839, call for hours) spends her winters in Puerto Rico and comes back to Block Island each year with a new collection of vintage treasures to sell at her colorful and expertly curated antique shop, which carries glassware, furniture, clothing, jewelry, and other collectibles.

ART GALLERIES

There are a handful of art galleries on Block Island, a place where artists of all genres have been summering or living year-round for decades. **Greenaway Gallery** (Water St. at Fountain Sq., 401/466-5331, www.malcolmgreenaway.com, call for hours) ranks among the most respected; it is the domain of contemporary photographer and island resident Malcolm Greenaway.

Spring Street Gallery (Spring St., 401/466-5374, www.springstreetgallery.com,

10am-6pm Mon.-Sat., 11am-7pm Sun. late May-mid-Sept.) is an artists' co-op, with a wide range of media that includes prints, photography, jewelry, and textiles.

The **Jessie Edwards Studio** (211 Water St., 401/466-5314, www.jessieedwardsgallery.com, 11am-5pm Wed.-Mon. mid-June-early Sept.), located above the post office, specializes in oil and watercolor paintings of local scenes by local artists in a rotating selection of two-week shows.

At the **Photo Dog Art Gallery** (189 Water St., 401/466-5858, www.lesleyanneulrich.com, 10am-10pm daily May-Sept., call for off-season hours), you can still buy analog film and develop pictures, or peruse the selection of frames, postcards, art, T-shirts, and a smattering of locally made gifts.

BOOKS

Up a hill by the post office and with the largest selection of books on the island, **Island Bound** (Water St., 401/466-8878, www.islandboundbookstore.com, call for hours) has a good children's section, stationery, some local history books, and a nice general selection of paperbacks and hardcover titles.

CLOTHING AND ACCESSORIES

The **Salty Dog** and the **Peppered Cat** (226 Water St., 401/466-5254, 10am-9pm Sun.-Thurs., 10am-10pm Fri.-Sat. May-early Sept., call for hours in off-season) reside in the same location, with the latter selling a mix of beachy items, including towels, flip-flops, saltwater taffy, coolers, T-shirts, boogie boards, and casual beachwear. The Peppered Cat specializes in more upscale women's apparel: shoes, designer jeans, handbags, jewelry, and more.

In addition to renting and selling surfboards, paddleboards and wetsuits, **Diamondblue** (Corn Neck Rd., 401/466-3145, www.diamondbluebi.com, 11am-4pm Mon.-Fri., 10am-5pm Sat.-Sun. May-Oct., call for winter hours) also carries its own line of surf-inspired clothing, jewelry, hats, and accessories. Beach chairs and umbrellas are available for rental as well.

Over the last three decades, **Glass Onion** (241 Water St., 401/466-5161, call for hours) has become a stalwart shopping experience for islanders looking for a unique selection of jewelry, books, bags, accessories, and other eclectic items.

A cut above the island's many T-shirt shops, **Block Market** (Water St. across from

BLOCK ISLAND
SHOPPING

vintage treasures at Red Right Return

the Statue of Rebecca, 401/282-0848, www. blvckmarket.com, 9am-10pm daily June-Sept.) sells original designs created by shop owner Sean Dugan, including men's and women's clothing, jewelry, and accessories.

GIFTS

Whether you pray to Buddha, Kokopelli, or the Virgin of Guadalupe, you'll find inspiration at **East of the River Nile Trading Company** (Chapel St., 401/466-3152, www. eastoftherivernile.com, 10am-8pm daily May-early Sept., 10am-5pm daily early Sept.-mid-Oct.), which peddles exotic tchotchkes from around the world, including Nepalese engraved copper pots, Peruvian nativity scenes, Chinese porcelain, and more.

GENERAL STORES

Block Island Health and General Store (High St., 401/466-5825, 8am-5pm daily) is something of a cross between a massive pantry and an offbeat variety store, stocking everything from snack foods and holistic vitamins to appliances and toiletries; the store also has a fax service. You can rent TVs, video players, and movies here, too.

Somewhat similar but with much more emphasis on gifts, beachwear, and touristy stuff, **Star Department Store** (1 Water St., 401/466-5541, 9am-9pm daily in high season, closed late Nov.-Easter) carries toys, souvenirs, and men's and women's sportswear, T-shirts, sweats, and hats.

Sports and Recreation

BEACHES

With 17 mi (27 km) of beaches encircling the island, beachcombers and solitude seekers need not worry about excessive crowds, even in the height of summer—it's usually possible to find at least a small stretch of beach that's nearly or entirely deserted. Keep in mind that only Benson and Ballard's beaches are staffed by lifeguards, and riptides are a serious problem in the waters surrounding Block Island. Pay close attention to water and wind conditions before venturing into unfamiliar waters.

★ Crescent Beach

The most famous but also most crowded swath of sand is 2-mi (3.2-km) **Crescent Beach**, which stretches along Block Island's east coast from Old Harbor to Clay Head Nature Preserve. The beach is comprised of different sections, the main one being **Fred Benson Town Beach** (or Benson Beach) off Corn Neck Road. This is one of the only beaches on the island where you'll find lifeguards and public amenities like changing facilities and showers, chair and umbrella

rentals, and a small snack bar (the other is Ballard's). There's also a large (free) parking lot with bike racks. This town beach, formerly run by the state, tends to draw the bulk of day-trippers and other visitors, especially on weekends.

South of Benson Beach, practically in Old Harbor, you'll find the shallow pools of **Baby Beach,** where families often bring children. It's a short walk from many hotels, and the tidal pools are fun for picking up fiddler and hermit crabs, collecting seashells, and swimming or wading.

On the other side, just north of Benson, the somewhat more secluded **Scotch Beach** section tends to draw a lot of summer workers, local teens, and the like. It's less suitable for families than Benson. North of here, beautiful **Mansion Beach** forms the northern end of this stretch. It lies beneath the remains of a mansion that burned in a fire long ago. There's not much parking here—many visitors arrive by bike. It's a very scenic and romantic spot, perfect for a picnic or some relative peace and quiet and yet more accessible than some of the island's most tranquil beaches.

Other Beaches

A lively spot that gets rowdy at night, **Ballard's Beach,** at the southern tip of Old Harbor's commercial district, is right by Ballard's seafood restaurant, just beyond the harbor's southern breakwater. This attractive span is popular with young singles and couples: Waitstaff scurries about, delivering beer and fruity drinks, revelers play volleyball, and live bands entertain the crowds on summer afternoons. The surf can be pretty intense at times, although it's perfectly safe for adults with swimming experience.

A short drive or bike ride from Old Harbor, **West Beach** (West Beach Rd.), with parking just past the town transfer station, is a relatively peaceful beach that's ideal for a stroll, especially at sunset. From here you can hike up the entire western shore of the island, heading north to North Lighthouse. Part of this area is a bird sanctuary, so dogs are not permitted, and humans are asked to stay below the high-tide line and avoid disturbing the dunes and wildlife.

There are several other smaller and more secluded beaches around the island, many of them known only among locals and accessible primarily on foot or by bike. Favorites among these include **Black Rock Beach** and **Vail Beach,** both of which are accessible from Snake Hole Road on the south shore of the island. Vail is a pretty (if rocky) spot in the shadow of Mohegan Bluffs and has some rough surf. Black Rock takes its name from the large black rock offshore; it has a series of secluded coves perfect for hiking or quiet sunbathing. You'll want to take a bike here, as the road to the beach is more than 1 mi long (1.6 km) and mopeds are forbidden. Given the seclusion of the area, some beachgoers may decide to make their excursion clothing-optional, although you didn't hear that from us.

BICYCLING

Few places in the Northeast are more ideally suited to bicycling than Block Island, where curving country lanes pass rugged bluffs and magnificent vistas alongside sweeping pastures and meadows. There are about 40 mi (64 km) of road, most with mild grades as no point on the island is higher than 250 feet; there are a handful of reasonably challenging hills and bluffs, however. There really aren't specific bike trails per se, but all of the island's roads are appropriate for cycling. The self-guided **Block Island Bicycle Tour,** which hits many of the island's highlights, is particularly fun.

Crescent Beach

Bringing a bike over on the ferry is easy and inexpensive, and there are several businesses on the island that rent bicycles by the day, week, or the hour.

SAILING

One of the yachting capitals of New England, Block Island has a couple of companies offering boat rentals and several more options for charters and tours. Probably the most prolific source of boat rentals of just about every kind is **Champlin's Marina** (80 West Side Rd., 401/466-2700, www.champlinsresort.com, call for pricing), where you can take out pontoon boats, paddleboats, kayaks, bumper boats, and zodiacs.

A favorite tour boat is the *Ruling Passion* (New Harbor, 401/741-1926, www.rulingpassionblockisland.com, $20-200 pp), a 45-foot trimaran that sails out of the New Harbor Boat Basin three times daily from June through September. The boat can carry up to 29 passengers, wine and cheese is served during the sunset cruise, and full moon sails are offered monthly. A less glamorous—but still fun—option are the **BIMI Harbor Tours** (401/500-3501, www.bimaritime.org, $20 pp, free for children under 5). Hosted by the Block Island Maritime Institute, these tours leave every Monday and Wednesday at 10am during the summer, and include educational talks about local history, folklore, and ecology.

CANOEING AND KAYAKING

Canoeing or kayaking is another great way to explore Block Island—take to Great Salt Pond, or venture out along the jagged coast. You can rent kayaks or sign up for a guided eco tour from **Pond and Beyond Kayak** (216 Ocean Ave., 401/578-2773, $25-35/hour), which schedules special kayaking trips for kids as well as full-moon paddles for adults. You can also rent kayaks at the concession at Fred Benson Town Beach, Champlin's Marina, and **Fort Island Kayaks** (40 Ocean Ave., 401/466-5392, $23-41/hour).

FISHING

There's more than saltwater fishing in these parts—many of the ponds on Block Island teem with perch, bass, and pickerel, but you'll need a license from town hall to fish these waters. In September, bonito swim up and feed off the shores of Block Island, delighting anglers who like a challenge. June is prime time for reeling in bluefish. Right in New Harbor Channel you can catch fluke, mackerel, and flounder. One of the best ways to fish out here is surf casting from the beach, but there are also charters available for deep-sea fishing.

Whether you're looking for a fly-fishing or surf-casting guide or lessons, a charter, or general advice on where and how to cast a line on Block Island look to **Block Island Fishworks** (40 Ocean Ave., 401/742-3992, www.sandypointco.com) as a one-stop source of information and guidance. This company does 4- to 8-hour charters on both large and small boats into some of southern New England's best fishing waters, which surround Block Island. It also offers both group and private fly-tying clinics and surf-casting lessons. Fishing tours start at $375 for a three-hour trip.

Shorter rides are available through **Hula Charters** (Water St., 401/263-3474, https://hulacharters.com) starting at $325 per person. Captain Matt King is an experienced, well-traveled angler (and former chef) who can probably teach you a thing or two about cooking what you catch as well.

HORSEBACK RIDING

Rustic Rides (West Side Rd., 401/466-5060, $40-55/hour) provides many kinds of horseback excursions on Block Island, from pony rides geared toward families and children to guided trail rides through some of the island's most magnificent preserves and open spaces.

WATER SPORTS

Surfing and paddleboarding are quite popular on Block Island, and you can rent boards at several locations, including the kiosk

Biking Block Island

a sculpture on the Block Island Bicycle Tour

Perhaps the most fun and convenient way to experience Block Island's beaches, bluffs, and bird sanctuaries is by bicycle, an eco-friendly and widely accepted mode of transportation for island visitors and locals alike. In 2014, the Block Island Tourism Council teamed up with www.so-new.org (a Southern New England tourism group) to create the **Block Island Bicycle Tour**, a self-guided, 7.5-mi (12-km) loop that includes nine stops at island landmarks and attractions at the southern end of the island, with an option to extend the tour by 8.5 mi (13.7 km) with three stops on the north end.

Each tour stop is marked with a station signpost; look for a blue and yellow bull's-eye marker with a QR code at the center. Cyclists can use their cell phones to scan the QR code, allowing them to access a short informational video about each stop on the route along with a tour map directing them to their next destination.

The tour includes many of the island's highlights, beginning at the **Visitor's Center** directly adjacent to the ferry landing, (where you can also pick up a paper map of the tour route if you'd rather not use your phone), and continuing on to **Abrams Animal Farm** and the historic **Springhouse Hotel**, where American icons from Mark Twain to the Kennedy family have enjoyed the view from the enormous veranda. From there the route continues on to the **Southeast Lighthouse**, the spectacular **Mohegan Bluffs**, and **Painted Rock**, an island tradition that began in the 1960s and continues to this day. This first leg of the tour will take you on to **Rodman's Hollow** nature preserve, and concludes at **Dead Eye Dick's**, a former piano bar with great seafood and one of the best sunset views on the island.

More ambitious cyclists will want to follow the route to its end by continuing on to marker number 9 at **Fred Benson Town Beach**, then on to **Great Salt Pond**, a popular spot for kayaking and paddleboarding (several marinas here offer rentals), or simply enjoying the plant and animal habitat of the marshes. From here, continue another 2 mi (3.2 km) north on Corn Neck Road to check out **North Lighthouse**, the northernmost point on the island. The area behind the lighthouse is a National Wildlife Refuge, with sandy paths and amazing ocean views.

The tour ends at marker number 12 in Old Harbor, where you'll likely want to reward yourself with a treat from one of the many restaurants and shops on Water Street.

at Frederick J. Benson Beach. To find out where the best breaks are, check with the folks at **Diamondblue Surf Shop** (corner of Dodge St. and Corn Neck Rd., 401/466-3145, www.diamondbluebi.com), where you can also buy or rent surfboards ($30/half day, $50/full day), paddleboards ($20/hour, $50/half day, $75/full day), and wetsuits ($20/day). The shop also offers surfing and stand-up paddleboarding lessons ($55-85 pp). **Ocean Adventures** (401/368-2611, www.oceanadventuresblockisland.com) offers surfing and stand-up paddleboard lessons

($50 pp) and rentals ($60/2 hours) on Great Salt Pond.

Another exciting way to see the island is with **Block Island Parasail** (401/864-2474, www.blockislandparasail.com, $80 and up), which takes passengers high above the water with the help of a large parachute sail for a true gull's-eye view of the island. The company, based on Old Harbor dock near Ballard's Beach, also offers banana-boat rides on gigantic inflatable yellow rafts pulled through the waves—dress appropriately, it's not a dry experience.

Food

UPSCALE

The lavish dining room at the ★ **Hotel Manisses** (1 Spring St., 401/466-2421, www.blockislandresorts.com, 6pm-9:30pm daily May-late Oct., $15-40) offers creative regional American fare, like seared scallops with baby kale, corn and marble potato succotash, or beef tenderloin filet mignon with celery root-potato dauphinoise. Both à la carte and prix fixe menus are offered. The flower-filled dining room or the lovely gardens of this stately old hotel make for a sublime setting. The house-made desserts are to die for and a children's menu is available as well.

Dining at the **Spring House Hotel** (52 Spring St., 401/466-5844, www.springhouseblockisland.com, 6pm-10pm daily late June-early Sept., reduced hours off-season, $22-36) is a lavish experience. Here you'll find contemporary continental fare, with main courses like lamb osso buco with saffron risotto and pine nut *gremolata,* or coriander-crusted swordfish with tomato confit, wilted greens, and Parmesan oil. The dining room, with white linen and Windsor chairs, overlooks the ocean. Reservations are recommended. The recently added Phone Booth Café and Juice Bar is open every morning, offering fresh-squeezed fruit and

vegetable juices (at $10 a pop), as well as coffee and pastries.

The **Restaurant 1879** at the **Atlantic Inn** (High St., 401/466-5883, www.atlanticinn.com, 6pm-10pm daily June-Aug., $21-30) offers tapas, creative cocktails, an award-winning wine list, and fresh seafood entrées in the comfortable dining room or on the gorgeous, wrap-around veranda overlooking the ocean. The food is impressive—think foie gras served with a pistachio sponge, pickled strawberries, oil-cured black olives, and black pepper sauce. The menu also caters to vegetarians, with options like organic tofu grilled with horseradish butter and maple gastrique.

SEAFOOD

A cheap and easygoing sister of the esteemed Hotel Manisses, ★ **The Oar** (221 Jobs Hill Rd., 401/466-8820, www.blockislandresorts.com, call for hours, $5-30) has a wonderful deck and dining room overlooking the sailboats and yachts on Great Salt Pond—a spectacular place for watching the sunset. Inside, the large room is decorated with dozens of hanging oars provided to the marina by boaters from all over the world. The menu leans on seafood, with lobster and blackened mahi-mahi rolls, peel-and-eat shrimp, grilled fish fillets, and the like. Southern fried chicken is also a specialty.

Seafood lovers take notice: **Finn's Seafood Restaurant and Fish Market** (212 Water St., 401/466-2473, www.finnsseafood. com, 11:30am-9pm daily mid-June-Oct., $4-38) has been serving up lobster dinners, rich chowders and stews, and heaping fried-clam platters for more than 40 years, and is somewhat of a Block Island institution. Situated by the ferry landing and overlooking the fishing boats sailing in and out of Old Harbor, Finn's fills up quickly, especially on warm days. Fortunately, the restaurant also has a takeout window with additional seating (without waiters) on another patio upstairs overlooking the harbor.

AMERICAN

Consider yourself lucky if you're able to score a table at **Eli's** (456 Chapel St., 401/466-5230, www.elisblockisland.com, 6pm-10pm daily in high season, call for off-season hours, $18-30), a hole-in-the-wall that locals speak of with solemn reverence. Executive chef Evan Wargo's tastes run from rustic Italian to Asian-inspired cuisine, using simple fresh and local ingredients that pop with natural flavor. Recent entrée standouts include grilled salmon with sunflower seed risotto, and grilled baby octopus with ginger aioli. A comprehensive vegetarian menu is available as well.

The **Mohegan Café & Brewery** (213 Water St., 401/466-5911, www.moheganbi. com, 10:30am-9pm daily mid-Mar.-late May, 10:30am-10pm daily late May-early Sept., 10:30am-9pm daily early Sept.-Oct., $10-25) is a great bet for lunch and dinner, and many evenings even hosts live music. The menu includes lots of fresh seafood as well as some distinctive Asian and Southwestern influences. The Mohegan is the island's only brewery, with four rotating drafts on tap (occasionally including house-brewed root beer or ginger beer for the kids). The dining room also has great views of the water, especially at dinnertime when the sunset lights up the harbor.

Right on Crescent Beach, attached to Yellow Kittens nightclub, ★ **Winfield's Restaurant** (Corn Neck Rd., 401/466-5856, www.winfieldsbi.com, 6pm-10pm daily late May-early Sept., 6pm-10pm Wed.-Sun. early Sept.-mid-Oct., $14-34) offers an improbable menu of upscale French, Italian, Asian, and Texan-inspired cuisine. If you don't think that's possible, try the grilled filet with jalapeño-cheddar polenta with chimichurri

sunset inside the Mohegan Café & Brewery

BLOCK ISLAND
FOOD

and grilled scallions. The dining room is comfortable and a bit rustic—a nice change of pace from the island's many crowded and noisier establishments.

The Beachhead (598 Corn Neck Rd., 401/466-2249, www.beacheadbi.com, 11:30am-9pm daily, call for hours in the off-season, $9-29) serves fresh seafood and American favorites in a space overflowing with art by island artists. The restaurant offers ample outside seating overlooking Crescent Beach, and hearty fare that includes crab mac 'n' cheese, seafood nachos, outstanding chili, and smaller portions for the kids.

ASIAN FUSION

A newer addition to the island is **Tigerfish** (126 Corn Neck Rd., 401/466-2300, 11am-7pm daily, $5-10), a fun, tiki-inspired lounge and restaurant serving pan-Asian cuisine along with some American favorites as well. Here you'll find spring rolls, udon noodle dishes, lobster fried rice, and a very enticing General Tso's crispy chicken and waffles.

COMFORT FOOD

The Poor People's Pub (33 Ocean Ave., 401/466-8533, www.pppbi.com, 11:30am-1am daily, $7-14) is a favorite place to grab simple, delicious food in a fun, relaxed atmosphere. Popular menu items include their famous mac 'n' cheese, to which you can add pulled pork, chili, or roasted chicken, and their award-winning lobster chowder. Outdoor seating is available, and the menu includes vegetarian entrées as well. This is a great option for travelers looking for good food on a tight budget, with a super friendly staff and a great selection of craft beer to boot.

Aldo's Restaurant and Pizzeria (130 Chapel St., 401/466-5871, www.aldosrestaurantblockisland.com, 11am-10pm daily late May-early Sept., $7-20), attached to a wonderful little bakery and ice-cream café, serves pastas, seafood, pizzas, and other Italian fare. Littleneck clams with drawn butter are a specialty, and pastas such as penne á

la vodka and seafood pesto (lobster, mussels, shrimp, scallops, and clams in a wine sauce over linguine) are made from scratch with fresh ingredients.

Club Soda (Connecticut Ave., 401/466-5397, http://places.singleplatform.com/club-soda-4/menu?ref=google, 3pm-1am daily year-round, $8-12), which has been a bar since the 1940s, occupies the basement of the Classic Highview Inn and is best known for serving delicious Southern barbecue. Other pub-like dishes include burgers, pizza, tangy buffalo wings, and the like. By the bar you'll find a series of murals depicting local scenes painted by local artist George Wetherbee. Dinner is served until 11pm, and the dining room is kid friendly until the older kids roll in in the evening.

Dead Eye Dick's (218 Ocean Ave., 410/466-2654, www.deadeyedicksbi.com, noon-3pm and 5pm-10pm daily, May-Sept., $9-34) is renowned as one of the best sunset spots on the island. Serving family-friendly meals even in the off-season, including blackened tuna, barbecue ribs, chicken Parmesan, and steak, also has a full bar and a nice selection of wines by the glass or bottle.

CAFÉS AND SANDWICH SHOPS

★ **Bethany's Airport Diner** (Block Island Airport, Center Rd., 401/466-3100, 6:30am-3pm daily June-Oct., call for hours in the off-season, $4-11) is more than just a stopover for a light bite before or after a plane ride—plenty of locals swear by its breakfast, which includes flapjacks, burritos, and crab cake Benedict. Tasty burgers, sandwiches, and chowders are served at lunch, and a fun, kitschy vibe and a view of the planes landing and taking off also make it a great spot for kids.

Drop by **Aldo's Bakery** (130 Weldon's Way, 401/466-2198, www.aldosbakery.com, 7am-9pm daily May, 6am-11pm daily June-Aug., 7am-9pm daily Sept., $4-8) for ice cream, muffins, Portuguese sweetbread, and designer coffees as well as the all-you-can-eat country-style breakfast buffet on weekend mornings. There's a row of outdoor tables and chairs in front, where on warm summer mornings locals nosh on eggs Benedict, French toast, and omelets (lots of fillings are available).

While the name is a bit misleading, **The Old Post Office Bagel Shop** (123 Ocean Ave., 401/466-5959, 6:30am-3pm daily May-Sept.) is an island favorite for coffee, gigantic muffins, and, yes, excellent bagels. Outdoor seating is available, but lines can get pretty steep in the high season. Breakfast tacos and egg sandwiches are also available for those looking for something more substantial.

At **Persephone's Kitchen** (235 Dodge St., 401/466-5070, 7am-3pm daily, www. persephoneskitchenbi.com) in Old Harbor, you'll find coffee, teas, smoothies, and espresso drinks as well as satisfying breakfast choices like daily frittata specials with rotating fresh ingredients and fresh-baked sourdough bread, avocado toast with sea salt and radish, and yogurt and granola bowls. Sandwiches, salads, and melts are also available during lunchtime.

Accommodations

It can be pricey to stay on Block Island, especially during high season, when room rates soar above $200-300 per night. Even during summer, however, you can often find specials (some advertised, some not), especially during midweek when demand is lower.

Reservation Services and House Rentals

The **Block Island Chamber of Commerce** (1 Water St., 401/466-2474 or 800/383-BIRI—800/383-2474, www.blockislandchamber. com) runs a reservation service that is especially useful if you're trying to find out about last-minute availability. **Block Island Hotel Reservations** (213 Water St., 800/825-6254, www. blockislandhotel.com) rents rooms at several hotels, inns, and private homes and also has entire houses and cottages available around the island. Many of the rentals can accommodate two to three couples.

In addition, hundreds of Block Island property owners rent out their homes for part or all of the summer, either on a weekly or multiple-week basis. In high season, expect to pay about $1,200-2,000 for a small and basic cottage that sleeps two, to more than $5,000 per week for a mansion. Renting can be very economical, however, for groups of four or more—factor in money saved by preparing some of your meals at home and it can be a bargain. Real estate agents that specialize in rentals include **Ballard Hall Real Estate** (401/466-8883, www.blockislandproperty.com); **Block Island Realty** (401/466-5887, www.birealty. com); **Sullivan Real Estate** (401/466-5521, www.sullivansalesandrentals.com); and **Phillips Real Estate** (401/466-8806, www. phillipsonbi.com).

$100-150

It's hard to miss the distinctive **Gothic Inn** (440 Dodge St., 401/466-2918, www. thegothicinn.com, Memorial Day-Columbus Day weekends, $110-210), decked with frilly verge board, sharp pointed gables, and striking finials. Set back from the road on a grassy lawn, the inn is backed by Crescent Beach and is steps from Old Harbor restaurants and shops. Room decor is simple and pleasant, with a clean, austere feel and Shaker-style furniture; from some windows you can enjoy views of the harbor. Also available are two-bedroom efficiency apartments, which are great for families and friends traveling together.

The **Gables Inn** (54 Dodge St., 401/466-2213, www.gablesinnbi.com, mid-Apr.-Nov.,

Block Island's Hotel Seasons

About a dozen of the nearly 60 accommodations on Block Island **stay open year-round**, but sometimes only on weekends in winter. The **larger hotels** in town are **open mostly from April or early May through late October**, some open or close a month earlier or later, and a couple stay open only Memorial Day through Columbus Day.

In **high season, July through August**, virtually every accommodation has a **two-night minimum on weekends**, and many a four-night or even seven-night minimum. These policies are based on supply and demand—in a slow week, or if there's iffy weather, you may get lucky and find a place willing to book your stay for just a night. Accommodations generally let the Block Island Chamber of Commerce know when there are last-minute availabilities or cancellations. So don't give up hope, even on a busy weekend, of finding a room on short notice—just keep in mind that your **options may be limited**.

Compared with Newport, Nantucket, the Hamptons, or many other upscale seaside resorts in the Northeast, **Block Island does not have exorbitantly priced rooms**. On a high-season weekend, you'll rarely see rooms with private baths renting for less than $150 but it's not impossible to find them. Budget travelers who don't mind a room with a shared bath will find a substantial selection on Block Island—sometimes for even less than $100 per night. On the other hand, rates at higher-end properties have been edging up during the past few years. It's now common to find rooms over $250 per night, and even over $350, that are not quite luxurious. Location and the laws of supply and demand, rather than amenities, seem to dictate these higher prices.

Because so many of Block Island's visitors stay for four days or more during the high season, **midweek rates generally don't fall by much**—but it is realistic to expect a drop of 10-20 percent at most places. You should also have more luck booking a single night's stay or scoring a last-minute room during the week. In the spring and fall shoulder seasons, rates on weekends drop 20-40 percent compared with summer; they can fall 30-50 percent at the few properties open in winter. Off-season weekdays usually see even more dramatic rate reductions. And even in the high season it's worth calling a property before deciding definitively that you can't afford it. On weekends with lower demand, for instance Memorial Day through Fourth of July or the last two weeks of August, hotels sometimes offer **"specials" with substantial reductions** on their high-season rates even if they are loath to drop their published rates overall.

$125-210) includes two 1860s Victorian inns with nice details like pressed-tin ceilings and vintage floral wallpapers. There are romantic, antique-furnished rooms here as well as more functionally furnished apartments and cottages better suited for longer stays and families with children. Amenities include barbecue grills and picnic tables, a laundry room, and bike racks. The inn is also very child-friendly; cribs and strollers are available upon request, and beach supplies like chairs, umbrellas, and coolers are available as well. Baby Beach is only a two-minute walk away.

The **New Shoreham House** (53 Water St., 401/466-2317, www.blockislandreservations. com, early May-late Oct., $100-150) is located directly across from the ferry landing and features 15 hostel-style rooms with shared bathrooms and ocean views. The accommodations aren't exactly luxurious, but the views (and the prices) make this a great bet for anyone traveling on a budget who doesn't mind staying right in the middle of all the action. Complimentary continental breakfast is included with your stay from July through Labor Day.

$150-250

Named after the Greek goddess of health, the lovely ★ **Hygeia House** (582 Beach Ave., 401/466-9616, www.thehygeiahouse.com, year-round, $145-295) has been meticulously

---

1: the Atlantic Inn overlooking the Atlantic Ocean
2: 1661 Inn and Hotel Manisses **3:** the historic Springhouse Hotel

restored by the great-grandson and family of the home's first owner, physician and hotelier John C. Champlin. The 1883 home has 10 guest rooms, most of them suites and all with views of the ocean or Great Salt Pond and New Harbor, fully updated bathrooms, and well-chosen Victorian antiques. Innkeeper and poet Lisa Starr has placed inspirational verses around the hotel along with books of poetry in each of the rooms to provide some contemplative gems during your stay.

The ★ **Sea Breeze Inn** (71 Spring St., 401/466-2275, www.seabreezeblockisland.com, year-round, $205-365) is a delightful compound of weathered cottages on a hillside overlooking marshes and swan ponds, and beyond that: the ocean. On the grounds you'll find aromatic and colorful perennial gardens and meadows carpeted with wildflowers. The 10 rooms are airy, uncluttered, and tastefully furnished with well-chosen country antiques. A two-night minimum is required for all stays.

About a 10-minute walk from Old Harbor, the **Rose Farm Inn** (Roslyn Rd., 401/466-2034, www.rosefarminn.com, mid-May-mid-Oct., $150-310) consists of two neighboring properties overlooking 20 acres of pastoral grounds. The rambling 1890s Farm House contains 10 period-furnished guest rooms, a large southern-exposure sundeck, and a stone front porch. Across the lane, the much newer Captain Rose House has nine guest rooms, some of which have double-whirlpool baths and a more modern feel. Second-floor units in the Captain Rose House are perhaps the most romantic, with dormer windows and decks overlooking the grounds, a working farm until the 1960s.

Considering its cheerful and friendly staff, breathtaking setting, and cute rooms, the ★ **Atlantic Inn** (High St., 401/466-5883 or 800/224-7422, www.atlanticinn.com, late Apr.-mid-Oct., $200-290) is one of the best choices on the island, perfectly balancing a grand setting with reasonable room rates. This white three-story hotel with a dark-gray mansard roof and 21 guest rooms sits high on a hill just a short walk from town. The interior overflows with character; think flowered wallpaper, tasseled lamps, and peacock feathers evoking a high-Victorian atmosphere. A continental breakfast (best enjoyed on the sunny, wraparound porch) is included in the rates.

Although it's set inland with no water views, the **Old Town Inn** (Old Town Rd., 401/466-5958, www.oldtowninnbi.com, late May-mid-Oct., $195-245) still has plenty going for it. The building consists of an 1820s main section and a similar-style newer wing, for a total of 10 warmly appointed rooms with private baths and a mix of antiques and more contemporary furniture. The inn is far enough away from the summer crowds to have peace and quiet, but not too far from restaurants and shops to be inconvenient. Rates include a full-breakfast buffet and afternoon hors d'oeuvres.

Consisting of two inns and several smaller nearby cottages, the ★ **1661 Inn and Hotel Manisses** (1 Spring St., 401/466-2421 or 800/626-4773, www.blockislandresorts.com, year-round, $150-450) offers an impressive and historic range of accommodations, plus one of the island's finest restaurants. The pale-gray Hotel Manisses has a five-story central tower and 17 guest rooms named for a famous Block Island shipwreck. Across the street, the 1661 Inn offers a similarly plush experience but with affordable options; four smaller units in the guesthouse share a bath and have considerably lower rates. Some rooms open onto sundecks with stunning water views, and others offer more privacy and quiet in cottages that range from quaint to modern, some with fireplaces and spa tubs. A champagne buffet breakfast, is served daily and included in the rates in the 1661's ocean-view breakfast room. Additional perks for all units include a guided island tour by van, a farm tour (Sat. only), late-afternoon wine and snacks, and a decanter of brandy in each room. When you factor in all the extras and the many types of accommodations, this well-operated resort is a great value.

Located on the main strip of Old Harbor within a short walk of the ferry, the **National**

Hotel (Water St., 401/466-2901, www.nationalri.com, early May-late Oct., $200-350) presents a dashing profile and more comfortable interior than the neighboring Harborside. It was built in 1888 and has 45 guest rooms with simple but comfortable furnishings and antiques. The interior may not be as fancy as some of the similarly priced Victorians up the hill, but the sunny lobby, enormous veranda, and proximity to beaches and downtown make this an excellent choice.

OVER $250

With its red mansard roof, and vast wraparound porch on a hillside overlooking Old Harbor Point, few hotels on the Eastern Seaboard strike a more commanding and regal pose than the ★ **Spring House Hotel** (52 Spring St., 401/466-5844, www.springhouseblockisland.com, Apr.-Oct., $200-400), which opened in 1852 to considerable excitement and was rebuilt in 1870 in grand Second Empire style. Since then, celebrity guests from Mark Twain to Billy Joel have enjoyed the spectacular ocean views from one of the hotel's 40 rooms and suites. Rooms in the main building are simply but attractively furnished with floral-print bedspreads, valances, and fabrics, pastel color schemes, and wicker dressers and nightstands; 10 similarly furnished additional guest rooms are next door in the Samuel Mott Building.

Victorian Inns by the Sea (401/466-5891 or 800/992-7290, www.blockislandinns.com, year-round, $250-400) consists of two main inns and a handful of smaller cottages, all of them quite upscale and with great locations. The late 1800s Blue Dory on Dodge Street is elegant yet unstuffy and inviting. From the back deck, a wooden doorway leads down the steps to the beach and crashing surf. The adjacent Waverly Cottage contains three large suites with kitchens, a living area, and whirlpool tubs. Around the corner, the Avonlea Inn is more spacious and airy, with a wraparound veranda overlooking the beach.

Champlin's Marina, Hotel, and Resort (80 W. Side Rd., 401/466-7777 or 800/762-4541, www.champlinsresort.com, May 15-Oct. 15, $265-335) isn't one of the island's old beauties, but it's an ideal accommodation for sailors and boaters. Set along a beautiful stretch of Great Salt Pond, the marina can accommodate about 250 boats. The hotel has 28 rooms, all with decks, and some with convertible sofas and kitchenettes. There's a restaurant on-site and a kitschy lounge called the Tiki-Bar. Additional amenities include an in-ground pool, bike rentals, a playground, kayak rentals, a movie theater, an ice-cream parlor, laundry facilities, and a bait-and-tackle shop.

CAMPING

Block Island has no campground, and in fact, camping is illegal throughout the island, except for a small tract of land owned by the Boy Scouts of America, on which only visiting scout troops may pitch tents.

Transportation and Services

GETTING THERE AND AROUND
Getting There
FERRY FROM POINT JUDITH

Most ferry travelers leave from Point Judith, the Narragansett fishing village just 10 mi (16 km) or so from the northern tip of Block Island. This is the only point from which ferries sail during the off-season (early Sept.-early June), and it offers by far the greatest number of crossings.

Conventional service is provided by **Interstate Navigation** (401/783-7996 or 866/783-7996, www.blockislandferry.com). There's always at least one, and usually 2-3, sailings each day, even in winter (except for Christmas Day, when there is no service). In fall and spring, service increases to four times most days and six times on weekends; in summer there are 8-9 sailings per day. Departure times vary widely, so call ahead or check the website for details. The round-trip fare is $23.75 per person for adults, $11.50 for children ages 5-11, and free for children under 4. The fare for cars is $79.20 round-trip, and $7 for bicycles. If you're planning on taking a car, it is wise to make a reservation and arrive early, especially in the high season. The trip takes about an hour.

Interstate Navigation also operates the **Island Hi-Speed Ferry** (866/783-7996, www.blockislandferry.com), a fleet of high-tech, passenger-only catamarans that will get you to the island in just 30 minutes. In summer, the ferry runs six times daily; in fall and spring, service is cut to five times daily. You'll pay a little more for these boats, $37.85 round-trip for adults, $21.50 for children ages 4-12, and $12 for children 3 and under. Bikes can be stowed for $8 round-trip. Many visitors think the quick and comfy ride is worth the extra cost, especially for those who tend to get motion sickness. Reservations are strongly recommended for these ships, and you can book either online or by phone. As with the traditional ferry, service is to Old Harbor.

Ferries depart Point Judith from Galilee State Pier, at the southern tip of the town of Narragansett. From points north, take I-95 to Route 4, follow this south to U.S. 1, and then exit in Narragansett at Route 108. From points south, follow I-95 to exit 92 in Connecticut, follow Route 2, turn right onto Route 78, and then follow U.S. 1 north to Route 108. From here, signs mark the way. There are numerous commercial parking lots within walking distance of the ferry, generally priced according to how close by they are. The closest lots are $10 per calendar day, meaning if you park at 6pm one night and get back the following day at 10am, you'll pay for two days. Driving times to Point Judith average an hour from New London, 50 minutes from Providence, and a little more than 90 minutes from Boston.

There are several ways to reach the ferry terminal without driving. You can take **Amtrak** (800/872-7245, www.amtrak.com) to Kingston station, a 12-mi (19.3-km), 20-minute ride by taxi from the terminal. Kingston station is about three hours by train from Manhattan and an hour from Boston. Cab companies serving the area include **Best Taxi** (401/781-0706).

You can also get to Point Judith using **Rhode Island Public Transit Authority (RIPTA) buses** (800/244-0444, www.ripta.

A ride on the Block Island Ferry makes getting there part of the fun.

com). Buses run to the ferry terminal from Narragansett; you can use RIPTA to get to Narragansett from T. F. Green Airport in Warwick, downtown Providence, and other parts of the state. This option requires a bit of planning and generally isn't worth the bother unless you're familiar with Rhode Island and used to regional bus systems or traveling on a tight budget (in which case you might want to skip Block Island entirely).

If you're flying into T. F. Green Airport, which is served by many major U.S. airlines, you can always catch a cab to the ferry terminal—it is much easier than taking a RIPTA bus, but also much more expensive. Contact **Best Taxi** (401/781-0706); the fare is about $60.

FERRY FROM NEWPORT

As with Point Judith, service from Newport is provided by **Interstate Navigation** (401/783-7996 or 866/783-7996, www.blockislandferry.com). The high-speed ferries leave from Newport at 9:45am and 12:30pm daily and return from Block Island at 11:15am and 5:10pm daily, late June through early September only; the sail time is about an hour. The fare is $50.50 for adults round-trip, $26 for children ages 5-11, free for children under 5, and $12 round-trip for bicycles.

The terminal is right downtown at Perrotti Park (39 America's Cup Ave.), and a public parking garage is located adjacent to the visitors center a few blocks away. The cost is $3 per car, per hour with a maximum of $24.50 for the day. Driving time to Newport is about 90 minutes from the Cape Cod canal crossing, and a little under two hours from Boston.

FERRY FROM NEW LONDON, CONNECTICUT

Service from New London is via high-speed passenger-only catamarans operated by **Block Island Express** (860/444-4624, www.goblockisland.com). The trip takes just 70 minutes, and ferries arrive on Block Island at Old Harbor. Late May through mid-June and mid-September through mid-October, Block Island Express runs only Friday through Sunday (as well as the Monday after Memorial Day and the Monday after Columbus Day), four times per day. Mid-June through mid-September Block Island Express runs daily, with four daily runs Monday through Wednesday and five daily runs Thursday through Sunday. The fare is $48.50 per person round-trip, and $24.25 for children ages 2-11 (there is no charge for infants), with a $10 charge for bicycles.

The New London ferry terminal is off Governor Winthrop Boulevard, just off I-95 (exit 84S from the south, exit 83 from the north)—follow signs from the exit. Long-term and short-term parking is available at the municipal **Water Street Parking Garage** (Atlantic St., just off Eugene O'Neill Dr., with rates from $6-15 per day, depending on the day of the week). Depending on traffic, it takes 2.5-3 hours to reach New London from Manhattan, and about an hour from Hartford.

The terminal is also just steps from New London's train station, which is served by **Amtrak** (800/USA-RAIL or 800/872-7245, www.amtrak.com), with service from many major cities, including Manhattan (about 2.5 hours), Hartford (about 3.5 hours, with a change in New Haven), and Washington DC (6-7 hours).

Greyhound (800/231-2222, www.greyhound.com) has service to New London from many major cities, including Manhattan (3-4 hours), Hartford (2.5-3 hours), and Washington DC (8-10 hours). The bus station is adjacent to the ferry terminal.

FERRY FROM LONG ISLAND, NEW YORK

Viking Fleet (631/668-5700, www.vikingfleet.com) runs from Montauk, New York, at the eastern tip of Long Island's south fork, to Block Island late May through mid-October. Boats leave once daily from Montauk at 10am, arriving at Block Island at 11am. The return departure to Montauk is at 5pm, arriving at 6pm (one additional boat departs Montauk at 3:30pm and Block Island at

11:30am Fri.-Mon. July-Aug.) The Montauk ferry arrives at Champlin's Marina in New Harbor rather than at the Old Harbor terminal. The adult fare is $40 one-way, $80 round-trip; the cost is $25 one-way or $50 round-trip for children 12 and under; $10 per bicycle or surfboard; automobiles are not carried.

BRINGING YOUR CAR

Cars can be brought over only on the ferries from New London and Point Judith. This can be a very tricky business, especially on weekends or virtually any day during summer. Unless you're hoping to obtain standby passage, make a reservation at least 4-5 months ahead for summer or holiday weekends; there's more flexibility on weekdays. On the day of passage, be at the ferry dock and check in at the ferry window at least one hour before departure—if you're late, you risk losing your reservation to those waiting on standby.

If you're traveling with your car off-season or you're flexible with time, consider going standby. In high season, standby is highly unreliable. Again, arrive at the terminal at least an hour before departure (a few hours ahead if you're trying to cross at a busy time). Once at the departure lot, check in with the attendant; he or she will give you a ticket that establishes your place in the line, and then you must remain with your vehicle if and until you're permitted to board (when it's not especially crowded, attendants sometimes let drivers leave their cars unattended for a bit). If you travel standby, you're not guaranteed return passage from Block Island—which means you may have to return at a different time or on a different day than you had hoped.

PLANE

Flying to Block Island may not be as expensive as you think, and the time it saves, to say nothing of avoiding potential ferry hassles, can make this option quite useful. **New England Airlines** (800/243-2460, www.block-island. com/nea) departs from **Westerly Airport** (56 Airport Rd.) daily from 7:30am-6:30pm, and from Block Island back to Westerly daily

from 8am-6pm. In summer, service runs a bit later, and additional flights to Block Island are offered on Thursday and Friday nights and back to Westerly on Monday morning. The fare is $64 one-way, $118 round-trip; for children $55 one-way, $110 round-trip; discounts are also available for seniors. New England Airlines also offers charter service to Block Island from virtually any airport in the continental United States.

You can reach Westerly Airport by **Amtrak** (800/USA-RAIL or 800/872-7245, www. amtrak.com). Amtrak trains stop in the town of Westerly, where you'll need to take a cab to the airport. Call **Eagle Cab** (800/339-2970); the fare is about $15. If you miss the last ferry, or if high winds or poor weather force cancellation of the ferry, it's a 20-25-minute drive from the ferry terminal in Galilee to the airport in Westerly, and a 35-40-minute drive from New London.

A few other charter airlines fly frequently in and out of Block Island, often to regional Northeastern airports. A reputable Block Island-based option is **Resort Air** (401/466-2000, www.resortaircharter.com).

Block Island Airport sits atop a hill in the center of the southern half of the island. The 2,500-foot runway is lighted, and taxis usually greet regularly scheduled flights and can easily be phoned to meet charters. There's a funky little restaurant here, Bethany's Airport Diner, and both car and bike rentals are available in summer. It's a pretty 20-minute walk into town from the airport: turn right out of the entrance and walk down Center Road.

Getting Around

You'll hear plenty of grumbling among islanders about the blight of **mopeds**—they are a frequent cause of accidents, and as a means of transportation they leave something to be desired. There aren't too many parts of the island that can't be managed on a **bicycle,** and, in fact, many roads to out-of-the-way beaches and trails are prohibited to mopeds. If you are staying for more than a few days or traveling with a large group, you might consider bringing a **car** over. Of course, islanders don't like visitors bringing their cars in high season, but politically correct or not, there's no question that a car is convenient, especially if you are lugging kids to and from the beach. If you'll be visiting for fewer than four days, however, and staying anywhere within a 10-minute walk of Old Harbor or New Harbor, where 90 percent of the island's accommodations are, you really need nothing more than a good pair of walking shoes to enjoy a vacation on Block Island.

If you do rent a **moped,** keep to the side of the road, always rent a helmet, and do not travel on the island's dirt roads, where wipeouts are a danger. Keep in mind that you cannot take mopeds out after dusk. There are about 170 mopeds for rent on the island, but you may encounter a few stares or glares from islanders who count themselves among the "no-peds" contingent.

One thing to keep in mind is that there are no street numbers on Block Island. The small signs mounted on the fronts of most houses and buildings are "fire numbers" used by the police and the fire department, but they are not in numerical order. Google maps recognizes most of these fire numbers as addresses, so using GPS to find your way around the island is certainly feasible.

BIKE, MOPED, AND CAR RENTALS

Bike rentals are offered at several shops, with rates running $15-25 daily. Mopeds cost up to $100 daily. Many of these same agencies rent cars. A quick tip: Before renting a bike or a moped, stop by a hotel or the chamber of commerce information booth, where you can frequently find flyers giving you $10 or 10 percent off the cost of a rental.

As you get off the ferry in Old Harbor, you'll find two rental agencies within steps of the terminal. **Island Moped and Bike** (Chapel St., behind the Harborside Inn, 401/466-2700, www.bimopeds.com) rents six-speed beach cruiser bikes, 21-speed mountain bikes, tandems and tag-alongs, mopeds, and safety equipment, and offers weekly

rates starting at about $45. Offering a similarly extensive selection of bikes and mopeds, **Old Harbor Bike Shop** (50 yards left of the ferry terminal as you disembark, 401/466-2029, https://blockislandmoped.com) also rents open-top Jeeps, vans, and other autos. **Beach Rose Bicycles** (1622 Roslyn Rd., www.beachrosebicycles.com, 401/466-5925, $40 per day) is another option, specializing in hybrid and mountain bikes, beach cruisers, and children's bicycles as well.

TAXIS

You'll see taxis lined up in Old Harbor and New Harbor, and also at the airport, waiting for passengers on scheduled ferry and plane crossings. You can also hail cabs on the street: Hold out your right hand and wave as one passes, even if it looks full or doesn't appear to be slowing down. If the driver can take you, the cab will pull over. If not, he'll often hold up his CB and wave it to you, indicating that he's calling for another cab to come to get you.

Island cab drivers can be a great source of information, and many of them offer hour-long tours of the island ($55 for 1-2 people, $10 more for each additional person, prices mandated by the town). For simple rides, cabs charge a flat fee and do not use meters. It's always quite reasonable, and fares are always displayed clearly in the cab. Fares are firm and set by the town; it's illegal to negotiate higher or lower fares. Cabs can be fined for taking too many passengers or for accepting passengers carrying open containers of alcohol.

If you need to phone a cab, try any of the following companies: **McGoverns' Cab** (401/862-6087); **O. J.'s Taxi** (401/741-0500), whose driver specializes in island history and photography tours; **Monica's Taxi** (401/742-0000); and **Mig's Rig Taxi** (401/480-0493), who is only bookable in advance and also gives interesting tours around the island.

VISITOR INFORMATION

For visitor information, contact the **Block Island Tourism Council** (P.O. Box 356, Block Island, RI 02807, 401/466-5200 or

800/383-2474, www.blockislandinfo.com). The council's offices double as the **Block Island Chamber of Commerce** (www. blockislandchamber.com), whose information center faces the Old Harbor ferry terminal. It's definitely worth popping in when you arrive on the island—brochures abound, including several that offer discounts on bike rentals or meals at restaurants, and there's an ATM, a fax and copier, and lockers for rent— ideal if you're on a day trip. Staff can also tell you which hotels and inns on the island have vacancies. Next door to the chamber you'll find public restrooms; there are also restroom facilities at the fire-police station, the Island Free Library, and North Light.

A few practicalities to keep in mind: Block Island has a water shortage—the situation has been grave at times, and visitors are asked to make every possible effort to conserve water. Also, do your best not to overuse electricity— the local utility company powers the island with diesel generators, and Block Island's electric rates are said to be higher than in any other town in the United States.

MEDIA

The weekly *Block Island Times* (401/466- 2222, www.blockislandtimes.com) is a great resource for anybody planning a visit of even a few days. Both the print paper and the online edition contain updated ferry information, news about upcoming events, and frequent features on local history.

The East Bay and Sakonnet

Driving east on I-195 out of Providence, travel-
ers might first find themselves crossing over the Massachusetts border
before driving back through Rhode Island and into the Sakonnet and
East Bay regions of the state.

The area's small townships distinguish themselves from the more
well-known Newport and South County by remaining small, close-knit
communities, where town beaches are a bit off the beaten path and unsupervised roadside farm stands still operate under the honor system.
Barrington, Warren, and Bristol comprise the East Bay section, characterized by unique downtown shopping districts, quaint B&Bs, and
a folksy fishing village vibe. Further south lay the towns of Tiverton

Highlights

Look for ★ to find recommended sights, activities, dining, and lodging.

★ **Blithewold Mansion and Arboretum:** Right up there with the lavish summer cottages found in Newport, Blithewold ranks among the most impressive house-museums in the state, with expansive and expertly maintained bayside gardens (page 169).

★ **Warren's Historic District:** This colonial shipbuilding center contains dozens of restored 18th- and 19th-century buildings, along with dozens of interesting shops, restaurants, and cafés (page 170).

★ **East Bay Bike Path:** This asphalt path is the most scenic of the state's biking routes, stretching from Providence down through the East Bay and with wonderful bay views along the way (page 174).

★ **Carolyn's Sakonnet Vineyard:** In peaceful and rural Little Compton, this vineyard produces some of the top wines in the state (page 181).

★ **Goosewing Beach and Nature Preserve:** A long stretch of sandy beach and a 75-acre nature preserve make this one of the most peaceful and scenic beaches in the state (page 184).

The East Bay and Sakonnet

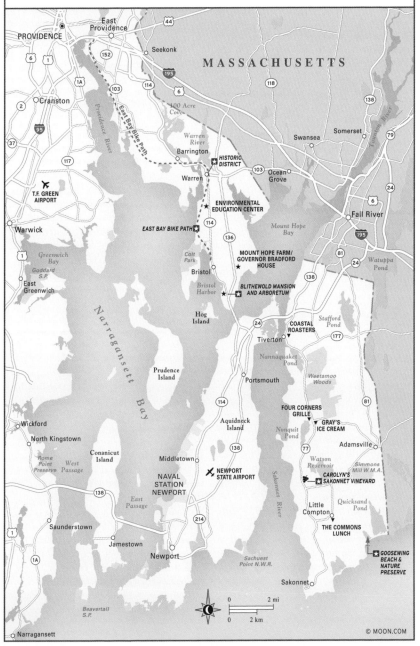

© MOON.COM

and Little Compton, made distinct by their proximity to the Sakonnet River, which separates them from Newport and Middletown to the west.

The region is ideal for travelers wishing to experience Rhode Island's gorgeous coastline without the long lines, exorbitant prices, and crowded attractions. Geographically speaking, the region is quite distinct as well. The peninsular towns of Barrington, Warren, and Bristol dangle jaggedly off the mainland like stalactites, fringed on various sides by Narragansett and Mount Hope Bays and the Seekonk, Warren, and Barrington Rivers. All told, the three towns share about 20 mi (32 km) of shoreline throughout Bristol County, as well as a handful of cultural and historical attractions to rival any other region in the state. Best of all, the entire area lies sheltered from—but completely accessible to—the Atlantic Ocean.

A short drive southeast, Sakonnet hugs the Massachusetts mainland on one side and the Sakonnet River on the other before coming to a point where the river meets the Atlantic. A summer drive headed south on Route 77 through Little Compton will reward adventurers with stretches of lush green farmland and rows of dazzling purple-blue hydrangeas (a popular fixture in many front yards).

PLANNING YOUR TIME

The East Bay and Sakonnet region is a quick day trip from Providence or Newport—although at least two days is recommended, especially during the warmer months when one of those days could easily be spent lounging on the beach. The appeal of this area is less in ticking off sights than it is in rambling along streets filled with colonial homes and antique stores or driving down sunny country roads lined with stonewalls. If you truly want to fall into the slow pace of life here, an overnight or two is a nice respite on a harried vacation.

The East Bay

The East Bay comprises a narrow swath of land that extends in a southeasterly direction from Providence down toward Aquidneck Island, where Newport is, and the Sakonnet Peninsula. To the east lies the Massachusetts border, and to the west is Narragansett Bay. Although it's a small area with just three towns—Barrington, Warren, and Bristol—the East Bay has its own distinct identity and is more than just a suburban extension of metropolitan Providence.

This is an area rich in museums, parks, B&Bs, and restaurants, especially in Bristol, the southernmost of the East Bay communities. At the north end, just below East Providence, the town of Barrington is a pretty suburb that's worth taking the time to drive through but lacks much in the way of actual diversions and businesses. In the middle, however, plan to spend a little time exploring Warren, a semi-industrial town with a rich shipbuilding heritage. It has steadily gentrified in recent years and contains a nice downtown historic district.

BRISTOL

If there were a competition for all-American town, Bristol would be a finalist. The main street is lined with flags left waving after the city's annual Fourth of July parade, the oldest in the country. The street itself is a vibrant vision of what main streets once looked like before malls, with boutiques and storefront cafés interspersed with solid granite buildings and picturesque colonial homes.

From such quaint environs, you'd hardly

Previous: Sakonnet Light; Blithewold Mansion and Arboretum; historic Downtown Warren.

Prudence Island

One of the state's strangest little places, Prudence Island—which is about 6 mi (9.7 km) long by 1 mi (1.6 km) wide—lies just a few miles southwest of Bristol in the middle of Narragansett Bay. Technically it is within the town limits of Portsmouth, just to the east. It was entirely wooded until the Revolutionary War, when the British used it as a source of lumber. Despite being the third-largest island in Rhode Island after Aquidneck and Conanicut, the island now has fewer than 100 year-round residents, including just a few summer homes and a small convenience store to pass for civilization.

Of course, that makes it a nature-lover's dream, with the densest white-tailed deer herd in New England, as well as wading birds such as great blue herons. It's an ideal spot for beachcombing, hikes, and taking advantage of nature lectures and strolls, which are sponsored by the Audubon Society of Rhode Island (401/949-5454, www.asri.org).

Near the boat docks at the southern end of the island and a -mi (6.4-km) bike ride or hike from the ferry landing, the Narragansett Bay National Estuarine Research Reserve (S. Reserve Dr., 401/683-6780, www.nbnerr.org, 11am-3pm Fri.-Mon., and by appointment), encompasses many acres of salt marsh, tidal flats and pools, forest, and even a historic farm site. Birding is a favorite activity at the reserve, where you'll also find a butterfly garden and several nature trails. A mile's (1.6 km) walk from the boat docks is the 25-foot-high Prudence Island Light (www.lighthouse.cc/prudence), which stands sentinel on the island's east side. The lighthouse itself is not open for tours, but the grounds are open from sunrise to sundown.

While this is a great place for exploring, keep in mind that deer ticks are a major problem on the island—take necessary precautions when exploring, especially in wooded areas. No bridges connect the island to the mainland or Aquidneck. Transportation is by the Prudence Island Ferry (147 Thames St., Bristol, 401/683-0430, www.prudencebayislandtransport.com, $10.80 round-trip for adults, $3.80 for children under 12) which runs several boats from Bristol sunrise to sunset daily. You can also dock your own vessel at the southern tip of Prudence Island. Unfortunately, camping is not permitted. Daytrippers be warned: other than at the ferry landing, there are no public restrooms (or coffee shops and restaurants) on the island, so plan wisely.

believe Bristol's contentious history. In the 17th century the land served as the primary encampment of the Wampanoags, led by King Philip, who staged the largest prerevolutionary Native American uprising. After Philip was defeated, the colonists who founded Bristol named it after one of Great Britain's greatest seaports, deriving a good bit of their commercial success in the infamous slave trade. After that ignominious start, Bristol was pummeled during the Revolutionary War. On October 7, 1775, the British sailed several warships into the town harbor and began an intense bombing campaign that damaged many buildings. A far worse attack occurred three years later, when about 600 British soldiers and Hessian mercenaries marched through the town and burned virtually every structure.

While never as well-to-do as Newport, Bristol's heyday as a shipping center after the Revolution led to many fine Victorian mansions and gardens being built on the outskirts of town. After slavery was outlawed, Bristol continued to rake in steep revenues on shipping and trade well into the mid-19th century, with ships sailing in and out of Bristol Harbor to China, the Mediterranean, northern Europe, the northwest coast of Africa, and the Caribbean. The town's legacy as a shipbuilding community continued through the efforts of the Herreshoff Manufacturing Company, which opened in 1863 in the factory space of the old rifle company, and became famous for creating the racing ships that helped the United States win the America's Cup sailing race year after year.

Industry led to an influx of Portuguese and Italian immigrants, many of whose descendants still influence Bristol's character—you'll find ample evidence of this heritage on local

Bristol

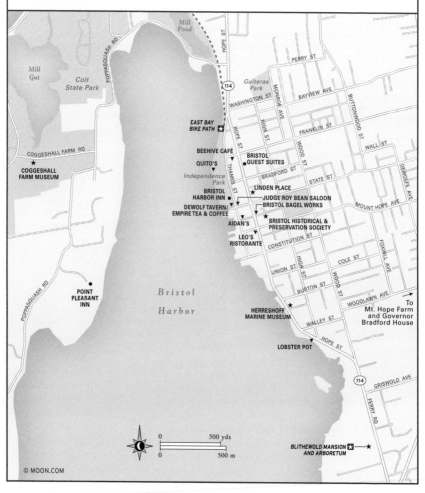

menus that include linguica sausage or puttanesca seafood dishes. Today the majority of residents are commuters from Providence and even Newport. The town is not really suburban in character or appearance, however, as it retains an organic small-town spirit with a clutch of restored, finely crafted historic homes. You'll see carved lintels, toothlike dentil molding, and pedimented windows and dormers on buildings up and down Hope Street.

Also known as Route 114, Hope Street is one of those slice-of-Americana thoroughfares that looks nearly flawless enough to be a movie set. Shops and restaurants line the west side of the street, grand colonial and Victorian mansions the other, and mature shade trees run along both. Restaurants range from upscale bistros to wiener joints and pizza parlors. It's a very family-friendly place: kids ride their bikes downtown, parents push strollers, and teens hang out on park benches in a way that you can't help but envy.

Downtown

Just off Hope Street, the **Bristol Historical and Preservation Society** (48 Court St., 401/253-7223, www.bhpsri.org, noon-3pm Sat. in summer and by appointment) overflows with photographs, letters, deeds, reports, and other historical artifacts spanning the town's several centuries. The displays are set in the 1828 jail, which was constructed with the granite ballast of incoming Bristol ships.

South of Downtown

At the southern tip of Bristol, the narrow Mount Hope Bridge arches steeply and gracefully over Narragansett Bay, connecting the mainland with Aquidneck Island (a left turn onto Route 24/138 leads to the Sakonnet towns of Tiverton and Little Compton, while a right turn onto Route 114 leads to Newport). When it was built in 1929, this $4 million structure with a main span of 1,200 feet was the 13th-longest suspension bridge in the world and the longest in New England. The road rises to 135 feet over the water below, and the two bridge towers are 284 feet tall.

Just across the bridge, **Mount Hope Farm** (250 Metacom Ave., 401/254-1745, www.mounthopefarm.com) dates to 1745 and is owned by a private trust that allows public access. Respectful pedestrians and bicyclists are free to explore the more than 200 acres of greenery, gardens, and trails overlooking Mount Hope Bay. (Bicyclists must stay on trails; cars are prohibited.) A farmers market happens every Saturday morning from 9am-12:30pm, year-round, and the farm hosts regular events like yoga classes and educational talks. There's also an inn, the **Governor Bradford House**, the interior of which has been restored to the colonial period.

To get a full sense of the agrarian life that also characterized this part of the state during much of the past few centuries, pay a visit to the **Coggeshall Farm Museum** (1 Colt Drive, 401/253-9062, www.coggeshallfarm.org, 10am-4pm Thurs.-Sun. Memorial Day-Labor Day, $5 adults, $3 children under 16), a living history museum that sits on 40 rolling acres overlooking Mill Gut Inlet, a sheltered expanse of Narragansett Bay. It's a nice place for a stroll in all seasons, made more interesting by the vintage and reproduction-antique farming tools and the yards of livestock. Throughout the year, historic interpreters conduct tours, lectures, and demonstrations, often in the farm's outbuildings, which include a blacksmith shop and a fieldstone springhouse.

Set on a 28-acre wildlife refuge on Narragansett Bay, **Audubon Society of Rhode Island's Environmental Education Center** (1401 Hope St., 401/949-5454 X3118, www.asri.org, 9am-5pm daily May-Sept., 9am-5pm Mon.-Sat., noon-5pm Sun. Oct.-Apr., $6 adults, $4 children 4-12, free for children under 4) contains the largest aquarium in the state along with well-executed 3-D natural history dioramas, marine-life touch tanks, and other provocative hands-on exhibits. This is an excellent resource for conservation education and great fun for children. Nowhere else in Rhode Island can you walk inside a 33-foot-tall life-size right whale, a species of baleen whales.

Herreshoff Marine Museum

You can get an intimate sense of Rhode Island's unique bond with the ocean at the **Herreshoff Marine Museum** (1 Burnside St., 401/253-5000, www.herreshoff.org, 10am-5pm daily May-Oct., $15 adults, $10 students, free for children 10 and under). Herreshoff has long been famous as one of the world's most respected and oldest manufacturers of ships. Brothers John Brown Herreshoff and Nathanael Greene Herreshoff, both named for legendary figures in Rhode Island history, founded the boat maker in 1863. John, famous for his photographic memory and keen sense of detail, laid out the plans for the craft, and Nathanael handled the execution. In its first year, Herreshoff produced nine sailboats, and it wasn't long before the company had taken over the old Burnside Rifle plant and produced several successful defenders of the America's Cup (beginning with the *Vigilant*

in 1893), plus powerful steamers, sleek yachts, and other fine craft.

Inside the museum's extensive exhibit hall you can admire about 45 Herreshoff boats as well as dozens of ship models and other historic memorabilia. Cruises are taken regularly aboard the 56-foot *Belisarius,* a vintage yawl that was Nathanael Herreshoff's final design—you'll usually see the boat tied up in the bay outside the museum. There's also a Discovery Center, geared for kids and families, where staff conduct workshops on sailing and boat construction.

★ Blithewold Mansion and Arboretum

Visitors to Rhode Island typically flock to Newport to tour the greatest homes of the Gilded Age, but serious mansion-goers should make a point of seeing Bristol's spectacular—and somewhat underrated—Blithewold Mansion and Arboretum (101 Ferry Rd., 401/253-2707, www.blithewold.org, Mansion: 10am-4pm Tues.-Sat., 10am-3pm Sun. early Apr.-mid-Oct.; Gardens 10am-5pm Mon.-Sat., 10am-3pm Sun., $15 adults, $6 children). Famous for its lush 33-acre grounds and its 1908 English manor house, the grounds here include 200 varieties of trees and more than 2,000 plants. A prize among these is a towering 90-foot sequoia, said to be the largest of its kind east of the Rocky Mountains. Inside the house's stone-and-stucco walls you can tour 45 rooms decorated mostly with pieces from the original family's impressive collection.

Linden Place

The name Samuel Colt is more associated these days with Connecticut; in Hartford you'll find the Colt factory village and former estate. However, Colt's more famous nephew, Samuel P. Colt, has roots in Bristol in the grand if garish 1810 mansion, now a museum, called Linden Place (500 Hope St.,

401/253-0390, www.lindenplace.org, 10am-4pm Tues.-Sat., noon-4pm Sun., early May-early Oct., $12 adults, $5 children), where his magnate grandfather, General George DeWolf, lived. The mansion, in Classic Revival style with major Victorian and Greek Revival alterations, eventually passed to Colt, who founded the U.S. Rubber Company (now Uniroyal) and the Industrial Trust Company (now Fleet Bank). Hollywood has connections to Linden Place as well: The matriarch of the famous Barrymore acting dynasty, Ethel Barrymore, lived here at one time, and parts of the mansion played a role in the 1974 film adaptation of *The Great Gatsby.* The mansion contains decadent furnishings from the period, outbuildings that date as far back as the 1750s, an elaborate ballroom from 1902, an 1820s carriage house, and neatly manicured grounds set with dramatic sculptures.

WARREN

At 6.2 square miles, making it the smallest town in the smallest county in the smallest state, Warren has continued to grow in popularity in recent years among professionals, educators, and artists. A mix of great historic buildings and affordable homes (compared to Newport or Boston) has helped encourage an emerging arts scene. It's an eclectic and economically diverse community with an unpretentious, easygoing vibe.

Originally part of the southern fringes of the Massachusetts town Swansea, Warren officially became part of Rhode Island in 1747 and developed rapidly into a shipbuilding and commercial center. During the Revolutionary War, the Redcoats targeted the community, along with Bristol to the south, for its contributions to the Continental Navy. In May of 1778, raiding troops burned some 75 boats as well as a large portion of the town's buildings. It took many years to recover fully from the war, but eventually Warren returned to its shipbuilding prominence and produced some of the 19th century's finest vessels. Since then, Warren has slowly shifted from manufacturing to tourism.

1: Audubon Society of Rhode Island's Environmental Education Center **2:** flowers at the Blithewold Mansion and Arboretum **3:** birds in Bristol Harbor

Warren

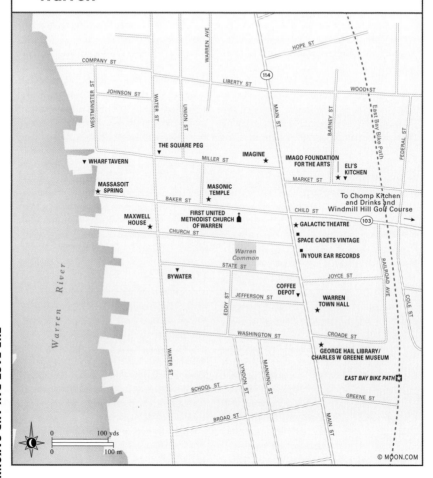

COMPANY ST

WARREN AVE

HOPE ST

WESTMINSTER ST

JOHNSON ST

WATER ST

LIBERTY ST

114

WOOD ST

UNION ST

MAIN ST

BARNEY ST

East Bay Bike Path

FEDERAL ST

THE SQUARE PEG

MILLER ST

IMAGINE ★

IMAGO FOUNDATION
FOR THE ARTS

ELI'S
KITCHEN
★ ▼

▼ WHARF TAVERN

MARKET ST

MASSASOIT
★ SPRING

BAKER ST

MASONIC
TEMPLE
★

To Chomp Kitchen
and Drinks and
Windmill Hill Golf Course

CHILD ST

103

MAXWELL
HOUSE ★

FIRST UNITED
METHODIST CHURCH
OF WARREN

★ GALACTIC THEATRE

CHURCH ST

■ SPACE CADETS VINTAGE

*Warren
Common*

STATE ST

■ IN YOUR EAR RECORDS

RAILROAD AVE

COLE ST

Warren River

▼
BYWATER

EDDY ST

JEFFERSON ST

COFFEE
DEPOT ▼

JOYCE ST

WARREN
TOWN HALL
★

WASHINGTON ST

CROADE ST

WATER ST

LYNDON ST

MANNING ST

★ GEORGE HAIL LIBRARY/
CHARLES W GREENE MUSEUM

EAST BAY BIKE PATH 🚲

SCHOOL ST

GREENE ST

BROAD ST

MAIN ST

0   100 yds
0   100 m

© MOON.COM

Warren's lack of chain stores and high-profile restaurants is refreshing compared to the glut of visitors in Newport and even neighboring Bristol. But there's quite a good bit to keep you busy here, especially if you're into shopping for antiques.

★ Warren's Historic District

An afternoon could easily be spent checking out the shops, galleries, and restaurants in Warren's historic center, a cute little

downtown neighborhood with bay views and some nicely preserved colonial architecture.

Just off Main Street is the 1844 **First United Methodist Church of Warren** (25 Church St., 401/247-9702, service 10:30am Sun.), whose 160-foot spire and clock tower defines the town's skyline. From the churchyard extends Warren's simple but appealing town common, which is fronted by several of the community's most striking old homes. You can easily combine your antique shopping with a tour of prominent sights, or just wander the streets around the intersection of Main Street (Route 114) and Child Street (Route 103) to take in the charm that Warren has to offer.

If you're interested in historical architecture, Baker Street has a couple of noteworthy buildings, including the hulking building at 39 Baker Street, the oldest continuously operated **Masonic Temple** in the country; it was built in 1799 with timbers from sunken British warships. Other notable structures nearby include the 1890 copper-domed **Warren Town Hall** (514 Main St., 9am-4pm Mon.-Fri.) and the Romanesque **George Hail Library** (530 Main St., 401/245-7686, 10am-8pm Mon.-Thurs., 10am-5pm Fri.-Sat.), built in 1889 and completely restored in the early 1980s. This structure also contains the **Charles W. Greene Museum** (2pm-4pm Wed. or by appointment, free), where you can examine a collection of artifacts from North and South American indigenous people, including beads, farming implements, and currency.

From this part of Main Street, you can take any intersecting street west a few blocks down toward the water to see Warren's bustling little dock, where oyster houses and boatyards thrive as they have for centuries. Views are especially good from the outdoor decks of the Wharf Tavern restaurant. These blocks cover what was once woodland and swamp settled by the Wampanoags under Massasoit and later his son King Philip. A bronze plaque at the foot of Baker Street marks the spot of **Massasoit Spring,** where King Philip presided over his people. You can learn more about Wampanoag history at **Maxwell House** (59 Church St., 401/245-0392, www.massasoithistorical.org, by chance and appointment, free), operated by the Massasoit Historical Association. Inside the 1750s Georgian colonial, a multitude of documents and exhibits concerning Warren's past are on display, including two beehive ovens and a mix of colonial and Victorian furnishings; hearth cooking demonstrations and other food programs are offered from time to time.

ENTERTAINMENT AND EVENTS

While the East Bay isn't a major center of nightlife, Bristol does have several pubs, most of them are near the waterfront and popular with a mix of students from nearby Roger Williams University, yuppies, blue-collar factory workers and fishers, and visitors. Favorites include **Judge Roy Bean's** (1 State St., Bristol, 401/253-7400, http://judgeroybeansaloon.com/, 4pm-1am Mon.-Thurs., noon-1pm Fri.-Sun.), and **Gillary's** (198 Thames St., Bristol, 401/396-9454, 11:30am-1am daily) by the waterfront. Both often have live music, plus various open mic and karaoke nights. Warren locals love **Jack's Bar** (294 Child St., 401/245-4052, 11am-9pm Wed.-Sat., 11am-10pm Fri.-Sat., noon-9pm Sun., 11am-9pm Mon.), a salty little dive bar with weathered wooden floors and chairs, and vintage sports ephemera hanging from the rafters.

Warren is home to one of the funnest little bar and music venues in the East Bay, ★ **Galactic Theatre** (440 Main St., www.galactictheatre.com, 7pm-1am Tues.-Sun.). In 2016, the Galactic began as a hybrid vintage store/movie theatre and gradually morphed into what it is today—a hole-in-the-wall cocktail lounge with a small stage right in the heart of Warren's downtown district. Charismatic bar-owner David Podsnap keeps the energy high in this tiny space, bringing in acts from bluegrass string bands, to vintage dance companies, to comedy circus performers and most things in between. You can still catch vintage movies on the big screen behind the bar on nights when no performers are scheduled.

Festivals and Events

No town in America has been celebrating the **Fourth of July** longer than Bristol, a community that ushers in this patriotic holiday with nearly fanatical fervor—notice as you stroll up Hope Street that even the fire hydrants are painted red, white, and blue. Nobody takes the parade through town lightly, and true devotees have been known to stake out space along the route days before the big event.

In mid-July, Rhode Island's favorite shellfish is feted at the **Warren Quahog Festival** (Burrs' Hill Park, S. Water St., Warren, 401/410-0045), which features chowders, cakes, and stuffies as well as displays by the many artists who have taken up residence in town.

A newer annual festival is the **Warren Folks Festival,** (30 Cutler St., Warren, 401/903-0969, https://thecollaborative02885. org, free) which happens each year in early September. Hosted by local arts nonprofit The Collaborative, the event features the best of the area's folk an American musicians as well as arts vendors, food trucks, pop-up bars, and more.

SHOPPING
Bristol

Hope Street is lined with cute boutiques and craft stores. **Green River Silver** (297 Hope St., 401/253-5005, www.greenriversilver. com, 10am-6pm Mon.-Sat., noon-5pm Sun.) has hundreds of different styles of sterling silver jewelry. A stone's throw away in a striking yellow colonial house, **Alfred's Gifts and Antiques** (331 Hope St., 401/253-3465, 10am-5pm daily) is one of Bristol's shopping highlights. There are several showrooms with an extensive selection of expensive and low-priced items, including Christmas decorations and home accessories. Nearby, **Kate and Co.** (301 Hope St., 401/253-3117, 10:30am-6pm Mon.-Sat., 10am-5pm Sun.) is a similarly inviting boutique with gourmet foods, gifts, accessories, and clothing—a nice mix of goods with a country bent.

Warren

Downtown Warren is lined with antique stores catering to every possible taste. One of the more unique is **Water Street Antiques** (15 Church St., 401/245-6440, noon-4pm daily), which specializes in kitsch and retro lamps along with furniture that would seem at home in Josie and the Pussycats' pad. Another

favorite, **Space Cadets: Destination Vintage** (450 Main St., 401/338-8163, 11am-5pm Mon.-Thurs., 10am-6pm Fri., 10am-4pm Sun.) sells vintage clothes, records, furniture, toys and games, posters, deadhead treasures, art, and anything else the shop's lovable hippie owners can get their hands on. It's an easy place to lose track of time.

The nonprofit **IMAGO Foundation for the Arts** (36 Market St., 401/245-3348, www. imagofoundation4art.org, 4pm-8pm Thurs., noon-8pm Fri.-Sat., 11am-3pm Sun.) shows a wide variety of works by local craftspeople and artists. You'll find photography, paintings, textiles, jewelry, ceramics, sculpture, and more. A huge three-story gift emporium that occupies what had been the Warren Antique Center, **Imagine** (5 Miller St., 401/245-4200, www.giftimagine.com, 10am-5:30pm Mon.-Sat., 11:30am-5pm Sun.) keeps inveterate shoppers busy for hours with its extensive array of quirky goods. There's unusual clothing and bedroom slippers, artful handmade jewelry, whimsical housewares and kitchen items, and gourmet knickknacks.

Warren also has a great record store, **In Your Ear Records** (462 Main St., 401/245-9840, www.iye.com, 11am-6pm Mon.-Sat., 11am-5pm Sun.), specializing in used and new LPs, from blues and jazz to rock, indie, reggae, folk, and beyond. The staff here is super friendly and helpful—often they'll let you throw a record on their turntable and give it a listen before you buy it. They also sell original art, posters, CDs, DVDs, and other music-related goods.

SPORTS AND RECREATION

One of the state's loveliest preserves and recreation areas, **Colt State Park** (off Hope St., 401/253-7482, www.riparks.com, sunrise-sunset daily, free) is a rolling waterside tract of about 460 acres with bike and walking trails (including a stretch of the East Bay

1: In Your Ear Records on Main Street in Warren
2: a section of the East Bay Bike Path in Bristol

Bike Path), numerous playing fields, fruit trees and flower gardens, and six picnic groves containing more than 400 picnic tables as well as an adorable chapel-by-the-sea. Other facilities include a boat ramp, fishing areas, and grills, which require reservations and cost $4 per hour. There is no beach here, however, and swimming is not permitted.

TOP EXPERIENCE

★ East Bay Bike Path

The 14.5-mi (23.3-km) East Bay Bike Path is a flat, 10-foot-wide, scenic paved trail that hugs many sections of eastern Narragansett Bay from India Point Park in Providence to Colt State Park in Bristol. The path also welcomes joggers, strollers, in-line skaters, and anyone not using motorized vehicles. The path, which follows the former Penn Central rail bed, covers a tremendously varied landscape from undeveloped waterfront to the lively commercial districts of Warren and Bristol. You can picnic at several spots along the way, and at several points on or just off the path you'll encounter places to stock up on snacks, deli sandwiches, and drinks. Bicyclists should keep to the right, others to the left. Dogs are permitted but must be on a leash. The path also passes by the **Audubon Society of Rhode Island's Environmental Education Center** (1401 Hope St., Bristol, 401/245-7500, www.asri.org, 9am-5pm daily May-Sept., 9am-5pm Mon.-Sat., noon-5pm Sun. Oct.-Apr.), a nice place to ditch your bike for a minute and explore the grounds, or birdwatch in the marsh.

For any bike issues along the trail, you can stop at the small but friendly **Your Bike Shop** (51 Cole St., Warren, 401/245-9755, www.yourbikeshopri.com, noon-5pm Tues.-Sat.) located in Warren right off the bike path. The agile mechanics can fix a flat or other mechanical problem while you wait; the shop also sells maps and bike gear.

For rentals, check out **Narragansett Bikes** (414 Warren Ave., East Providence, 401/434-3838, www.nbxbikes.com, 10am-6pm Mon.-Fri., 10am-5pm Sat. noon-5pm Sun.). Rental rates run $35-50 for a full day.

The **Rhode Island Department of Transportation** (401/222-4203, ext. 4033, www.dot.ri.gov/community/bikeri) offers a great collection of bike maps available for download on its website. The site also has links to cycling organizations and lots of other useful information. Additionally, the RIPTA buses that traverse the state are equipped with bike racks; the rack on the front of each bus holds up to two bicycles, and there is no additional fee to use them.

Beaches

While none of these towns front the ocean, they offer some nice spots for sunbathing, swimming, and playing in the sun. You'll find the most popular of the region's expanses at **Bristol Town Beach** (Colt Dr., off Rte. 114, 401/253-7000, www.bristolri.us/parks), a sprawling complex that includes athletic fields and tennis and basketball courts, where the beach is long and attractive. The **Barrington Town Beach** (Bay Rd. 401/247-1925, www.barrington.ri.gov) has parking for residents only unless you arrive after 5pm, but it's also just a short detour from the East Bay Bike Path.

Fishing

There's great saltwater fishing in Mount Hope and Narragansett Bays and along the banks of the Warren and Sakonnet Rivers. Bluefish, snappers, scup, tautog, and flounder are among the most common catches. Fishing licenses can be obtained online at www.ri.gov/DEM/saltwater.

Golf

There is one decent public golf course in the East Bay. The **Windmill Hill Golf Course** (35 Schoolhouse Rd., Warren, 401/245-1463, www.windmillgolfri.com, 7am-1 hour before sunset daily, $15-25) has nine par-three holes ranging 118-220 yards. There's also a nice little restaurant open for breakfast, lunch, and early dinner daily.

Sailing, Boating, and the Outdoors

As one of the world's great sailing hubs, it's not surprising that Bristol has an excellent school for this leisurely summer activity. The **East Bay Sailing Foundation** (401/257-6774, www.eastbaysailingfoundation.org) offers adult and youth sailing training on several kinds of sailboats.

There are also public boat launches throughout the East Bay, including the Town Beach, off Bay Road in Barrington; Haines Memorial Park, off Narragansett Avenue in Barrington; by the commercial fishing pier, off Water Street in Warren; at Bristol Narrows, off Narrows Road in Mount Hope Bay, which is off Route 136 in Bristol; at Colt State Park in Bristol; and at the foot of State Street, off Route 114 in downtown Bristol. The latter two launches are the most popular and scenic, and they put right into Bristol Harbor, from which you have good access to Narragansett Bay, the Sakonnet River, and the ocean.

You'll also find public marine facilities with water, electricity, and other amenities at the following marinas: **Ginalski's Boat Yard** (14 Johnson St., Warren, 401/245-1940); **Stanley's Boat Yard** (17 Barton Ave., Barrington, 401/245-5090, www.stanleysboatyard.com); **Bristol Marine** (99 Poppasquash Rd., Bristol, 401/253-2200, www.bristolmarine.com); and **Striper Marina** (26 Tyler Point Rd., Barrington, 401/245-6121, www.stripermarina.com). Striper Marina also offers full-day and half-day sportfishing charters on seven vessels.

Bird-watchers, hikers, and outdoors enthusiasts take to the nature trails at the **Osamequin Wildlife Sanctuary** (Rte. 114, Barrington, sunrise-sunset daily).

FOOD

Considering the East Bay's small size and proximity to culinary powerhouses of Providence and Newport, the peninsula has a surprisingly varied and polished dining scene. You'll find some great seafood restaurants in Bristol, most of them downtown along or near Hope Street and the waterfront. In recent years, Warren's dining scene has stepped it up a notch with a handful of eclectic farm-to-table eateries cropping up in formerly empty storefronts. It's easy to find a great meal here without spending a bundle of cash, and without enduring the excessive wait times often encountered in Providence and Newport.

Seafood

A fixture overlooking Bristol Harbor since 1929, the **Lobster Pot** (119 Hope St., Bristol, 401/253-9100, www.lobsterpotri.com, 11:30am-9pm Mon.-Sat., noon-9pm Sun., $10-40) really must be experienced during daylight hours to be appreciated: Window-side tables put you directly on the water, and at dusk you can watch the sun slowly fall over the islands of Narragansett Bay. This is a spacious and somewhat dressy spot, though it is still casual, and service is excellent. The menu varies from fairly simple and light bites (lobster salad sandwiches, broiled scallops) to considerably more formal dinners—the usual surf-and-turf options, a decadently rich seafood casserole baked with butter and bread crumbs, and blackened swordfish. But the real pull is the fresh-caught lobsters, which are available in several sizes boiled, broiled, grilled, or baked and stuffed.

Housed in an historic 1857 brick building on Hope Street, **Bristol Oyster Bar** (448 Hope St., Bristol, 401/396-5820, www.bristoloysterbar.com, 4pm-10pm Mon.-Tues., noon-10pm Wed.-Sun., $9-22), is a light, airy space serving fresh oysters farmed right in the Narragansett Bay. The raw bar here is certainly the highlight—it serves shrimp, lobster, and littlenecks in addition to oysters—and the rest of the menu is simple but fresh and delicious. Recent dishes include seared sea scallops, with leek, fennel, and fava bean risotto and lemon herb gremolata, and pan-seared halibut with avocado, crab, fresh local sweet corn, crispy squash blossoms, and pistachio cream.

Another Bristol institution is **DeWolf Tavern,** (259 Thames St., 401/254-2005, www.dewolftavern.com, 11:30am-10:30pm Mon.-Fri., 8am 10:30pm Sat., 8am-9:30pm Sun., $13-34) which made its home in a renovated 1818 warehouse overlooking the bay back in 2004. The interior is truly beautiful and the menu includes favorite New England fare like stuffed lobster, steaks, and mussels.

American

At **Bywater** (54 State St., Warren, 401/694-0727, www.bywaterrestaurant.com, 5pm-10pm Mon.-Thurs., 5pm-midnight Fri.-Sat., $9-29), guests can enjoy the hip and modern vibe in the nautically inspired dining room and some new American cuisine from the kitchen. Start with the Cape Cod mussels steamed in coconut milk, ginger, and lemongrass, then try the mustard rubbed smoked pork chop with a cabbage ragout, herbed spaetzle, or the grilled striper with white beans and olive oil, charred local carrots, haricot verts, and citrus salad.

Another favorite in Warren is **The Square Peg** (51 Miller St., 401/215-3831, www.squarepegwarren.com, 11:30am-10pm Tues.-Sat., 11:30am-midnight Fri.-Sat., $12-27) a cute little corner restaurant serving creative takes on tacos, burgers, fish and chips, and salads. Expertly-made cocktails and a killer

house-made sangria make this spot that much more appealing.

Simple, local, and delicious food is the motto at ★ **Eli's Kitchen** (40 Market St. Warren, 401/245-1809, www.eliskitchen warren.com, lunch: 11am-4pm Wed.-Fri., dinner: 5pm-9pm Wed.-Thurs., 5pm-10pm Fri.-Sat., 4pm-9pm Sun., brunch: 9am-4pm Sat., 9am-2pm Sun., $7-16) a homey and inviting space with tinplate ceilings, and earthy, thoughtful decor. Small dishes include things like the Cubano Panini, with citrus and oregano braised pork and house-smoked ham, or the Chana Dal Burger, with mango chutney and pickled red onion. Larger plates include things like ricotta gnocchi made with local cheese and mushrooms, wilted kale, and parmigiano, or shrimp and grits with house-smoked ham, bacon, green peas, and fresh lemon. The menu is locally sourced, has plenty of vegetarian and vegan options, and an excellent menu for the kids. You will not find a better meal in the East Bay for these prices.

Comfort Food

A very true rendering of an Irish pub, **Aidan's** (5 John St., Bristol, 401/254-1940, www. aidanspub.com, 11:30am-10pm Mon.-Thurs., 11:30am-11pm Fri.-Sat., 11am-10pm Sun.,

Bywater restaurant in Warren

$6-14) makes a lovely diversion, whether killing time before boarding the ferry to Prudence Island, catching live music on a weekend evening, or hanging out over pints of stout and food like burgers, fish-and-chips, bangers and mash, and pot pies. Across the street from Rockwell Waterfront Park, Aidan's also has a nice outdoor deck overlooking the bay.

If you've never had a mac 'n' cheese burger or frickles (fried pickles), you might plan a stop at ★ **Chomp Kitchen and Drinks** (440 Child St., Warren, 401/289-2324, www.chompri.com, 4:30pm-9pm Tues.-Thurs., 11:30am-10pm Fri.-Sat., 11:30am-9pm Sun., $8-19), where indulgent and creative sandwiches got them named "Best Burger in America" by *Restaurant Hospitality Magazine* in 2015. An extensive craft beer and cocktail menu (try the Hot Guava Margarita with Luna Azul tequila, citrus, guava nectar, Ancho Reyes Chili liqueur, and salt) amps up the already delicious offerings here, like the mini stuffed quahogs with smoky pork, jalapeños, and pickled red onions or the Shumai Burger with kimchi, chili lime aioli, and crispy wontons.

Decent American and continental fare—lobster thermidor, broiled lamb chops—can be found at the **Wharf Tavern** (215 Water St., Warren, 401/245-5043, www.thewharftavernri.com, 11:30-9pm Sun.-Thurs., 11:30am-10pm Fri.-Sat., $10-38), most famous for its excellent view of the town's busy dock area and Narragansett Bay; it's especially nice at sunset. The pub-like dining area has varnished woods, maritime memorabilia, and oil lamps on each table, and there's live entertainment on weekend evenings.

Just about every kind of seafood comes deep fried at **Quito's** (411 Thames St., Bristol, 401/253-4500, www.quitosrestaurant.com, 11:30am-9pm Mon.-Sat., 11:30am-8pm Sun., $10-26), a family-owned restaurant that started out as a fish market in 1954. Situated right at the edge of Independence Park in downtown Bristol, Quito's is a tiny but attractive little building that sits right on the harbor. Seafood chowders, stews, and bisques, fried clam strips, and clam cakes are big sellers here. Steamed mussels, shrimp scampi, and lobster casseroles are popular as well.

Asian Fusion

Jackie's Galaxy (383 Metacom Ave., Bristol, 401/253-8818, 11:30am-10pm Mon.-Thurs., 11:30-am-10:30pm Fri.-Sat., noon-9:30pm Sun., $9-18) is a beloved small Rhode Island chain of restaurants serving Asian cuisine and sushi. The Bristol location features Szechuan-, Hunan-, and Hong Kong-style menus, as well as a classic sushi menu with standards like the Boston roll (salmon, cucumber, and lettuce), and spicy tekka tuna with avocado and spicy mayonnaise sauce. The interior here bears an unfortunate resemblance to a banquet hall with dizzying carpets and heavy striped drapes, but the food should make up for whatever the place lacks in ambience.

Cafés and Sandwich Shops

Break up a day spent cycling on the East Bay Bike path with refreshments at ★ **Beehive Café** (10 Franklin St., Bristol, 401/396-9994, www.thebeehivecafe.com, 7am-4pm Sun.-Wed., 7am-9pm Thurs.-Sat., $4-15), a cute café overlooking Independence Park and Bristol Harbor. Grab a table and chill out over smoothies, lattés, tea (the chai is terrific), freshly made croissants, and fantastic chocolate cookies, or pop in for dinner and try the pulled pork sandwich, the butternut squash sandwich, or the vegetable pot pie. Seating on the rooftop deck is optimal if you can get it. Lines at the counter tend to get quite long here but move quickly thanks to a friendly and efficient staff.

Just a block from the ferry to Prudence Island, **Leo's Ristorante** (365 Hope St., Bristol, 401/253-9300, www.leosristoranteri.com, 11am-8pm Sun.-Thurs., 11am-9pm Fri.-Sat., regular-size pies $12-23) opened in 1948 and is one of Bristol's favorite dining spots. The handsome old-fashioned storefront shop has high pressed-tin ceilings and ample sidewalk seating during the warmer months; it's a great spot for a light bite or a full meal after biking or strolling along Hope Street. Try the pizzas or sample or a meatball sub. Beer and wine are served as well.

Downtown Warren's ★ **Coffee Depot** (501 Main St., Warren, 401/608-2553, 6:30am-8:30pm Sat. and Mon.-Thurs., 6:30am-6pm daily, $3-9) is a fun spot with an artsy atmosphere and the best coffee in town. It's a nice place to people watch at one of the sidewalk tables over iced coffee in the summer, or lounge around playing board games or reading the paper on a rainy day. The extensive tea list, irresistible pastries and baked goods, and friendly staff are nice perks as well.

Empire Tea & Coffee (251 Thames St., Bristol, 401/618-1388, www.empireteaandcoffee. com, 6am-5pm daily, $2-$7) is an airy little coffee shop right on the harbor with a great selection of teas, excellent coffee, and fresh-made pastries like scones, muffins, and cookies. If you get there early enough, they may even have some egg sandwiches left.

Bristol Bagel Works (420 Hope St., Bristol, 401/254-1390, www.bristolbagelworks. com, 6:30am-2:30pm Mon.-Fri., 7am-2pm Sat.-Sun., $2-7) is another appealing spot for lunch or a snack break. It is a sunny little café with blond-wood tables and Windsor chairs where you can choose from a selection of about 15 kinds of bagels and spreads; traditional sandwiches are also offered.

ACCOMMODATIONS

You'll find a smattering of B&Bs in Bristol and Warren, but it's also easy to explore the East Bay as a day trip from Providence or Newport, where there are many more lodging options. Also, just across the Massachusetts border in Seekonk, Swansea, and Fall River, you'll find a full range of chain hotels and motels.

$150-250

In Bristol, **William's Grant Inn** (154 High St., Warren, 401/253-4222, www. williamsgrantinn.com, $159-200) is a family-owned bed-and-breakfast in an 1808 colonial home just two blocks from the waterfront and a short walk to downtown shops

and restaurants. Rooms are outfitted with Victorian decor, like four-poster beds, lace curtains, and flowery wallpaper. Sleek and modern they are not, but they're comfortable and homey, and the innkeepers provide a full breakfast to be enjoyed in the dining room or outside on the cute garden patio.

Bristol House Bed & Breakfast (14 Aaron Ave., Bristol, 401/396-9066, $109-239) is a cape-style B&B with comfortable rooms decorated with a nautical New England flare—the Harbor Room has starfish pillows and seashell wall art, and the Independence room has a star-spangled quilt. Complimentary gourmet breakfast is served in the light, airy dining room, and you can play a game of croquet in the backyard garden patio. There are only four rooms available here, so reservations will need to be made well in advance.

The East Bay's largest property, the 40-room **Bristol Harbor Inn** (259 Thames St., Bristol, 401/254-1444 or 866/254-1444, www. bristolharborinn.com, $129-289) was reconstructed along the scenic waterfront from a former bank and a rum distillery dating to about 1800. Guest rooms are simply decorated with rather unremarkable decor—but who needs wallpaper when you have a view of the harbor outside your window? Continental breakfast is served in the room where rum casks were once filled; wireless Internet is available throughout the hotel. On-site amenities include docking facilities, bike and boat rentals, and quick access to waterfront restaurants.

You can imagine yourself as lord of the manor at the ★ **Governor Bradford House** (250 Metacom Ave./Rte. 136, Bristol, 401/254-9300, www.mounthopefarm.com, $140-250). Situated on Mount Hope Farm, a 200-acre preserve of fields, ponds, and woodlands, the house was once owned by an early Rhode Island governor and later by Rudolf Haffenreffer of Narragansett Brewing Company fame. And, of course, George Washington stayed here in 1793 when he was an old man. The five guest rooms are decorated with a designer's eye with canary or lime-green walls and grand four-poster beds; some guest rooms have working fireplaces.

Bristol Guest Suites (649 Hope St., Bristol, 401/396-9560, www.bristolguestsuites. com, $100-195) are three well-kept apartments that are great options for either weekend or weeklong stays. The three are The Sailor's Loft, a 500-square-foot studio overlooking Bristol Harbor; The Garden Loft, a small but airy one-bedroom; and The Harbor Loft, a two-bedroom suite with harbor views as well. All have wireless Internet, queen beds plus a queen couch pullout, flat-screen televisions, and small but functional kitchen areas.

Over $250

Perhaps the East Bay's most lavish and luxurious accommodations, the **Point Pleasant Inn** (333 Poppasquash Rd., Bristol, 401/253-0627 or 800/503-0627, www.pointpleasantinn. com, $295-375) sits on Poppasquash Point overlooking the sailboats of Narragansett Bay. The six guest rooms are over-the-top elegant, veering toward the slightly gaudy, with rates to match. All have furnishings like leather chairs, four-poster beds, antique mahogany tables and dressers, and oil paintings. This 33-room mansion was built by a local business executive in 1940 and is run today like a small European-style hotel, with a staff that works hard to pamper guests. Facilities include an in-ground pool, free use of bikes, a tennis court, croquet, an exercise room, an outdoor hot tub, a sauna, a billiards room, and an area for fishing in the bay.

INFORMATION AND SERVICES
Visitor Information

Pamphlets, brochures, and visitor information are available from the **East Bay Chamber of Commerce** (16 Cutler St., P.O. Box 588, Warren, RI 02885, 401/245-0750 or 888/278-9948, www.eastbaychamberri.org), whose offices occupy the restored Cutler Mills in downtown Warren. The town of Bristol also has a helpful website (www.explorebristolri. com), with maps, directories, and event listings.

Media

East Bay Newspapers (401/253-6000, www.eastbayri.com) publishes a number of local papers, including the *Barrington Times*, *Warren Times-Gazette*, *Bristol Phoenix*, and the *Sakonnet Times* (covering Tiverton and Little Compton, Rhode Island). While they're geared toward locals, visitors will find useful information on the website, www. eastbayri.com.

A small glossy arts and entertainment magazine called *The Bay* (www.thebaymagazine. com) is also published monthly, and can be found for free in many of the area's restaurants and coffee shops.

GETTING THERE

Most visitors to the East Bay use a car to get around. Driving from Providence, it's a quick 12-mi (19.3-km), 20-minute trip down I-195 and Route 114 to Warren and 18 miles (29 km), 25 minutes, to Bristol. From Newport, it's a 15-mi (24-km), 25-minute journey to Bristol and 20 miles (32 km), 35 minutes, to Warren. The area is also accessible by the East Bay Bike Path, which stretches from the East Side of Providence straight through East Providence, Barrington, Warren, and Bristol, for a total distance of about 14 mi (22.5 km).

To reach the East Bay towns, you can also manage with **Rhode Island Transportation Authority (RIPTA) buses** (401/781-9400, www.ripta.com), which pass through the busy town centers of Bristol and Warren and connect with Newport, Providence, and other large towns in the region. Buses from Providence to Bristol take 30 minutes and stop at the corner of Hope and State Streets. Fares are a bargain at $2 regardless of the distance.

GETTING AROUND

Within the towns, the central districts are small enough that you can see many of the key attractions on foot or by bicycle. There's ample street parking in Barrington, Warren, and Bristol, and there are municipal lots in Warren and Bristol.

Sakonnet

Originally named Pocasset by the Seaconnet Native Americans who lived here before selling the land to the Plymouth Colony in 1680, Tiverton and Little Compton (to the south) make up the Sakonnet Peninsula. It is not a true peninsula, since it shares a land border with Massachusetts to the east, but the area is nevertheless physically cut off from the rest of Rhode Island except by way of the Sakonnet Bridge (Route 24/138).

Sakonnet is a quiet and picturesque corner of Rhode Island; both Tiverton and Little Compton are small and pastoral, with acres of flat farmland surrounded by trim stone walls and gray-shingled farmhouses. After exploring them both, it's interesting to consider that these two towns have a land area considerably larger than either Aquidneck Island (home to Newport, Portsmouth, and Middletown) or the East Bay towns of Barrington, Bristol, and Warren. Suburbia has been slowly creeping into both towns, especially the northern reaches of Tiverton, but the two communities still remain pleasingly rural. Little Compton has a large and close-knit summer community, many of the families having been regulars for generations. There are no miniature golf courses or amusements, however, just a handful of informal eateries, a yacht club, and a smattering of beach houses, most of them down quiet dirt lanes out of the public eye. Tourism isn't discouraged in these parts, but you won't find many places to stay or things to do, and that's just the way the locals and many visitors like it.

TIVERTON

Although Plymouth settlers bought the land that is now Tiverton in 1680, the town wasn't incorporated until 1694. No provisions for a church or school were made until 1746, shortly before the area, along with its East Bay neighbors to the north, were transferred to the Rhode Island colony.

During the Revolutionary War, however, the town's high bluffs overlooking the Sakonnet River and Aquidneck Island had tremendous strategic importance. From the town's shores, the Continental Army launched

an antique shop at Historic Tiverton Four Corners

several raids on the British, who had settled comfortably in Newport and elsewhere on Aquidneck Island. Aside from the war, for its first 300 years Tiverton maintained a mostly agricultural existence, with a smaller but still significant fishing industry.

Attractions are few, but shoppers will want to congregate around **Historic Tiverton Four Corners** (www.tivertonfourcorners.com), a village of mostly 18th-century houses full of boutiques, galleries, and cafés. It's at the junction of Routes 77 and 179, a few miles south of Route 24, the main road through the peninsula. Beachcombers should wander along **Grinnell's Beach** (Rte. 77), a narrow spit of sand where an old stone bridge used to cross the Sakonnet River before the towering Sakonnet Bridge replaced it. It's a scenic place to admire the river.

LITTLE COMPTON

Once the domain of the Seaconnet Native Americans, who were ruled in the late 1680s by a female chieftain named Awashonks, **Little Compton** holds a special place in the hearts of Rhode Islanders, many of whom have dear memories of summer bike rides, country drives, and campfires on the beach. The town's history as a summer resort predates even the Civil War, making it one of New England's oldest retreats. Like Tiverton, it has also drawn heavily on fishing and agriculture to support itself. You can reach it most easily and scenically by driving south from Tiverton either on Route 77, on the west side of town, or Route 81, on the east side.

As you explore the west side of Little Compton by car or by bike, you can enjoy great views of the Sakonnet River and the many historic homes along Route 77. On your left, not long after crossing from Tiverton into Little Compton, you'll reach the **Wilbor House** (Rte. 77, 401/635-4035, tours 2pm-5pm Wed.-Sun. mid-June-mid-Sept., free), a lovely old clapboard farmhouse with several restored outbuildings. Parts of the house date to the 1690s, but it has been added onto several

times through the centuries. You can also picnic on the grounds.

★ Carolyn's Sakonnet Vineyard

Still farther south along Route 77, **Carolyn's Sakonnet Vineyards** (162 W. Main St., Rte. 77, Little Compton, 800/919-4637, www.sakonnetwine.com, 11am-6pm Sun.-Fri. 11am-7pm Sat.) has transcended New England's reputation for lackluster grapes to produce some exceptionally fine wines. Back when wine was a mostly West Coast phenomenon, Susan and Earl Samson rolled the dice in Rhode Island, where they surmised the cool microclimate could support vines similar to those in France's Loire Valley. Founded in 1975, the vineyard has since been a smashing success—one of the first in New England and still among the best. Acres of grapevines produce several wines from the winery's signature vidal blanc grape, a French-American hybrid with floral aromas and fresh acidity. Also notable is the aromatic gewürztraminer. Sakonnet produces about 30,000 cases of wine each year, proving that it's far more than a boutique winery. Along with over 50 acres of scenic vineyards, the winery features tours, tastings, and special events. In 2012, jewelry manufacturing magnate Carolyn Rafaelian (founder of Alex and Ani) purchased the vineyard and sullied some of its charm by tacking her first name onto the title. Fortunately, no amount of hubris can spoil the vineyard's exceptional beauty, The tasting room and expansive front lawn seating area here overlook the vineyard and the Sakonnet River just beyond.

Continuing South

South of Sakonnet Vineyards down Route 77, make a left on Meeting House Lane; at the end of this short road you'll come to **The Common,** perhaps the most enchanting little town green in Rhode Island. Almost entirely without commercial enterprise, the grassy plot stretches out beneath the towering spire of the United Congregational Church, most

of it covered with gravestones, some of which date to the 1600s. Across from the church you'll find the legendary town commissary, The Commons Lunch.

For even more quaint scenery, at the far end of the peninsula on Sakonnet Point is a collection of pleasingly ramshackle fishing villages with a strand of sandy beach just past the Sakonnet Yacht Club. Each summer the small harbor fills with sailboats and yachts; sunbathers crowd the local beach, but this vacation community remains sleepy and laid back, looking much as it probably did a century ago. Some 600 yards offshore on an iron pier, **Sakonnet Point Light** (www.lighthouse.cc/sakonnet) is a majestic 66-foot-tall cylindrical tower still lit at night.

Adamsville

East of The Common is an even more backwater part of the peninsula named **Adamsville**. A brass plaque erected in 1925 sits at the center of the village, commemorating the Rhode Island Red, a type of chicken that was developed in Adamsville and revolutionized chicken farming, as it was the first to both lay eggs and provide meat.

On Main Street you'll find the 1788 **Gray's Store** (4 Main St., Adamsville, 401/635-4566, 6:30am-8pm daily), reputedly the oldest continuously operating store in the United States, until it closed in 2012 (it opened back up again in 2013). It still has the original soda fountain and penny-candy case along with a mini-museum of historical ephemera. A little farther east along Main Street (Route 179), just before the state border marker for Westport, Massachusetts, you'll pass a quirky old shop on your right called **Gray's Gristmill** (508/636-6075, www.graysgristmill.com, noon-4pm Tues.-Sun.). Here you can buy authentic Gray's Old-Fashioned Rhode Island Johnny Cake Corn Meal as well as gifts, homemade jams, a few odd furnishings, and

inexpensive bric-a-brac ranging from junk to some neat little finds.

To get to Adamsville from Little Compton Common, continue east along Simmons Road, make a left on East Main Street, and follow it north as it jogs up to Peckham Road. Make a fast right and then a left again onto Long Highway, make another quick right onto Colebrook Road, and follow it into Adamsville.

SHOPPING

In Tiverton, you'll find several fine shops and art galleries at **Historic Tiverton Four Corners** (Rtes. 77 and 179, Tiverton, www.tivertonfourcorners.com), most of them inside the restored 18th- and 19th-century houses of the village's original residents. Among the highlights is the **Metal Works** (3940 Main Rd., Tiverton, 401/624-4400, www.themetalworkscorp.com, 8am-4:30pm Mon.-Fri.), which specializes in antique lanterns but can also custom create all kinds of home furnishings and arts. At **Peter's Attic** (8 Puncatest Neck Rd., 401/625-5912, 11am-5pm Thurs.-Sat., noon-5pm Sun.), you'll find three floors of fine country and colonial antiques. **Salt** (3845 Main Road, 401/816-0901, 10am-5pm Mon.-Sat.) carries casual and hip clothes, jewelry, handbags, and gifts, while **Cutie Curls** (3852 Main Rd., 401/837-0777, 10am-3pm Thurs.-Fri., 10am-5pm Sat., noon-5pm Sun.) sells upscale consignment clothes for children.

In Little Compton, **Wilbur's General Store** (50 The Commons, Little Compton, 401/635-2356, 7am-6pm Mon.-Sat., 7am-5pm Sun.) is a reminder of life before Home Depot and Walmart: a small shop stuffed with groceries, housewares, beach pails, hardware, and a deli counter with gourmet food.

Just southwest of Adamsville Center, the **Old Stone Orchard** (33 Cold Brook Rd., Little Compton, 401/635-2663, 10am-5pm Thurs.-Sun. fall only) has pumpkins, apples, and similar fall fare.

1: grapevines at Carolyn's Sakonnet Vineyard **2:** sailboats at Sakonnet Point **3:** a roadside stand in Little Compton in fall

END

SPORTS AND RECREATION

There aren't many formal venues for recreation in this region, but it's a wonderful place for many kinds of activities, especially on-road bicycling. The terrain is relatively flat, and excellent views of the sea and rolling meadows are to be had in both towns, especially Little Compton.

You'll find great birding and hiking, as well as beachcombing, down at the southeastern tip of Little Compton at **Goosewing Beach Preserve** (off South Shore Rd., Little Compton, 401/331-7110, www.nature.org). There's a beach parking fee of $15 a day during the week and $20 per day on weekends Memorial Day through Labor Day; at other times it's free. The Nature Conservancy oversees this pristine barrier beach and neighboring Quicksand Pond, and guided nature walks are given throughout the summer.

Fishing enthusiasts will find great opportunities for saltwater fishing from **Grinnell's Beach,** by the old Stone Bridge site off Route 77 in Tiverton, and also a bit farther south at Sapowet Point.

Hiking

In Tiverton, the **Emilie Ruecker Wildlife Refuge** (116 Seapowet Ave., Tiverton, 401/949-5454, www.asri.org) has some 50 acres of marsh environment crisscrossed by trails. Bird-watching blinds offer a chance to see snowy egrets, glossy ibis, and a breeding pair of ospreys.

Northwest of the Common in Little Compton on the way to Adamsville, you'll pass the turnoff for **Simmons Park,** a 400-acre plot laced with trails, shrub wetlands, a red maple swamp, and oak and American beech woodland. Here you can spot cottontail rabbits, foxes, mink, wood and mallard ducks, ospreys, and owls. Wild turkeys were released here in recent years and have become somewhat common. Note that this is also the town hunting grounds; all visitors *must* wear fluorescent orange when walking through the preserve during hunting season (Oct.-Feb.).

Beaches

★ **GOOSEWING BEACH AND NATURE PRESERVE**

The 75-acre **Goosewing Beach and Nature Preserve** (also called South Shore Beach) (125 South Shore Rd., 401/331-7110, www.nature. org) is an historic landmark and a favorite spot among Rhode Islanders who appreciate its out-of-the-way location and its relative lack of tourists, beach traffic, or commercial enterprise. Purchased by the Nature Conservancy in 1989 in an effort to preserve the endangered populations of Piping Plover and Least Terns that nest here, the beach has since opened the doors of a small environmental education center (accessible by crossing over the beach from the parking lot) offering seasonal nature walks and events. This spectacular expanse of sandy barrier beach narrowly divides the sea from a series of pristine coastal ponds. There are limited camping spots available, on-duty lifeguards, and restrooms during daytime hours, and, unlike many of Rhode Island's state beaches, campfires are permitted on the shore. Goosewing is also a favorite surf spot with locals; it's a nice sandy beach break with minimal rocks. There's a parking fee of $15 a day during the week and $20 per day on weekends Memorial Day through Labor Day; at other times it's free.

The Sakonnet Peninsula has a number of attractive beaches with considerably smaller crowds than those in nearby Newport. **Grinnell's Beach** (Main Rd. at Old Stone Bridge) is a sandy crescent at the head of the Sakonnet River and is popular with surf fishers; it has a lifeguard, changing rooms, and restrooms.

FOOD

Although not as limited in dining possibilities as in places to stay, Sakonnet has but a few eateries. Quality and quirky ambience are hallmarks of dining in these parts—the restaurants are generally quite good and in some cases worth a trip from anywhere in the state.

American

Situated on the shore of the Mount Hope Bay, Boat House (227 Schooner Dr., Tiverton, 401/624-6300, www.boathousetiverton.com, 11:30am-9pm Mon.-Thurs., 11:30am-10pm Fri.-Sat., 11am-9pm Sun., $14-39) offers waterfront dining in a cozy atmosphere that caters to a polo-shirt-and-boat-shoe-wearing crowd. Dishes like pan-seared yellowfin tuna with fennel piperade, Maine soldier beans, and kalamata tapenade are mouthwatering (and expensive). Boat House is owned by the Newport Restaurant Group, owners of Rhode Island staples Hemenways and the Castle Hill Inn among others. The food here will no doubt be delicious, even if the ambience is slightly corporate and stiff.

The top pick in this area when it comes to special occasions, ★ Four Corners Grille (3841 Main Rd., Tiverton, 401/624-1510, www.4cornersgrille.com/home, 11am-9pm Mon.-Fri., 11am-9pm Fri., 8am-9pm Sat.-Sun., $6-17) is nothing fancy on the outside, but this neighborhood spot with cozy wooden booths, warm lighting, down-to-earth service, and limited parking excels in the food department, presenting a consistently excellent menu of regional American and Italian dishes at fair prices. In season, try the softshell crab scampi. Other treats include shrimp Mozambique, herb-crusted grilled scrod with Maryland-style creole crab cakes, several kinds of burgers, tuna-steak sandwiches, and seafood bisques.

At Crowther's (90 Pottersville Rd., Little Compton, 401/635-8367, www.crowrest.com, 4pm-midnight, Mon.-Thurs. noon-midnight Fri.-Sun., $6-17) the warm, wood-planked dining room and small-town vibe complement an unpretentious but very appealing menu. Regionally inspired entrées like Portuguese littlenecks sautéed with chourico and white wine punctuate a menu that is

otherwise heavy with hearty and traditional American fare—think meatloaf, chicken Parmesan, and homemade blueberry pie. This is one of the few spots in the area where you can enjoy decent draft beer and creative cocktails late into the evening—if you feel so inclined.

Comfort Food

★ Gray's Ice Cream (16 East Rd., Tiverton, 401/624-4500, www.graysicecream.com, 6:30am-9pm daily summer, call for winter hours) occupies a low-slung shingle building at Tiverton Four Corners. Since 1923 it has been making fans of frozen sweets happy with such homemade flavors as blueberry, coconut, maple walnut, peach brandy, and ginger. Swarms of devotees check in regularly to order their favorites and try out the new flavors added each season.

Near the Sakonnet River and overlooking Nanaquaket Pond, Evelyn's Drive-In (2335 Main Rd., Rte. 77, Tiverton, 401/624-3100, www.evelynsdrivein.com, 11:30am-8pm daily, $2-15) delivers a somewhat more substantial variety of short-order goodies, from grilled tuna and swordfish to the usual lobster rolls, fried oysters, and chowders. It's perfect after an outing at the beach.

One of the Ocean State's great culinary institutions, ★ The Commons Lunch (48 Commons, Little Compton, 401/635-4388, 6am-3pm Mon.-Wed., 6am-8pm Thurs.-Sat., $2-10) boasts an epic menu of diner-esque favorites, including massive but thin—almost crepe-like—johnnycakes. Breakfast is served all day, but the lunch menu includes seafood rolls, quahog chowder, and even old-timer favorites like liverwurst sandwiches. Few desserts hit the spot better than the strawberry ice cream with freshly made strawberry sauce. This endearing little restaurant is named for the town common, which it faces.

The Barn (15 Main Rd., Adamsville, 401/635-2985, 7am-noon Mon.-Sat., 7am-1pm Sun., $3-10) occupies an elegantly weathered 200-year-old clapboard barn. It's all about

breakfast here—the place closes at noon on weekdays and 1pm on weekends. More than a few foodies claim The Barn serves the best breakfasts in Rhode Island, and the lines on summer weekends are maddeningly long. A specialty is Eggs on the Bayou, poached eggs on English muffins with crab cakes and creole hollandaise sauce. If you have a sweet tooth, you can dig into raspberry-filled French toast with crème anglaise, toasted almonds, and fresh berries. Be sure to order a side of ostrich sausage.

Cafés and Sandwich Shops

The best coffee in the Sakonnet area can be found at ★ **Coastal Roasters** (1791 Main Rd., Tiverton 401/624-2343, 6:30am-5pm daily, $2-6), situated on the Sakonnet River right on Route 77. It also has smoothies, espresso, tea, and baked goods, and it's a convenient stop on the way to the beach. It's a tiny little roadside place—the interior has only a couple of tables but there's nice outdoor seating overlooking the water.

Provender (3883 Main Rd., 401/624-8084, www.provenderfinefoods.com, 9am-5pm Tues.-Sun. during summer, call for winter hours, $3-9) occupies the ground floor of a very cool three-story Second Empire house crowned with a tall, square cupola. There are long, wooden benches on the wraparound porch, which is a lovely place to sit in the shade and enjoy the imaginative, high-quality sandwiches and sweets, tea, coffee, and other refreshments. The Provender also has fresh picnic supplies and a nice choice of goods for a bike ride, as well as olive oil, fancy relishes, and sauces.

ACCOMMODATIONS

Your options for spending the night, short of befriending a resident, are greatly limited in Tiverton and Little Compton. You'll find just two inns, both in Little Compton, and a few bed-and-breakfasts. Still, it's a short and easy drive to Sakonnet from Newport, Bristol, and Fall River, Massachusetts, all of which have ample lodging choices.

One dependable option in Little Compton is **Harmony Home Farm Bed & Breakfast** (465 Long Hwy., Little Compton, 401/635-2283, www.harmonyhomefarm.com, $130-175), where the rooms and cottages either have their own entrances and private porches or come with fully equipped kitchens.

The newly reopened **Stone House Inn** (122 Sakonnet Pt. Rd., Little Compton, 401/635-2222, www.newportexperience.com/stonehouse, $235-350) is located almost at the end of Sakonnet Point in an historic 1854 building overlooking a salt pond just steps away from the Atlantic. Guest rooms are luxurious, with state-of-the-art tubs, ocean views, balconies, and beautifully restored interiors. The property has 14 such suites, beach access, and an outdoor fire pit for guests to enjoy. It's definitely the best bet in the area, if you can afford it.

INFORMATION AND SERVICES
Visitor Information

There's no formal visitors center on the Sakonnet Peninsula. For pamphlets, brochures, and visitor information, your best bet is the **Newport County Convention and Visitor's Bureau** (23 America's Cup Ave., Newport, 800/976-5122, www.discovernewport.org).

GETTING AROUND

As in the East Bay towns, a car is the only viable way to get around Sakonnet. These are quiet little towns where parking is easy to find, usually off the street, except in summer by the beach in Little Compton.

1: Goosewing Beach and Nature Preserve in Little Compton **2:** Provender, a bakery and sandwich shop at Tiverton Four Corners

South County

Misleading though it may be, South County is not actually a county. Rather, locals use this name lovingly to refer to a coastal area of southern Rhode Island (much of which is technically in the domain of Washington County).

Starting from Westerly, at the far southwest corner of the state, the Atlantic coast traces the towns of Charlestown, South Kingstown, and Narragansett, where it turns sharply north, separating North Kingstown from the Narragansett Bay. Known for its long, sandy coastlines and sleepy back-road landscapes, South County offers first-rate beaches, fresh-caught seafood, lots of low-key motels and inns, and in the summer months, some of the most authentically Rhode Island

Highlights

Look for ★ to find recommended sights, activities, dining, and lodging.

★ **Wickford Village:** The charming waterfront village of Wickford contains about 40 boutiques, most of them independent, including fine-art galleries, gourmet food shops, and clothing stores (page 192).

★ **Gilbert Stuart Museum:** For a glimpse into the life of colonial America's foremost portraitist, visit this estate of Gilbert Stuart, whose depiction of George Washington graces the dollar bill. Its scenic grounds and gardens here are part of the draw (page 192).

★ **Narragansett Town Beach:** With its bikini-clad surfers and iconic view of The Towers, this roughly 19-acre stretch of sandy coastline is classic New England (page 193).

★ **The Fantastic Umbrella Factory:** This outgrowth of a 1960s hippie community now serves as an eclectic compound of funky stores in clapboard buildings, with a petting zoo, a café, greenhouses, and a bamboo forest (page 197).

★ **Misquamicut Beach:** This family getaway is chock-full of miniature golf courses, ice-cream stands, seafood shacks, and relatively affordable motels and beach cottages (page 199).

South County

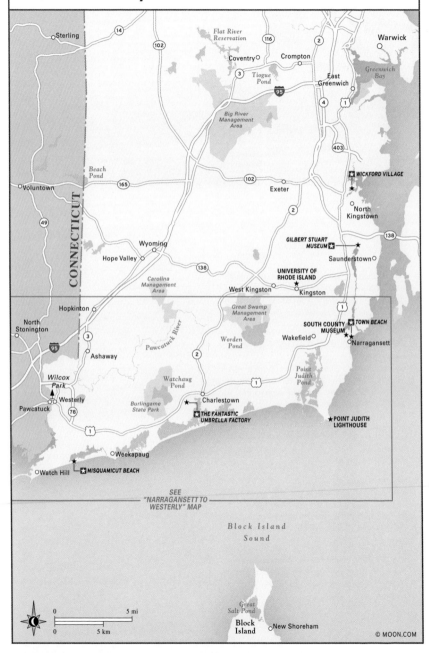

Sterling
14
102
Flat River Reservation
116
2
Warwick
Coventry
Crompton
3
Tiogue Pond
East Greenwich
Greenwich Bay
95
4
1
Big River Management Area
403
WICKFORD VILLAGE
Beach Pond
165
102
Exeter
North Kingstown
Voluntown
49
2
CONNECTICUT
GILBERT STUART MUSEUM
138
Wyoming
Hope Valley
138
Saunderstown
Carolina Management Area
UNIVERSITY OF RHODE ISLAND
West Kingston
Kingston
1
Hopkinton
Great Swamp Management Area
SOUTH COUNTY MUSEUM
TOWN BEACH
North Stonington
95
3
Pawcatuck River
Worden Pond
Wakefield
Narragansett
Ashaway
2
Point Judith Pond
Watchaug Pond
1
Wilcox Park
Burlingame State Park
Charlestown
Pawcatuck
78
Westerly
THE FANTASTIC UMBRELLA FACTORY
POINT JUDITH LIGHTHOUSE
1
Weekapaug
Watch Hill
MISQUAMICUT BEACH

SEE "NARRAGANSETT TO WESTERLY" MAP

Block Island Sound

0   5 mi
0   5 km

Great Salt Pond
Block Island
New Shoreham

© MOON.COM

experiences a person can have. If you've never rolled up your pants and gone quahogging, spent an afternoon sipping Narragansett tall boys at the Ocean Mist, or dipped a deep-fried clam cake into a bowl of steaming "chowda," now's your chance.

South County is, for the most part, happily old-fashioned and uncluttered by strip-mall excess. High-rise hotels and massive condo communities are scarce or nonexistent, and where high-density beach housing has been allowed, it's mostly tasteful and unflashy in the traditional New England style.

Watch Hill, in Westerly, looks like the set of an old movie, with its dainty harbor and small shopping district. Up the coast on Narragansett Bay, in North Kingstown, the village of Wickford is one of the best-preserved colonial villages of its size anywhere in the region, and nearby Kingston is dominated by the many stately old granite buildings of the University of Rhode Island.

Punctuating the shoreline are vast tracts of protected wilderness preserves and sheltered saltwater ponds in Charlestown and Westerly, while further inland, the towns of Exeter, Hopkinton, and Richmond offer nature preserves, hiking trails, and winding drives through farmland and small historic villages.

PLANNING YOUR TIME

Because South County is one of Rhode Island's most family-oriented destinations, and also a great area for hiking, sunbathing, sailing, surfing, and the like, you might want to make this your base if you're traveling with kids or pursuing outdoor recreational activities. Watch Hill, with its carousel, bumper cars, and mini golf, is a particularly nice beach for the kids, while older kids and teens will prefer the action at Misquamicut Beach, as will young adults and couples. Many visitors to this part of the state, especially in summer, rent cottages or efficiencies for a week or more. From South County, you can easily explore other parts of the state on day trips or overnighters.

Otherwise, South County is probably a part of the state that you can enjoy in a relatively short period, especially in the winter. You'll find a smattering of sophisticated restaurants and shops in the area, especially in the towns of Wickford and Narragansett, and there are some historic attractions in the South County Museum and Gilbert Stuart Museum, but the best of what the area has to offer is located outdoors. If beachcombing, hiking, fishing, and swimming aren't your thing, you're probably better off spending your time in Providence, Newport, and even the East Bay.

Sights

NORTH KINGSTOWN

North Kingstown was once home to many thriving farms, many of which are still in operation or have now become museums. A highlight of the area is Wickford, a cute little village situated around a cove in the Narragansett Bay. Just minutes east of busy U.S. 1, Wickford has lots of beautifully preserved colonial houses from the 18th and 19th centuries, all pleasantly weathered and peeling. Many boutiques and galleries have taken up shop here as well, making this a nice place to wander around for an afternoon.

Just north of Wickford, don't expect to see battlements at **Smith's Castle** (55 Richard Smith Dr., off U.S. 1, just north of Wickford, 401/294-3521, www.smithscastle.org, noon-4pm Thurs.-Mon. June-Aug., noon-4pm Fri.-Sun. May and Sept.-Oct., or by appointment, grounds free, house $10 adults, $5 children

Previous: Watch Hill Lighthouse; the Gilbert Stuart Museum in North Kingstown; evening at Narragansett Town Beach.

6-12, free for children under 6). In fact, the neatly restored mansion is the oldest surviving plantation house in the country. Its fascinating history mirrors the checkered history of Rhode Island; during the state's slave-trading heyday in the early 18th century, this manor was a slave-holding plantation, producing tobacco, grains, apples, and vegetables as well as sheep, cattle, and pigs. After slavery was outlawed, the plantation lay dormant for a century before functioning again as a small dairy in the early 20th century. Guided tours of the house given by historical interpreters in period clothing are available throughout the summer months, and you can walk the grounds year-round, admiring the cove that looks across to Queens Island and strolling through the lush gardens.

★ Wickford Village

Almost nothing about Wickford suggests the last half-century, except perhaps the occasional jet rushing overhead from nearby T. F. Green Airport. It seems like a movie set depicting a time many decades ago, and, indeed, the town inspired the setting for John Updike's novel *The Witches of Eastwick*. Follow Main Street from the village's commercial district out to the town pier on Wickford Harbor, which opens to Narragansett Bay. Here you can walk alongside stacks of lobster traps, listen to the squawk of aggressive seagulls, breathe in the briny air, and look back over the dozens of masts in the harbor toward town.

★ Gilbert Stuart Museum

Open up your wallet and chances are you'll find an example of the work of Gilbert Stuart, best known for his portrait of George Washington that graces the dollar bill. Stuart's life and work are encapsulated at the **Gilbert Stuart Birthplace and Museum** (815 Gilbert Stuart Rd., Saunderstown, 401/294-3001, www.gilbertstuartmuseum.com, 10am-4pm Thurs.-Mon., May-June and Sept.-Oct., 10am-4pm daily July-Aug., $12 adults, $6 children 6-12, free for children under 6), centered

Lay of the Land: South County Villages

To an out-of-towner, it may seem like South County delights in confusing travelers, as each of the major towns is divided into several villages with obscure Native American names or maddeningly similar sobriquets. A quick guide, then:

- **North Kingstown** contains the villages of Quonset Point, Saunderstown, and Wickford.

- **Narragansett** includes Galilee and Point Judith.

- **South Kingstown** encompasses Jerusalem, Kenyon, Kingston, Matunuck, Peace Dale, Wakefield, and West Kingston.

- **Charlestown** includes Cross Mills and Quonochontaug; and **Westerly** contains Avondale, Misquamicut, Watch Hill, and Weekapaug.

around the red gambrel-roofed colonial house where Stuart was born on December 3, 1755. He lived in the house only until he was seven, at which time his family moved to Newport; soon after, people began to notice his prowess as a painter.

The house has been preserved as it functioned both as a home and a small colonial factory of sorts. Each room contains a corner fireplace, and many of the original woodworking and construction details are still intact, from the wooden door latches to the hand-blown windowpanes. Reproductions of Stuart's works hang throughout the house. In the common room you'll see a display of colonial cooking utensils and tools. Costumed docents are often on hand to demonstrate colonial activities, such as fulling wool and grinding meal.

The house occupies scenic grounds near a pond and a stream; on the grounds is the restored gristmill in which two massive grinding stones made the cornmeal used in johnnycakes. There is an herb garden where plants commonly used in colonial times are grown, and a children's activity garden with educational and interactive outdoor exhibits.

Saunderstown

South of Wickford on Route 1A is the village of Saunderstown. Here you'll find **Casey Farm** (2325 Boston Neck Rd./Rte. 1A, 401/295-1030, www.historicnewengland. org, 1pm-4pm Tues. & Thurs., 9am-1pm Sat. June-mid-Oct., $6 adults, $5 seniors, $3 students), which dates to 1750 and has beautiful ocean vistas over Narragansett Bay; it was also the site of several small battles during the Revolutionary War. Today this 300-acre working farm is a rare parcel that preserves the agrarian ways of colonial times in coastal New England. Hiking trails lace the property. Special events throughout the summer and fall include hayrides, farmers markets, and demonstrations.

NARRAGANSETT

Wedged between Charlestown and the bay that bears its name, this small community is the easternmost of South County's coastal resorts—it runs along the southeastern tip of the oceanfront and then up the western side of Narragansett Bay. The northern section of town, along the bay, is called Narragansett Pier. Sandy beaches line the shore along with large and stately summer homes, cottages, and smaller residences. Other than the fishing and boating business down at Galilee and Point Judith, Narragansett is very much a tourist town due to its exceptional beaches (namely Town Beach, Salty Brine, Scarborough, and Roger Wheeler), although plenty of folks also live and work here, or commute to Providence, just 30 mi (48 km) north.

South County Museum

Located on the estate of a former state governor, the **South County Museum** (Strathmore St., off Rte. 1A, 401/783-5400, www.southcountymuseum.org, 10am-4pm Tues.-Sat., July-Aug., 10am-4pm Fri.-Sat., May-June and Sept., $12 adults, $10 seniors, $5 children 6-12, free for children under 6) offers an engaging and useful overview of a gentleman's farm, a carpenter's shop, a blacksmith shop, a general store, a one-room schoolhouse, and many other historic venues that you might find in colonial and then Victorian coastal Rhode Island—you'll find more than 20,000 period artifacts and implements spread among these exhibits. The museum organizes dozens of events, including apple-pie-eating contests, fall harvest fairs, Victorian teas, and quilt shows. Displays here are geared largely to kids and families and include an exhibit on the railroads of South County. Many rotating exhibits are also shown. The museum sits on 175-acre Canonchet Farm, which dates to the 18th century and was once the home of Rhode Island governor William Sprague.

Narragansett Pier

Ocean Road then becomes Route 108 and turns north following the shore. This 5-mi (8-km) road passes Scarborough State Beach and some very posh residential neighborhoods near the ocean before entering the village of Narragansett Pier, which came into its own as a Victorian resort where wealthy vacationers arrived in droves by steamship and train. Until it burned down in 1900, the draw of the neighborhood was the Narragansett Casino Resort, still famous as the location where the popular clams casino dish was invented. Only the majestic arch of **The Towers** (35 Ocean Rd., 401/782-2597, www.thetowersri. com, tours by appointment, free) survives in all of its late-19th-century elegance. Now the building hosts a small museum with old photographs as well as lectures, dances, and live music. Numerous beach cottages and quite a few shops and restaurants also line the streets of Narragansett Pier. Watching tourists, beachgoers, and surfers from the seawall is a favorite summer pastime.

★ Narragansett Town Beach

At the center of Narragansett Pier is

Narragansett Town Beach, (39 Boston Neck Rd., www.narragansettri.gov, 401/783-6430), at which you can enjoy nearly 19 acres of sandy waterfront and some of the best swimming and surfing in the state, or simply sit and soak up the sun and admire the view of The Towers in the distance. This is a broad beach with shallow bathing, a pavilion with showers and a snack bar, and plenty of parking. Surfing lessons and board rentals are available onsite most days in the summer ($30-60), but if you're not inclined to ride the waves, it's fun enough just to be a spectator. From Memorial Day through Labor Day, parking costs $10 per day during the week and $15 on the weekends, but be warned: You'll also be charged an additional fee of $10 just to walk on to the beach. If you're lucky enough to find a spot, you can also park on Ocean Road at the southern end of the beach.

Galilee and Point Judith

South of U.S. 1, Point Judith Road (Route 108) runs 4 mi (6.4 km) to the turnoff for Galilee, a bustling port opposite Jerusalem. This whole area is more generally part of Point Judith, which is a tiny community in terms of population; it ranks fifth, however, on the East Coast and a formidable 17th in the nation among fishing ports, producing annual fishing revenues of $37 million. Approximately 250 boats call Point Judith home. You'll also find many of the area's summer homes, plus superb clam shacks, charter fishing operations, and some of the state's top beaches. From here you can book whale-watching tours ($35-48) and other excursion boats, and this is also where you catch the ferry to Block Island, which runs year-round from Point Judith ($23.75 round-trip).

Back out on Route 108, the road leads a bit farther south, eventually ending at the **Point Judith Lighthouse** (www.newenglandlighthouses.net/point-judith).

1: Point Judith Lighthouse 2: flower gardens at The Fantastic Umbrella Factory 3: the Gilbert Stuart Birthplace and Museum

Fans of lighthouses should explore the grounds of the 1857 structure, a 51-foot octagonal tower that is the third incarnation to be built on this spot; the original Point Judith Lighthouse went up about a half-century earlier. The current lighthouse, which underwent a major restoration in 2000, is not open to the public.

SOUTH KINGSTOWN

In keeping with Rhode Island's confusing place names, South Kingstown lies about 6 mi (9.7 km) south of North Kingstown and includes the village of Kingston (not to be confused with Kingstown) and Wakefield (not to be confused with Wickford). Get a bird's-eye view of the territory at the **Wooden Observation Tower** (3481 Kingstown Rd., U.S. 1 and Rte. 138, dawn-dusk, free). The 100-foot-tall tower with an open-air observation deck sits on one of the county's higher points, MacSparran Hill, and affords stunning views of Narragansett Bay, Conanicut and Aquidneck Islands (and the bridges that connect them), and the South County shoreline.

University of Rhode Island

West on Route 138, the county seat **Kingston** was formerly known as Little Rest, some say because during colonial times it was home to several taverns providing room and board. It's one of the state's better-known towns today because it's home to the **University of Rhode Island** (URI, www.uri.edu), founded in 1892 as Rhode Island College of Agriculture and Mechanic Arts. URI has a student body of about 13,000 undergrads and 2,000 graduate students. One notable facility on the campus is the **Thomas M. Ryan Center,** a 200,000-square-foot athletic arena that seats 9,000 and hosts major sporting events and big-name concerts.

The public is also welcome to visit the **URI Fine Arts Center Galleries** (105 Upper College Rd., 401/792-2775, www.uri.edu, free), which include the Main, Photography, and Corridor exhibit spaces. The hours for each vary, so it's best to phone ahead or visit the website.

Kingston

Just down the street, the 1802 **Helme House** (2587 Kingstown Rd., 401/783-2195, www.southcountyart.org, 1pm-5pm Wed.-Sun., free), one of the town's most stately Federal buildings, is headquarters to the South County Art Association. Art classes are given, like drawing, painting, pottery, and photography, and there's a small gallery with frequently changing exhibits.

Kingston has had two impressive courthouses through the years, one of which is now the **Courthouse Center for the Arts** (3481 Kingstown Rd., 401/782-1018, www.courthousearts.org, 10am-4pm Mon.-Fri., 10am-2pm Sat., free), a tall and imposing granite structure built in 1896. It houses art galleries and a shop selling locally produced arts and crafts, as well as classrooms for various visual and performing arts workshops. This is also a live music and performing arts venue throughout the year. The other is an immense 1775 structure that served on a rotating basis 1776-1791 as the Rhode Island State House, and is now the **Kingston Free Library** (2605 Kingstown Rd., 401/783-8254, http://www.skpl.org/728/Library-Services, 10am-6pm Mon.-Tues., 10am-8pm Wed., noon-8pm Thurs., 10am-5pm Fri., 9am-noon Sat.).

Wakefield and Matunuck

In Wakefield, the administrative center of South Kingstown, you'll find the usual array of prosaic shopping centers and strip malls, but follow Main Street west away from U.S. 1 into downtown and you'll find a more attractive stretch of mostly late-Victorian and early-20th-century shop fronts and buildings. The Saugatucket River passes through the center of town, and a number of excellent small businesses and restaurants have opened here in an attempt to revitalize the downtown area and make it a destination. The town has also worked hard to develop a greenway along this historic river, once industrial and polluted. It is now lined by a walking path that's nice for strolling and bird-watching.

About ten minutes south of Wakefield is the tiny village of Matunuck, home to a small seaside community comprised mostly of small beach cottages, campers, and rentals interspersed with a few larger waterfront homes and working farms. It's also home to Theatre-by-the-Sea (364 Cards Pond Rd., 401/782-8587, www.theatrebythesea.com), a historic theater and playhouse that comes to life each summer with productions for both adults and children. Past shows include Saturday Night Fever, *Funny Girl*, and *Legally Blonde*.

Tiny as it may be, Matunuck is also home to several beautiful beaches, many of which are preferred by locals who want to avoid the crowds and pricey parking fees at larger beaches like Scarborough and Narragansett Town Beach. East Matunuck State Beach, South Kingstown Town Beach, and Moonstone Beach are all located here, the latter of which is an excellent spot for experiencing the bioluminescent marine life that washes up on shore on late summer evenings. The **Wood-Pawcatuck Watershed Association** (203 Arcadia Rd., Hope Valley, 401/539-9017, www.wpwa.org) occasionally leads a "Bioluminescent Paddle" ($20 pp) just down the road on Ninigret Pond on summer evenings toward the end of August, when the bioluminescent comb jellyfish start showing up in coastal waters. Boats are provided, but the events fill up fast, so advanced registration is necessary.

CHARLESTOWN

East of Westerly is the large rural town of Charlestown, one of Rhode Island's great recreation hubs, with outstanding beaches as well as several extensive tracts of undeveloped and preserved land. The town itself is dominated by two large parks on either side of Route 1; on the north side of the road, signs point the way to Burlingame State Park. On the south side of the road is a parcel divided into Ninigret

National Wildlife Refuge and Ninigret Park. This land borders another of South County's big saltwater ponds, Ninigret Pond.

★ The Fantastic Umbrella Factory

Coming from the west, bear right on Route 1A to find one of the more unusual sights in Rhode Island, or anywhere, really: the eclectic collection of shops, farmland, and animal exhibits known as **The Fantastic Umbrella Factory** (4820 Old Post Rd./ Rte. 1A, Charlestown, 401/364-6616, www. fantasticumbrellafactory.com, 10am-6pm Wed.-Mon., call for winter hours). When the back-to-the-land movement was in full swing during the 1960s, a small group of hippies took up residence in the backwoods of Charlestown, where they created a curiosity shop and flower nursery that has grown over the years into a veritable Wonka-esque fantasyland. Guinea fowl and emus prowl the grounds among shops selling everything from handmade toys, crystals, and drums, to African masks, rain sticks, and samurai swords, while a greenhouse full of Technicolor perennials dazzles the eye. It's a great place to buy unique gifts, to let the kids gawk at the animals, or just to wander around and explore. Be sure to check out the bamboo forest in the back!

WESTERLY

Named for its location on the far end of the Rhode Island coast, Westerly is a picturesque town with solid granite buildings from the 19th and early 20th centuries built with stones from nearby granite quarries. The granite made the little town rich, and its residents gained a deep appreciation for the arts, a tradition that carries on to the present day.

As with most Rhode Island municipalities, the town of Westerly is a large area that takes in several small villages, among them Westerly proper, Watch Hill, Misquamicut, Weekapaug, and Bradford. Hopkinton and Ashaway lie just northeast. Most visitors spend their time in Watch Hill, Misquamicut,

and Weekapaug, three popular summer resort communities on the Atlantic Ocean.

If you are interested in a walking tour of the town, most of the town's civic buildings, as well as several of its largest and grandest homes, are on or near **Wilcox Park** (bounded by High St., Broad St., Granite St., and Grove Ave.), a broad and rolling 18-acre green with mature shade trees, a duck pond, and several distinctive fountains and sculptures. At the edge of the park, notice the **Westerly Public Library** (44 Broad St., 401/596-2877, www. westerlylibrary.org, 9am-8pm Mon.-Thurs., 9am-6pm Fri., 9am-4pm Sat.), a brick and red granite structure with a red-tile roof accented with terra-cotta trim. It was built in 1894 as a memorial to local Civil War veterans and originally included a bowling alley, gymnasium, art gallery, and community space for the Grand Army of the Republic.

The **Babcock-Smith House** (124 Granite St., 401/596-5704, www.babcock-smithhouse. com, 2pm-5pm Sat. May-Oct., 2pm-5pm Thurs.-Sun. July-Aug., $5) is Westerly's de facto local history museum; the 1734 early Georgian-style house was built for physician Dr. Joshua Babcock, later appointed the chief justice for Rhode Island. Inside you'll find a collection of 18th-century furnishings, varying from primitive pieces to an ornately wrought Federal sideboard and a towering highboy from Connecticut.

Watch Hill

The village of Watch Hill—named because it was used as a lookout position during the Revolutionary War—is a quaint resort community occupying the rocky point at the south end of Westerly. At the turn of the 20th century, an enterprising local rented out rooms in the lighthouse at the top of the hill; grand old hotels followed, and high society, including Clark Gable, Douglas Fairbanks, and Henry Ford, came to cool their heels by the sea. It still draws its fair share of vacationers and second-home owners, plus some workers from other parts of Rhode Island, as it's just a 45-minute commute to Providence and even closer to the

Narragansett to Westerly

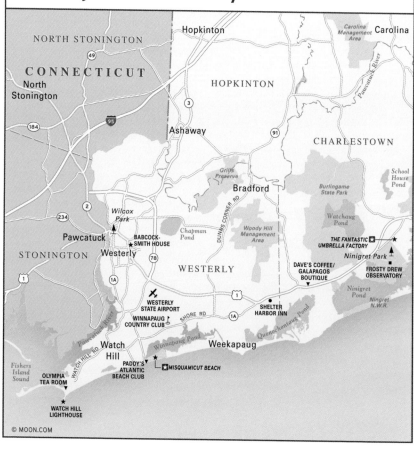

© MOON.COM

many businesses in Warwick, Cranston, and eastern Kent County.

The commercial center of the village runs along Bay Street for about 400 yards and contains a mix of cafés, galleries, boutiques, and a handful of accommodations. It's a tight-knit little town with a friendly personality, and it's completely devoid of the modern development that characterizes South County's beach communities farther east. High above Bay Street, a parallel road called Bluff Avenue has the grandest of Watch Hill's summer homes, one of which belongs to Taylor Swift.

The beach at Watch Hill is quite well known, at least among southern Rhode Islanders and others who live nearby—this long strand largely unblemished by development ranks among the prettiest beaches in southern New England. It's also one of the most popular with young kids because of the **Flying Horse Carousel** (Bay St., 401/348-6007, 11am-9pm Mon.-Fri., 10am-9pm Sat.-Sun., $1). Built in 1876, it is thought to be the oldest carousel in the country. The name comes from the fact that the wooden horses are suspended by metal chains, causing them to fly farther out the faster the carousel spins.

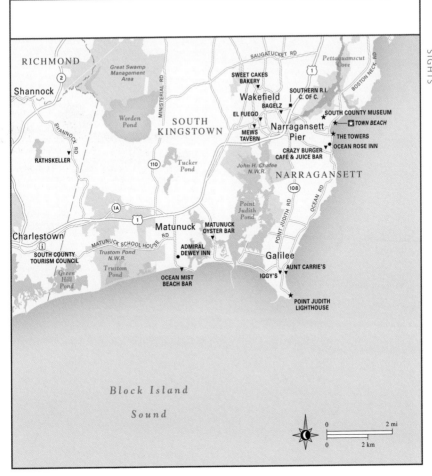

While the carousel has been renovated many times over the years, the horses still have leather saddles and genuine horsehair manes. During the ride, kids can reach for the famous brass ring to win a free ride.

The **Watch Hill Lighthouse** (14 Lighthouse Rd., no phone, www.watchhill lighthousekeepers.org, grounds 8am-8pm daily, museum 1f-3pm Tues.-Thurs. July-Aug., free) lies just south of the village center off of Bluff Avenue, down a private road that is closed to unauthorized vehicles but open to foot traffic and bicycles. For nearly 200 years, Watch Hill has been known for its lighthouse,

which was commissioned in 1806 and established the town. The unadorned granite tower, which is closed off to guests, isn't the prettiest lighthouse in the world, but its vantage point is spectacular.

★ Misquamicut Beach

Three mi (4.8 km) east of Watch Hill on Route 1A is Misquamicut (mih-SKWAH-mih-cut), which has a gracious 3-mi-long (4.8 km) stretch of sand. Unlike Watch Hill, Misquamicut was not settled until the very end of the 1800s, and it really only began to flourish as a resort community around 1910.

This community is a traditional shore strip of pastel-hued clapboard cottages, houses, and motels. The larger places facing the beach offer clear ocean views and guest rooms just steps from the surf; many have kitchenettes, and most have their own fairly predictable seafood and chops restaurants. There are no franchise restaurants or hotels in Misquamicut. Instead, you'll mostly find properties that have been in the same family for generations, catering to successive generations of guests. Plenty of these hotel employees know their guests' names on sight, and vice versa. It's the sort of tight-knit community where kids grow up together as their families visit every summer.

In the center of Misquamicut is the actual Misquamicut State Beach (257 Atlantic Ave., Westerly, 401/596-9097, www.riparks. com), with a large and attractive beach pavilion, a big playground, changing rooms, and other facilities. This is a beautiful and well-kept stretch of sand. The section of the community just east of the state beach is less pristine, but it is an excellent place to bring kids, mostly due to the presence of the Atlantic Beach Park (321 Atlantic Ave., 401/322-0504, www.atlanticbeachpark.com, 11am-10pm daily Memorial Day-Labor Day), which features an early 20th century carousel, amusement rides, and a video arcade. Farther east along Atlantic Avenue is Dunn's Beach, a long swath of summer houses punctuated by just a few businesses.

Entertainment and Events

South County has a lot going on in performing arts, especially considering that the area is in no way urban, but much of this activity doesn't really start up until late spring and dies just as quickly by October. The one area institution that keeps South County lively during the colder months is URI, which presents music and theatrical events throughout the school year and whose students keep several bars crowded year-round.

There are dozens of mostly low-key taverns along the shore in South County, and a few spots inland in Westerly and Wakefield are popular with students of nearby URI. Especially in summer, the bars and taverns near the shore can get pretty wild, with a mix of summer-break college students, youngish visitors and vacationers, and gruff fishers, depending on the venue. In Misquamicut, where you'll find the greatest number of beach hotels and motels, much of the action takes places in bars at the resorts themselves. You can hear live music at a number of places, and sports pubs are also relatively common.

BARS AND CLUBS
South County isn't exactly known for its nightlife, but there are a number of spots that are particularly nice to sit and have a drink, especially on summer evenings.

In Narragansett, George's of Galilee (250 Sand Hill Cove Rd., 401/783-2306, www.georgesofgalilee.com, from 11am daily) and the Bon Vue Inn (1230 Ocean Rd., www.1230oceanbistro.com/bonvue.htm, 401/789-0696, kitchen 11am-1am daily) are laid-back beach bars with occasional live music throughout the summer. The interiors may be unremarkable, but the ocean views make up for what the bars themselves lack in personality.

Farther south, a hugely popular spot with college students and everybody else in South County, the Mews Tavern (456 Main St., Wakefield, 401/783-9370, www.mewstavern. com, 11am-1am daily) has the area's best selection of craft beers on tap and is often one of the most crowded South County hangouts,

1: sailboats in the harbor in Watch Hill
2: Misquamicut Beach

To the Lighthouse

It's fitting that a state nicknamed the Ocean State should have some of New England's prettiest and most historic lighthouses along its coastline. Rhode Island's waters are notoriously treacherous, with sunken reefs and narrow passages throughout Block Island Sound and Narragansett Bay. Twenty-one lighthouses still stand along the coastline, 13 of them in use today to guide ships. Of these, only a few are open to the public, but there's nothing to prevent you from exploring the grounds and snapping pictures to your heart's content. Here are ten worth checking out:

EAST BAY & SAKONNET

- **Pomham Rocks Light** (1871; Willett Ave., East Providence). An unusual 40-foot octagonal tower atop a Second Empire Victorian house on a small island in the Providence River. Site closed, but visible from East Bay Bike Path.

- **Prudence Island** (Sandy Point) Light (1852; Sandy Point, Prudence Island). Active 30-foot octagonal tower has an unusual "birdcage" lantern on top; grounds open.

- **Sakonnet Light** (1884; Little Compton). Active 66-foot cylindrical tower located on an island off Sakonnet Point, accessible only by boat.

NEWPORT & JAMESTOWN

- **Castle Hill Light** (1890; Castle Hill Point, Newport). Active 40-foot granite tower; grounds open.

especially on weekend nights. The building's original circa 1947 bar has a jukebox and is plastered with dollar bills, while the newer dining room here is more conducive to a sit-down meal.

Also in South Kingstown, the ★ **Ocean Mist Beach Bar** (895A Matunuck Beach Rd., 401/782-3740, www.oceanmist.net, 10am-1am daily) in Matunuck has live music and draws a rowdy bunch of sunburned beachgoers on summer nights. Some serious coastal erosion has brought the crashing tides closer and closer to the building's foundation, threatening to wash it away completely—in the meantime, the bar is within walking distance from East Matunuck State beach, and you can enjoy a drink and a burger on the back deck while listening to the waves crashing directly underneath you.

In Westerly, the bar at **Paddy's Restaurant** (159 Atlantic Ave., Misquamicut, 401/596-4350, www.paddysbeach.com, 11am-1am daily in summer) is a popular spot right on the beach where you can order all sorts of froufrou tropical drinks like banana rumrunners and frozen mudslides. The bar hosts live local bands throughout the summer. The Knickerbocker Music Center (35 Railroad Ave., 401/315-5070, www.knickmusic.com, call for hours) hosts live music with an emphasis on blues, reggae, country, and Americana acts. The venue is also home to a taproom with food. It tends to draw an older, mellow crowd. The Malted Barley (42 High St., 401/315-2184, www.themaltedbarleyri.net, 11am-1am daily) is a craft beer bar in downtown Westerly with a fun, casual atmosphere and a nice back deck when the weather is nice. Try the Grey Sail Flying Jenny EPA, brewed right in Westerly, or the Whaler's Ginger Wheat, made just down the road in Wakefield. The food menu is mostly limited to one basic thing—housemade pretzels, pretzel sandwiches, and pretzel desserts—but it does this one thing very well. Salads are also available if pretzels don't do it for you.

- **Rose Island Light** (1870; Newport). Active 35-foot octagonal tower; site accessible by ferry during summer.

- **Beavertail Light** (1749; Beavertail Point, Jamestown). Active 68-foot handsome gray-granite square tower with a museum inside, open during summer.

SOUTH KINGSTOWN

- **Point Judith Light** (1810; end of Rte. 108, Narragansett). Active 51-foot octagonal tower, one of the most picturesque in the state; grounds are open daily.

WESTERLY

- **Watch Hill Light** (1808; Lighthouse Rd., Watch Hill). Active 45-foot square granite tower with white cylindrical top; the tower is closed, but grounds are open, as is a small museum in the keeper's house during summer.

BLOCK ISLAND

- **Block Island North Light** (1829; Sandy Point). Active 51-foot octagonal brick tower; grounds are open daily, and a small museum inside is open during summer.

- **Block Island Southeast Light** (1875; Mohegan Bluffs). Active 52-foot octagonal brick tower dramatically situated on seaside bluffs; museum and tower are open to tours in summer.

PERFORMING ARTS

Many of the arts events in South County revolve around URI, including the **University of Rhode Island Theatre** (Fine Arts Bldg., Kingston, 401/874-5843, www.uri.edu/artsci/the), which presents four plays a year, including musicals and classic works. The **Music Department** (Fine Arts Bldg., 401/874-2431, www.uri.edu/artsci/mus) presents a wide range of works during the school year, including choral programs, classical concerts, and live jazz. For bigger shows, the **Thomas M. Ryan Center** (1 Lincoln Almond Plaza, Kingston, 401/788-3200, www.theryancenter.com) hosts national performers (past performers include Bob Dylan and Steve Martin) in an 8,000-seat auditorium. Inside a Romanesque granite building, the **Courthouse Center for the Arts** (3481 Kingstown Rd., West Kingston, 401/782-1018, www.courthousearts.org) features indie films, community theater, and local musicians.

South County also has a number of small theaters that present a variety of dramatic and musical works. In Westerly, the professional **Granite Theatre** (1 Granite St., 401/596-2341, www.granitetheatre.com) stages about eight classic plays April through September and Thanksgiving through Christmas. The theater occupies a former church, a Greek Revival structure built in 1849 that lost its spire during the 1938 hurricane. **Theatre-by-the-Sea** (364 Cards Pond Rd, Matunuck, 401/782-8587, www.theatrebythesea.com) is a seasonal stage in a converted 1880s barn near the ocean, with productions for both adults and children. Past shows included *Young Frankenstein, The Little Mermaid*, and *Mama Mia!* The **Colonial Theatre** (Westerly, 401/596-7909, www.colonialtheatreri.org) hosts free Shakespeare in the Park productions at Wilcox Park each July and August.

FESTIVALS AND EVENTS

Summer and fall are major event seasons in South County, especially for seafood, specifically quahogs, which are celebrated with great fervor.

In mid-June the Rhode Island Air Show (Quonset Point Air National Guard Base, North Kingstown, www.rhodeislandairshow.com) features high-flying displays of several exciting planes, including fighter jets and bombers. Many planes are also exhibited on the ground and can be toured up close. It's free and a fun event for kids—just remember to bring ear protection, as some of the planes are quite loud.

In July, Wickford Village comes alive with the Wickford Art Festival (401/294-6840, www.wickfordart.org), when hundreds of artists set up booths in the town center.

In early August, the Charlestown Seafood Festival (401/364-4031, www.charlestownrichamber.com/seafoodfestival.html) draws hundreds of chowder and quahog aficionados to Ninigret Park. Activities include bungee jumping, a rock wall, car show, kayaking, amusement rides, and live music. And of course, just about every type of seafood popular in the Ocean State is available, including raw oysters and clams, steamed lobsters, clam cakes, fish-and-chips, and fried whole-belly clams. Later in August, locals turn out in big numbers for the Washington County Fair (Rte. 112, Richmond, 401/539-7042, www.washingtoncountyfair-ri.com), an agricultural, arts and crafts, family-oriented festival that makes it hard to believe the urban hub of Providence is just 35 minutes away.

In early September, the Rhythm & Roots festival (Ninigret Park, 888/855-6940, www.rhythmandroots.com) is one of the area's most popular music festivals, an eclectic mix of Cajun and zydeco, bluegrass, folk, and rockabilly. It's a multicultural event, with excellent food stalls that have items from all over the world, along with arts and crafts vendors.

Shopping

NARRAGANSETT

Narragansett Pier Marketplace (Ocean Rd.) is a small collection of tourist shops, including Polka Dot Panda (18A Pier Marketplace, Narragansett, 401/792-4885, www.pdpanda.com, 11am-8pm daily), which specializes in luxury and designer children's clothing with onsite embroidery for personalized gifts. There's a T-shirt shop in the market, a gift shop, a shoe store, and a great ice-cream parlor called Nana's. Adjoining the market is the Coast Guard House restaurant.

WICKFORD

Wickford has about 40 shops and boutiques, most of them independently owned. The vast majority are along West Main and Brown Streets, Wickford's main drag. At the Woven Path (11 Brown St., 401/667-3722, www.thewovenpath.com, 11am-4:30pm Wed.-Sat.), you'll find hand-woven scarves, shawls, and handbags all made right in the shop on a 1979 Harrisville Loom. The shop also features original art including watercolor and oil paintings, photography, lithography, pottery, and jewelry all handmade by local artists. Village Reflections (2 W. Main St., 401/295-7802, 10am-6pm Mon.-Thurs., 10am-8pm Fri., noon-6pm Sun.) offers contemporary women's clothes and beautiful jewelry with an earthy, hippie flair.

Green River Silver Co. (83 Brown St., 401/295-0086, www.greenriversilver.com, 10am-6pm Mon.-Sat., noon-5pm Sun.) sells fine sterling jewelry from around the world. Since 1990, the shop owners here have been selecting handmade pieces during their travels to the southwestern U.S., Mexico, India, Bali, Israel, Poland, and Thailand. Midnight Sun (13 West Main St., 401/316-0505, 10am-5pm daily) offers unique clothes and jewelry from around the world, as well as drums, jewelry, incense, and tapestries.

You can browse for art at the Wickford

Back Roads and Antique Shops

While some of southern Rhode Island's tiny villages don't seem to warrant a visit on their own, the collective area is certainly one of the most scenic for lazy summer drives through winding back roads flanked by wildflowers and farmland. It's also a great area to go digging for treasures in one of the region's antique shops and consignment stores, of which there are many. If you're heading south from Providence, here are a few to get you started: If you're in search of home decor, or vintage furniture and art of the high-end variety, check out RĒ (7512 Post Rd., North Kingstown, 401/667-5996, www.rerhodeisland.com), an estate buyout shop with a knowledgeable and keen-eyed staff. From there, keep heading south via Route 1, then head west past rolling farmland on Route 138 into Richmond, where you'll find Jules Antiques and General Store (320 Kingstown Rd., 401/539-2925, www.julesantiquesri.com), located in an 8,000-square-foot red farm building that showcases the wares of more than 70 different dealers. Here you'll find everything from beat-up books and farm furniture, to more valuable and rare antiques.

From there, keep driving west about 4 mi (6.4 km) into the small village of Hope Valley, where you'll find The Remnant Shop (1081 Main St., 401/539-2900, www.remnantshopinc. vzwebsites.com), located in a cool old brick building on the corner of Main and Bank Streets. The shop's ground floor is full of both new and vintage fabrics and leather, while the giant upstairs room is filled with used furniture, books, tableware, jewelry, and other ephemera from decades past. From here, head toward the coast and continue south onto Switch Road for about 4 mi (6.4 km) before turning right onto 91 West, a winding route that is at times lined by fragrant pine trees, flanked by stone walls and farmland, and at points even interrupts the sprawl of giant sod fields. After about 5 mi (8 km), turn left on 216 headed south into the tiny village of Charlestown, where you'll find Rusty Rabbit Antiques (5219 Old Post Rd., 401/322-1111), a cute little shop in a yellow cottage that specializes in nautical tchotchkes, like antique model ships and art made from old buoys.

If you haven't had enough at this point, continue south on Route 1 into Westerly. Just beyond downtown is the Jonnycake Center (23 Industrial Dr., 401/377-8069 www.jonnycake.org/thrift), a nonprofit that operates an enormous thrift store where you can find unbelievably inexpensive furniture, clothing, books, ceramics, kitchenware, vintage linens, and antique art. The best part? The money you spend here helps support the center's mission of helping needy families in the Westerly area—so you don't need to feel guilty about buying more things you probably don't need.

Art Association Gallery (36 Beach St., 401/294-6840, www.wickfordart.org, 11am-3pm Tues.-Sat., noon-3pm Sun.), a nonprofit cooperative with about 300 members.

KINGSTON

Near URI, Kingston Hill Store (2528 Kingston Rd., Kingston, www.abgbooks. com, 401/792-8662, 10am-5pm daily) is a fine source of rare and antiquarian books, with quite a few titles on Rhode Island history.

A few miles west of URI, off Route 138, Peter Pots Pottery (494 Glen Rock Rd., West Kingston, 401/783-2350, www.peterpots. com, 10am-5pm Mon.-Sat., noon-5pm Sun.) has been an acclaimed shop and gallery since

the 1940s; it's a source of beautiful yet functional stoneware, including coffee mugs, table accessories, wine decanters, lamps, and pitchers. The showroom is set inside a circa-1700 stone mill.

WAKEFIELD

Downtown Wakefield has a smattering of antique shops and other independent stores and boutiques. The Purple Cow (205 Main St., Wakefield, 401/789-2389, www. thepurplecowco.net, 10am-6pm Mon.-Wed., 9am-8pm Thurs.-Fri., 10am-6pm Sat., 11am-4pm Sun.) is an offbeat gallery with custom-made clothing, jewelry, greeting cards, and other gifts. At One More Time (406 Main St.,

Wakefield, 401/782-8414, 10am-5pm daily), you can choose from an array of gently used upscale men's and women's clothing, shoes, accessories, and jewelry.

Located in a former art deco gas station, the **Glass Station** (446 Main St., Wakefield, 401/788-2500, www.theglassstationstudio. com, 10am-8pm Mon.-Sat., 10am-3pm Sun.) is now the studio and gallery of glassblower Eben Horton, who creates vases inspired by ocean waves and whimsical glass fish. In addition to beautiful handblown vases and ornaments, beginner glassblowing workshops are also available on-site ($40 and up). **Dove & Distaff** (365 Main St., 401/284-1170, www. doveanddistaffruggallery.com, 10am-4pm Mon.-Sat.) sells area rugs, bags, throws, pillows, lampshades, wallpaper, bed linens, and other home goods out of their showroom in an historic 19th-century building.

WESTERLY AND WATCH HILL

Westerly has several good antique shops, among them **Homespun Cottage** (25 High St., Westerly, 401/322-9800, www.homespunantiques.com, 10am-5pm Wed.-Mon.), which boasts two floors of eclectic wares full of New England charm. **Woodmansee's Gift Shop & Boutique** (27 Broad St., 401/596-2310, www.woodmanseesri.com, 10am-5pm Mon.-Sat.) has been catering to the seaside sensibilities of Westerly residents for over a century—it specializes in clothing and jewelry for sophisticated ladies, like floppy hats and comfortable but fashionable clothes made with natural fabrics and dyes. Younger ladies can find more hip and trendy clothes next door at Woodmansee's sister store, **Woodee's** (33 Broad St., 401/596-0200, www.woodeesri. com, 10am-6pm Mon.-Sat.).

You can reward kids you've dragged into countless grown-up stores with a visit to the **Candy Box** (14 Fort Rd., Watch Hill, 401/596-3325, 10am-8pm daily), where you can find old fashioned fudge, gum drops, and saltwater taffy.

CHARLESTOWN

★ **The Fantastic Umbrella Factory** (4820 Old Post Rd./Rte. 1A, 401/364-6616, 10am-6pm daily, call for winter hours) is just off U.S. 1, down the Old Post Road from Ninigret Park, and qualifies as a certifiable tourist attraction. This collection of buildings (amidst flower gardens, a bamboo forest, and a petting zoo) includes the General Store, which carries a fairly bizarre assortment of collectibles and gifts—kites, jewelry, soaps, greeting cards, mugs, toys, wood carvings, and weird socks are among the goodies. At Small Axe Productions, you can find handblown glassworks, crystals and gemstones, jewelry, stoneware pottery, and handwoven clothes. Also on the grounds are an art gallery, an eyeglass store, and the Small Axe Café, which specializes in natural foods. The "factory" was founded in 1968, and it definitely maintains its hippie sensibilities.

You never know what you'll find at the **General Stanton Flea Market** (General Stanton Inn, 4115 Old Post Rd., 401/364-8888, www.generaljosephstantoninn.com, 8am-3:30pm weekends and holidays May-Oct.). Under the tents you'll find anything from comics and collectibles, antique glass and textiles, furnishings, vintage clothes and from dozens of dealers. If you're looking for something a little more modern, try **Galapagos Boutique** (5193 Old Post Rd., 401/322-3000, www.shopgalapagos.com, 9am-6pm daily), which stocks trend-conscious clothing and specializes in designer jeans. At **Charlestown Village** (U.S. 1 at Rte. 2), you'll find a smattering of eclectic shops selling a variety of things like T-shirts, chocolates, and nautical ephemera.

Sports and Recreation

BEACHES

Narragansett is Rhode Island's beach-bumming capital, its crown jewel being **Roger Wheeler State Beach** (Sand Hill Cove Rd., off Rte. 108, Narragansett, 401/789-3563, www.riparks.com), a typically packed swath of golden sand at Point Judith, with among the best facilities in the county, including an excellent playground, a picnic area, and a bathhouse. Just west of Roger Wheeler in Galilee is **Salty Brine State Beach** (254 Great Rd., Galilee, 401/789-8374, www.riparks.com), a short span that's popular with teens and college students. On the Narragansett Bay side of town, **Scarborough State (North) Beach** and **Scarborough South Beach** (both off Ocean Ave., Narragansett, 401/789-2324 or 401/782-1319, www.riparks.com) connect and provide a total of about 3,000 parking spaces and roughly a half-mile of sand. These are both hot spots for college students, and the crowds can get a bit rowdy from time to time. Farther up Ocean Avenue at Narragansett Pier is **Narragansett Town Beach** (39 Boston Neck Rd., 401/783-6430), a very popular

beach with a full slate of facilities, and plenty of parking. But be warned: this is the only beach in Rhode Island where beachgoers will pay to park and will also be charged an additional fee of $10 just to walk on to the beach.

It may not seem like a huge area, but South County has about 100 mi (161 km) of shoreline, most of it accessible to the public, including some of the best stretches of sand in New England—especially along the secluded coast of Charlestown, a gem that locals know but outsiders usually do not. As you move west to east in the county from the Connecticut border, you'll first come to the beaches of Watch Hill, which include **Watch Hill Beach** (off Route 1A, 401/596-7761), with restrooms and a bathhouse on a pretty stretch of sand; the half-mile of beach leads farther out to isolated **Napatree Point** (401/596-7761), which juts into Long Island Sound, and has a well-deserved reputation for bird-watching, as many migrating shorebirds frequent these sands at various times during the year. Parking here is available at two paved lots on Bay Street. Parking at Watch Hill is available

the General Store at The Fantastic Umbrella Factory

in two small private lots for $10 per day and space is quite limited—but the upside is that you won't typically find swarms of people here for this reason.

Farther east, Misquamicut State Beach (257 Atlantic Ave., off Route 1A, 401/322-1026, www.riparks.com) offers a half-mile of very popular and heavily used beachfront—it's among the most developed in the state. In mellow Weekapaug, to the east, there's shore access at Quonochontaug Beach (off West Beach Rd.), which has very limited facilities but is overseen by lifeguards. A lot of people choose to swim in the eponymous salt pond that borders the beach; like Napatree, this is a fine place for bird-watching.

A secluded and modest barrier beach, with ocean on one side and the west end of Ninigret Pond on the other, Blue Shutters Town Beach (off East Beach Rd., off U.S. 1, 401/364-1206) has a few parking spaces, a snack bar, and changing facilities with showers. Remote East Beach is reached on foot by walking farther along the shore; this is an uncrowded and largely unsupervised area that's nice for swimming at your own risk. Charlestown Town Beach (off U.S. 1, 401/364-1208, parking $20) is a good bet for beating the crowds, although avid outdoorsy types love it for its big crashing waves and wide beach (note the volleyball court). The beach has full changing facilities, restrooms, picnic areas, and lifeguards.

A rather narrow stretch of South Kingstown cuts down to the ocean between Charlestown and Narragansett; here you'll find a pair of excellent beaches. By far the most popular is East Matunuck State Beach (off 950 Succotash Rd., 401/789-8585), which has a 700-car parking lot, lifeguards, and full changing facilities. This half-mile-long beach is close to South Kingstown Town Beach (Matunuck Beach Rd., 401/789-9301, www.riparks.com), which is just over 1,000 feet long but has sports facilities, grills and a picnic grove, changing rooms with hot showers, a playground, and an ice-cream shop in close proximity.

FISHING

Home to the third-most-profitable fishing port in New England, Point Judith is the place for fishing enthusiasts. Several companies offer fishing charters, including Frances Fleet (33 State St., Galilee, 401/783-4988, www.francesfleet.com), which hosts a variety of trips, including cod-fishing excursions at sunrise, nighttime bluefish and striped bass runs, and tuna trips far out at sea. Other fishing boats include Adventure Rhode Island Fishing Charters (401/359-1785, www.adventurecharters.org) and C-Devil II Sportfishing (401/374-1439, www.cdevilsportfishing.com).

BOATING

Frances Fleet (33 State St., Galilee, 401/783-4988, www.francesfleet.com) also offers whale-watching cruises out of Narragansett, while Rhode Island Bay Cruises (Quonset Point, North Kingstown, 401/295-4040, www.rhodeislandbaycruises.com) offers tours on a sightseeing catamaran, exploring different themes like lighthouses, Newport Harbor, and the Tall Ships.

For information on the more than 50 party boats that sail from South County, contact the Rhode Island Party and Charter Boat Association (401/737-5812, www.rifishing.com). A full list of boats and contact information appears on the website along with links to websites for many individual boats.

Near the Cross Mills section of Charlestown, Ocean House Marina (60 Town Dock Rd., off Post Rd./Rte. 1A, Charlestown, 401/364-6040, www.oceanhousemarina.com, 9am-5pm Mon.-Fri., 8:30am-2pm Sat.) was built as the town meetinghouse and later came to be run as a summer resort. Today it's a marina renting all types of boats along with a bait-and-tackle shop. It sits right on Ninigret's salt pond, from which you can reach Block Island Sound.

1: beach in South County 2: the boardwalk at South Kingstown Town Beach 3: fishing off the rocks in Watch Hill 4: a surfer at Matunuck Beach

CANOEING AND KAYAKING

Freshwater boaters and anglers should check out the **Wood River**, the state's best trout-fishing stream—it meanders down through Exeter and Hope Valley, passing through the southwestern corner of the state before emptying into the Pawcatuck River in Westerly and flowing south to the ocean. If you tackle the full navigable length of the river, it'll take a good seven hours by canoe or kayak (the river is nearly 14 mi/22.5 km long). One of the most popular put-ins is off Route 165 in Exeter (follow it west from Rte. 3, just south of the I-95 overpass); head toward Beach Pond State Park until you reach the bridge over the Wood River. This upper stretch is relatively brisk but without any rapids.

Another popular access point is Hope Valley Road Landing, just off Route 3 in the village of Hope Valley. From here it's a quite smooth run for about 6 mi (9.7 km) down to Alton Dam. This lower stretch is especially picturesque, the riverbanks lined with dense maple and oak woodland.

Another excellent spot for canoeing, kayaking, or fishing is **Great Swamp,** a dense swath of South County marshland that is inaccessible except by boat. The main route begins at the launch in West Kingston off Route 138, known as Taylor's Landing. From here you enter a very narrow stretch of the Chipuxet River and paddle south; after a while the trickle of water opens to a much wider and more stable stretch of river. After about 3 mi (4.8 km) of fairly easy paddling you'll enter one of the larger freshwater bodies in the state, Worden's Pond. There are all sorts of opportunities for wildlife sightings on this trip. There's also a put-in and takeout area at the south end, off Worden's Pond Road.

The **Kayak Centre** (562 Charlestown Beach Rd., Charlestown, and 9 Phillips St. in Wickford, 401/295-4400, www.kayakcentre. com, 9am-6pm Mon.-Sat., 11am-5pm Sun.) is an excellent resource, renting and selling kayaks and offering tours, lessons, and advice. Another place for kayak rentals and instruction is **Quaker Lane Bait and Tackle** (4019 Quaker Lane, North Kingstown, 401/294-9642, www.quakerlanetackle.com, 5am-8pm Mon.-Fri., 4:30am-8pm Sat., 4:30am-7pm Sun.).

SURFING

South County has several great surf spots, some of them more accessible than others. Beginners and those looking to take lessons should start at **Narragansett Town Beach** (39 Boston Neck Rd., 401/783-6430), where you can rent boards of varying sizes by the day or hour. The folks just around the corner at **Narragansett Surf & Skate Shop** (74 Narragansett Ave., 401/789-7890, www. narragansettsurfandskate.com, 10am-7pm Mon.-Sat., 10am-5pm Sun.) set up shop in the parking lot of the beach during the summer and offer lessons for individuals and groups. They also rent stand-up paddleboards and wetsuits. This is an easy beach break on most days, and very popular with kids and families.

More advanced surfers will want to check out the waves at the **Point Judith Lighthouse** (1470 Ocean Rd., Narragansett), a point break that's accessible by scrambling down the (often very slippery) rocks in front of the parking area. The waves can be fun here but be mindful of the rocks and boulders, which can be hidden or not, depending on the tide.

Another favorite spot, especially for longboarders, is a fisherman's beach known as **Deep Hole** (Matunuck Beach Rd., South Kingston) in Matunuck. This is a rocky point break with a small beach and a small dirt parking area that can get very crowded when the surf is up, but parking is free, if you can find it. This is also a popular spot for stand-up paddleboarding and windsurfing.

HIKING

South County, both near the beach and inland, contains a vast cache of preserved, undeveloped land, especially in the town of Charlestown. Near the shore is the **Ninigret National Wildlife Refuge** (50 Bend Rd., off

Hiking in Exeter, Hopkinton, and Richmond

Just north of Westerly and Charlestown, Exeter, Hopkinton, and Richmond don't abound with formal attractions, but they do possess some of the state's best hiking, canoeing, fishing, and camping areas, namely the Long Pond and Ell Pond trails in Hopkinton, and the Arcadia Management Area, nearly 14,000 forested acres spread throughout the three towns.

A favorite trail among locals is the one that cuts through the **Long Pond-Ell Pond Nature Preserve** in Hopkinton. This rocky, and at times steep, trail winds through fragrant pine trees, white cedars, red maples, hemlocks, mountain laurel, and some of the tallest wild rhododendrons in the state. Late spring or early summer is the time to go if you want to catch the rhododendrons in bloom, but the trail is pretty spectacular at just about any time of the year. To access the trailhead: Take exit 2 from I-95 and continue south on Route 3 for about 2.5 mi (4 km). Make a right onto Canonchet Road, and travel about 2.5 mi (4 km) until the road ends. Make a left here at North Road, and follow it until it becomes a dirt road. The Ell Pond trailhead begins just beyond a small parking lot on your left. The trail here is about 4 mi (6.4 km) long, but some of the most breathtaking views occur within the first mile (1.6 km). (Fun fact: Parts of this trail were used as the set for several scenes in the 2012 Wes Anderson film *Moonrise Kingdom*.) You can find more information about this trail at the Nature Conservancy's website, www.nature.org.

While the Arcadia Management Area is spread out among Exeter, Hopkinton, and Richmond, several of the major access points for its various trails are located in Exeter. One of the most accessible trails here is **Breakheart Trail**, which circles around Breakheart Pond, and is shaded by tall pines and oaks. It's just a short 1.5mi (2.4-km) loop around the pond, but more ambitious hikers can choose the option of a longer hike by following the yellow-blazed trail markers and completing the entire hike (about 6 mi/9.7 km). To access the trailhead: Take exit 5A from I-95, then merge right onto RI-102, headed south. Continue just under 1 mi (1.6 km) and turn right to follow RI-3 south for 1.3 mi (2.1 km). At the stoplight, turn right onto RI-165 West and continue for 2.8 mi (4.8 km) before turning right onto Frosty Hollow Road. Continue down this gravelly road for another mile (1.6 km), taking another right when the road comes to a T. Follow this road until it ends at a dirt parking lot overlooking the pond. For more information about hiking in Arcadia, visit www.riparks.com.

U.S. 1, 401/364-9124, www.fws.gov/refuge/ninigret), a broad, rolling space that leads down to the shores of Ninigret Pond, one of several massive salt ponds in the region. The preserve has almost no facilities but has some excellent hiking trails, including a gentle 1.4-mi (2.3-km) loop that ends at Grassy Point, where you can climb to an observation platform and gaze out over Ninigret Pond.

Adjacent to and east of the preserve and with an entrance off Route 1A, **Ninigret Park** (401/364-1222) is the more activity-oriented section of the Ninigret lands. Facilities include athletic fields, public tennis courts, a children's playground, a paved bike trail, hiking areas, fishing in Ninigret Pond and a small freshwater pond with a beach, and picnic groves. The **Frosty Drew Nature Center** (401/364-9508, www.frostydrew.

org, 10am-1pm Sat. July-Aug.) in the park contains exhibits on natural history and offers weeklong nature programs for kids 6-10 throughout the summer. Nature Center staff members regularly give walks, talks, and other programs, usually on Saturday mornings in summer. Near the nature center is the **Frosty Drew Observatory** (61 Park Ln., Charlestown, 401/596-7688, www.frostydrew. org), a nonprofit center that hosts many programs open to the public, usually on Friday nights. A retractable roof allows the observatory's powerful telescope to peer into the brilliant night sky. In summer the observatory is open after dark, and during the fall you can typically visit at about 6:30pm.

The western and northern parts of South County are more remote and less crowded, making them ideal for horseback riding, camping, and hiking. The 72-mi (116-km) North-South Trail runs from the northern boundary of the state all the way through South County before ending at the coast. It enters lower Washington County near the junction of Routes 138 and 112, in Wyoming east of I-95 exit 3, and it terminates at Charlestown's Blue Shutters Town Beach. Highlights and good access points along the trail include Burlingame State Park, Indian Cedar Swamp, and the Carolina Management Area. The website http://outdoors.htmlplanet.com/nst/nst_map00.htm has a good detailed map of the trail as it runs through the state.

Some of the best area hikes are in Hope Valley and Hopkinton around Blue Pond, Long Pond, and Ell Pond. Marked trails meander around these lakes and through groves of hemlock and clusters of rhododendrons. Long Pond makes for an especially nice hike—follow Route 138 west from Hope Valley and turn left at Rockville village onto Canonchet Road. After about 1 mile (1.6 km) you'll come to a parking area for the Narragansett Trail, which leads west along the south shore of Long Pond. From the same parking area, a different trail cuts south toward Asheville Pond. The terrain in these parts is somewhat challenging, sometimes passing over steep rock ledges and leading to relatively high bluffs. The best time to go is in early June, when the many stunning rhododendron bushes that line the trail are in bloom.

BICYCLING

Taking advantage of South County's mostly flat topography is the William C. O'Neill Bike Path (www.southcounty.com/bikepath), which runs 7 mi (11.3 km) from Kingston Amtrak station, just off Route 138, to Mumford Road in Narragansett. From there an additional 2 mi (3.2 km) of on-road biking will get you to Narragansett Pier. To keep up with the trail's status and learn more about sites along the way, visit the website.

You can also check for maps and more info on biking in Rhode Island on the website of the state Department of Transportation (www.dot.ri.gov/community/bikeri).

Bikes can be rented at Narragansett Bikes (922 Boston Neck Rd., Narragansett, 401/782-4444, www.nbxbikes.com, 10am-6pm Mon.-Fri., 10am-5pm Sat., noon-5pm Sun.). Rates are around $50 per day, $100-120 per week.

GOLF

South County is Rhode Island's golfing capital, and greens fees at South County courses are among the most reasonable you'll find in southern New England. Among the best in the area is Winnapaug Country Club (Shore Rd., Westerly, 401/596-1237, www.winnapaugcountryclub.com, $25-60), an attractive 18-hole course with very nice views of Winnapaug Pond. The layout was designed by acclaimed architect Donald Ross, and a nice little restaurant is open for lunch and dinner.

A nice short nine-holer is the new Rose Hill Golf Club (222 Rose Hill Rd., Wakefield, 401/788-1088, $15-25).

Fairly close to the URI campus, Laurel Lane Golf Course (309 Laurel Lane, West Kingston, 401/783-3844, www.laurellanecountryclub.com, $27-58) is a short but pleasant 18-hole course; it also has a lounge and snack bar. This is an exceptionally well-cared-for course, with beautiful greens and fairways.

TENNIS

The town of South Kingstown has public tennis courts at several of its town parks, including Brousseau Park (Succotash Rd.), Old Mountain Field (Kingstown Rd.), and West Kingston Park (Rte. 138). Call South Kingstown's recreation department (401/789-9301) for details.

ICE-SKATING

At URI's Ryan Center, the snazzy Boss Ice Arena (1 Lincoln Almond Plaza, URI campus, Kingston, 401/788-3200, www.bossicearena.com, $7) is open to the public

South County Seafood

With so many excellent seafood options to choose from—from informal clam shacks to fancy oyster bars to dockside fish markets—where does one begin in a quest for the best seafood in South County? If you're craving something crispy, breaded, and fried, you'd be smart to head to Point Judith at the intersection of Ocean and Point Judith Roads. This is where **Aunt Carrie's** (1240 Ocean Rd., Narragansett, 401/783-7930, www.auntcarriesri.com, 11:30am-9pm daily May-Sept.) has been dishing out fried fish, clams, scallops, and clam cakes (or clam fritters, depending on who you talk to) since 1920. Just across the street, equally delicious clam cakes and chowder (plus legendary doughboys) can be found at **Iggy's** (1157 Point Judith Rd., 401/783-5608, www.iggysri. com, 11am-9pm Mar.-Columbus Day). Its original location in Warwick has been operating since 1924, so they definitely know what they're doing. Lines for both of these unassuming little shacks are known to twist around the block on summer nights, so be prepared to make an evening of it.

If you're looking for a more upscale experience, try the **Coast Guard House** (40 Ocean Rd., Narragansett, 401/789-0700, www.thecoastguardhouse.com, 11:30am-9pm Mon.-Thurs., 11:30am-10pm Fri.-Sat., 10am-10pm Sun.), a historic former Coast Guard station located next to The Towers in the Pier district. Open since the 1940s, this is another stalwart of the South County dining scene, serving up fresh-caught lobster, salmon, and seafood chowders and bisques at one of the choicest waterfront locations in the area. If oysters are more your thing, check out **Matunuck Oyster Bar** (629 Succotash Rd., 401/783-4202, www.rhodyoysters.com, 11:30am-10pm daily), specializing in farm-to-table and pond-to-plate, locally harvested food. Situated right on Potter's Pond and just a short walk to East Matunuck State Beach, this is definitely one of the best and most favored raw bars in the state.

If you'd rather cook your own, try **Ocean Catch Seafood** (566 Kingstown Rd., 401/789-3474, www.oceancatchseafoodri.com, 9am-7pm daily) in Wakefield, or **Ferry Wharf Fish Market** (296 Great Island Rd., 401/782-8088, 9am-6:15pm daily in Narragansett. Both have plenty of fresh, locally caught fish, shellfish, lobster, crabs, and all of the fixings you'll need to make a culinary masterpiece of your own.

daily for skating and pickup games of ice hockey. In Westerly, the Washington Trust Community Skating Center (61 Main St., 401/637-7902, www.oceancommunityymca. org, $8 adults, $5 children) is open to the public from November through March.

Food

NARRAGANSETT AND SOUTH KINGSTOWN
Spanish
Spain of Narragansett (1144 Ocean Rd., Narragansett, 401/783-9770, www.spainri. com, 4:30pm-9:30pm Tues.-Thurs., 4:30pm-10pm Fri.-Sat., 1pm-9pm Sun., $21-38) is one of the more dramatic dining spaces in South County—its high-ceilinged dining room is anchored by a gurgling fountain. This isn't a tapas restaurant per se, but you will find a number of nicely prepared starters, from clams casino to garlic-smoked chorizo. Sole lightly egg-battered and pan-sautéed in a lemon Chablis sauce and chicken Andaluza (stuffed with pine nuts, diced smoked ham, spinach, and manchego cheese, topped with fresh cilantro and tomatoes) are excellent entrées.

Seafood
Few restaurants in Rhode Island are as universally loved as the ★ **Matunuck Oyster Bar** (629 Succotash Rd., Matunuck, 401/783-4202,

www.rhodyoysters.com, 11:30am-10pm daily, $12-44), which overlooks Potter's Pond, where oyster farmer and restaurateur Perry Raso founded the Matunuck Oyster Farm in 2002. Today the restaurant enjoys a reputation for having some of the freshest and most delicious oysters in the state, as well as for providing a variety of other locally sourced and farm-fresh ingredients. The dining room is no frills, with a small bar where it's fun to sip on a martini and watch the staff deftly shuck oysters, while the deck overlooks the pond and has an excellent sunset view. Obviously, the oysters here are the thing to try, but if shellfish are not your thing, try the beet and goat cheese salad with grilled salmon or the pistachio encrusted Atlantic Cod.

American

A decent spot for inspired yet reasonably priced American food, Turtle Soup (113 Ocean Rd., Narragansett, 401/792-8683, www.turtlesouprestaurant.com, 11:30am-1am daily, $11-20) is on the ground floor of the distinctive twin-gabled Victorian beach hotel, the Ocean Rose Inn, with nice views of the water across the street—it's an elegant space but unfussy, as one would expect of a beach restaurant. The menu offers a nice range of options, including pork tenderloin with honey-Dijon mustard cream, and sesame tuna with ginger and white-wine reduction. Less expensive sandwiches (burgers, chicken clubs) are also available, and you can order from a fine selection of appetizers to create a good meal—pan-seared crab cakes with a smoked jalapeño rémoulade are a fave. Service is low key and friendly.

Beloved by locals and vacationers alike, ★ Crazy Burger Café and Juice Bar (144 Boon St., Narragansett, 401/783-1810, www.crazyburger.com, 8am–9pm Mon.-Thurs. 8am–9:30pm Fri.-Sat. $5-24) serves breakfast, lunch, and dinner, as well as fresh juices, smoothies, and espresso. The interior combines a humble diner style with funky pastel colors, and the covered patio out back is decked with flowers in the summer. Inspired by the 1970s health-food movement, this is one of the few places in South County where one can find dishes tailored specifically to vegans and vegetarians. All of the food is conceptualized and prepared in-house from scratch, and, as the name promises, the burgers are indeed crazy (the Luna-Sea Burger is a popular favorite, made from ground salmon and wrapped in phyllo dough). Be warned, the restaurant does not take reservations, and waits in excess of an hour are common, especially on weekends and nice beach days. Don't let this deter you from experiencing one of the best restaurants in the area.

Mexican

If you find yourself craving tacos after a day at the beach, try ★ El Fuego (344 Main St., Wakefield, 401/284-3353, www.elfuegomexicangrill.com, 11am-9pm Tues.-Sat., $5-10), a laid-back taco shop in downtown Wakefield. Fish, pork, beef, and vegetarian burritos, tacos, and quesadillas here are cheap, quick, delicious and satisfying. The interior has comfortably scuffed-up hardwood floors, colorfully painted walls, and large, sunny windows.

Thai

You can find delicious Thai food at Luk Thai Cuisine (249 Main St., Wakefield, 401/284-4370, www.lukthaifood.com, 11am-9:30pm Mon.-Thurs., 11am-10:30pm Fri.-Sat., noon-9pm Sun., $11-17) in Wakefield. Anything from beef and pork to duck, mussels, or squid can be added to classic dishes like pad Thai and drunken noodles, and spicy food lovers can customize their dish even further by choosing the "mouth explosion" or "hot as hell" modifications. The atmosphere is simple but comfortable, many items can be made gluten free, and BYOB is permitted.

Japanese

Kabuki (91 Old Tower Hill Rd., Wakefield, 401/788-0777, www.kabukicuisine.com, 11:30am-10:30pm Mon.-Wed., 11:30am-11pm Thurs.-Sat., 1pm-10:30pm Sun., $8-15) is an Asian bistro, serving creative Japanese food, sushi, and a smattering of Thai and Vietnamese dishes. Try the Blackberry Salmon or the Wakefield sushi roll, with spicy king crab meat, shrimp tempura, and honey-wasabi sauce.

Middle Eastern

A great deli specializing in Middle Eastern and Lebanese food, **Pick Pockets** (160 Granite St. Westerly, 401/637-7900, www. pickpocketswesterly.com, 10am-9pm daily, $4-10) stays open through the dinner hour each evening. It's a good place to pick up sandwich supplies and other goodies.

Comfort Food

The quintessential house of good cheer, ★ **Mews Tavern** (456 Main St., Wakefield, 401/783-9370, www.mewstavern. com, 11am-1am daily, $7-16) serves outstanding burgers along with dozens of other hearty dishes: scallops carbonara, seafood pie pizzas (scallops, shrimp, crab, smoked salmon, and a blend of cheeses), stuffed portobellos, Cajun steaks, teriyaki chicken wings, and beef-and-bean burritos. Of course, plenty of people descend on this rambling faux log-cabin ski lodge in the center of downtown Wakefield for the huge liquor list, including 70 microbrews on tap, more than 200 single-malt scotches, and three-dozen tequilas.

Although coastal erosion has threatened to wash it straight into the sea, the ★ **Ocean Mist Beach Bar** (895A Matunuck Beach Rd., 401/782-3740, www.oceanmist.net, 10am-1am daily) continues to serve up burgers, burritos, and chowder to hungry beach bums, bikers, surfers, and anyone else who happens to stroll in. The front windows of the bar and dining room look straight out onto the Atlantic, and you needn't worry about washing the sand off of your feet before entering. This is a truly laid-back beachfront restaurant and the food is surprisingly good, especially during Sunday brunch.

More than a few Rhode Islanders believe that **Aunt Carrie's** (1240 Ocean Rd., Narragansett, 401/783-7930, www. auntcarriesri.com, call for hours, $9-22) serves not only the best clam cakes and chowders in South County but the best in the state—maybe even in southern New England. This handsome little casual eatery sits on the bay in Point Judith and has ample outdoor and indoor seating, but its immense popularity results in lines most summer days—although a bring-your-own-booze policy makes the wait a little more pleasant for some patrons. After putting your name on the invariably long list for a table, you can wander around the grounds or even hike down by the beach, which is nearby. The brightly painted dining room buzzes with chatter every night as customers indulge in fried lobsters with drawn butter, whole-belly fried clams, and other fruits of the sea.

On the road to Jerusalem, **Cap'n Jack's** (706 Succotash Rd., Wakefield, 401/789-4556, www.capnjacksrestaurant.com, 11am-9pm daily, $7-17) has been serving big portions of seafood and pasta since 1972—the cavernous restaurant is always packed, and nobody seems to mind the rather dull decor. What you come for is lobster bisque with a hint of sherry, broiled scallops in a lemon-butter sauce, shrimp *fra diavolo,* baked scrod with mussels, and a few non-fish items such as gnocchi with meatballs and chicken teriyaki. The restaurant also makes its own pastries and desserts, which are just as hefty as the seafood platters. If you'd rather take your food to the beach, Cap'n Jack's has a takeout counter as well.

Cafés and Sandwich Shops
Wickford on the Water (85 Brown St., Wickford, 401/294-7900, www. wickfordonthewater.com 7am-9pm Sun.-Thurs., 8am-10pm Fri.-Sat., $6-10) is a cute little sandwich shop with a large deck overlooking the harbor in Wickford Village. It offers a full breakfast menu, daily lunch and dinner specials with sandwiches and fish-and-chips, a full bar, and extremely friendly service.

Near the sleepy little village of Peace Dale, ★ **Sweet Cakes Bakery** (1227 Kingstown Rd., South Kingstown, 401/789-5420, www.sweetcakesbakeryri.com, 7am-5pm Mon.-Sat., 8am-2pm Sun., $3-8) occupies the ground floor of a tiny pink clapboard house. It's easy to miss but you'll want to stop in for the gigantic fresh-baked scones and cinnamon buns or delicious savory breakfast sandwiches served on buttery croissants. It also serves soups, salads, and other lunch items, and excellent spicy chai. The adjoining screened in porch is an especially pleasant spot to eat, with flowery vintage tablecloths and cool breezes in the summer.

Those willing to overlook the silly name will be rewarded at ★ **Bagelz** (90 Pershing Rd., Wakefield, 401/783-9700, www.bagelzri.com, 6am-3pm daily, $2-9), a boiled-then-baked bagel bakery that also serves excellent fair-trade coffee, tea, espresso, pastry, deli sandwiches and fresh salads. Family-owned and operated for more than 20 years, Bagelz makes some of the best in the state—try the Nova Scotia Lox sandwich on an everything bagel with onion and tomato or a whole wheat bagel with walnut raisin cream cheese. Bagel "loverz" will not be disappointed.

CHARLESTOWN AND WESTERLY
American
The Bistro at the Ocean House (1 Bluff Ave., Watch Hill, 855/678-0364, www.oceanhouseri.com/culinary/the-bistro, 11:30am-2:30pm and 5:30pm-9:30pm Mon.-Sat., $12-36) offers all of the dishes you'd expect from a restaurant housed in one of the state's ritziest lodgings; oysters Rockefeller, seared lamb chops, filet mignon, and shrimp cocktail, served with some of the most exquisite ocean views in the state.

Opened as a quaint lunch spot and ice-cream parlor in 1916, the ★ **Olympia Tea Room** (74 Bay St., Westerly, 401/348-8211,

---

1: a sunny table at the Ocean Mist Beach Bar in Matunuck 2: the Olympia Tea Room in Watch Hill

www.olympiatearoom.com, 11:30am-9pm Mon.-Sat., noon-9pm Sun., $14-33) has gradually evolved through the years into one of Watch Hill's most dynamic and inventive restaurants. The handsome dining room with a black-and-white checked floor, salmon-pink walls, and lazily whirring ceiling fans serves a wide range of regional American cuisine, from grilled Kansas City sirloin to littleneck clams with sausage simmered in marinara with linguine. Specials change often and have included Connecticut River shad roe pan-fried with butter and baked in cream, and a Watch Hill fried oyster po'boy with spicy red tartar sauce, vine-ripened tomatoes, and shaved red onion.

Ella's Food & Drink (2 Tower St., Westerly, 401/315-0606, www.ellasfinefoodanddrink.com, 11:30am-9pm Wed.-Thurs., 11am-10pm Fri.-Sat., 11am-8pm Sun., $12-48) is 200-seat restaurant with an outdoor terrace serving up French-Asian dishes and whatever else strikes chef Jeanie Roland's fancy. Try the pan-seared, miso-infused Faroe Island salmon with toasted coconut-dusted forbidden black rice, chili bok choy, ginger, and sesame butter or the "dynamite oysters"—baked local oysters with spiced chili-ginger infusion.

Serving excellent food without pretense, **Bridge** (37 Main St., Westerly, 401/348-9700, www.bridgeri.com, 11:30am-10pm Mon.-Sat., 10am-10pm Sun., $11-24) is situated in a refurbished mill overlooking the Pawcatuck River. The menu is heavy on farm-fresh ingredients and local seafood—favorites such as lobster rolls, steamed mussels, grilled swordfish tacos, and calamari share the menu with vegetarian options like roasted vegetable tamales. The garden patio is a great spot to hang out on summer evenings.

Comfort Food
One of the largest dining rooms on the beach, **Paddy's** (159 Atlantic Ave., Misquamicut, 401/596-4350, www.paddysbeach.com, 11am-1am daily in summer, call for winter hours, $14-25) serves unexpectedly good and often creative food, especially considering

the crowds that pile in on many summer weekends. Favorites include penne in pink vodka sauce with lightly fried calamari and Parmesan cheese; the "bucket" of mussels with a sweet-and-spicy Thai butter sauce and grilled focaccia; and pan-seared tuna served rare over mashed potatoes with miso vinaigrette. The kitchen does a nice job balancing hearty and uncomplicated favorites with some nicely inventive fare. The ocean views from the restaurant make the food taste that much better.

A former speakeasy during the Prohibition era, the ★ **Rathskeller** (489a Old Coach Rd., Charlestown, 401/792-1000, www.thecharlestownrathskeller.com, 11am-1am daily) in Charlestown reopened in 2014 after several years of closure. The resurrected bar and restaurant is mostly shiny and new, but details like a stone fireplace and several wall murals in the dining room dating back 80 years have been preserved. The food here is delicious—try the German sausage plate with knackwurst, bockwurst, and smoked bratwurst with sauerkraut, or the littleneck clams with linguini. The restaurant's back patio is also nice—complete with horseshoe games, volleyball and bocce courts, and a fire pit around which you can enjoy a beer on summer nights.

Cafés and Sandwich Shops

At the far west corner of the state, you'll find **Dave's Coffee** (5193 Old Post Rd., Charlestown, www.davescoffeestore.com, 401/322-0006, 6am-6pm daily, $2-5), a certified organic roaster and coffee shop situated inside a cute little clapboard colonial on Route 1. If you're in the Charlestown area, this is the place to pick up first-rate espresso, fresh-baked muffins, breads, and other pastries (some of which are vegan and/or gluten free) before you head out to the beach. In colder weather, their cozy café is a nice place to spend a relaxing afternoon reading or playing board games.

In Westerly, the **Cooked Goose** (92 Watch Hill Rd., Westerly, 401/348-9888, www.thecookedgoose.com, 7am-7pm daily summer, 7am-3pm daily Columbus Day-Memorial Day) is one of the best sources in the county for gourmet foods, both prepared and packaged. You can also pick up takeout sandwiches, breakfasts, and the like. Specialties include fresh H&H Bagels delivered from New York City, quiche (the selection changes daily), curried chicken salad, and gourmet sandwiches like the Avondale (smoked turkey, Havarti cheese, and cranberry mayo on pumpernickel). Fresh-baked pies, Louisiana bread pudding, and lemon squares are among the dozens of desserts available each day.

A Westerly coffee hangout that also doubles as a wine bar is **Perks and Corks** (62 High St., Westerly, 401/596-1260, www.perksandcorks.com, 11am-1am Sun.-Fri., 9am-1am Sat., $2-12), a living-room-style café with plush sofas and armchairs and a slightly bohemian vibe. You can also order bagels, fresh-baked breads, desserts, and fine wines and cocktails, along with organic teas, lattes, and the like. Check the website for occasional live music and open mic nights.

Accommodations

In some respects, South County is a throw-back to another era when it comes to accommodations. Of the more than 100 options in the area, the vast majority are closer than 1 mile (1.6 km) from the ocean. Very few are chain properties, and very few offer the sort of upscale accommodations you'd find in Newport or Block Island. South County is a community where family-run, comparatively simple hotels, motor lodges, and motels dominate the landscape. It's fairly easy to find accommodations that sleep 4-8 guests with kitchen facilities and plenty of social- and activity-oriented amenities like playgrounds, pools, shuffleboard courts, and boat launches. Especially in Misquamicut, you'll find several properties directly on the beach.

A drawback of sorts is that it's rather difficult to find seaside properties with character; the expectation is that visitors to South County aren't likely to spend a whole lot of time in their rooms. There are a couple of historic properties in Watch Hill, and you'll find a smattering of atmospheric inns both near the shore and inland. Also, while accommodations aren't fancy or super expensive, they're generally not bargain-basement cheap in summer, at least near the water. During July and August weekends it can be tough to find accommodations for less than $100. The most economical deals tend to be hotels that have efficiencies or cottages available by the week—these are especially economical if you're booking a unit that sleeps a few people.

$100-150

The Surfside Motel (334 Narrow Lane, Charleston, 401/364-1010, $99-150) is one of the least expensive independently owned motels in South County, with a great location just off Route 1, close to both the Ninigret National Wildlife Refuge and several of the state's most pristine beaches. The rooms are simple but bright and tastefully decorated, with all of the standard amenities; some rooms have kitchenettes. Guests also have access to grills, picnic tables, and a fire pit. Especially if you plan on spending most of your time outdoors, the price-to-quality ratio here is a best bet.

Another inexpensive option for those wishing to be close to the beach is the **Scarborough Beach Motel** (901 Ocean Rd., 401/783-2063, www.scarboroughbeachmotel. com, $125-175). The rooms might leave something to be desired aesthetically speaking, but it's a clean and comfortable base from which to enjoy the ocean, the shops, and restaurants of Narragansett Pier, and the views at Point Judith. Guest rooms have Wi-Fi, televisions, and air-conditioning, and there's a small grassy yard with picnic tables.

A short walk from the beaches in Matunuck, the ★ **Admiral Dewey Inn** (668 Matunuck Beach Rd., 401/783-2090, www.admiraldeweyinn.com, $150-180) is a towering 1898 summer beach house whose upper floors afford exceptional views of the ocean and Block Island Sound. The inn opened as a boardinghouse back at the turn of the 20th century; these days you can expect somewhat fancier accommodations, but the 10 guest rooms are still happily uncluttered and informal, with hardwood floors, brass and carved-wood headboards and beds, and Victorian furnishings and wallpapers. Most rooms have private baths, and half offer ocean views. A buffet breakfast is set up in the dining room or, when weather permits, on the porch. Just across the street is Matunuck's Theatre-by-the-Sea.

One of the best economy motels in Rhode Island, the **Hamilton Village Inn** (642 Boston Neck Rd., North Kingstown, 401/295-0700, www.hamiltonvillageinn.com, $100-149) is a dapper white structure that sits along the road between Wickford village and the bridge to Jamestown—it's close to Casey

Farm and the Gilbert Stuart Museum and not far from the beaches. Rooms are clean, and suites have fully equipped kitchens. The grounds consist of nicely cared-for gardens and towering trees, and the diner-style on-site restaurant, Sea View Station, serves three meals a day.

$150-250

Blue Oaks Bed and Breakfast (146 Boston Neck Rd., Wickford, 401/268-3902, www.blueoaksbedandbreakfast.com, $199-249) is a traditional early-20th-century four-square clapboard home with five warmly-furnished guest rooms, each with a private bath. Decor is a nice balance of modern and Victorian era, with luxury linens and robes, and fresh-baked breakfast pastries and coffee served each morning. For the price and the quality, this location can't be beat.

A six-room Second Empire farmhouse dating to the 1870s, Langworthy Farm (308 Shore Rd., Westerly, 401/322-7791, www.langworthyfarm.com, $175-210) is an upscale bed-and-breakfast with four charming guest rooms and a pair of suites. In the Weekapaug section of Westerly, the inn has ocean views from some rooms. One suite has two full bedrooms, each with its own private bath. Some rooms have whirlpool tubs. The farm also has a small winery.

If you're looking to stay inland in the Wyoming and Hope Valley area, not far from the University of Rhode Island, consider the Stagecoach House Inn (1136 Main St., Wyoming, 401/539-9600, www.stagecoachhouse.com, $159-199), a former 18th-century stagecoach inn. The hotel is just off I-95, overlooking a peaceful river, and all guest rooms—which are in a newer motor-lodge-style unit—have gas fireplaces and tubs with jets. Continental breakfast is included, and the inn sits directly across from the Wood River Inn, a popular restaurant with a nice selection of draft beer.

An easy walk from Town Beach in Narragansett, the 1870s Blueberry Cove Inn (75 Kingstown Rd., Narragansett, 401/792-7865, www.blueberrycoveinn.com, $100-260) has seven guest rooms, including one suite with a whirlpool tub and fireplace. The white Victorian presides over well-trimmed lawns and gardens, and rooms are decked with luxurious Egyptian-cotton linens, canopy beds, televisions, air-conditioning, and tasteful (if a bit flowery) Victorian furnishings. A lavish full breakfast is included.

OVER $250

A large clapboard hotel right on the bay in the heart of Narragansett Pier, the Aqua Blue Hotel (1 Beach St., Narragansett Pier, 401/783-6767, www.aquabluehotels.com, $250-410) has 62 fairly large and contemporary rooms with typical chain-hotel-style furnishings. The big reason to stay here is location: It's adjacent to The Towers at Narragansett Pier and within walking distance of the beach, many shops and restaurants, and the South County Museum. Pluses include whirlpool tubs in most rooms, balconies, and a full-service spa. There's also a lounge with a sundeck and two restaurants.

A popular spot facing Narragansett Bay, the ★ Ocean Rose Inn (113 Ocean Ave., Narragansett Pier, 401/783-4704, www.oceanroseinn.com, $200-350) describes itself as "beach chic." The main inn dates to 1901 and contains nine gorgeous guest rooms with polished hardwood floors, four-poster beds, and decor that's hip and fresh without being pretentious. Some rooms have private decks, and all have fabulous water views. There's also a long veranda with chairs looking out over the water. A second, contemporary building contains 18 guest rooms, many of which also enjoy very nice water views—these accommodations have less character but are more practical for kids. All rooms in both buildings have private baths. The Turtle Soup restaurant, on the ground floor of the main inn, serves very good contemporary fare.

1: the Admiral Dewey Inn in Matunuck
2: the historic Ocean Rose Inn in Watch Hill

As one of the only boutique hotels in South County, **The Break** (1208 Ocean Rd., Narragansett, 401/363-9800, www. thebreakhotel.com, $250-450) is a trendy, 16-room hotel decorated in bright, modern colors, and upscale, colorful furnishings. Located just a few minutes away from Point Judith and the beaches at Narragansett Pier, The Break offers a heated outdoor pool and sundeck, a gym and spa, complimentary beach bags and chairs available to borrow, an onsite restaurant, and complimentary breakfast served on the rooftop lounge.

A stately gambrel-roofed house near both Misquamicut and Watch Hill is **The Villa** (190 Shore Rd., Misquamicut, 800/722-9240, www.thevillaatwesterly.com, $300-450). The grounds have flower gardens, an in-ground pool, and a hot tub, and the Mediterranean-inspired house contains six guest suites, some with whirlpool tubs, fireplaces, and private terraces. These are cushy, couples-oriented rooms that are perfect for special occasions; one has a skylight situated directly above its double whirlpool bath, while the master suite's double whirlpool bath faces the gas fireplace. In warm weather, breakfast is served on the lanai overlooking the pool and gardens.

At the comparatively quiet west end of Misquamicut Beach, still an easy walk or bike ride from the boardwalk and with glorious views of the ocean and plenty of beachfront, the **Pleasant View Inn** (65 Atlantic Ave., Misquamicut, 401/348-8200, www. pvinn.com, $250-350) is this community's largest hotel, with 112 rooms, many of them overlooking the ocean. Room rates depend on the view, size, and amenities, but all rooms have cable TV and most have private balconies; suites have microwaves, refrigerators, and wet bars. The Pleasant View has a pair of restaurants, one more casual and serving lighter snacks, but neither of them is overly formal.

A Victorian-inspired inn that actually dates to 1939, the **Weekapaug Inn** (25 Spray Rock Rd., Weekapaug, 401/322-0301, www.weekapauginn.com, $450 and up) is a long building with a roofline punctuated by more than a dozen gables, overlooking Quonochontaug Pond and the ocean just beyond that. Its uncomplicated rooms are tidy and attractive, well-tended by the fourth generation of Buffum family innkeepers. However, you won't find TVs or phones in these rooms—guests who favor the Weekapaug are seeking the peace and quiet of the sea. Entertainment tends to revolve around playing board games in the lobby or taking in one of the many guest lectures or storytelling events frequently set up by the innkeepers. Outdoor amenities are many: shuffleboard, lawn bowling, croquet, bicycles, canoes, sailboats, and tennis courts. Children's activities, including arts and crafts and nature walks, are organized each day. This is an all-inclusive resort, so while rates begin at nearly $450 per double-occupancy room per night, they include three very good meals each day, plus all activities and facilities (children are charged about $150 per person per night).

CAMPING

Burlingame State Park (Sanctuary Rd., follow signs north from U.S. 1, Charlestown, check station 401/322-7994, camp store 401/322-2629, www.riparks.com, $18/night) is an enormous reserve of about 2,100 acres with about 750 simple campsites; you can stay as long as two weeks, and there are washing facilities and toilets near the sites. You'll also find a general store, excellent swimming, and abundant peace among the fragrant pine trees. Other park facilities include a boat launch, ample covered and open picnic facilities, and fishing. Picnic sites cost $2 per day, and the group picnic shelters cost $35. As at all Rhode Island state parks, except the beaches, there's no day-use fee.

An easy drive from the ocean is **Whispering Pines Campground** (41 Saw Mill Rd., Hope Valley, 401/539-7011, www.

whisperingpinescamping.com, $43-59 per night), which has 200 sites for tent and RV camping, some with water and electricity hookups, all with free Wi-Fi. Facilities include a sizable swimming pool, mini-golf course, bocce and horseshoes, basketball and volleyball courts, athletic fields for softball and soccer, a game room, snack bar, and playground. You can also fish in a catch-and-release freshwater pond, which has a beach with complimentary canoes and paddleboats. If you're looking for a more peaceful, secluded wilderness experience, this is not it—noisy power generators from the many RVs run throughout the night, and weekend entertainment like DJ nights and karaoke are not uncommon.

Inland a few miles but along a pretty freshwater pond, **Worden's Pond Family Campground** (416A Worden's Pond Rd., Wakefield, 401/789-9113, www.wordenpondfamilycampground.com, May-mid-Oct., $50 per night) is a 65-acre spread with about 200 campsites nestled in the woods. Amenities include showers, restrooms, fishing, swimming, and a playground. Oddly enough, the campground does not offer tent-camping—RVs only are permitted, and a one-week minimum is required in July and August.

Transportation and Services

GETTING THERE AND AROUND
Airports
Westerly Airport (U.S. 1 and Rte. 78, in Connecticut I-95 exit 92 from the south, in Rhode Island I-95 exit 1 from the north) is South County's regional air facility. It's primarily used by private planes and charters, and it's where you can catch flights on several airlines to Block Island. **New England Airlines** (800/243-2460, www.block-island.com), the regular airline between Westerly and Block Island, can be booked for charters from Westerly to many other parts of the country. Of course, as for all of Rhode Island, Warwick's T. F. Green Airport is the main way to reach South County by air.

Buses
Rhode Island Public Transit Authority (RIPTA) (401/781-9400, www.ripta.com) runs several buses connecting South County with Providence, Newport, and other parts of the state.

Driving
U.S. 1 runs west-east near the shore to Narragansett and then north near the bay through North Kingstown. Route 4 cuts northwest from it and joins I-95 as the most direct route from South County to Providence and points north. For taxis, contact **Eagle Cab** (Narragansett, 401/783-2970). You can also rent a car from **Enterprise** (6980 Post Rd., North Kingstown, 401/885-7558, www.enterprise.com).

I-95 skirts the upper half of South County and is the best way to reach the area from Connecticut and points south, but the main road through lower South County is U.S. 1, a busy four-lane highway and a fairly quick route except on summer weekends and at rush hour. Route 1A is the more scenic route, running mostly parallel to U.S. 1 as it jogs along the coast, offering access to beaches and many of the quaint shoreline communities. Route 138 runs west-east through the county's midsection and then continues to Jamestown and Newport. For taxi service, contact **Wright's Taxi** (Westerly, 401/596-8294).

Trains
One of two Rhode Island train stations served by Amtrak, **Kingston Railroad Station**

(1 Railroad Ave., off Kingstown Rd./Rte. 138, www.trainweb.org/kin, 6am-10:45pm daily) is a handsome clapboard building on the National Register of Historic Places, built in 1875 in the Victorian stick style with influences of a European chalet. **Amtrak** (800/872-7245, www.amtrak.com) stops in Westerly at 14 Railroad Avenue.

VISITOR INFORMATION

The **Narragansett Chamber of Commerce** (36 Ocean Rd., 401/783-7121, www.narragansettcoc.com) runs a visitors center in The Towers in Narragansett Pier. For info on Wickford and the rest of North Kingstown, contact **North Kingstown Chamber of Commerce** (8045 Post Rd., North Kingstown, 401/295-5566, www.northkingstown.com).

For information on Westerly, stop by the **Greater Westerly-Pawcatuck Chamber of Commerce** (1 Chamber Way, 401/596-7761, www.westerlychamber.org), which runs a comprehensive visitors center off of Route 1.

For Charlestown, contact the **Charlestown Chamber of Commerce** (4945 Old Post Rd., 401/364-3878, www.charlestownrichamber.com).

For information on all of South County, contact the **South County Tourism Council** (4808 Tower Hill Rd./U.S. 1, Wakefield, 401/789-4422 or 800/548-4662, www.southcountyri.com). To learn more about South Kingstown, contact **South Kingstown Chamber of Commerce** (230 Old Tower Hill Rd., Wakefield, 401/783-2801, www.skchamber.com).

MEDIA

This part of South County produces two newspapers: *The Standard-Times* (401/789-9744, www.ricentral.com) and the *Narragansett Times* (401/789-9744, www.ricentral.com), which comes out twice weekly. Get local news and entertainment information from the *Westerly Sun* (401/348-1000, www.thewesterlysun.com), published daily.

Background

The Landscape

A tiny state of just about **1,500 square miles,** Rhode Island contains about 400 mi (645 km) of shoreline, including inlets, rivers, estuaries, and bays. Nearly every inch of the state lies within 20 mi (32 km) of the ocean or Narragansett Bay, which begins at the northern end of the state, first as the Seekonk River and then the Providence River, and a large chunk of the state is on the islands of Aquidneck, Conanicut, Prudence, Block, and a few others. And while Rhode Island has a very high population density, the state actually feels fairly rural and undeveloped in many places.

Despite the nearly constant proximity of water frontage, Rhode Island has a distinct inland region, which has a personality that is much like that of the rest of interior southern New England. The southern end of the state, however, from Napatree Point in the extreme southwest to Point Judith to the east, is one long and scenic expanse of beautiful golden sand, punctuated only by the occasional inlet. Directly behind these beaches are long and deep salt ponds, created by occasional breaks in the beach that allowed saltwater to pour in and that have then been sealed by shifting sands. These salt ponds are sheltered havens for wildlife watching, water sports, and fishing.

At Point Judith, the endless string of beaches gives way to the mouth of enormous Narragansett Bay. Beaches extend, off and on, up the western shore of the bay nearly to Providence. A little more than 1 mi (1.6 km) across Narragansett Bay lies the long and narrow Conanicut Island and, another mile (1.6 km) east of that, the considerably larger Aquidneck Island. About 10 mi (16 km) due south of Point Judith, well away from the mainland, lies the summer resort community of Block Island. And another couple of miles east of Aquidneck is the final bit of Rhode Island's oceanfront, Sakonnet. Another 5 mi (8 km) east and you're in Massachusetts.

The thin swath of land fringing the ocean from Napatree Point clear up around Narragansett Bay to Providence is characterized by its low elevation and sandy soil. The East Bay and Sakonnet areas are slightly higher in elevation and are composed mostly of sandstone and other rock that hasn't eroded to nearly the degree that the low coastal plain has through the eons. Most of Rhode Island, however, is characterized by rolling terrain with peaks rising occasionally to 700 or 800 feet—not terribly high compared with northern New England or even the highest points in nearby northeastern Connecticut and central Massachusetts. But compared with other small states that fringe the Eastern Seaboard—New Jersey and Delaware, for example—Rhode Island is relatively hilly and offers a nice balance for anybody who loves to admire both the ocean and the hilly countryside.

GEOLOGY

Geologically speaking, Rhode Island offers a classic view of how **glaciers** form the land. Virtually every square foot of the state owes its general appearance to the encroachment and then recession of a massive glacial formation that ended just a split second ago in geological terms, around 8000 BC.

Except for a narrow strip of coastal plain near the ocean, the western two-thirds of Rhode Island sits atop very **ancient igneous and metamorphic rock.** The eastern third (where you'll find Providence and the Blackstone River Valley, the islands of Narragansett Bay, the East Bay towns, and the Sakonnet Peninsula) lies on younger and softer sedimentary rock. The land underlying Block Island and that little strip of **coastal plain** in South County, however, originally came from much farther north.

A block of ice perhaps a mile high drifted down from Canada as far south as the present tip of Rhode Island during the most recent ice age. This catastrophic action scarred the soil, lifting boulders, rocks, and sediment from northern New England and carrying them hundreds of miles south to the ocean. As the earth's temperature rose and the glacier on top of Rhode Island slowly melted, a stream of debris-laden water flowed downhill toward sea level, building up piles of rocks at the leading edge of the glacier—and forming the terminal moraine that underlies Block Island.

As the glacier continued to recede northward, it likely paused for a time, leaving another deposit of sand and debris called a recessional moraine. It now forms the narrow

The Name Game

The genesis of how and why Rhode Island acquired its official name—technically known as Rhode Island and Providence Plantations—has never been definitively nailed down. The region has no particular history linking it to the Greek island of Rhodes, and it is quite clearly not an island. So how did it come to be known as Rhode Island?

The history of the name is a jumble of vague associations and mistaken identities, but it's believed that the name Rhode was first used to describe Block Island by 16th-century Italian explorer Giovanni da Verrazano, who wrote that it reminded him of the Greek island. In the next century, sailors passing by another small Narragansett Bay island, today known as Aquidneck, mistook it for the island Verrazano had identified, and started calling it Rhode Island. Later, as Providence developed, the entire region became known as Rhode Island and Providence Plantations.

Confused? No doubt the state's residents were, too, which may be why they later shortened the state's name to simply Rhode Island. Legally, however, it remains Rhode Island and Providence Plantations—the longest name in all the United States, ironically held by its smallest state.

fringe of sandy coastal plain that lies along the shore.

While most of the land of Rhode Island was not deposited by glaciers, every inch of it was shaped by glacial movement. Before the ice age, this land would have stood many yards higher in elevation and would have looked much different from the way it does today. The land that has now been displaced by Narragansett Bay would have been soft rock and soil that gave way easily to the tremendous weight and pressure exerted by the massive glaciers—this soil was pushed out into the ocean by the glacier's steady and massive push.

The islands of Aquidneck, Conanicut, and Prudence, along with the jagged peninsulas that poke into the bay from Bristol, Warwick, and other Narragansett towns, resisted the glacial erosion more effectively. The earth here is chiefly composed of ancient igneous and metamorphic rock—it's not as hard and erosion-resistant as the western and northwestern interior sections of the state, and so it's not nearly as hilly. But these islands and peninsulas provided a substantial enough resistance to survive the ice age above sea level, while the glaciers carved out what is now the bay around them.

Throughout the state's interior, you'll see other evidence of glacial activity. Some of the state's many freshwater ponds and natural reservoirs were formed when a chunk of glacier broke off and melted, forming a so-called kettle pond. And everywhere you'll find boulders and rocks made up of granite, quartz, and other materials that were carried out this far by glacial activity.

The glacier is also partially responsible for eroding the softer soil that once covered much of western Rhode Island, revealing the harder igneous and metamorphic rock below the surface. Those rocks were formed by molten lava that pushed its way out from the earth's mantle and cooled beneath the surface over many millions of millennia. Where that surface has been eroded, jagged and sharp rocky ridges now rise out of the soil.

The mostly sedimentary rock that forms the eastern third of the state is rather new by geological standards, perhaps a couple of million years old. This rock was formed by deposits of mud, gravel, and sand over a lower bedrock of igneous and metamorphic rock, which over eons of shifting and faulting earth were compressed and in some cases pushed up to the earth's surface. Some of this muck compressed into coal, of which small deposits have been found in Portsmouth, Cranston, and other parts of Rhode Island through the years; these are among the easternmost coal deposits found on the North American continent.

CLIMATE

Compared with some other regions of New England, Rhode Island enjoys a fairly **moderate climate,** especially in the parts of the state that lie within 15 mi (24 km) or so of the ocean and the bay (meaning most of the state). The presence of the Atlantic Ocean and Narragansett Bay keep temperatures a bit warmer in winter than inland, meaning that big snowstorms in Massachusetts often take the form of rain here. Conversely, in summer, hot weather is often cooled by sea breezes, especially out on Block Island and the southern tips of Westerly and Newport.

Its position on the Gulf Stream ensures rather unpredictable weather, especially during hurricane season (midsummer through mid-fall), as ocean-driven winds often sweep across the entire state. Major damage-inducing storms rarely hit more than once every 5-10 years, however. The state has a long growing season by Northeastern standards, generally commencing in late April through early May and lasting through the better part of October (it's longer, obviously, along the coast).

Statewide, the average low temperature in January is about 21°F, and the average high in July is about 83°F. Annual precipitation (in both rain and snow) averages about 42 inches per year and ranges anywhere from 25 to nearly 70 inches. The state, at least in the northwestern hills, usually sees its first real snowfall in late November to early December, and the last one is in April. Rainfall tends to be consistent throughout the year, with 3-4 inches monthly (the lowest amounts are in summer, but passing and not infrequent late-afternoon and evening thunderstorms can dump significant amounts of rain).

Environmental Issues

As nice as it is for wildlife watchers to be in such close proximity to fauna, it's also unfortunate because wild animals have become increasingly dependent on people and dangerously abundant in areas with heavy traffic and an environment that barely supports them. Where there is overpopulation, they are a nuisance in the eyes of many people—blamed for spreading **Lyme disease,** ravaging gardens and yards, and causing traffic accidents. Rhode Island does have some areas that are sparsely populated by people, especially the western and northwestern sections of the state—you'll even find a few designated hunting grounds. But anybody who drives on a daily basis in Rhode Island is sure to see deer leaping across the road, usually at night—sadly, many have been struck.

With all the talk these days of **encroaching suburban sprawl**—and it's true that this trend is one of the greatest threats facing the state in the 21st century—it's easy to forget that most of Rhode Island was already deforested by the early 1800s, when the state's economy was almost entirely agrarian.

Ironically, the region's woodlands were saved not so much by conservation efforts, which didn't develop in earnest until the 20th century, but by the Industrial Revolution. In places where the hilly, rocky terrain made fast and simple transportation routes difficult, or where a lack of rivers made hydropower impractical, the land was left largely to revert to woodland, and some areas were even reforested to increase the supply of lumber.

Despite this, the amount of undeveloped land has consistently diminished at a rapid rate since the late 19th century. In Rhode Island's countless river valleys, fields of crops gave way to mills and factories. Farms still thrive in a few parts of the state, but their number has decreased dramatically.

Rhode Island's regulatory economy has ensured that much of the area enjoys clean air and water, as efforts have been made to clean up the pollution of the mills and factories that boosted the economy in the 20th century. Isolated **chemical factories and power plants** continue to cause problems in some areas.

One of the most contentious ongoing issues in the region is the controversy over how to manage coastal fish and shellfish effectively. Rampant **overfishing** had decimated cod, flounder, and other groundfish species by the mid-1980s. At that point, the federal government seized fisheries all over New England in a bid to restore populations using quotas and periodic bans. While the effort has been successful at restoring some species, such as haddock, bluefish, and many species of shellfish, others still languish at severely reduced levels. In addition to overfishing, many cold-water species like cod are moving farther north as southern waters increase in temperature. While many of the state's fishing ports are still thriving, **climate change** will continue to have a direct impact on the fisheries in southern New England as populations of warmer-water species move in, and the effects of water acidification play out on shellfish like lobster, oysters, and clams.

Plants

TREES AND SHRUBS

About **50 species of tree** are common to New England, but only a fraction are present in Rhode Island. The state is about 60 percent forested, with slightly more than 400,000 acres of woodland. Common conifers ("evergreens") throughout the state include the conical eastern red cedars, towering reddish-brown tamaracks, prickly blue spruces, white and red pines, hemlocks, and right along the shore in some spots, gnarled pitch pines.

While you don't hear as much about leaf peeping in Rhode Island as you do in other New England states, Rhode Island's broadleaf trees put on a spectacular show each fall, especially in places with sugar, silver, and red maple trees—the red maple, also known as the swamp maple, is Rhode Island's state tree. The peak time for watching them burst with bright foliage is late October in most of the state and mid-October in the most northwestern and hilly areas. There are 11 species of oak in Rhode Island, and they can be quite brilliant in the fall—you're most likely to see white, scarlet, bear, swamp white, scrub, pin, post, chestnut, and black oak trees.

Some of the other tall Rhode Island broadleaf species include beech, birch (the pretty white birch are more prevalent in the north), dogwoods (which flower beautifully all spring), elms (although many of these perished from disease during the middle of the last century), holly, poplar, honey locust, hickory, and weeping willow.

Smaller broadleaf trees and shrubs that dot the landscape, many of which bloom with a riot of colors, include speckled alder, dogwood, sumac, pink azalea, rhododendron, multiflora and beach rose, northern bayberry, and pussy willow.

Hundreds of varieties of **wildflowers** bloom across the state, beginning most vibrantly in June and remaining vital well into early fall. Also look for **beach plum,** a shrub bearing hard plumlike fruit that is ubiquitous on the coast in Rhode Island and puts on quite a show with its pretty fuchsia flowers.

Animals

Much of Rhode Island's flora and fauna is typical of southern New England. The state is a haven for **bird-watching,** as the coast and Narragansett Bay are on a major migratory bird route. Several parks and preserves near the water have been established specifically for this purpose.

There's actually a misconception that the farther north you go in New England, the more likely you are to see wildlife. In fact, in Vermont, New Hampshire, and Maine, so much of the land is undeveloped that many animals steer clear of roads, villages, and people—they have the luxury of rarely having to leave their remote habitats, and they maintain a healthy fear of mankind. Rhode Island, however densely populated it may be, is actually an easy place to spot a variety of animals. The state is heavily wooded, with quite a few parks and preserves, and yet it is also heavily developed. Wildlife and human life coexist in close proximity, and mammals in Rhode Island tend to be less afraid of people and better able to feed themselves by scavenging through backyards, compost heaps, and garbage cans.

INVERTEBRATES

Coastal Rhode Island has long had a reputation for its abundance of shellfish, but during much of the 20th century pollution and overfishing combined to deplete or spoil the region as a source of seafood. Thankfully, immensely ambitious efforts to clean up the waters off Rhode Island, along with careful harvesting regulations, have restored the region's stock of these tasty creatures.

A great range of marine invertebrates are found off Rhode Island's shoreline, including a number of **jellyfish** and **sea anemones,** most of which are harmless, except for the large and extremely dangerous lion's mane jellyfish, which is more common in northern waters. Scour the beaches and rocks during low tide and you'll find **marine mollusks** of every ilk, from Atlantic dogwinkles and edible common periwinkles to large (up to six inches long) knobbed whelks that live in those pretty yellow-gray shells that kids are prone to hold to their ears in hopes of hearing the seashore. You'll also see tons of lively hermit crabs sidling along the beach line, living safely inside the mobile homes they've fashioned out of gastropod shells.

Tasty **blue mussels** cling to rocks and pilings. **Bay scallops** and **Eastern oysters** are found in shallow waters, as are clams. A true Rhode Islander knows how to identify clams—long, thin razor clams, hard-shell **Northern quahogs** (which include the prized cherrystones and littlenecks, the latter often found minced in clam chowder and atop pizzas), **Atlantic surf clams,** and most deliciously, soft-shelled "steamer" clams. Also found in shallow waters among the rocks and mudflats are sea urchins (which are dangerous if stepped on), common green crabs, rock crabs, sand fiddlers, and the famously delicious **blue crabs.** Farther out, beginning in about 10 feet of water, **sea scallops** and **lobsters** make their homes, coming closest to the shore in summer.

Less engaging to most people are the many land invertebrates that slither and crawl around the state, and indeed some of these—**ticks, mosquitoes, horseflies** and **deerflies, carpenter ants, yellow jackets, cockroaches, Japanese beetles**—are a genuine nuisance. But on summer nights it's a comfort to fall asleep to the distinct chatter, trill, and staccato of the zillions of katydids and tree crickets. **Spiders** munch on most pests and rarely bother humans, as is true of the many beautiful **dragonflies, butterflies,** and **ladybugs** that swarm around flowerbeds.

BIRDS AND FISH

Given the Ocean State's coastal location, many islands, and extensive shoreline, Rhode Island is rich with sea creatures and birdlife, and fishing and bird-watching are among Rhode Islanders' favorite pastimes. Fairly close to shore in season (May to Nov.) are bluefish and striped bass. Many other varieties of fish are found in deeper and farther reaches of the Atlantic. People sometimes overlook the fact that Rhode Island also has dozens of freshwater ponds, lakes, and rivers; inland species common in the state include trout (many ponds are stocked with them), bluegills, bass, and perch.

Rhode Island lies in the middle of a common migratory route for many species of North American birdlife. The state's coastal areas and many wildlife preserves contain a veritable who's who of the bird world, especially in spring as birds fly from warmer climes toward Canada, and in fall when they head south again. Large, dramatic species such as peregrine falcons and blue herons can be spotted throughout the year, while smaller species, including warblers, sparrows, and thrushes, congregate at beaches and other low-lying areas during the summer and fall.

REPTILES AND AMPHIBIANS

Thirteen species of snake live in Rhode Island, none of them poisonous. Rattlesnakes and copperheads, common to other parts of New England, are considered all but extinct here, although there may be some slithering around the western and northwestern hills. Note that many nonvenomous snakes resemble their venomous cousins; **Eastern hognose snakes** look like copperheads, for instance.

Turtles are the other type of reptile commonly found in Rhode Island, especially painted turtles, which are known to sunbathe in groups around rivers and swamps. Respect the space of the **snapping turtle,** whose sturdy jaws can leave you with a nasty bite. You won't see them very often, but they do love to swim and cavort in muddy-bottomed rivers and other bodies of water.

Among amphibians, **newts** and **salamanders** aren't easy to see, as they often blend in well with their surroundings, but the yellow-spotted and red varieties do stand out a bit. They tend to be found around creeks and live under rocks and logs, and they are most visible March through October during the day. **Frogs** are often known for their loud choruses on spring and summer nights when they seek out mates. Spring peepers, bullfrogs, and Woodhouse's toads frequent ponds and swamps, while common American toads and wood frogs prefer yards, fields, and wooded areas. In spring, unfortunately, thousands of frogs and toads are hit by automobiles in areas where large numbers of them are moving toward popular breeding grounds.

MAMMALS

The mammals you're mostly likely to see around Rhode Island are **white-tailed deer, raccoons, opossums, Eastern chipmunks, Eastern gray squirrels,** and **striped skunks.** All of these species are common in secluded woodlands, developed suburbs, and even some urban areas, and most of them are not easily startled by the presence of human beings.

Skunks, opossums, and raccoons are primarily nocturnal, and if you see one during the day, you should keep your distance, especially if it's behaving erratically or aggressively; there's a chance it's carrying rabies. If you come into physical contact with such a creature, you should immediately contact an emergency physician.

Less commonly sighted animals, which you have the best chance of seeing in state parks and preserves, include **black bears** (only rarely in northwestern Rhode Island), **Eastern cottontail rabbits, woodchucks, beavers, meadow voles, coyotes** (again mostly in the northern part of the state, but they are becoming increasingly common despite once being

virtually extinct), **gray and red foxes, fishers, mink,** and **river otters.**

Whale-watching cruises operate off Rhode Island's coast—these dramatic sea mammals, once hunted to near-extinction, often inhabit the state's waters. Finback, humpback, and minke whales are sighted most often, as is the occasional school of bottlenose dolphins. Whales are most common spring to fall, with small numbers summering off the coast and the majority passing through in April through May on their way north and back south again in October through December during their migration to warmer waters.

Both harbor and gray seals, which have always been fairly common from Maine to Cape Cod, have made a recent comeback along Rhode Island's shoreline, primarily in Narragansett Bay.

History

BEFORE 1636

The land that is now Rhode Island was occupied by a handful of Algonquin Native American groups through much of the early part of the last millennium—Narragansetts, Niantics, Nipmucs, Pequots, and Wampanoags all lived here, and not always at peace with one another. The nations shared a common genealogical heritage and similar languages and other cultural traits, but they also observed their own distinct rituals, laws, and other practices. Even today, many Rhode Island place-names have Native American roots: Conanicut Island, for example, is named for Canonicus, a 17th-century leader of the Narragansetts; Pawtucket translates as "place with the waterfall"; and Sakonnet means "land of the wild goose."

Contrary to what some history books might have schoolkids believe, the colonists from England who arrived in the New World in the 1620s did not find an impenetrable wilderness but rather a network of Indian villages, staked-out fishing areas, and cleared and tilled fields. Even the forests were open and parklike, the result of frequent burnings to aid in hunting.

Among Rhode Island's indigenous peoples, women took on many of the most labor-intensive tasks, cultivating and harvesting the fields, tanning hides, and maintaining order at home. In warmer months the people settled in open fields, and with the coming of cold weather they moved to wooded valleys and other sheltered areas.

When Roger Williams and his followers settled in Rhode Island, the area was home to perhaps 20,000 Native Americans. Although Williams himself worked peacefully with the people he encountered near Providence, within 50 years the effects of European settlement almost wiped out the population. The settlers spread smallpox and other diseases that Europeans were immune to, but Native Americans were not; they systematically removed Native Americans from the best land, and eventually from all the land; they introduced alcohol, murdered many who fought to keep their land, and sold many more into slavery.

Before the first Europeans established a permanent settlement in Rhode Island, quite a few explorers passed near the shore or spent time on land, and some left accounts of their time here. A few early state histories asserted that the Vikings were Rhode Island's first European inhabitants, but it is now believed that those settlements were many miles north of present-day New England in Canada's Labrador. One early explorer to survey the coast appears to have been Portuguese navigator Miguel Corte-Real, who sailed through

1: birds at a nature preserve on Block Island 2: green pastures in South County 3: The industrialization of America began when engineers turned to the river to power their machinery.

234

BACKGROUND
HISTORY

in 1511. The most celebrated explorer, however, is no doubt Giovanni da Verrazano, a Florentine sailing in the New World under the French flag; in 1524, he explored the waters around New York City (the Verrazano Narrows Bridge, which connects Brooklyn to Staten Island, is named for him) and up to Rhode Island. Dutch traders later explored the coast, among them Adriaen Block, for whom Block Island is named.

COLONIAL SETTLEMENT

The founder of modern Rhode Island's first permanent European settlement is Roger Williams, who arrived in 1636 in what is now Providence. This happened a year after an odd and reclusive Anglican clergyman named William Blackstone (for whom the river and valley are named) established a camp in what is now Cumberland, but Blackstone lived alone, largely as a hermit, and no true community emerged in his wake. Williams arrived with the intention of establishing a settlement, and he did so quickly. More remarkably, he arrived after having been banished from the Massachusetts Bay Colony, where his beliefs in the separation of church and state and that the Puritans should completely break their ties with the mother country's Anglican Church greatly angered the colony's rigid and autocratic powers. Faced with an arrest warrant and the threat of deportation, Williams gathered a handful of sympathizers and traveled to the confluence of the Woonasquatucket and Moshassuck Rivers.

He secured a tract of land there through negotiations with his Narragansett friend Canonicus, and within two years he had convinced a group of about a dozen other settlers to encamp at this new plantation he called Providence (in recognition of "God's providence" to Williams during his time of distress). Providence grew quickly and adopted a civil democratic form of government that tolerated all religious beliefs from the start. In 1639, he and a fellow resident of Providence baptized each other and then 10 others in founding what has become the modern-day

Baptist Church of the United States. By 1640, Providence functioned as its own independent political entity, with a board of governors who conducted local business according to the will of the entire community.

Providence came to be the most influential of four independent communities that would eventually unify as the Rhode Island colony. Like Providence, Portsmouth, Newport, and Warwick were also formed by political dissidents from Massachusetts. John Clarke and William Coddington were banished from the Massachusetts Bay Colony in 1638 for publicly asserting their differences with Puritan governmental and religious authority. They came to Providence, consulted with Williams, and decided to settle in the northernmost section of Aquidneck Island. Later that year, their friend and political inspiration in Massachusetts, Anne Hutchinson, joined them at this new settlement, originally named Pocasset.

But Hutchinson, Clarke, and Coddington could not resolve their power ambitions, and in 1639 the latter two ultimately left with a small group of allies to form their own settlement, Newport, at the southern tip of the island. Pocasset came to be called Portsmouth. While Hutchinson and the Clarke-Coddington groups maintained some autonomy, they also recognized the strength in numbers, and in 1640 agreed that the two communities would submit to joint rule, with Coddington as governor of this new "colony." A few years later the island then known as Aquidneck adopted the name accidentally assigned to it many years earlier—Rhodes—and in 1644 it officially took the name Rhode Island.

Warwick was settled in 1638 by yet another of the dissidents who originally came to Portsmouth, Samuel Gorton. An idealist and ideologue who made trouble everywhere he went, Gorton was banished first from Plymouth and then ultimately from Portsmouth, where he drew the ire of Hutchinson and her followers. He took up residence in Providence for a time and then in 1645 moved with a small group to Pawtuxet, the original village of Warwick. He arranged a deal with the Narragansetts to transfer that land to the English Crown, and a year later he sailed to England, where he enlisted the aid of an old friend, the Earl of Warwick, to secure a royal guarantee of title from parliament. In honor of the earl's assistance, he named the settlement Warwick in 1648.

As the four individual settlements grew, Roger Williams began to recognize their vulnerability, especially given the proximity of the two colonies in Massachusetts that so despised them all and the growing colony to the west, Connecticut. In 1643 Williams sailed to England to secure a parliamentary grant that would guarantee all four communities a legal basis for existence; the grant, which he secured from the Earl of Warwick in 1644, named the new colony "The Incorporation of Providence Plantations in the Narragansett Bay in New England." Originally the grant referred only to Providence, Portsmouth, and Newport; Warwick was admitted to this new union during the colony's first legislative session in 1647. That first session met in Portsmouth, and for a time subsequent sessions met in different cities, with Newporters typically serving as president of each session. At that time, Newport had the largest population (about 300), much more than Providence's 200 residents.

New towns were added to the Rhode Island colony through the rest of the 17th century, including Westerly in 1661, Block Island in 1664 (incorporated as the town of New Shoreham), Kings Towne in 1674 (it split into North Kingstown and South Kingstown in 1723), East Greenwich in 1677, and Jamestown (the town name for the island of Conanicut) in 1678. In Massachusetts during these years, the towns of Barrington, Little Compton, and Bristol were all formed; after a boundary dispute was resolved, these three communities became part of Rhode Island.

REVOLUTION

Even as it was consolidating itself as an independent entity, trouble was brewing with

the original inhabitants of Narragansett Bay and would eventually boil over into the bloody conflict known as King Philip's War. Rhode Islanders are quick to point out that the war had its origins not in their state but in Massachusetts, even if most of it was fought in Rhode Island. Despite the good relations Roger Williams enjoyed with the Native Americans, the same could not be said of his neighbors to the north in Plymouth Colony. The colony's governor, William Bradford, originally got along well with the Wampanoag chief, Massasoit, but tensions began to simmer after the deaths of two leaders of settlers on the Rhode Island-Massachusetts border. Eventually colonists arrested Massasoit's son Alexander on spurious charges. During the march he was forced to make to Plymouth, he fell ill and died. Foreseeing the inevitable conflict, Massasoit's younger son, Metacomet, whom the colonists called Philip, launched a preemptive raid on the Massachusetts town of Swansea. The colonists counterattacked by invading the Wampanoag camp at Mount Hope in Bristol, forcing 1,500 Indians to escape across the river on rafts.

The war that followed drew together many of the Native Americans in New England in a last-gasp attempt to push back English expansion. Despite burning Providence and many other towns in the yearlong campaign, the Indians were defeated by their lack of supplies and treachery among infighting groups as much by the English arms. By the time peace was agreed on in 1676, Philip and more than 5,000 Indians had been killed, with many more sold into slavery; on the English side, 500 colonists had been killed. After the war, many Native Americans were permanently relocated to South County, near Charlestown, effectively ending autonomous Indian presence in the state. Eventually, of course, even those settlements were removed in the westward march of Europeans across America.

Despite the bloodiness of the war, it was not the only conflict that Rhode Islanders had to deal with. During much of the next century and beyond, there were an amazing number

The Five Indigenous Tribes of Rhode Island

When Europeans first began to explore what is now Rhode Island in the 1500s, there were five indigenous groups living here: the **Pequots**, the **Nipmucs**, the **Niantics**, the **Narragansetts**, and the **Wampanoags**.

PEQUOTS

Among the five, the **Pequots**—who lived mostly in what is now southeastern Connecticut but also in southwestern Rhode Island—exercised the greatest degree of autonomy and defiance of the settlers. This warlike mentality quickly led to their near-extinction as colonists killed them and even turned friendlier tribes, such as the Narragansetts and the Connecticut Mohegans, against them.

In the 1630s the Pequots killed a pair of British merchants whom they encountered sailing up the Connecticut River on a trading mission. They further raised the ire of the settlers when they killed the respected explorer John Oldham off the coast of Block Island in 1636, an act that led to immediate reprisals in the form of burnings and raids by English troops. The Pequots continued to strike, attacking and murdering several Wethersfield families during the winter of 1636-1637 and unsuccessfully attempting to establish a warring pact with their neighbors, the formidable Narragansett Indians of nearby Aquidneck Island.

These tensions escalated the following spring into the great Pequot War of 1637, during which about 130 European settlers from the Connecticut River towns, along with 70 allied Mohegans, developed a plan to destroy their enemy. Believing it wise to approach from the least likely side, the group attacked from the east, sailing to Rhode Island's Narragansett Bay and marching west with a force of about 400 Narragansetts looking on.

The Pequots were concentrated in a pair of encampments near what is now Norwich, Connecticut, each of these a several-acre enclosure of a few dozen wigwams. The settlers, led by John Mason, struck the largest Pequot community at dawn and killed most of its inhabitants, burning the wigwams and shooting any who attempted to flee. The second Pequot encampment attempted to thwart the invasion but was easily driven to retreat. During the next two months, the remaining members of the severely crippled Pequot league moved west toward New York but were met in a massive swamp, which would later become Fairfield, by Mason and his battalion. Again most of the Indians were killed, with the remaining 180 Pequots taken hostage and brought to Hartford.

The Pequots could not have been conquered without the assistance of the Mohegans and the Narragansetts, with whom the English signed a treaty of friendship in 1637. But peace between the Native Americans and the English would last only a few decades, until King Philip's War.

NIPMUCS

The **Nipmuc** Indians lived principally in central Massachusetts but also occupied some land in Northern Rhode Island. Their fate after King Philip's War, in which they battled the colonists, is little documented, but it's believed that most survivors fled west into Canada, and those who stayed behind joined with the few Indian groups that remained friendly to the colonists.

NIANTICS

Rhode Island's **Niantics,** distinct from but related to the Niantics of southeastern Connecticut, lived in the southern part of mainland Rhode Island, where the sea borders modern-day Westerly and Charlestown. Their leader, Ninigret, managed to prolong their viability by keeping distance from the Native Americans who rebelled against the colonists. Ninigret met on several occasions with colonists, and he even refrained from participating in King Philip's War. This tribe of Narragansetts (as colonists increasingly came to call all Rhode Island Indians) continued to live on their land through the late 1800s. By that time, their numbers had dwindled, and eventually their final bits of land were taken from them.

NARRAGANSETTS

Rhode Island's modern-day **Narragansetts** are mostly of Niantic descent, but they're joined by some who descend from the actual Narragansett nation, which was, perhaps, the largest tribe in Rhode Island during the 17th century. By the time of King Philip's War, there were 5,000 Narragansetts living throughout Rhode Island. Their larger numbers are explained in part by their not succumbing to the diseases that brought down the more powerful Wampanoags, who lived mostly in southeastern Massachusetts but also in part of eastern Rhode Island. As the Wampanoags declined, the Narragansetts took over their territory on the islands of what is now Narragansett Bay.

WAMPANOAGS

It was with Narragansett and **Wampanoag** leaders that Roger Williams socialized and negotiated a land treaty on his arrival in the 1630s. Canonicus was the sachem, or ruler, of the Narragansetts and would become a close friend of Williams until his death in 1647; Massasoit headed the Wampanoags, and Williams assisted in bringing some degree of peace between these two nations. He also made peace between the Native Americans of Rhode Island and the colonists of Massachusetts, who had arrested and banished Williams in the first place.

By the 1670s, the Narragansetts were led by a descendant of Canonicus named Canonchet. The leader of the Wampanoags, Philip, the son of Massasoit, sought to unify New England's many Native American groups in an ambitious and perhaps desperate attempt to overthrow the Puritan grip on the region. An Indian who was a Christian convert loyal to the settlers betrayed King Philip's intentions and was quickly killed by Philip's men. The settlers escalated the conflict by capturing and killing the people who had killed the informant, and so began King Philip's War, which would ultimately seal the fate of Native Americans in the northeastern United States.

The war was fought near the Rhode Island-Massachusetts border, where the Wampanoags occupied a fort at Mount Hope, today part of the Rhode Island community of Bristol. After several colonists in the town of Swansea were killed, thousands of colonial troops descended on Mount Hope. The Indians managed to destroy about a dozen colonial settlements and significantly damage another 40; in all, roughly half the English villages in New England during the 1670s were damaged. More than 800 colonists and about 3,000 Native Americans were killed. The Indians lost about 15 percent of their total population, while the colonists lost perhaps 1.5 percent.

AFTER KING PHILLIP'S WAR

In the end, although many colonists were killed, tragically all of the region's Native Americans were ultimately contained. At the onset of the war, Canonchet and his Narragansetts adopted a neutral stance, but the colonists attacked the Narragansetts preemptively, and Canonchet then led several of the violent raids against the colonists, destroying houses in Providence and Warwick. King Philip spent time in northern New England attempting to unify other tribes into a greater resistance. Canonchet was captured and executed near Stonington, Connecticut, in 1676. Soon after, King Philip was captured and killed near Mount Hope. The last remaining Narragansett royal, Quaiapen, sister of Niantic leader Ninigret, died shortly thereafter in a battle at Warwick. By summer 1676, the Narragansetts had been broken and the Wampanoags decimated; Philip's surviving family members were sold into slavery. The end of King Philip's War signified the end of the Native American way of life in Rhode Island as it had existed before European settlement.

The Dorr Rebellion

Rhode Island governed according to its colonial charter, granted in 1663, for longer than any other Northern state. By the 1840s, the governing principles laid out in this document had become a poor fit for the state, especially given Rhode Island's rapid industrialization and growing immigration. What rankled many citizens was the antiquated criteria for voting rights—only men owning land worth $134 (a large amount in 1663, and still in 1840) were permitted to participate in the electoral process.

The unjust effect of these rules seemed particularly appalling given Rhode Island's track record on freedom of religion—and its vehement protests against taxation without representation during the American Revolution. Here, more than 60 years after the United States had secured independence, Rhode Island was letting a comparatively wealthy minority set policies and laws for the general population. Of course, the state legislature was made up chiefly of well-to-do landowners who knew that any concessions toward universal men's suffrage would severely diminish their power and influence. They fought to keep this enormous chunk of the population disenfranchised.

Thomas Dorr, a resident of the still-rural village of Chepachet in western Rhode Island, thought it was time for Rhode Island's lawmakers to recognize the changing times and extend full voting rights to all male residents, as neighboring states had done. Of course, women would not be empowered to vote in Rhode Island or in any U.S. state until well into the 20th century, so even with reform, half the adult population would continue to be excluded from the political process.

Interestingly, Dorr was from neither an immigrant nor an industrial background. Born in 1805 to a wealthy Rhode Island family, he became a successful lawyer and around 1840 began rallying for popular legal reforms to liberalize the state's voting laws. Dorr's People's Party, frustrated with the lack of headway they were able to make against the state's conservative incumbent legislators, called its own constitutional convention in October 1841 to amend the antiquated state constitution. During the convention, Dorr's party ratified what they called the People's Constitution. Of course, this entire process was outside the laws of Rhode Island, and the new constitution was not recognized by the sitting legislature, which overwhelmingly voted down the People's Party's attempts at reform.

In effect, Rhode Island suddenly found itself with competing legislatures, each acting in defi-

and variety of border disputes created by a legacy of conflicting land deeds and purchases from Native Americans as well as frequent claims on chunks of what is now Rhode Island by Massachusetts and Connecticut.

Within the first two decades of Rhode Island's formation, religious dissidents from around the world began to learn of the small colony's reputation for tolerance. Quakers arrived in the New World in 1657 with the hope of spreading the word through the colonies. Their proselytizing in Massachusetts was met with fiery resistance, to the point that one Quaker, Mary Dyer, was hanged in Boston in 1660 for attempting to make converts out of Puritans. But they were welcomed in Newport, many of whose residents actually joined the Society of Friends during the city's first several decades. Providence and Roger

Williams were less enthusiastic about the Quakers, but consistent with their beliefs, they made no efforts to curtail this freedom of religion; Williams even engaged in a three-day debate with a Quaker spokesperson in 1671.

Jewish settlers from Holland came to Newport in 1658 and swiftly established the Jeshuat Israel congregation. The community thrived for more than a century, until Britain occupied Newport during the Revolutionary War. The settlement's Touro Synagogue, still in use, is the oldest in the United States.

A major shift in political power in England, the restoration of King Charles II in 1660, caused concern for the leaders of the young Rhode Island, so a group sailed to the mother country in 1663 and successfully secured a royal charter to supersede the parliamentary grant issued by the Earl of Warwick in

ance of the other. The federal government decided not to intervene and rather encouraged the dual governments to work things out. Matters worsened on April 18, 1842, when Dorr's party elected him the new governor of Rhode Island, while the original state government reelected incumbent Samuel H. King. By May, Thomas Dorr had rallied a team of supporters to stage a coup on the Providence Armory, in hopes of turning the military to his side and ultimately taking over the State House and other official state offices. Relatively few Dorrites took part in the mission on the armory, and Thomas Dorr and his followers were easily turned back. Several weeks later, Dorr decided to call his new government to assemble at Sprague's Tavern in Chepachet (which still operates today as a restaurant, the Tavern on Main). Governor King sent the Rhode Island militia to silence this rebellion. Dorr's own small militia waited at Acote's Hill, about 0.25 mi (0.4 km) south of where present-day U.S. 44 crosses through Chepachet, but on realizing that King's troops were far greater in number and firepower, Dorr and his group retreated to the tavern.

King and his men marched to Sprague's Tavern, where they ordered the Dorrites out at gunpoint. During the standoff, more words were exchanged than bullets, although one of King's men did manage to fire a shot through the keyhole of the locked tavern, striking a Dorrite in the thigh.

After the standoff, Dorr fled the state. The appropriately named governor King took a rather autocratic approach to restoring order: He declared martial law and had Dorr arrested and charged with high treason. The rival government was completely shut down, and many of Dorr's followers were arrested.

Although disgraced by the state's official government, Thomas Dorr was hailed a hero by many, and the goals of the so-called **Dorr Rebellion** were eventually largely accomplished. Fearing a backlash and continued civic unrest, the conservative state legislature amended the constitution, dramatically liberalizing the requirements for voting rights. In 1843, Rhode Islanders took to the polls and approved the new Rhode Island constitution.

The rest of Dorr's life was quite sad, however. He was found guilty of treason in 1844 and harshly sentenced to hard labor for the rest of his life. Many Rhode Islanders and even some dignitaries rallied for his pardon, which was granted after he had served a year in prison. Still, Dorr was demoralized and physically weakened by this ordeal, and he died just a few years later.

1644. Interestingly, this charter—which fully asserted the religious tolerance of the state—remained in effect until 1843, well after the United States had secured independence from England.

Rhode Island developed a reputation as a rather ruthless little shipping powerhouse during the latter half of the 17th century. Newport and other communities outfitted a number of privateering ships, mostly during the myriad colonial wars of that time—the Anglo-Dutch trade wars of the 1650s-1670s and the French and Indian Wars of the following century. Privateering, where private armed ships were enlisted to attack and capture enemy ships, was not even formally outlawed by the Rhode Island Assembly until the very end of the 17th century. Even then, illegal privateering, which is really just a nice way to

say piracy, took place regularly at the hands of Rhode Island crews.

From the late 1600s onward, Rhode Island developed into one of the world's busiest trading hubs, establishing commercial ties with virtually every other colony and many other countries, including England, the Atlantic islands colonized by Portugal, western Africa, and the West Indies. Most colonists still made their living as farmers until well into the 18th century, but increasingly and especially in port communities such as Providence, Newport, Bristol, Westerly, Wickford, and Pawtuxet, many residents made their living in the merchant trade or related professions such as shipbuilding.

Slave trading was easily the most lucrative form of commercial enterprise during this period, and Rhode Island raked in more money through this abhorrent practice than just about any other state. (Despite the colony's infamy as a slave-trading hub, in 1774 Rhode Island became the first state to ban the slave trade; in 1784 the state outlawed owning slaves entirely.) A huge percentage of the New World's slave ships during the late 17th to late 18th centuries were registered to Rhode Island. Generally these ships sailed to Africa with rum and other goods in exchange for enslaved people, who were mostly brought to the West Indies or to South Carolina, where they were sold and distributed across the South. Many enslaved people were brought directly to Rhode Island and forced into domestic or agricultural service. From the West Indies, the ships brought molasses to Rhode Island, where it was distilled into the rum that the ships carried to West Africa to obtain more slaves. The process came to be known as the Triangle Trade.

With its prominent shipping interests, Rhode Island was one of the first New World colonies to object strenuously to the many trade regulations and taxes imposed by Britain through the mid-18th century. Some laws put limits on the manufacturing of goods in Rhode Island, forcing colonists to engage in expensive trade for such items, while other edicts placed onerous duties on molasses and other imported wares. Another practice that enraged the colonists was that of British ships whose "press gangs" randomly kidnapped Americans and forced them to enlist in the English navy. Whatever fame the Boston Tea Party may have as the opening blow of the Revolutionary War, in effect it merely followed in a tradition of vigilante attacks on British ships established by Rhode Islanders.

By 1765—eight years before the Sons of Liberty spilled their tea in Boston Harbor—resentment had turned to outright hostility in Rhode Island, and on one particular night in June, a posse of nearly 500 Newport men and boys cut loose a boat attached to a British ship that had been used for impressing colonists, dragged it to shore, and set it on fire. A few years later another band of Newporters destroyed a British revenue ship, the *Liberty*, and in 1772 perhaps the most notorious of these acts of insurrection further intensified anger between the British and the Rhode Island colonists: On a warm June evening a group from Providence sneaked out to the British revenue ship the *Gaspée* and set it on fire. This event galvanized support in Rhode Island for a full-scale war against the mother country—the *Gaspée* incident has been described by some as the colony's own Battle of Lexington. Rhode Island's governor at the time, Newport's Joseph Wanton, walked a political tightrope after the *Gaspée* incident, issuing a warrant for the arrest of the men who burned the ship but making little effort to capture them.

The Battle of Lexington in April 1775 stirred Rhode Island into a formal and fervent state of war. Within 24 hours of news of the Lexington and Concord battles reaching Rhode Island, the tiny colony put together a militia force of about 1,500. Governor Wanton, who was sympathetic to the colonial cause but skeptical that war would bring about positive change, declined to officially sanction military action. The assembly convened in October 1775, voted to depose Wanton, and immediately replaced him with Providence assemblyman Nicholas Cooke, who authorized Rhode Island's participation in the military campaign against Britain.

On May 4, 1776, the Rhode Island Assembly became the first colony in the New World to formally declare its independence from England—eight weeks before the Continental Congress in Philadelphia issued the unified Declaration of Independence. Rhode Island, therefore, can claim to be the oldest independent state in the United States, and legally, at least, could be considered an independent country for the brief two months before the rest of the states joined in. On July 18, 1776, the General Assembly convened and officially named its former colony the State of Rhode Island and Providence Plantations.

Rhode Island's shipping prowess became evident yet again during the Revolutionary

War; Esek Hopkins, the brother of noted statesman and 1750s governor Stephen Hopkins, was the first commander-in-chief of the Continental Navy, and many in the colony served at sea during the campaign. Warwick son General Nathanael Greene successfully turned around the colonists' failing efforts in the South when he led his troops to victory over the British in March 1781 at Guilford Courthouse, northwest of Greensboro, North Carolina.

Meanwhile, Newport—which was occupied by British troops from December 1776 to October 1779, when colonists abandoned the city to provide reinforcements in New York City—played an important role toward the end of the war: It was here that General Rochambeau and his French troops encamped in March 1781 and where he conferred with General George Washington to plan out the sneaky and successful assault on Yorktown. A detachment of the Rhode Island regiment, led by Captain Stephen Olney, also took part in the Yorktown battle.

The British occupation of Newport, however, proved devastating to that city, which had been well on its way to becoming one of the nation's most dynamic and important ports. The population of the city declined by nearly 50 percent after the war, in part because many Tory sympathizers had lived there during the British occupation—as the war drew to a close, they fled permanently to British North America, mostly Nova Scotia. In general, Rhode Island's economic prospects were gloomy for the first few decades after the war, and shipping trade was reduced to a trickle.

STATEHOOD AND THE INDUSTRIAL REVOLUTION

Although Rhode Island made the earliest declaration of independence of any colony, it also took the longest to agree to join the Union, and existed essentially as an independent state from 1776-1787. Almost wholly reliant on trade, its residents resented having to conform to trade restrictions and controls set by the entire Union. The notion of joining with the other colonies struck at least some Rhode Islanders as no better than having to submit to British rule. The idea of having to funnel a share of state shipping revenues to the federal government, in the form of taxes, was totally unacceptable.

At the Constitutional Convention in Philadelphia in 1787, it was decided that Rhode Island would be made to join the Union—the colony itself sent no delegates to the convention in something of an act of protest. It was not until May 29, 1790—after much internal debate and external pressure from the newly formed U.S. Congress—that the state assembly convened in Newport and ratified the federal Constitution by an extremely close vote of 34 in favor, 32 against. At the time, the new state of Rhode Island comprised 30 towns and had a population of 70,000, nearly 10 times greater than in the previous century.

Rhode Islanders remained divided on a number of issues facing the state and the young nation in the decades after the war, including whether to support Alexander Hamilton's Federalist agenda or Thomas Jefferson's Republican, pro-French stance. Sympathies were also split during the War of 1812, which hurt Rhode Island financially more than it did almost any other state because of its stifling effect on maritime trade. But one Rhode Island military star did make a name for himself during this war: South Kingstown's Oliver Hazard Perry, who commanded the victorious U.S. fleet during the Battle of Lake Erie in 1813. Having secured U.S. control of Lake Erie, Perry paved the way for General William Henry Harrison's short-lived invasion of Canada. Perry's younger brother, Matthew, earned fame by opening commercial trade with Japan in 1854. Bristol native General James DeWolf also contributed admirably against the British during the war.

While the state's shipping economy declined after the Revolution and its agricultural industry had been shrinking for the past century, Rhode Island was about to become a different kind of economic superpower.

The Industrial Revolution

After the Revolutionary War, Great Britain sought to cut its losses by preventing the export of technology and industrial innovation to the United States. Passengers on U.S.-bound ships were forbidden from taking with them blueprints, books, and materials containing the information that had made England an industrial superpower. Also prevented from leaving the country were workers with considerable experience in English factories.

Samuel Slater, a 21-year-old who had worked as a manager in England's technologically advanced Arkwright Mills, found a way around this policy. As the story goes, he snuck aboard a ship in attire and with baggage that gave no hint of his social and professional standing. He sailed to the United States, arriving first in New York, where he found few opportunities for employment. A newspaper ad placed by Moses Brown, of the famous Providence Brown family, caught Slater's attention, and he traveled to Pawtucket. Brown had sought an individual with experience in textile manufacture. With Slater's knowledge and Moses Brown's capital, Pawtucket quickly became the site of the nation's first textile factory. The new enterprise prospered beyond anybody's wildest expectations.

With the success of Slater's mills, investors quickly began pumping money into the region, building new cotton and wool mills as well as factories for tool manufacture, textile production, hat making, and shoe making. The tremendous competition spurred constant innovation and technological improvement, and in this hothouse the United States came of age as an industrial nation. Farmers with irregular income based on the whims of nature were lured to these fast-growing mill villages with the promise of steady, albeit difficult, work. Mill owners ran their operations like fiefdoms, exploiting workers, hiring young children and women for some of the most difficult and dangerous jobs, creating inhumane working conditions, and controlling just about every aspect of the mill workers' lives. Workers were expected to attend church, remain sober, and buy all goods from a company store. Owners controlled housing, schools, roads, churches, and shops. The practice of employing and providing for entire families to work the mills came to be known as the Rhode Island system of manufacturing.

The child-labor practices of the day seem almost unbelievable in the 21st century. Mill workers were as young as six. In 1826, for instance, the superintendent of the Providence Thread Company was a 19-year-old man; he had 11 years of experience in the factory by that time. Children generally worked 12-14 hours per day, suffered frequent injury and illness, and being small and nimble, were often assigned the dangerous jobs that involved fast-moving machine parts. They were paid perhaps $1 per week.

Through the early 19th century, cotton mills and machine shops huffed and puffed along the banks of the river in tremendous numbers. In 1809, President Madison gave a great boost to the local textile industry when he wore a woolen suit manufactured in Pawtucket. Dr. Timothy Dwight, an early president of Yale College, detailed his travels in the young country in his diaries, in which he observed in 1810: "There is probably no spot in New England, of the same extent, in which the same quantity of variety [and] manufacturing business is carried on."

In early 1790s Pawtucket, Moses Brown—one of the Providence Brown brothers, after whom the university is named—financed a young textile worker from England, Samuel Slater, who had secretly traveled to the United States in hopes of profiting from his extensive knowledge of Britain's advanced mill technology (at this time it was illegal for British subjects to share their knowledge of technology with other nations). Slater almost single-handedly oversaw the formation of the U.S. textile industry, and in so doing played as important a role as anybody in sparking the American Industrial Revolution. Within a few years, several powerful and highly mechanized mills had sprung up in Pawtucket and neighboring towns of the Blackstone River Valley, a superb source of water power. Textile mills opened in Warwick, Coventry, and other cities within a few years. Twenty-five

By 1815, there were 16 cotton mills in Rhode Island, Connecticut, and Massachusetts with 119,310 spindles (there were said to be about 350,000 spindles in the entire country at that time). The number of spindles in the nation grew to 1.5 million by 1830, and 2.3 million by 1840. By then, the leading cotton-manufacturing states were Massachusetts (278 mills, 666,000 spindles) and its much smaller neighbor, Rhode Island (209 mills, 519,000 spindles).

With the growth of factories all over northern Rhode Island and elsewhere in southern New England, transportation infrastructure improved rapidly and radically. A canal was opened in 1828 alongside the Blackstone River, and the Providence and Worcester Railroad followed in 1847, ending the canal business. Road improvements continued all the while.

SINCE 1900

Because it attracted families from all over Europe and the New World, the Rhode Island system of manufacturing encouraged tremendous diversity of ethnicity and religion, a mix unheard-of in Puritan New England before the Industrial Revolution. Rhode Island had already been a haven for religious freedom and practice, hosting New England's first significant communities of Quakers, Catholics, Baptists, and Jews. As mills ran out of local farmers to populate their mill villages, they began recruiting from afar. Through the decades, workers arrived from Ireland, Scotland, England, Germany, the Netherlands, Italy, Greece, Portugal, Ukraine, Sweden, Armenia, Poland, Lithuania, Finland, and Syria. And perhaps most prominently in northern Rhode Island, huge numbers of job-hungry French Canadians came to work in these enormous factories. In the middle of the 20th century, African Americans came to the region from the Southern states, as did Latin Americans and Asians.

By the 1940s, about 75 percent of Pawtucket's 75,000 residents were foreign born. There were about 50 textile mills in Pawtucket, but these were outnumbered by about 60 general factories producing everything from machine parts to metal goods and jewelry.

The mills raised the bar worldwide for industrial productivity by the late 19th century as production soared to all-time highs. But by the early 20th century, cheaper labor, more land, and better water sources in the South began to cause industrial decline in New England. Labor problems caused disruption and closures, and mill owners began investing their capital in more hospitable parts of the country.

By the 1920s, the South accounted for half of the industrial output in the United States. The downward spiral of the Northeast translated to less capital, outmoded factories and machines, increasingly disgruntled workers, and more mill closures. Only about 10 percent of the textile mills in operation at the end of World War II remain open today. Many of the former mill villages of the Blackstone River Valley appear downtrodden and dispirited today, and quite a few of the old mills have been abandoned or demolished. However, a new interest in vintage mill architecture has resulted in restoration and retrofitting of at least some of the most important buildings in the valley.

years after Slater designed the first waterpowered textile mill in Pawtucket, Rhode Island had about 25,000 workers employed in textile production, spinning about 30,000 bales of cotton annually into nearly 30 million yards of cloth. The boom continued through the 19th century, with capital expenditure in cotton textile production in Rhode Island rising from about $7 million in 1850 to more than $30 million in 1880.

Following on the heels of Rhode Island's cotton-textile milling success, the state developed into a leader in woolen and worsted production. By 1850 extensive worsted woolen mills ran in Cranston, North Kingstown, Hopkinton, Peace Dale, North Providence, Pawtucket, Woonsocket, and Providence. Innovations such as the carding machine, developed in Peace Dale by Rowland Hazard, and steam power, used in Providence at the Providence Woolen Manufacturing Company, further established the state's industrial preeminence. By 1890, Providence was second only to Philadelphia in woolen manufacturing.

MODERNIZATION AND INDUSTRY

Inventor George H. Corliss developed a proper steam engine for the Providence Dyeing, Bleaching, and Calendaring Company in 1848, and soon the Corliss Steam Engine was famous all over the world for saving time and labor. Eventually, Corliss became the largest steam engine producer in the country. Numerous related industries, especially machine-tool making, sprang up during the textile boom.

Another industry that expanded rapidly during the 19th century, especially in Providence, was the manufacture of jewelry, especially the costume variety. Seril and Nehemiah Dodge, brothers from Providence, had developed a cheap and fairly easy way to electroform metal, thus enabling them to produce popular jewelry at extremely low prices. Nehemiah later expanded his business greatly, employing journeyman goldsmiths and silversmiths and apprentices to become the nation's first mass producer of discount jewelry.

One of the Dodge apprentices, Jabez Gorham, went from making silver spoons and selling them door-to-door to founding the now-famous Gorham Manufacturing Company in Providence. The early 19th century saw a rapid increase in production, with dozens of shops making jewelry and silverware by 1810. By 1880, Rhode Island led all U.S. states in the percentage of residents employed in jewelry manufacture.

Rhode Island didn't revise its constitution, which had been in place since the Royal Charter of 1663, until 1842, by which time a growing number of residents had begun to recognize the unfairness of a governing document that allowed only owners of more than $134 worth of land to vote. Slavery had been banned 60 years earlier, and sentiments

favoring egalitarianism had been intensifying. The new constitution was therefore revised, after the constitutional crisis known as the Dorr Rebellion, to grant universal suffrage to all men in Rhode Island. Women remained without a voice, as they did throughout the United States, until 1920.

At the onset of the Civil War, Rhode Islanders actively supported the Union efforts, furnishing thousands of troops early on, the first regiment under the noted Colonel Ambrose E. Burnside (who later moved permanently to Rhode Island). The state governor at the time, William Sprague, served in the Battle of Bull Run. All told, 14 Rhode Island regiments went to battle during the Civil War, including an artillery regiment, the 14th, consisting entirely of African American men who aided valiantly in the defense of New Orleans. (Despite the immortalization of the Massachusetts 54th in the 1989 film *Glory*, the Rhode Island 14th actually suffered more casualties than any other African American regiment in the war.) Rhode Islanders participated in nearly every major battle—an interesting legacy for a state that profited from slavery for so many years.

Throughout the 19th century, as the state's industrial prowess grew, economic and technological advances followed. Gas lighting was introduced to the streets of Newport and Providence in the early 1900s, several state banks were chartered, steamboats connected Providence to Newport and then to many other locations, the Blackstone Canal was dug between Providence and Worcester, and railroad tracks linking Providence to Boston, southeastern Connecticut, and Worcester were laid between 1835 and 1847. In 1880 the state received telephone service, and around the end of the 19th century, Providence houses were illuminated with electricity. Also around this time, the present State House in Providence was constructed, with the first General Assembly convening there on New Year's Day 1901. Since that day, Providence has been the sole capital of Rhode Island—before then, it alternated with Newport.

Rhode Island's economy, and its intake of immigrant workers, grew precipitously after the Civil War. In addition to producing large quantities of textiles and jewelry, by the turn of the 20th century Rhode Island factories specialized in various types of metal manufacture (wire, hardware, stoves, fire extinguishers), rubber goods and footwear, paints, yacht and ship equipment, sewing machines, chemical and drug products, and baking powder. By 1900, the Providence-based manufacturer Brown and Sharp (it moved to North Kingstown in the 1960s) was the nation's largest producer of machine tools. There were about 150 machine shops and 250 costume-jewelry manufacturers in the state.

Conditions in factories were miserable, in some cases brutally inhumane, throughout the 19th century. In the early 19th century, men earned about $5 per week at mill jobs, women less than half that, and children a little over $1. A workweek consisted of six 12- to 14-hour days. Workers lived in tightly supervised mill villages—employers supplied the houses, schools, hospitals, churches, and shops; they effectively controlled every aspect of their employees' lives. And early on, at least, these villages were bleak and depressing.

A few mill owners made an effort to promote culture and education within their communities, but this was the exception rather than the rule. As early as 1836, the Children's Friends Society of Rhode Island was formed to rally on behalf of child workers' rights, and in 1840 a state law was passed requiring that children under 12 attend at least 12 months of schooling before beginning their "careers" in the mills.

Other unions formed gradually during the 19th century, as an increasing number of workers began to rebel against the horrid conditions. But mills simply imported foreign workers, who were less organized, less able to unionize, and more willing to accept harsh conditions. Immigration was mostly from French-speaking Canada, Ireland, Britain, Italy, Poland, and Portugal. It was not until 1909 that the state actually formed a board to oversee and regulate labor conditions in its factories, but even this organization had little success in improving working conditions until 1923, when the state Bureau of Labor was established. Strikes occurred regularly during the early 20th century, and some of these were intensely bitter and violent.

World War I, to which Rhode Island sent 29,000 troops (of which 600 perished), interrupted Rhode Island's steadily growing industrial power for a time. After World War I, as companies fled the increasingly strong labor unions of New England, Rhode Island began losing textile factories to the cheap labor of the South. But by the 1930s, even with the Depression in full swing and an increasing number of companies leaving the Northeast, Rhode Island had become the most highly industrialized state in the Union—more than half of the working population of 300,000 in 1930 was employed in manufacturing.

By 1940, the population of Rhode Island had grown to nearly 700,000. World War II interrupted everyday life there as it did all over the world; about 92,000 Rhode Islanders served in the war, and 2,157 were killed. The Ocean State, with its many factories, contributed tremendously to the war effort with the production of boots, knives, parachutes, munitions, and other supplies.

WORLD WAR II TO THE PRESENT

After the war, the advent of cheap suburban housing, a fast-growing and convenient interstate highway system, and a steady decline in urban industry inspired a rapid out-migration from Providence and other cities into neighboring towns. Even where jobs remained in the cities, at least for a while, workers no longer had to live near their places of employment. The 1950s marked the beginning of nearly four decades of wretched economic decline, high crime, and deterioration in Rhode Island's urban areas. Providence's 1950 population of about 250,000 dropped by 75,000 over the next 20 years. Economically, the state stagnated badly from the 1950s through the 1970s, and by the 1980s it had one of the least favorable climates for doing business in the country.

Suburbs such as Warwick, Cranston, Johnston, and North Kingstown blossomed over this period, and today as you drive through these communities you'll see thousands of suburban homes built between World War II and the 1970s, not to mention scads of shopping centers and a handful of large indoor shopping malls that also date to this period. In cities, urban renewal efforts led to the clearance of many so-called slums, including the destruction of some wonderful Victorian housing. But Providence, and Rhode Island in general, did a better job preserving its most important historic homes and neighborhoods than many other parts of New England; some of the most beautiful historic districts in the nation are in Rhode Island.

One industry that thrived in Rhode Island after World War II was the military—the U.S. Navy was the state's largest civilian employer during the 1950s and 1960s. The naval shipyard just outside Newport was responsible for building the nation's cruiser-destroyer fleet. But this industry crashed in 1974 when the Navy moved these operations to the South. Yet again, the relatively high operating costs and wages in New England sent business packing. Newport was left reeling, but the city rebounded by turning itself into a full-scale year-round destination. The tourism industry remains the most important in Newport today.

The tourism rebound of Newport and the general renaissance in Providence have been important factors in the great improvement in the state's image over the past few decades. There have also been failings, such as a slew of extremely embarrassing political scandals concerning bribery, extortion, misuse of funds, and other unethical misdeeds that shattered the public's faith in state and local government during the 1980s. But the reforms that grew out of these incidents ultimately helped to clean up government—at least to a degree.

Government and Economy

GOVERNMENT

Rhode Islanders have long marched to their own drummer when it comes to politics. The colony was founded by Massachusetts Bay Colony dissidents who believed strongly in religious freedom and the separation of church and state. From the very beginning of the colony's settlement, there was tension between the southerners on Aquidneck Island and the northern residents of Providence.

The state operated under a Royal Charter issued in 1663 until well into the 19th century. Although this document proved antiquated and awkward by that time, it was replaced only in 1842 after a near civil war, the Dorr Rebellion.

Early on, Rhode Island was represented by a general assembly comprising six men from each of the original towns. As new towns incorporated, the assembly grew. Sessions were held at private homes until the first colony house was constructed in Newport in 1690, but for some time after that, the assembly often met in homes in other parts of the state. Even the revised state constitution of 1842, which finally granted suffrage to all male adult Rhode Islanders, authorized that General Assembly meetings could convene in Newport, Providence, South Kingstown, Bristol, or East Greenwich. In 1854, the Assembly pared this list of towns to two, and from then until 1900 the legislature met alternately in Newport and Providence. It wasn't until 1900, when Providence had grown to become the state's hub of economics, education, and population, that it became the definitive state capital.

Until the 20th century, the General Assembly was made up of equal numbers of representatives from every town in the state. Eventually the law was changed so that the Senate's representation was based purely on population distribution. Currently, there are 75 state representatives and 38 state senators.

Before 1992 the governor of Rhode Island held office for a term of just two years, but this was extended to four years; the governor may serve a total of two full terms.

Rhode Island has two members in the U.S. House of Representatives in addition to its two U.S. senators.

POLITICAL PARTIES

Generally speaking, Rhode Island's popularly elected officials tend to be rather socially progressive; fiscally they're more varied but still pretty liberal. Like its neighbor Massachusetts, Rhode Island tends to vote overwhelmingly Democratic. Patrick J. Kennedy, son of Senator Ted Kennedy, decided not to seek reelection in 2010, which opened the state to the first truly contested U.S. congressional election in years. The vast majority of the state's elected Republicans have been considered moderate in relation to the national party as a whole. In 2014, newly elected Democratic governor Gina Riamondo became the first woman to serve as governor of Rhode Island.

Of course, many people think of the former longtime mayor of Providence, Buddy Cianci, when they discuss Rhode Island politics—and, indeed, he represents the best and worst of local politicians: forward-thinking, bold, and genuinely solicitous of the people he served while at the same time completely captive to political interests and prone to backroom dealings that both skirted and crossed the line of the law.

ECONOMY

With its history of wealthy shipping magnates and ostentatious summer cottages, coupled with its legacy of industry and manufacturing, Rhode Island is a state with quite a few extremely wealthy citizens and a huge core of working-class wage earners. The median household income of $63,870 is just above the national average, though far below the average for its New England neighbors, and indeed the state's positive and negative economic attributes tend to balance each other out.

There's something refreshingly down-to-earth about some of the state's old mill towns and interior highways. They remind you that Rhode Island is not simply a summertime playground of beachgoers and boaters. In fact, although Newport's Gilded Age in the early 1900s imbued the state with a reputation for privilege and excess, Rhode Island is mostly a place where middle-class, egalitarian values prevail, as they have since Roger Williams founded Providence Plantation as a haven for religious and political freedom in the early 1600s.

MANUFACTURING

The state's industrial clout continues to decline even today, but a rapid increase in the number of retail and service-oriented jobs has contributed to an overall economic boom not seen for many decades. Providence especially has benefited, and it has become a poster child for the urban renaissance that has swept across many American cities in the past 15 years or so.

Manufacturing jobs in Rhode Island still continue to disappear—according to the Bureau of Labor Statistics, the number of state residents employed in manufacturing fell from about 56,000 to 42,000 between 2005 and 2015. Other major areas include leisure and hospitality (55,000 workers); trade, transportation, and utilities (76,000); education and health services (the leader, with 106,000); professional and business services (65,000); government (60,000); and construction (15,000). Rhode Island also continues to have a prolific commercial fishing industry.

In the manufacturing sector, the main business endeavors are primary metals, fabricated metals, machinery, and electrical equipment. Jewelry and silverware production remains a manufacturing force still larger than in any other state, and Rhode Island still has many people employed in textile production, even if the numbers are a small fraction of those a century ago.

TOURISM, EDUCATION, AND HEALTH CARE

As noted, about 55,000 Rhode Islanders work in the leisure and hospitality and tourism industry. After the U.S. Navy moved out of Newport in the 1970s, that city turned to tourism as its leading industry. Block Island also relies chiefly on tourism, although plenty of Block Islanders still make a living the way that they have for generations, in fishing. To a lesser extent, parts of South County—specifically the beach communities—are heavily dependent on tourism.

In recent years, with its vastly improved reputation, even Providence has come to depend heavily on tourism, a notion almost unthinkable during the city's darkest economic years in the 1960s and 1970s. In 2014, Providence was named "America's Favorite City," by *Travel & Leisure*, America's "Best Small City" by *Architectural Digest*, and in 2015, the "Coolest City," by *GQ* magazine. Still, for all of its recent favorable press, Providence has a way to go in building its tourism infrastructure to accommodate large numbers of visitors, and outside of the Northeast, many people remain unaware that the city has much to offer.

Rhode Island's other big service sectors are health and education. The former is especially significant in Providence and its suburbs, where there are many hospitals and health providers. Education is a big contributor to the economy in Providence and several other parts of the state. The University of Rhode Island, in Kingston, has the largest student enrollment in the state, while in Providence there are Brown University, Johnson & Wales, the Rhode Island School of Design, Rhode Island College, and Providence College. Other notable schools in Rhode Island include Bryant College in Smithfield, Salve Regina University in Newport, and Roger Williams University in Bristol.

People and Culture

Rhode Island is sometimes described as the nation's only city-state, a tempting designation given its diminutive size and high population density. Here again, there are some contradictions at work. On the one hand, most of Rhode Island is served by one metro bus system and one main newspaper; you can commute to Providence from virtually anywhere in the state. In certain respects, the day-to-day events of Providence are the events of Rhode Island—and perhaps in no other state does one city wield so much influence.

On the other hand, only 178,000 Rhode Islanders actually live in Providence—that's barely more than 15 percent of the state's population. By comparison, about 25 percent of all Nevadans live in Las Vegas, and more than 20 percent of all Illinois residents live in Chicago. Rhode Island was founded as a collection of distinct communities, all headed by dissidents and freethinkers who had become unwelcome in Puritan Massachusetts. The towns of Rhode Island continue to function with very much their own autonomy and individual spirit. Newport sees itself as entirely distinct from and independent of Providence, and it always will. A Block Islander would laugh aloud if accused of living in Greater Providence, despite that the island lies just 40 mi (64 km) from the state capital. Woonsocket is only 10 mi (16 km) northwest of Providence, but these two cities have about as much to do with each other as Philadelphia and Pittsburgh—or so their residents might insist.

1: day cruise boats out on Narragansett Bay
2: surfers in Matunuck

Liberians in Rhode Island

One of the more recent immigrant groups to make their presence known in the state has been Liberians, an ironic turn of events given that Liberia was established by people freed from slavery who returned to Africa after emancipation—and that Providence prospered hugely during colonial times through the slave trade. Modern-day Liberia has been ravaged economically and politically by a devastating civil war through the 1990s. In 1991, the U.S. State Department granted provisional immigration status to Liberian refugees, and since that time more than 6,000 of the people to receive this status have settled in Rhode Island, many with the aid of the refugee resettlement services headed by the Dorcas International Institute of Rhode Island.

Although it's the smallest state in the Union, Rhode Island has more people living within its borders than Montana, Delaware, either of the Dakotas, Alaska, Vermont, or Wyoming. Roger Williams and the other early settlers hailed from England, and from the 1630s through the 1850s the population was largely white, of British descent, and Protestant. Within 50 years of European settlement in Rhode Island the Native American population had almost disappeared. The colony did possess a slightly more diverse population in the 1600s than other parts of New England. The founding doctrine protecting the worship of all religions contributed to an early influx of Quakers (most came from England) and Jews (mostly from Spain and Portugal). Catholics, mostly from France, began settling in Rhode Island in small numbers after the American Revolution, when locals became quite appreciative and fond of the French troops stationed in Newport under Rochambeau.

During the past 150 years, the industrialization of Rhode Island has led to other dramatic changes in demographics.

POPULATION

In the mid-19th century, Ireland's residents faced famine, poverty, and blight, and many moved to the young United States in search of better opportunities. Along with a number of Scottish and English immigrants, they became the earliest foreigners to work in Rhode Island's factories.

By around 1850, Rhode Island's population included quite a few foreign-born citizens, particularly in the textile hubs of Pawtucket and Central Falls; about 97 percent of them hailed from Ireland, Scotland, Wales, and England. The next big wave of immigrants, from Quebec, first arrived during the Civil War to work in mills in northern Rhode Island, the vast majority of them settling in Woonsocket. They would remain a tight-knit and prolific force for many years, and even today there is a strong and vibrant French Canadian community in Woonsocket. As the mills have largely closed, however, many younger people from this area are moving elsewhere for better opportunities.

Perhaps the largest immigrant group to settle in Rhode Island are the Italians, and to this day Italian culture continues to be important in the social fabric of the state. The biggest wave of Italian immigration happened just as the French Canadian migration slowed, about 1900-1915, but the Italians arrived in smaller numbers for many years after—the majority from Sicily, Naples, and other southern Italian regions. Today, Rhode Island's most pronounced Italian American communities are in Providence, especially the Federal Hill area, which has a Little Italy-style restaurant and shopping scene that's on par with any in the Northeast. There are other Italian enclaves in other parts of Providence, such as the North Side and Silver Lake, some of them dating to the early 1900s, and also large contingents in Cranston, Bristol, and Westerly.

Other immigrant groups that have contributed to Rhode Island's eclectic population include Poles, who arrived in the greatest numbers 1895-1905 and settled heavily in Central Falls, Providence, Pawtucket, Cranston, Johnston, Warren, and Woonsocket; and Portuguese, especially those from the Azores, Madeiras, and Cape Verde island groups, who were recruited by the state's whaling industry in the 1850s and 1860s. As the whaling industry died out, many of the Portuguese settled in fishing communities, while others worked as farmers and both skilled and unskilled laborers. In smaller but still significant numbers, Swedes, Germans, Armenians, Greeks, Lithuanians, Finns, and Syrians settled in the Ocean State during the early 20th century.

DEMOGRAPHICS

Outside the big cities, Rhode Island is predominantly a state of Caucasians, chiefly of English, Irish, and Italian ancestry. As of 2019, about 80 percent of Rhode Islanders identify themselves as white; about 6 percent identify as black; and about 14 percent of Rhode Islanders are of Hispanic or Latino origin.

As of the last census estimate in 2019, the state population stood at 1,056,738. The population has doubled since 1900 but has increased only slightly since 1970, when it stood at 950,000. As is true all over the Northeast, cities in Rhode Island have mostly lost population in the past half-century, while suburban areas have seen tremendous growth. Providence, for instance, had a population of nearly 250,000 around the time of World War II, and the number dropped to just 160,000 in a matter of 25 years. In 1900 Providence was the 12th-largest city in the nation; today it ranks around 143. Since 1990, however, Providence has seen a roughly 7 percent increase in population to 179,000.

Towns just outside Providence have grown rapidly since the migration from the cities to the suburbs that began after World War II. The population has nearly quadrupled in Warwick, doubled in Cranston, tripled in Barrington and Johnston, and increased more than six times in North Kingstown.

Rhode Island was one of the few states in the country to lose population during the 1980s, so the recent stabilization of population is a welcome indicator that Rhode Island's economic future looks more promising. It appears the state's economy has bounced back somewhat since the recession of the early 1990s and has mostly weathered the more recent economic crisis. Of course, this is the second-most densely populated state in the Union, with just over 1,000 people per square mile; only New Jersey's density is higher, and not by much. Of Rhode Island's 39 towns, almost half have population densities greater than 1,000 per square mile, so it will probably never be a state that grows at a rapid rate—there simply isn't room to put a lot of new people.

On the other hand, if you're looking for a sparsely settled part of the state, fear not: Block Island, West Greenwich, and Foster all have fewer than 100 people per square mile (although Block Island is crowded in the summer with seasonal visitors). Little Compton, Exeter, Glocester, Hopkinton, Richmond, and Scituate have plenty of breathing room, too.

Rhode Island On-Screen

Rhode Island has lobbied as hard as any state in New England to attract filmmakers, and the results have been impressive.

TELEVISION

Providence, which aired 1999-2002, did much to promote the capital city. The hit show, which starred Melina Kanakaredes, Mike Farrell, and Paula Cale, was filmed largely in Los Angeles, but the show shot a number of scenes each year on location in Providence and towns nearby—about twice each year the cast and crew traveled to Rhode Island to shoot on-site footage. Even former Providence mayor Vincent "Buddy" Cianci made a cameo on the show. The animated Fox TV show *Family Guy* is also set in Rhode Island and has even featured a fictitious Buddy Cianci High School. It was created by Seth MacFarlane, who studied animation at Providence's Rhode Island School of Design. Continuing the streak, the TV series *Brotherhood* aired on the cable network Showtime for three seasons 2006-2008 to critical acclaim, including a Peabody Award, even though it never grew outside of a cult audience. Filmed almost entirely on location in Providence, it dealt with familiar themes of an Irish-American politician and his brother, who happened to be a capo in the Irish mob. (The show was based on the Bulger brothers in Boston, who were also the subject of the Martin Scorsese movie *The Departed*.)

FILMS

Rhode Island's history as a filmmaking fave is rather recent, although a handful of classics were shot here. Newport, for instance, was the film locale for the 1956 Grace Kelly, Bing Crosby, and Frank Sinatra movie *High Society*. Newport, in fact, has been the location for a number of pictures, perhaps most notably the 1974 adaptation of F. Scott Fitzgerald's *The Great Gatsby,* starring Robert Redford, Mia Farrow, and Sam Waterston. The mansion scenes were shot at Rosecliff Mansion. Other Newport-filmed movies include *The Betsy* (1978, starring Laurence Olivier, Robert Duvall, and Katharine Ross), *True Lies* (1994, starring Arnold Schwarzenegger and Jamie Lee Curtis), *Thirteen Days* (2000, starring Kevin Costner), *Mr. North* (1988, starring Anthony Edwards, Robert Mitchum, and Lauren Bacall), *Heaven's Gate* (1980, starring Kris Kristofferson, Christopher Walken, and John Hurt), and *Amistad* (1997, starring Morgan Freeman, Nigel Hawthorne, and Anthony Hopkins). Scenes in *Amistad* were also shot in Pawtucket and Providence, including one at the Rhode Island State House.

Religion

Still true to the principles of its founder, Roger Williams, Rhode Island continues to embrace religious diversity. Interestingly, the largest religious group in the state, Catholicism, is the one that was actually least tolerated for the longest time, but the huge influx of Irish, Italian, and French Canadian immigrants between the 1850s and the 1930s, and the fact that Catholics often produced larger families than non-Catholics, have contributed to Rhode Island's overwhelmingly Catholic character.

Rhode Island was never a Puritan colony, as Massachusetts was, so its village commons are rarely anchored by a Congregational church and cemetery. Nevertheless, there are large numbers of Protestants all over the state, the majority of them belonging to the Congregational Church. Various other Protestant sects and other Christian groups

One last Newport-filmed movie was *Me, Myself & Irene* (2000, starring Jim Carrey and Renée Zellweger), written and directed by perhaps Rhode Island's most famous moviemaking team, brothers Bobby and Peter Farrelly. The Farrellys have become rather notorious for reinventing the "gross-out" genre with such ribald films as *There's Something About Mary* (1998, starring Ben Stiller, Matt Dillon, and Cameron Diaz), which was shot in part in Providence. And although they didn't direct it, the Farrelly brothers wrote and produced the Alec Baldwin and Shawn Hatosy movie *Outside Providence* (1999), which was indeed shot outside Providence, specifically in Woonsocket.

Outside Providence was directed by another Rhode Island son, Pawtucket's Michael Corrente, who also directed *Federal Hill* (1995, starring Corrente himself), which traced the lives of five young men living in Providence's famed Little Italy. Corrente also directed the screen adaptation of David Mamet's *American Buffalo* (1996, starring Dustin Hoffman and Dennis Franz), which was filmed in Pawtucket. Corrente's movies offer an especially gritty and realistic look of urban Rhode Island.

Keep your eyes open while watching a few other Rhode Island-filmed movies, including *Mystic Pizza* (1988, starring Julia Roberts, Lili Taylor, and Annabeth Gish), which was shot mostly over the border in southeastern Connecticut but also had scenes in Watch Hill and Westerly; *Meet Joe Black* (1998, starring Brad Pitt and Anthony Hopkins), which was filmed in part at Warwick's Aldrich Mansion; *The Last Shot* (2004, starring Alec Baldwin, Matthew Broderick, Toni Collette, and Tony Shalhoub), a mob comedy set partly in Providence; *Reversal of Fortune* (1990, starring Jeremy Irons, Glenn Close, and Ron Silver), based on the true-crime book by lawyer Alan Dershowitz about the attempted-murder trial of Claus von Bulow—much of it was filmed in Newport; and *Wind* (1992, starring Matthew Modine, Jennifer Grey, and Cliff Robertson), which was shot in Jamestown. In more recent years, filming in Rhode Island has tapered off, but the state has served as the primary location for the Steve Carrell vehicle *Dan in Real Life* (2007; look for a cameo by the Book and Tackle Shop in Watch Hill) and *Little Children* (2007), the critically acclaimed film starring Kate Winslet.

Most recently, Wes Anderson's *Moonrise Kingdom* (2012) was filmed in parts of southern Rhode Island, and Woody Allen's 2015 film *Irrational Man* (starring Joaquin Phoenix and Emma Stone) was filmed mainly in Newport and Providence.

have congregations scattered throughout the state.

Ironically, although Rhode Island is home to the oldest synagogue in the United States, the Ocean State has a relatively small Jewish population, a legacy of their flight from their religious center in Newport during the Revolutionary War. Providence and other towns in the state do have Jewish congregations, and Providence—because of its strong ethnic diversity—also has mosques and other places of worship that serve the many non-Christians living in and around the city.

In keeping with Rhode Island's rather socially left-of-center reputation, fundamentalist and conservative Christians are in the minority in the state and among political candidates, who tend to vote progressively on controversial issues such as abortion, school prayer, gay rights, and school vouchers.

Essentials

Getting There

Rhode Island is tiny, crossed by a major interstate highway and railway tracks, served by New England's third-largest airport and within a two-hour drive of three other major airports, and easily reached from every major city in the Northeast. Few other states are more easily accessible from corner to corner than Rhode Island.

For general information on commuting, getting to and from Rhode Island, and getting around the state, contact the **Rhode Island Department of Transportation** (401/222-2450, www.dot.ri.gov). Its website offers extensive information on numerous publications,

traveler resources, road conditions, licenses and permits, upcoming roadwork and projects, legal notices, and construction bid notices.

AIR

Rhode Island is served by **T. F. Green Airport** (2000 Post Rd., Warwick, 401/691-2000, www.pvdairport.com), which is 8 mi (12.9 km) south of downtown Providence off I-95 exit 13—it's a significant alternative to Boston's Logan Airport, as well as a pleasant, easy-to-use facility that readers of *Condé Nast Traveler* magazine have voted among the top airports in the world. It's served by several airlines: Delta, Frontier, JetBlue, Southwest, United, and American have flights to numerous U.S. cities as well as the Caribbean and Canada. About 100 flights arrive at Green Airport daily, with an equal number of departures.

Green's recent expansion has resulted in lots of extra parking spaces; rates at the on-site garage range $17-25 per day (check out the airport's website for special-rate coupons). Just south of the airport, the long-term parking lot costs $17 per day and $85 per week. For the latest parking information, call 401/737-0694. There are also a number of commercial lots near the airport, several of which provide free shuttle service to and from the terminal.

GROUND TRANSPORTATION

Rhode Island Public Transit Authority (RIPTA) (401/781-9400, www.ripta.com) provides frequent service daily from T. F. Green to downtown Providence (Bus 20, 35-45 minutes) and from T. F. Green to Newport (Bus 14, 1 hour). The fare is $2 one-way. **Airport Taxi and Limousine Service** (401/737-2868, www.airporttaxiri.com) serves Warwick and neighboring communities and also provides regularly scheduled shuttle service from the airport to downtown Providence hotels, colleges, the convention center, and the train and bus stations. The cost is $15 per person to Providence for the shuttle; taxi rates vary by destination.

Transportation from T. F. Green to South County, Newport, and some of the farther-away sections of Rhode Island is covered in detail in individual chapters of this book. **Arrow Prestige Limousine** (2329 Post Rd., Warwick, 800/220-5466, www.arrowprestigelimo.com) offers all manner of ground transportation from T. F. Green Airport, including chauffeured limos and shuttle vans.

CAR RENTAL

Major car rental agencies at T. F. Green Airport include **Alamo** (401/737-4800 or 888/327-9633, www.alamo.com), **Avis** (401/736-7500 or 800/331-1212, www.avis.com), **Budget** (401/739-8986 or 800/527-0700, www.budget.com), **Thrifty** (401/732-2000 or 800/367-2277, www.thrifty.com), **Enterprise** (401/732-5261 or 800/325-8007, www.enterprise.com), **Hertz** (401/738-3550 or 800/654-3131, www.hertz.com), and **National** (401/737-4800 or 800/227-7368, www.nationalcar.com).

BUS

Peter Pan Bus Lines (800/343-9999, www.peterpanbus.com) runs from Rhode Island to a number of New England cities. Examples include an express run from Newport to Boston, which runs several times a day and takes about 90 minutes. The fare is around $29 round-trip. Service from Boston to Providence runs several times daily, takes about an hour each way, and costs about $16 round-trip, $24 if you take the bus straight from Logan Airport.

There's also bus service from Providence to Albany (New York); Falmouth, Hyannis, and Woods Hole on Cape Cod; New Bedford, Pittsfield, Springfield, and Worcester; Logan Airport in Boston (Massachusetts); Hartford, and the University of Connecticut in Storrs

---

Previous: Newport at sunset.

Driving Distances from Providence

Albany, New York	185 mi (300 km)	New Haven, Connecticut	102 mi (164 km)
Boston	50 mi (81 km)	Newport, Rhode Island	34 mi (55 km)
Burlington, Vermont	267 mi (430 km)	New York City	180 mi (290 km)
Chicago	971 mi (1,563 km)	Philadelphia	274 mi (441 km)
Cleveland	640 mi (1,030 km)	Portland, Maine	162 mi (261 km)
Concord, New Hampshire	119 mi (192 km)	Toronto	565 mi (909 km)
Hartford, Connecticut	73 mi (118 km)	Washington DC	407 mi (655 km)
Hyannis, Massachusetts	75 mi (121 km)	Westerly, Rhode Island	44 mi (71 km)
Montreal	361 mi (581 km)	Worcester, Massachusetts	39 mi (63 km)

Interestingly, few state capitals are closer together than Providence and Hartford, but they are not directly connected by an interstate highway. You either have to drive down I-95 to the coast and then continue east to Route 9 in Connecticut or take another road combination.

Five cities that share Providence's approximate latitude: Salt Lake City; Beijing; Baku, Azerbaijan; Ankara, Turkey; and Madrid.

Three cities that share Rhode Island's approximate longitude: Quebec City, Canada; Santo Domingo, Dominican Republic; and Cuzco, Peru.

(Connecticut). Newport also has service to New York City and Boston's Logan Airport.

Peter Pan bus terminals are in Newport (23 America's Cup Ave.), in the north end of Providence (1 Peter Pan Way, off I-95 exit 25), and downtown Providence (1 Kennedy Plaza). The stop used in Providence depends on the route, so check ahead.

You can find connections to a great many locations in New England and across the country from **Greyhound** (800/231-2222, www.greyhound.com), the largest national carrier. Stations are in Newport (23 America's Cup Ave.) and Providence (1 Kennedy Plaza) at the same locations as Peter Pan, but Greyhound's fares tend to be slightly higher; it can be worth it on the buses that offer free Wi-Fi, however.

TRAIN

Amtrak (800/872-7245, www.amtrak.com) runs trains through the state daily. This is a fairly hassle-free way to get here from Boston, New York City, Philadelphia, and other major metropolitan areas. The one Amtrak route in Rhode Island passes through on the way between Washington DC, and Boston, with stops at Providence, Kingston, and Westerly. From Boston it's about 40 minutes to Providence, another 10 minutes to Kingston, and another 20 minutes to Westerly. Many of the Amtrak runs are Acela express trains that stop at Providence but not Kingston or Westerly. From the south, train times (the shorter times are for the high-speed trains) to Providence are 6-7 hours from Washington DC; 4.5-5 hours from Philadelphia; 3-3.5

hours from New York City; and 1.5-2 hours from New Haven.

Massachusetts Bay Transit Authority

The **Massachusetts Bay Transit Authority** (617/222-5000, for route and schedule information 617/222-3200, www.mbta.com), the nation's fourth-largest public transportation system, offers weekday commuter rail service between Boston's South Station and downtown Providence on the Attleboro/Stoughton line, with many stops in southeastern Massachusetts along the way. Trains depart Providence on weekdays about a dozen times daily from 5am to about midnight; the ride takes about 70 minutes, and the fare is $10.50 one-way. The station is located at 100 Gaspee Street, just below the Rhode Island State House. Fewer trains run on weekends, generally 6am-11pm Saturday and 11am-11pm Sunday.

Getting Around

It's as easy to get around Rhode Island as it is to get to it. The well-maintained network of roads will get you anywhere in the state. For almost any destination it's also possible to rely on public transportation; for most of the state, that means the bus system, the Rhode Island Public Transportation Authority (RIPTA). For larger destinations (Providence, Newport, Westerly, Kingston) it's possible to rely on the train and larger bus carriers.

DRIVING

Rhode Island's main thoroughfare, I-95 is a convenient if rather dull road that runs from the southwestern corner of the state northeast through Providence before entering Massachusetts. A bypass highway, I-295, cuts around the west side of Providence, from Warwick nearly to Woonsocket and then east to Attleboro, Massachusetts. I-195 cuts east from Providence through the northern tip of the East Bay and into Massachusetts. These roads will get you where you need to go, but especially around Providence, they are prone to rush-hour traffic jams.

Route 146 is a convenient limited-access highway running northwest from Providence, and U.S. 6 is a similar highway heading west from Providence, but both of these become regular four-lane roads once they're out of the metropolitan area. U.S. 6 and parallel U.S. 44 are generally fast roads with little commercial development that pass through the pretty wooded countryside of western Rhode Island; they're a smart way to get to Connecticut, even with the occasional traffic light. U.S. 1, the main shore road in South County, runs from Westerly east to Narragansett and then north to intersect with Route 4 in North Kingstown. Route 4 then leads back up to I-95. This route is generally fast, with some limited-access stretches. U.S. 1 north of North Kingstown is a slow, heavily developed road through Warwick, Cranston, Providence, and Pawtucket—it should be used only for local traffic, not as a way to get through the area quickly.

Top picks for scenery on other highways include Route 102 (from North Smithfield south to North Kingstown), Route 138 (from the Connecticut border at Exeter east to Newport and then northeast through Tiverton), Routes 77 and 81 (up and down the Sakonnet Peninsula), Route 122 (from Pawtucket through the Blackstone River Valley to Woonsocket), Route 94 (from Chepachet south through Foster), Route 14 (west from Providence over Scituate Reservoir through Kent to the Connecticut border), and Route 1A, which hugs the coast intermittently through South County, both along the ocean and then up beside Narragansett Bay.

1

2

MASS TRANSIT

Because Rhode Island is small, and a significant chunk of the state is urban, mass transit is quite useful and efficient, at least in terms of buses and, to a limited extent, ferryboats. There are no subways, commuter trains, or light-rail services in Rhode Island, although Amtrak makes stops in a few towns and the Massachusetts Bay Transit Authority (MBTA) provides commuter rail service connecting Providence with Boston's South Station.

It's quite possible and economically feasible to visit some parts of the state without using a car. If, for example, you're going to Block Island, Providence, Newport, parts of South County, and parts of the East Bay, you could get into town from Boston or New York City with a combination of bus, train, and (for Block Island) ferry, and then use a bus or cabs to get around locally—in some of these towns you can cover quite a bit of ground on foot. To make the most of western or northwestern Rhode Island, or the more remote coastal areas (Sakonnet, Jamestown, upper Aquidneck Island), you really need a car—it's also most practical to use one in Providence's suburbs, from Pawtucket to Woonsocket down to Warwick, although buses do serve all of these towns and are fine in a pinch.

For optimum convenience and freedom to explore, a car is your best bet for covering the state as a whole. Even Providence has a fair amount of street parking and plenty of garages. In summer, Newport is almost congested enough that a car defeats its purpose, but if you're planning to explore the outlying areas and your hotel or inn provides off-street parking, it's a good idea to bring one. Block Island, especially in summer, is best visited without a car. It's a small island with good public transportation, and it's excellent for biking; almost all accommodations are within walking distance of Old Harbor or New Harbor, where you'll find most of the island's shops and restaurants. If you're staying for a while, your accommodations offer off-street parking, or if it's off-season, a car can make sense and give you a little more flexibility, but it's really not a necessity at any time of year. And everybody living on Block Island will be quite pleased if you arrive without a car that would add to the traffic during the summer high season.

Intercity Buses

Rhode Island is small enough that much of the state is served by Providence's city bus system, operated by the **Rhode Island Public Transit Authority (RIPTA)** (401/781-9400, www.ripta.com). Most buses originate in Providence, but others start and end in other parts of the state. For example, you can use RIPTA buses to get from Newport to Providence or the University of Rhode Island in Kingston; from Bristol to Providence; from Providence to Burrillville; or from Coventry to Providence. The base fare is $2 per ride; charges increase as you travel through different zones. RIPTA's website is very useful in terms of plotting your exact trip.

1: sunset commute on a highway bridge in Providence 2: passenger ferry pulling into Block Island

Sports and Recreation

BIRD-WATCHING

Many a Rhode Islander seems to be taking up bird-watching these days, especially folks who live around the coastal regions, with Block Island ranking among the best spots. Its popularity makes a lot of sense, as hobbies go, as it is not expensive and is highly educational. Best of all, birds are abundant in the state year-round, although which individual species can be seen depends on the season.

More than 400 species of birds live in Rhode Island. Much of the best birding is along the coast, where you'll see myriad waterfowl year-round and magnificent blue heron October through April. Peregrine falcons, hawks, and osprey regularly fly around marshes and estuaries, and in August through September you'll see warblers and thrushes. A huge population of sparrows descends on coastal points during the fall. Owls are not easy to find, but they do live around the state.

The Rhode Island chapter of the **Audubon Society** (12 Sanderson Rd., Smithfield, 401/949-5454, www.asri.org) is a useful resource for bird enthusiasts. The society's website has helpful links for birders, including a bimonthly newsletter and information on recent sightings downloadable from its website. At the society's headquarters in Smithfield, the **Hathaway Library** houses a vast collection of books, publications, videos, and software related to birding in general and in Rhode Island, specifically. You can also pick up books, tapes, and other birding materials at the two Audubon Society gift shops in the state, one at the headquarters and the other at the **Audubon Environmental Education Center** (1401 Hope St., Bristol, 401/245-7500).

The society owns or oversees about 9,500 acres of preserves throughout Rhode Island, several of them open to the public and excellent for bird-watching. **Kimball Wildlife Sanctuary** (180 Sanctuary Rd., Charlestown) is a 29-acre property with a 1.5-mi (2.4-km) hiking trail through fields and forests. Another birding Valhalla is the **Emilie Ruecker Wildlife Refuge** (286-2 Seapowet Ave., Tiverton), overlooking the Sakonnet River. The salt marshes here are a favorite spot

a nature preserve on Block Island

for observing migrating birds during the fall and spring; there are blinds set up for watching and photographing the wildlife.

Another excellent spot is the **Headwaters of the Queen's River** (Henry Bowman Rd., reached via New London Turnpike and Rte. 102), a remote woodland that connects Fisherville Brook Refuge (owned by the Rhode Island Audubon Society) to the state-administered Big River Management Area. Walking along trails here, you're apt to see many kinds of forest interior birds, including hawks. Another excellent Nature Conservancy preserve for bird-watching is the **Francis C. Carter Memorial Preserve** (Route 112, Charlestown), a large coastal preserve frequented in summer by species that include eastern towhee, scarlet tanager, and prairie warbler. Contact the Rhode Island chapter of the **Nature Conservancy** (159 Waterman St., Providence, 401/331-7110, www.nature.org) for directions to and descriptions of these and more than a dozen other pristine preserves around Rhode Island.

On Block Island, the Nature Conservancy works in partnership with several local organizations to preserve a huge section of the island from being developed—these preserves are among the state's most exceptional venues for bird-watching.

FISHING

Among the state's many great fishing holes and swift rivers, the Wood, Pawcatuck, Moosup, and Falls Rivers are among the best sources of trout fishing. A number of stocked ponds throughout the state are designated only for kids under 15. Stocked trout ponds are closed for fishing March 1 to the second Saturday in April, which marks the beginning of trout-fishing season. For a complete list of trout-stocked ponds and rivers in Rhode Island, and for other details about fishing in the Ocean State, contact the **Division of Fish and Wildlife** (4808 Tower Hill Rd., Wakefield, 401/789-0281, www.dem.ri.gov/programs/fish-wildlife). The website also has links to all state fishing and hunting

regulations, lists legal minimum sizes and possession rules, provides information on obtaining licenses, lists all of the state's freshwater and saltwater boat launches (and regulations concerning these launches), and provides tidal charts, lengths of fishing seasons, and scads of additional information.

Other common freshwater catches, some tasty and some usually thrown back, include banded sunfish, black crappie, bluegills, smallmouth and largemouth bass, and yellow perch. Largemouth bass and certain varieties of trout may also be found in brackish waters, and some species of anadromous fish (those that spawn in freshwater but live most of their lives in salt water) can be found, notably shad and herring, which were recently reintroduced to the Blackstone River, where they had thrived before mills and dams rendered the waters inhospitable in the mid-19th century.

Along Rhode Island's shoreline, bluefish, sturgeon, striped bass, and cod are popular game fish, as a variety of shellfish, including mussels, oysters, lobsters, crabs, and Rhode Island's most famous saltwater treasure, the quahog clam, which is found up and down the Eastern Seaboard but is especially prevalent in the Ocean State. The quahog (pronounced "CO-hog" in these parts but "KWAH-hog" in some other places), also known as a steamer, is a hard-shelled, vaguely round clam that can be found in many sizes; the little ones are typically called cherrystones, the midsize variety are littlenecks, and the largest ones are called—and are used to make—chowders (they're also used in clam cakes, fritters, and other delicacies). For a chance to fish for these and New England's many deep-sea species—such as haddock, black sea bass, bonito, mackerel, bluefin tuna, and swordfish—consider booking a trip on any of the state's many private fishing charter boats.

Recreational saltwater fishing does not require a license if you're a passenger on a charter boat, but you will need a license for shell fishing ($200 for the season or $11 for 14 days), and only for nonresidents—just be sure to observe all the rules on minimum-size limits. Recreational lobster fishing is permitted only for Rhode Island residents who buy a $40 license. Freshwater (and anadromous) fishing, if you're age 15 or older, requires a seasonal license, which costs $18 for residents, $35 nonresidents. Or, for just $16, out-of-state visitors can buy a three-day fishing license. These may be obtained at town halls and a number of bait-and-tackle shops. Fishing licenses expire on the last day of February each year, regardless of when you buy it. If you're fishing for trout, salmon, or char—or fishing in a catch-and-release or fly-fishing-only area—you must buy a trout conservation stamp along with your license for $5.50.

BEACHES

You simply cannot visit the Ocean State without visiting its beaches. Even in the wintertime, the blustery Rhode Island coastline has a particular charm, especially when viewed from a cozy seaside restaurant or during a sunny afternoon drive.

But of course, the optimal time to experience the beach here is during the summer, when waters are relatively warm (about 72 degrees Fahrenheit at their peak in August) and easy to enjoy. The state offers all variety of coastline—from rocky bluffs towering 150 feet over the sea, to soft, sandy beaches perfect for sunbathing and swimming. If surfing's your thing, there are plenty of opportunities for that; if you prefer a coastal hike with dramatic scenery, try **Beavertail State Park** or **The Cliffwalk** in Newport. Taking the kids? **The Atlantic Beach Park** in Misquamicut has soft sand, fun waves, and a video arcade and bumper cars to boot.

But if you're just looking to relax, most any beach will do. Head to South County where the drive south along Route 1 is dotted with more than a dozen different state and town beaches to visit. For a list, visit www.riparks.com.

BOATING

Rhode Island loves boating, so much so that the purchase of boats (along with any equipment bought the same day) is tax-free. There are aquatic outfitters and tour providers throughout the state, with the most popular river sports (such as canoeing and kayaking) along the Wood River, the Seekonk River, sections of Narragansett Bay, and many of the salt ponds in Newport and South Counties. For information on boating safety and regulations throughout Rhode Island, visit www.boatsafe.com/Rhode_Island.

Contact the **Rhode Island Party and Charter Boat Association** (P.O. Box 3198, Narragansett, RI 02882, 401/737-5812, www.rifishing.com) for a full list of private fishing, sightseeing, and sailing charter boats in the state as well as links to many charter operators.

Many of the state's lakes and ponds allow boating, and there are marinas and launches strung along the shore from Westerly to Little Compton. For a complete list of public boat launches, contact the **Rhode Island Department of Environmental Management (DEM)** (401/222-4700, www.dem.ri.gov); the website has links to information on tidal charts, licensing, and Rhode Island boating safety.

GOLFING

Rhode Island's number and variety of courses—from winding, relatively flat, and rather tight links to lush, narrow, and hilly woodland layouts—have increased rapidly through the years, especially in South County, which has become Rhode Island's golfing capital.

If you live or play regularly in Rhode Island it makes sense to join the **Rhode Island Golf Association** (1 Button Hole Dr., Providence, 401/272-1350, www.rigalinks.org). The association's website lists dozens of member clubs, upcoming local tournaments, and many additional resources.

CAMPING

Rhode Island has two basic forms of camping: the more primitive tent-and-backpack activity that's offered at both commercial campgrounds as well as at the state-operated Fisherman's Memorial State Park Campground, the George Washington Management Area, and the Ninigret Conservation Area; and the RV camping that's offered mostly at commercial sites but also at the state parks. There's also tent camping at three municipal facilities: **Fort Getty Recreation Area, Melville Ponds Campground,** and **Middletown Campground.**

The charge for camping sites at most state parks is $18 per night for residents, and $36 for nonresidents if you're only bringing a tent. Additional fees apply for sites with water, electrical, and sewer hookups, and for use of septic dump stations. Some parks have camping cabins available. For details on which state parks have camping and accept reservations, contact the **Rhode Island Department of Environmental Management** (Parks and Recreation, 2321 Hartford Ave., Johnston, RI 02919, 401/667-6200, www.riparks.com).

There are private commercial campgrounds throughout the state, most of them in the rural western and northwestern areas. Popular camping areas include:

- **Burlingame State Park** (1 Burlingame State Park Rd., Charlestown, campground information 401/322-7337, park information 401/322-8910).

- **Charlestown Breachway** (follow signs from Charleston Breachway exit from U.S. 1, Charlestown, 401/364-7000, www.riparks.com).

- **East Beach** (Ninigret Conservation Area, E. Beach Rd., Charlestown, 401/322-8910, www.riparks.com).

- **Fisherman's State Park Campground** (1011 Point Judith Rd., Rte. 108, Narragansett, 401/789-8374, www.riparks.com).

- **Fort Getty Park** (Fort Getty Rd., Jamestown, 401/423-7260, www.jamestownri.gov/town-departments/parks-rec/fort-getty).

- **George Washington Management Area** (2185 Putnam Pike, U.S. 44, West Gloucester, 401/568-6700 or 401/723-7892, www.riparks.com).

- **Melville Ponds Campground** (181 Bradford Ave., Portsmouth, 401/682-2424, www.melvillepondscampground.com).

- **Second Beach Family Campground** (474 Sachuest Rd., Middletown, 401/846-6273, www.middletownri.com).

Travel Tips

STUDENT TRAVELERS

Providence is one of the most student-friendly cities in the country, whether you're studying here or visiting. Especially along Thayer and Wickenden Streets in Providence, you'll find cafés, shops, and other businesses catering to students. You'll also find all kinds of resources and like-minded company at the libraries and student unions of Brown, the Rhode Island School of Design, the University of Rhode Island, and other schools across the state. Unfortunately, though, there are no youth hostels in Rhode Island.

TRAVELERS WITH DISABILITIES

Rhode Island is on par with other Northeastern states in the degree to which establishments conform to the guidelines set by the Americans with Disabilities Act (ADA). With new hotels, larger and recently built restaurants, and most major attractions, you can expect to find wheelchair-accessible restrooms, entrance ramps, and other required amenities. But Rhode Island has many hole-in-the-wall cafés, historic house-museums with narrow staircases or uneven thresholds, tiny bed-and-breakfasts, and other buildings that are not easily accessible to people using wheelchairs. If you're traveling with a service animal, always call ahead and even consider getting written or faxed permission to bring one with you to a particular hotel or restaurant.

A useful resource is the **Society for the Advancement of Travel for the Handicapped** (212/447-7284, www.sath. org).

TRAVELING WITH CHILDREN

Rhode Island is an excellent state for families and travelers with children. The only real drawback is that the most visited destination in the state, Newport, is more geared toward adults than children; many Newport inns and higher-end hotels tend to frown on children as guests, as do some of the rowdier or more sophisticated restaurants and bars.

Providence and the metropolitan region have some terrific attractions that may be of more interest to kids than lavish Newport mansions, such as the RISD Museum in Providence, Slater Historic Site in Pawtucket, and—of course—the Providence Children's Museum.

The hands-down capital of family travel in Rhode Island, however, is South County. From Watch Hill to Misquamicut to Narragansett, you'll find great beaches, miniature golf, amusement parks, events tailored toward kids, and family-friendly accommodations. Block Island is a little more sedate and less commercially kid oriented, but it also has both hotels and cottage rentals that are perfect for families.

WOMEN TRAVELING ALONE

Rhode Island is generally a safe and progressive state when it comes to women traveling alone. Although Providence does have the same crime concerns that most major cities do, it's a fairly easy city to get around, and the handful of inns and bed-and-breakfasts are particularly popular with single female travelers. If you ever find yourself in any state of concern or crisis, contact the **Women's Center of Rhode Island** (401/861-2761, www.womenscenterri.org), which has a 24-hour hotline (401/861-2760) and emergency beds available at any time. The organization's mission is primarily to assist women (and children) coping with abusive situations or homelessness, but counselors here can assist women experiencing any kind of challenge.

SENIOR TRAVELERS

Rhode Island is less famous as a destination among senior travelers than Cape Cod or certain parts of coastal Maine that draw many visitors in their senior years, but it's definitely a place where travelers over 50 or even over 65 will not feel at all out of place. Depending on the attraction or hotel, you may qualify for certain age-related discounts—the thresholds can range from 50 to 65. It can also help if you're a member of **AARP** (888/OUR-AARP—888/687-2277, www.aarp.org). For a nominal annual membership fee, you'll receive all sorts of travel discounts as well as a newsletter that often touches on travel issues. **Road Scholar** (800/454-5768, www. roadscholar.org) organizes a wide variety of educationally oriented tours and vacations geared toward older individuals or couples with one member in that age group.

GAY AND LESBIAN TRAVELERS

Close to such gay-popular vacation spots as Provincetown (Massachusetts), Fire Island (New York), Ogunquit (Maine), and Northampton (Massachusetts), and with several major cities with visible and vibrant gay neighborhoods, Rhode Island is a relatively progressive and accepting state when it comes to gay issues—gay marriage has been legally recognized here since August of 2013. Discrimination on the basis of sexual orientation is illegal (as it is on the basis of race, religion, gender, and age), and the vast majority of the restaurants, hotels, inns, and businesses in the state are quite accustomed to and comfortable with the presence of same-sex couples.

While there are currently no gay newspapers in Rhode Island, you can find information online at **Options** (www.optionsri.org), where you'll find articles and entertainment listings for an LGBT audience. In Providence, you'll find bars and clubs with a specifically and predominantly gay clientele—on the whole, the city has a dynamic gay scene, and the Rhode Island School of Design, Brown, and Johnson & Wales all have active gay student groups. Newport is also a very gay-friendly city; a few of its inns have an especially gay following. For information on these and other gay-friendly businesses in the city, contact **Newport Out** (44 Catherine St., Newport, 401/849-9600, www.newportout.com). For information on Rhode Island's annual Pride festival in mid-June in Providence, visit www.prideri.com.

ACCOMMODATIONS

Many destinations celebrate their peak seasons in the summer when the weather is the nicest; not so in the noncoastal areas of Rhode Island. Peak travel in Providence is in the fall, particularly in late September through October, when the foliage is at its most dramatic and students are pouring into area colleges. Many hotels jack up their prices by a factor of two or even three during this brief crowded season. If leaf peeping isn't your thing, you can save a lot of money by traveling in late August through early September when the summer humidity has dissipated but hotel prices haven't yet skyrocketed.

Of course, the opposite holds true for the state's many beach destinations; Newport in particular gets incredibly congested with beachgoers in the summer. Rhode Islanders make the most of the brief period of heat between Memorial Day and Labor Day, so do yourself a favor and schedule your beach vacation before or after these magical dates, when you'll beat both the crowds and high prices.

Along with the rest of the country, Rhode Island has seen a steady rise in the price of accommodations at all levels, making it difficult to find any bargains among the major-name hotels. Bed-and-breakfasts, especially in more rural areas, can be a nice alternative; often run by couples or families, they can offer dirt-cheap prices without sacrificing amenities or homeness. Those who prefer the anonymity of a motel will find more bargains (though less consistency) in independent operations. Gone are the days when a Super 8 or Motel 6 offered a $39 double—$139 is more like it. Of course, you can always find rooms and private apartments on Airbnb, with a wide range of prices and comfort levels.

Health and Safety

WILDLIFE ENCOUNTERS

Because it has relatively few truly wild areas, Rhode Island presents few chances to encounter dangerous or menacing animals. Rabies is a fairly rare problem, occurring most often in skunks, opossums, raccoons, and other mostly nocturnal animals. The state is rarely visited by bears or other potentially dangerous mammals such as coyotes and moose. Watch out for ticks, however, as incidences of Lyme disease continue to be a persistent problem.

LYME DISEASE

The close proximity of deer with human beings has contributed to a painfully debilitating disease named for the small Connecticut town, just 25 mi (40 km) west of the Rhode Island border, where it was first diagnosed: Lyme disease. Symptoms, unfortunately, vary considerably from victim to victim, and one common problem is delayed diagnosis—the longer you go without treating the problem, the more likely you are to have severe effects.

In many, but not all, cases, a victim of Lyme disease exhibits a red ring-shaped rash around the bite of a deer tick, somewhat resembling a little bull's-eye and appearing from a week to many weeks after the incident. Flulike symptoms often follow—fever, achy joints, and swelling. If left untreated for more than a couple of months, chronic arthritis or debilitation of the nervous system may set in. It is in no way a disease to be taken lightly.

Unfortunately, testing for Lyme disease is unreliable at best; in the absence of reliable blood tests, you should consult with your health-care provider the moment you develop any of the symptoms outlined above—especially if you've been spending time in areas where ticks and deer are commonplace: wooded terrain, meadows, and coastal scrub.

Better yet, avoid getting bitten by ticks in the first place; when spending time in wooded areas, wear a long-sleeved shirt or jacket and long pants, and tuck your pant legs into your boots or socks. It's also a good idea to don light-colored clothing, as you'll have an easier time sighting ticks, which are dark. Remember that the more-common wood ticks do not carry the disease, and that deer ticks are extremely small, about the size of a pinhead.

HOSPITALS

Because of Rhode Island's high population density, you're never terribly far from a hospital when you're in the Ocean State. Some major hospitals include **Kent Hospital** (455 Toll Gate Rd., Warwick, 401/737-7000 or 800/892-9291, www.kentri.org), **Miriam Hospital** (164 Summit Ave., Providence, 401/793-2500, www.miriamhospital.org), **Newport Hospital** (20 Powel Ave., Newport, 401/846-6400, www.newporthospital.

org), **Rhode Island Hospital** (593 Eddy St., Providence, 401/444-4000, www.rhodeislandhospital.org), **Roger Williams Medical Center** (825 Chalkstone Ave., Providence, 401/456-2000, www.rwmc.org), **Our Lady of Fatima Hospital** (200 High Service Ave., North Providence, 401/456-3000, www.fatimahospital.com), **South County Hospital** (100 Kenyon Ave., Wakefield, 401/782-8000, www.southcountyhealth.org), and **Westerly Hospital** (25 Wells St., Westerly, 401/596-6000, www.westerlyhospital.org).

PHARMACIES

You'll find pharmacies, many of them open until 9pm or 10pm, throughout Rhode Island, the only exceptions being the more remote towns in the western and northwestern part of the state and Sakonnet. The leading chain in Rhode Island is CVS (www.cvs.com). Pharmacies open 24 hours include **Cranston CVS** (681 Reservoir Ave., Cranston, 401/943-7186), **East Providence CVS** (640 Warren Ave., East Providence, 401/438-2272), **North Providence CVS** (1919 Mineral Spring Ave., North Providence, 401/353-2501), **Johnston CVS** (1400 Hartford Ave., Johnston, 401/861-0312), **Pawtucket CVS** (835 Newport Ave., 401/726-0724), **Woonsocket CVS** (1450 Park Ave., Woonsocket, 401/762-3174), **Wakefield CVS** (11 Main St., Wakefield, 401/783-3384), **Warwick CVS** (767 Warwick Ave., 401/467-7788), and **Westerly CVS** (150 Granite St., Westerly, 401/348-2070).

TRAVEL INSURANCE

Buying travel insurance makes sense if you've invested a great deal in a trip with prepaid accommodations, airfare, and other services, especially if you have any reason to be concerned about your ability to make the trip (if you have medical concerns, however, check the fine print regarding preexisting conditions). It's a good idea to buy insurance from a major provider, such as **Access America** (800/284-8300, www.etravelprotection.com) or **Travel Guard International** (877/540-6575, www.

travelguard.com). Typically these policies can cover unexpected occurrences such as trip cancellations, interruptions, and delays, as well as medical expenses incurred during your travels.

CRIME

Crime is not a major problem in Rhode Island, although random acts of both serious violent crime and petty theft are about as common in the state's urban areas as they are in New York City or Boston. In other words, most crime occurs in the rougher parts of town, well away from tourist attractions and the heart of downtown. The crime rate has dropped sharply in every major city in the state, just as it has elsewhere in the Northeast, and virtually no community in Rhode Island is dicey such that you shouldn't feel safe driving around and walking on major thoroughfares.

In an emergency, dial 911.

Information and Services

MONEY

Banks are plentiful throughout Rhode Island, although they are fewer and farther between in rural areas, including Sakonnet and the western and northwestern parts of the state. There, finding a bank that's open can require looking around a bit. Most banks are open 9am-3pm or 5pm Monday through Friday and 9am-noon Saturday.

ATMs are abundant in Rhode Island; most of those found at banks are open 24 hours and accept a wide range of bank cards (typically Cirrus or Plus network cards) and credit cards. You'll also find ATMs in airports and at many bus and train stations, in many convenience stores and gas stations (especially larger ones that keep late hours), hotel lobbies, and increasingly in some bars and taverns. ATMs typically charge a fee ranging $2-4, the exception being when you're using a bank card issued by the same bank as the ATM.

Credit cards and bank cards are acceptable forms of payment at virtually all gas stations and hotels, many inns and bed-and-breakfasts (but not some of the small ones), most restaurants (except some inexpensive places, small cafés, diners, and the like), and most shops (except some small, independent stores).

Currency Exchange

Rhode Island receives very few international visitors directly from their countries of origin—at T. F. Green Airport, foreign flights are handled only from Canada and a few Caribbean nations. Therefore, currency-exchange booths and services in the state are limited. It's best to make these exchanges in whatever city you fly into from your country of origin. Rhode Island is far enough from Canada that Canadian currency is not generally accepted in the state.

COMMUNICATIONS AND MEDIA
Phones and Area Codes

For the time being, Rhode Island has just one area code, 401; when dialing within the state, it's unnecessary to use the area code.

Note when reading about establishments in this book, where there is one, the local telephone number precedes any toll-free number.

Pay phones are becoming increasingly rare with the widespread adoption of cell phones. When you can find them, they tend to be expensive, generally charging $1 for local calls, and they also add a surcharge for collect calls or for using a calling card. Most hotels charge a $1-2 surcharge for local calls, toll-free calls, or just about any other kind of call placed from their phones; long-distance rates can be outrageous at many hotels, and it's generally a good idea—if you don't already have a cell phone with an economical calling plan—to use your own calling card or buy a prepaid one. Calling cards are available at many convenience stores and gas stations at a wide range of prices. If you're a member of Costco, Sam's Club, or another wholesale discount store, consider buying one of the prepaid phone cards sold at these stores.

Cell Phones

It's illegal to jabber away on your cell phone while driving, unless you're using a hands-free device. Text messaging while driving is also illegal, and subject to fines of up to $100.

Internet Access

The best and most convenient place to check email and use the Internet is the public library; there's one in virtually every Rhode Island town, most with public computers. Many libraries in the state have high-speed wireless connections you can access from your own wireless-enabled devices. Libraries at Rhode Island's several universities and colleges are also open to the public, but their policies vary regarding computer use; some allow computer access only to students, faculty, and staff. Libraries generally allow you to use their computers for short periods of 15 minutes-1 hour.

Most cafés around the state offer high-speed wireless (Wi-Fi) hot spots for customers. You can always try a **FedEx Office,** which has branches in Warwick (1020 Bald Hill Rd., 401/826-0808), Middletown (7 E. Main Rd., 401/848-0580), and Providence's East Side (236 Meeting St., 401/273-2830); all are open 24 hours. This is an excellent traveler's business and work resource, as it's also a place to make copies, buy some office supplies, use FedEx and other shipping services, print copies, scan photos, and so on.

It's also standard for inns and hotels—even small ones—to provide Wi-Fi Internet access to guests.

Media

Rhode Island has about 20 newspapers, five TV stations, and nearly 40 radio stations. A few local magazines and periodicals cover individual regions within the state, some of them distributed free at visitors centers and in hotels.

The glossy magazine *Rhode Island Monthly* (401/649-4800, www.rimonthly.com) has good dining, arts, and events coverage. The *Providence Journal* (401/277-7300, www.providencejournal.com) has an informative website with information on local dining, arts, music, travel, kids-oriented activities, and more. *Providence Monthly* (www.providenceonline.com) is another resource for arts and events coverage, as is the subpar alternative newsweekly *Motif* (www.motifri.com).

TIME ZONE

Rhode Island is entirely within the Eastern Standard Time (EST) zone. Like most U.S. states and Canadian provinces, Rhode Island observes Daylight Saving Time (EDT).

VISITOR INFORMATION

The statewide information bureau is the **Rhode Island Office of Tourism** (315 Iron Horse Way, Suite 101, Providence, RI 02908, 401/278-9100, www.visitrhodeisland.com), which runs a visitor information center on I-95 between exits 2 and 3, and can send you a free Rhode Island travel planner by mail.

In downtown Providence, a well-stocked info center run by the **Providence Warwick Convention & Visitors Bureau** (10 Memorial Blvd., 401/751-1177, www.goprovidence.com) occupies the bottom floor of the downtown convention center.

In addition, there are a number of visitors centers throughout the state, some of which are unstaffed and others that are open only Memorial Day through Columbus Day.

Resources

Suggested Reading

Rhode Island hasn't exactly been written about to death, but there are a number of useful and colorful books on the Ocean State. Most of those listed below focus exclusively on Rhode Island or at least southern New England, but a number of additional titles—general guidebooks and historical reviews—discuss the state as a component of its greater identity, New England.

DESCRIPTION AND TRAVEL

Bergenheim, Roger. *Rhode Island: A Photo Portrait of the Ocean State*. Providence, RI: Providence Business News, 2013. Coffee-table-style photography book with stunning images of daily life in Rhode Island.

Lehnert, Tim. *Rhode Island 101: Everything You Wanted to Know About Rhode Island and Were Going to Ask Anyway*. Lunenburg, Nova Scotia: MacIntyre Purcell Publishing, 2010. A nice primer on everything from awful-awfuls to "The Call of Cthulhu" that will have you speaking like a native in no time.

Sikorsky, Gary J. *101 Things to Do in Rhode Island*. Atglen, PA: Schiffer Publishing, 2016. This book pairs specific sight-seeing and activity suggestions with photographs for a helpful, easy-to-use book providing exactly what the title promises, from champagne brunches on Block Island to visiting an historic lighthouse on tiny Rose Island.

MAPS AND ORIENTATION

There are a number of decent folding maps on Rhode Island, and if you contact the state tourism office (800/556-2484, www.visitrhodeisland.com), you'll be sent the free annual *Rhode Island Travel Guide*, which contains a very good general state map, which can also be downloaded online.

Kappa Map Group (www.kappamapgroup.com), available in most bookstores, makes some of the best maps of the state, from full state atlases to pocket maps of several towns and cities. The most recent is the *Rhode Island, SE Massachusetts & SE Connecticut State Road Atlas*, published in 2018.

Very precise maps of the state are published by Rand McNally, whose foldout maps *Rand McNally Connecticut/Rhode Island* and *Streets of Providence/Newport* are published annually and are more up to date, and they include excellent city coverage.

Providence also has a cool little map store, **The Map Center**, located at 545 Pawtucket Ave. Suite A114 in Pawtucket. (401/421-2184, www.mapcenter.com, 10am-5pm Mon.-Fri.). The owner is extremely knowledgeable and helpful.

HISTORY

Conley, Patrick T. *Rhode Island's Founders: From Settlement to Statehood*. Charleston,

SC: The History Press, 2010. A recent take on the brave and quirky iconoclasts Roger Williams, Anne Hutchinson, and others, written by the state's foremost historian.

Douglas-Lithgow, R. A. *Native American Place Names of Rhode Island*. Bedford, MA: Applewood Books, 2000. Provides the lore behind countless Rhode Island rivers, villages, lakes, and other features from the state's Native American history.

Eno, Paul F., and Glenn Laxton. *Rhode Island: A Genial History*. Woonsocket, RI: New River Press, 2005. This is a first-rate, readable history of the state's curious past.

Geake, Robert A. A History of the Narragansett Tribe of Rhode Island. Mount Pleasant, SC: The History Press, 2011. A history of Rhode Island's native inhabitants, chronicling their encounters with early European settlers up to their return to sovereignty in the 1900s.

Laxton, Glenn. *Hidden History of Rhode Island: Not-to-Be-Forgotten Tales of the Ocean State*. Charleston, SC: The History Press, 2007. An admittedly quirky grab bag of tales from Rhode Island history, this makes an entertaining travel companion for those long bus and ferry rides.

Raven, Rory. *Wicked Conduct: The Minister, the Mill Girl, and the Murder that Captivated Old Rhode Island*. Charleston, SC: The History Press, 2009. A true-crime history that reads like a novel, this book details an 1830s murder in Tiverton that reverberated throughout young America.

Works Progress Administration. *Rhode Island—A Guide to the Smallest State*. Boston, MA: Houghton Mifflin, 1937 (out of print). Arguably the best treatment of the state ever written is this dense and fascinating work compiled by the Works Progress Administration (WPA) Workers of the Federal Writers' Project. Part of the amazingly well-executed and thoroughly researched American Guide Series, the book is long out of print; many titles within this series have been picked up in recent years and reprinted by current publishing houses, but not yet Rhode Island. Your best hope of finding a copy of this wonderful tome is by scouring the racks of used bookstores or websites such as eBay. Depending on its condition and age, and whether it has its original cover and map, this guide should sell for $15-75.

SPECIAL INTEREST

Allio, Mark R., and Mary Jane Begin. *R is for Rhode Island Red: A Rhode Island Alphabet*. Chelsea, MI: Sleeping Bear Press, 2005. An exquisitely illustrated picture book that provides a nice backdrop for young children as they tour the state.

Beaulieu, Linda. *The Providence and Rhode Island Cookbook: Big Recipes from the Smallest State*. Guilford, CT: Globe Pequot Press, 2005. In a great state for dining, this book by talented food writer and restaurant critic Linda Beaulieu is a must.

Brennan, John T. *Ghosts of Newport: Spirits, Scoundrels, Legends, and Lore*. Charleston, SC: The History Press, 2007. An engaging and, dare we say, "spirited" guide to the undead pirates, heiresses, and commoners that purportedly still crowd Newport's streets.

HIKING AND RECREATION

Kricher, John C., and Gordon Morrison. *Peterson Field Guide to Eastern Forests North America*. Boston, MA: Houghton Mifflin, 1998. For more than 20 years, the best all-around guide on New England's geology, flora, and fauna.

Matheson, Christie. *Discover Rhode Island: AMC Guide to the Best Hiking, Biking, and Paddling*. Boston, MA: Appalachian

Mountain Club Books, 2004. An excellent all-around guide to the outdoors by a long-time New England travel writer.

Mirsky, Steve. *Best Easy Day Hikes Rhode Island*. Guilford, CT: Globe Pequot Press, 2010. A wealth of ideas for short nature hikes in the state for those wanting to enjoy the outdoors without too much strain or stress. Also available in Kindle and iPhone editions.

Peterson, Roger Tory. *Peterson Field Guide to Birds of Eastern and Central North America*. New York, NY: Houghton Mifflin Harcourt, 2010. The definitive guide for birders by the godfather of the hobby is newly updated in its sixth edition.

Samson, Bob. *Fishing Connecticut and Rhode Island: A Guide for Freshwater Anglers,* and *Fishing the Connecticut and Rhode Island Coasts.* Toronto, CN: Burman Books, 2007 and 2003. Excellent guides to the state for fresh- and saltwater anglers by an experienced outdoor writer.

Weber, Ken. *Weekend Walks in Rhode Island: 40 Trails for Hiking, Birding, & Nature Viewing* Woodstock, VT: Countryman Press, 2005. A good reading companion for avid strollers.

Wilson, Alex. *AMC River Guide: Massachusetts—Connecticut—Rhode Island*. Boston, MA: Appalachian Mountain Club, 2006. The Appalachian Mountain Club publishes a favorite book of kayakers, rafters, canoeists, and fishing enthusiasts.

...

Internet Resources

TOURISM AND GENERAL INFORMATION
Official State of Rhode Island Home Page
www.ri.gov
The official state website comes in handy when you're looking for detailed information on state and local politics, regional demographics, the state library, and local laws.

Official State of Rhode Island Tourism Home Page
www.visitrhodeisland.com
The mother of all Rhode Island travel and tourism websites, it has links to the state's regional tourism sites: Blackstone River Valley as well as northern and northwestern Rhode Island (www.tourblackstone.com), Block Island (www.blockislandinfo.com), Newport, Aquidneck Island, and Sakonnet (www.discovernewport.org), Providence (www.goprovidence.com), South County

(www.southcountyri.com), and Warwick (www.visitwarwickri.com). Within each site you'll find a trove of links to regional attractions, dining, lodging, events, transportation, and other information.

Providence Journal
www.providencejournal.com
This website, produced by the state's most widely read newspaper, is probably the most comprehensive and informative online news resource in Rhode Island. Here you'll find the same news coverage as in the print edition, with the added benefit of archived stories, and more up-to-date coverage for breaking stories.

Providence Monthly
www.providenceonline.com
The *Providence Monthly* is another glossy lifestyle magazine, and its website is a good resource for the latest on new restaurants,

museum exhibitions, live music, movies, and other goings-on in Providence. The coverage is chiefly about Providence, but you'll also find listings for the metro area, including Warwick, Cranston, and Pawtucket.

Rhode Island Monthly
www.rimonthly.com

This site contains stories, reviews, and information from the state's glossy lifestyle magazine *Rhode Island Monthly*. Included is a regularly updated events calendar and links to top picks in the magazine's annual "Best of Rhode Island" feature.

TRANSPORTATION

Several sites are very useful for exploring the different transportation possibilities in Rhode Island, including air, bus, train, and ferry options.

Amtrak
www.amtrak.com

Home page for the national rail service, which makes several stops in Rhode Island.

Block Island Ferry
www.blockislandferry.com

Find out about rates and schedules for the ferry that serves Block Island.

Peter Pan Bus Lines
www.peterpanbus.com

Details on interstate bus service to and from Rhode Island.

Rhode Island Department of Transportation
www.dot.ri.gov

Provides extensive information on numerous publications, traveler resources, road conditions, licenses and permits, upcoming roadwork and projects, legal notices, and construction bid notices.

Rhode Island Public Transit Authority (RIPTA)
www.ripta.com

The site for Rhode Island's in-state bus line; it's an excellent, easy-to-use site with maps and schedules that show all of the bus routes throughout the state.

T. F. Green Airport
www.pvdairport.com

Find out about parking, airlines, check-in information, and arrivals and departures at the state's main airport.

SPORTS AND OUTDOORS

Audubon Society
www.asri.org

Great site for birding, with specifics on the society's Rhode Island chapter.

Rhode Island Chapter of the Nature Conservancy
www.nature.org

Hikers might want to visit this site, which contains information about the Nature Conservancy's many Ocean State refuges and preserves.

Rhode Island Department of Environmental Management (DEM)
www.dem.ri.gov

Among Rhode Island's top Internet resources for outdoors enthusiasts, the DEM home page provides information and policies pertaining to boating, hiking, going to the beach, and many other activities.

Rhode Island Division of Fish and Wildlife
www.dem.ri.gov/programs/fish-wildlife/

Covers rules, licenses, boat launches, and tidal charts.

Rhode Island Golf Association
www.rigalinks.org
Here golfers can learn all about the state's
many public courses.

**State of Rhode Island Division
of Parks and Recreation**
www.riparks.com
This site provides links to every property
in the state park system and also has information on primitive camping at state parks.

Index

INDEX

List of Maps

Photo Credits

Title page photo: Liz Lee;

All interior photos © Liz Lee, except page 7 © (bottom left) RISD Museum; page 8 © (top) Sean Pavone | Dreamstime.com; pages 10-11 © Marie Elena Sager | Dreamstime.com; pages 12 -13 © (top) Lei Xu | Dreamstime.com; (bottom) Alpha and Omega Collection / Alamy Stock Photo; page 14 © Shashwatgupta1998 | Dreamstime.com; page 15 © (top) Daniel Logan | Dreamstime.com; page 16 © Jerry Coli | Dreamstime.com; page 19 © Bratty1206 | Dreamstime.com; page 20 © (right) Enfig74 | Dreamstime.com; page 23 © Ezumeimages | Dreamstime.com; page 24 © Ken Cole | Dreamstime.com; page 25 © Lei Xu | Dreamstime.com; page 26 © Allan Wood Photography | Dreamstime.com; page 28 © (right) RISD Museum; page 45 © (top) RISD Museum; page 85 © Marianne Campolongo | Dreamstime.com; page 86 © (top left) Demerzel21 | Dreamstime.com; (top right) Stuart Monk | Dreamstime.com; page 102 © (left middle) Chee-onn Leong | Dreamstime.com; (right middle) Demerzel21 | Dreamstime.com; (bottom) Arenacreative | Dreamstime.com; page 107 © Jerry Coli | Dreamstime.com; page 110 © (bottom) Teconley | Dreamstime.com; page 127 © (bottom) Allan Wood Photography | Dreamstime.com; page 168 © (top left) Nicole Duperre | Dreamstime.com; page 194 © (top left) Luckyphotographer | Dreamstime.com; page 200 © (bottom) Ritu Jethani | Dreamstime.com; page 220 © (bottom) Allard1 | Dreamstime.com; page 225 © Arenacreative | Dreamstime.com; page 232 © (bottom) James Kirkikis | Dreamstime.com; page 249 © (top) Jerry Coli | Dreamstime.com; page 254 © Ptphotos | Dreamstime.com; page 258 © (top) Kevin James Sousa | Dreamstime.com; (bottom) Jerry Coli | Dreamstime.com

ROAD TRIPS AND DRIVE & HIKE GUIDES

MOON
Drive & Hike
APPALACHIAN TRAIL
THE BEST TRAIL TOWNS, DAY HIKES, AND ROAD TRIPS IN BETWEEN
TIMOTHY MALCOLM

MOON
BLUE RIDGE PARKWAY
Road Trip
INCLUDING SHENANDOAH & GREAT SMOKY MOUNTAINS NATIONAL PARKS
JASON FRYE

MOON
CALIFORNIA
Road Trip
SAN FRANCISCO, YOSEMITE, LAS VEGAS, GRAND CANYON, LOS ANGELES, & THE PACIFIC COAST HIGHWAY
STUART THORNTON

MOON
NASHVILLE TO NEW ORLEANS
Road Trip
NATCHEZ TRACE PARKWAY • MEMPHIS • TUPELO • MISSISSIPPI BLUES TRAIL
MARGARET LITTMAN

MOON
NEW ENGLAND
Road Trip
BOSTON, ACADIA NATIONAL PARK, WHITE MOUNTAINS, BERKSHIRES, NEWPORT, AND CAPE COD
JEN ROSE SMITH

MOON
NORTHERN CALIFORNIA
Road Trip
SAN FRANCISCO, WINE COUNTRY, SONOMA, REDWOODS, LAKE TAHOE, SHASTA, LASSEN, YOSEMITE, BIG SUR
STUART THORNTON & KAYLA ANDERSON

MOON
PACIFIC COAST HIGHWAY
CALIFORNIA, OREGON & WASHINGTON
IAN ANDERSON

MOON
Drive & Hike
PACIFIC CREST TRAIL
THE BEST TRAIL TOWNS, DAY HIKES, AND ROAD TRIPS IN BETWEEN
CAROLINE HINCHLIFF

MOON
PACIFIC NORTHWEST
Road Trip
SEATTLE, VANCOUVER, VICTORIA, THE OLYMPIC PENINSULA, PORTLAND, THE OREGON COAST & MOUNT RAINIER
ALLISON WILLIAMS

MOON.COM | ROADTRIPUSA.COM

MOON

ROUTE 66
Road Trip

JESSICA DUNHAM

MOON

SOUTH FLORIDA & THE KEYS
Road Trip

WITH MIAMI, WALT DISNEY WORLD, TAMPA & THE EVERGLADES

JASON FERGUSON

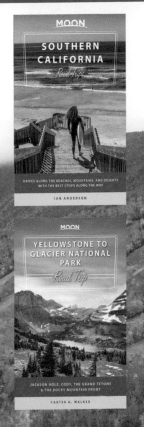

MOON

SOUTHERN CALIFORNIA
Road Trip

DRIVES ALONG THE BEACHES, MOUNTAINS, AND DESERTS WITH THE BEST STOPS ALONG THE WAY

IAN ANDERSON

MOON

SOUTHWEST
Road Trip

LAS VEGAS, ZION & BRYCE, MONUMENT VALLEY, SANTA FE & TAOS, AND THE GRAND CANYON

TIM HULL

MOON

VANCOUVER & CANADIAN ROCKIES
Road Trip

VICTORIA, BANFF, JASPER, CALGARY, THE OKANAGAN, WHISTLER & THE SEA-TO-SKY HIGHWAY

CAROLYN B. HELLER

MOON

YELLOWSTONE TO GLACIER NATIONAL PARK
Road Trip

JACKSON HOLE, CODY, THE GRAND TETONS & THE ROCKY MOUNTAIN FRONT

CARTER G. WALKER

Road Trip USA

Covering more than 35,000 miles of blacktop stretching from east to west and north to south, *Road Trip USA* takes you deep into the heart of America.

This colorful guide covers the top road trips including historic Route 66 and is packed with maps, photos, illustrations, mile-by-mile highlights, and more!

MOON

Road Trip USA

CROSS-COUNTRY ADVENTURES ON AMERICA'S TWO-LANE HIGHWAYS

FIND YOUR ADVENTURE

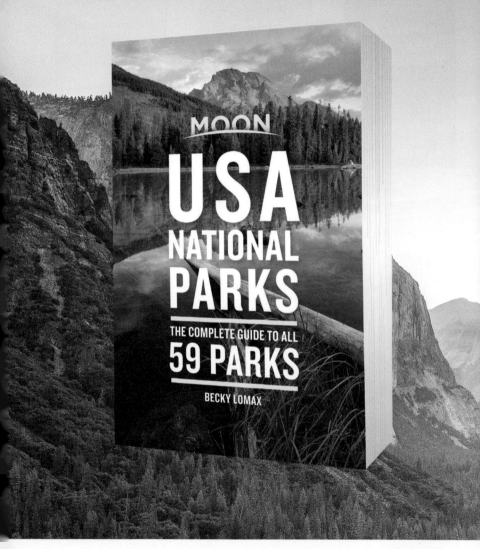

MOON

USA
NATIONAL
PARKS

THE COMPLETE GUIDE TO ALL
59 PARKS

BECKY LOMAX

Join our travel community!
Share your adventures using **#travelwithmoon**

MOON.COM
@MOONGUIDES

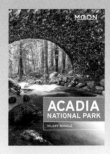

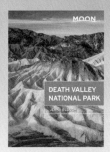

ACADIA
NATIONAL PARK
HILARY NANGLE

MOON

ARCHES &
CANYONLANDS
NATIONAL PARKS
W. C. McRAE & JUDY JEWELL

MOON
BANFF
NATIONAL
PARK
HIKE·CAMP·KAYAK
ANDREW HEMPSTEAD

DEATH VALLEY
NATIONAL PARK
JENNA BLOUGH

GLACIER
NATIONAL PARK

MOON
GRAND
CANYON
KATHLEEN BRYANT

MOON
GREAT SMOKY
MOUNTAINS
NATIONAL PARK
HIKE·BIKE·CAMP
JASON FRYE

MOON

MOUNT RUSHMORE
& THE BLACK HILLS
Including the Badlands
LAURAL A. BIDWELL

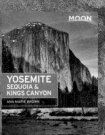

ROCKY MOUNTAIN
NATIONAL PARK
ERIN ENGLISH

MOON
YELLOWSTONE
& GRAND TETON
HIKE·CAMP
SEE WILDLIFE
BECKY LOMAX

MOON

YOSEMITE
SEQUOIA &
KINGS CANYON
ANN MARIE BROWN

MOON

ZION &
BRYCE
Including Arches, Canyonlands,
Capital Reef, Grand Staircase-
Escalante & Moab
W. C. McRAE & JUDY JEWELL

In these books:

- Full coverage of gateway cities and towns
- Itineraries from one day to multiple weeks
- Advice on where to stay (or camp) in and around the parks

GO BIG AND GO BEYOND!

These savvy city guides include strategies to help you see the top sights and find adventure beyond the tourist crowds.

OR TAKE THINGS ONE STEP AT A TIME

#TravelWithMoon

MAP SYMBOLS

══════	Expressway	○	City/Town	✈	Airport	⚓	Golf Course
┅┅┅┅	Primary Road	◉	State Capital	✈	Airfield	🅿	Parking Area
═════	Secondary Road	⊛	National Capital	▲	Mountain	⛪	Archaeological Site
┄ ┄ ┄	Unpaved Road	★	Point of Interest	✛	Unique Natural Feature	⛪	Church
────────	Feature Trail	•	Accommodation				Gas Station
- - - - - -	Other Trail	▾	Restaurant/Bar		Waterfall		
··············	Ferry	▾	Restaurant/Bar	▲	Park		Glacier
═════	Pedestrian Walkway	■	Other Location	⬛	Trailhead		Mangrove
⅏⅏⅏⅏	Stairs	⋀	Campground	⛷	Skiing Area		Reef
							Swamp

CONVERSION TABLES

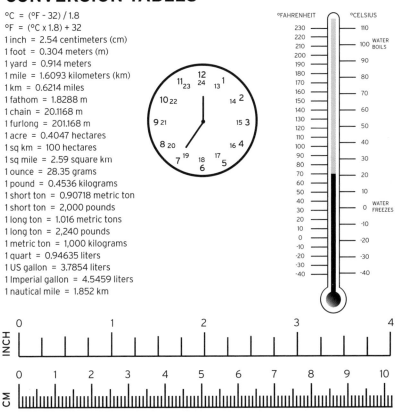

°C = (°F - 32) / 1.8
°F = (°C x 1.8) + 32
1 inch = 2.54 centimeters (cm)
1 foot = 0.304 meters (m)
1 yard = 0.914 meters
1 mile = 1.6093 kilometers (km)
1 km = 0.6214 miles
1 fathom = 1.8288 m
1 chain = 20.1168 m
1 furlong = 201.168 m
1 acre = 0.4047 hectares
1 sq km = 100 hectares
1 sq mile = 2.59 square km
1 ounce = 28.35 grams
1 pound = 0.4536 kilograms
1 short ton = 0.90718 metric ton
1 short ton = 2,000 pounds
1 long ton = 1.016 metric tons
1 long ton = 2,240 pounds
1 metric ton = 1,000 kilograms
1 quart = 0.94635 liters
1 US gallon = 3.7854 liters
1 Imperial gallon = 4.5459 liters
1 nautical mile = 1.852 km

MOON RHODE ISLAND

Avalon Travel
Hachette Book Group
1700 Fourth Street
Berkeley, CA 94710, USA
www.moon.com

Editor: Kimberly Ehart
Acquiring Editor: Grace Fujimoto
Series Manager: Kathryn Ettinger
Copy Editor: Kelly Lydick
Graphics and Production Coordinator:
  Lucie Ericksen
Cover Design: Faceout Studios, Charles Brock
Interior Design: Domini Dragoone
Moon Logo: Tim McGrath
Map Editor: Kat Bennett
Cartographers: Andrew Dolan, Karin Dahl,
  Kat Bennett
Indexer: Greg Jewett

ISBN-13: 978-1-64049-832-7

Printing History
1st Edition — 2003
5th Edition — May 2020
5 4 3 2 1

Text © 2020 by Elizabeth Lee and Avalon Travel.
Maps © 2020 by Avalon Travel.
Some photos and illustrations are used by permission and are the property of the original copyright owners.

Hachette Book Group supports the right to free expression and the value of copyright. The purpose of copyright is to encourage writers and artists to produce the creative works that enrich our culture. The scanning, uploading, and distribution of this book without permission is a theft of the author's intellectual property. If you would like permission to use material from the book (other than for review purposes), please contact permissions@hbgusa.com. Thank you for your support of the author's rights.

Front cover photo: Castle Hill in Newport © Cate Brown/RobertHarding.com
Back cover photo: Narragansett Bay by Newport © Darryl Brooks | Dreamstime.com

Printed in China by RR Donnelley

Avalon Travel is a division of Hachette Book Group, Inc. Moon and the Moon logo are trademarks of Hachette Book Group, Inc. All other marks and logos depicted are the property of the original owners.

All recommendations, including those for sights, activities, hotels, restaurants, and shops, are based on each author's individual judgment. We do not accept payment for inclusion in our travel guides, and our authors don't accept free goods or services in exchange for positive coverage.

Although every effort was made to ensure that the information was correct at the time of going to press, the author and publisher do not assume and hereby disclaim any liability to any party for any loss or damage caused by errors, omissions, or any potential travel disruption due to labor or financial difficulty, whether such errors or omissions result from negligence, accident, or any other cause.

The publisher is not responsible for websites (or their content) that are not owned by the publisher.